# ITALY

# ITALY

# THE ENDURING CULTURE

Jonathan White

CONTINUUM
London and New York

Continuum
370 Lexington Avenue, New York, NY 10017–6503

First published in the UK 2000 by Leicester University Press
First published in the USA 2001

**British Library Cataloguing-in-Publication Data**
A catalogue record for this book is available from the British Library.

ISBN 0–8264–5293–0 (hardback)

**Library of Congress Cataloging-in-Publication Data**
White, Jonathan Charles, 1945–
    Italy: the enduring culture/Jonathan White.
        p. cm.
    Includes bibliographical references and index.
    ISBN 0–7185–0257–4—ISBN 0–7185–0258–2 (pbk.)
    1. Italy—Civilization. 2. Civilization, Modern—Italian influences. I. Title.

DG442. W48 2001
945—dc21                                                                    00–061217

Typeset by YHT Ltd
Printed and bound in Great Britain by Biddles, Guildford & King's Lynn

# CONTENTS

# LIST OF PLATES

# LIST OF ILLUSTRATIONS

# PREFACE

This study of dynamic continuities as well as crises and fissures in Italian culture from Dante to the present takes an interdisciplinary approach to many topics not as yet commonly thus treated. Its coverage extends, among other things, to literature, art history, opera, film, sexuality, urbanism, the mafia, and population movements of emigration and (latterly) immigration. The book hence bucks the trend of specialization by looking in a highly comparative way at several different ages in the formation of modern Italy, from the rapid rise of merchant cities before and including Dante's time to millennial change of the present technological age. To write with this ambitious scope, the art works, events or cultural 'moments' chosen as representative had each to be seen in a specific historical context, but always as far as possible in relation to the present. If, in Croce's terms, all real histories are histories of the present – in this case, ways of seeking to understand how one major European culture, that of Italy, evolved into the specific configurations characterizing it at the beginning of a new millennium – then my enquiries had to reveal both continuities and, by contrast, what has become unfamiliar to our current imaginations because of material and spiritual changes in our ways of living. For these purposes, the sheer otherness of specific *past Italies* had to be reimagined in ways able to be understood in the here and now. This historical juggling act between past and present, so as to reconstruct ongoing 'past presences', has been my greatest challenge in writing the book. My desire is that it succeed in communicating the underlying excitements to readers, in the form of many new discoveries for them also.

Implicitly the book is asking at every point how modern culture and society in Italy have emerged from earlier configurations, and how far and for what reasons they differ from individual past moments. Italy led the West in forms of urbanism which fostered a post-feudal world. That

is the point I start from. In now consigning to its readers a work I have
lived with for years, my hopes are to engage others in ongoing
discussion – based on varied but informed views of earlier centuries – of
how far Italy might, in the quite critical conditions of 'meltdown' in
which she has found herself in recent times, be considered a kind of
political laboratory in which Western cultures can read their own
futures. In other words, how far does Italy again (or should we say still)
hold the status of paradigm, such that our reflections upon Italianness
past and present are bound also to throw light on those other cultures?

   Though the book's shortcomings are all my own, many people,
known or unknown to me, have played constructive roles in my writing
of it. I began learning Italian as an adolescent, in Saturday-morning
classes in Melbourne where many of my classmates were, unlike myself,
sons or daughters of Italian emigrants. My father, a geneticist, had spent
much of his own childhood in Italy, and would occasionally venture
beyond genetics by quoting Dante to me. I like to think he would have
wished his son to continue with this tradition and deep love of Italy,
which in a sense is what the book seeks to do. As I tackled its separate
chapters I was able to rely upon the support of near and distant
colleagues, of friends, and of family.

   In Italy, Lorenzo Bianchi of the Università di Ca' Foscari a Venezia
and his wife Caterina De Luigi and their four sons have accepted me and
mine over many years as extended family at their warm hearth in
Venice, and were my constant sources of information and materials for
study of that city. Silvano Vicarelli of the Università degli studi di Siena
and Nara Mechini, together with their son Leonardo, likewise offered
repeated hospitality in Siena, and a wealth of further perspectives,
economic as well as artistic and social, onto my work. In Palermo, my
visits have been graced by the companionship and teaching invitations
extended to me by Elio Di Piazza and by Daniela Corona, both of the
Università degli studi di Palermo. They helped me to grasp at least some
fraction of the enduring fascination of Sicilian culture, in part
paradigmatic of Italy in general, in part so very different and mysterious
in its own right. Among many others in the School of Humanities and
Comparative Studies at Essex University, I have been particularly
sustained by the encouragement, advice, criticism and above all the
friendship of Peter Hulme and Jules Lubbock, both of whom have long
believed in a number of the deeper concerns of the book, and helped me
to clarify my own understanding of them. Teaching trips to Florence

over several years enabled me to formulate ideas in debate with engaging year-groups of Essex students on our Tuscany course, and to discuss the intricacies and richnesses of Italian culture with present or former colleagues from our Art History and Theory Department: in particular, Michael Podro, Thomas Puttfarken, Evelyn Welch and Lisa Wade. Years ago, before even embarking on the writing of this work, I had confirmed the values of exactitude and rigorous questioning of documentary and other forms of evidence by attending seminars on Italian history given by Stuart Wolf in Essex. At a much later stage Gino Moliterno of the Australian National University in Canberra kindly made available to me his incomparable archive of modern issues in the Italian press for my work on the treatment and status of immigrants in the 1990s. Zygmunt Baranski of the Italian Department at the University of Reading read and commented productively on earlier versions of my Introduction and of my first chapter, on Dante. Maurizio Calbi, now at the Università degli studi di Salerno, was for several years a Ph.D. student at Essex, and although working in a rather different field of study – a topic in English drama and related texts of the early modern period – provided me with refreshing doses of *italianità* in informal discussion, as well as lucid insights into philosophies of history and of culture, and very searching responses to earlier versions of the chapters of this book which I gave as seminar papers. Another present Essex Ph.D. student, Pietra Palazzolo, has been particularly generous in helping me with letters to Italy seeking photographic reproductions and permissions. I thank too my editor Janet Joyce for the wisdom and firmness of her advice to me in the various stages of the book's production. Also at Continuum in London, the assistance of Valerie Hall during the period of submission of the manuscript, together with her subsequent work on it – especially in sorting out photographs, captions and rights and permissions issues – has been deeply appreciated. At a somewhat later stage of production Philippa Hudson and Sandra Margolies have been invaluable in the final editing processes.

At a particular midway point of the enterprise, when I seemed to myself in rather a dark wood (students of Dante will follow the allusion), guidance came in the form of Felicity Baker, of the Department of French at University College London. Her enthusiastic perceptions about the project as a whole, and her critical reading of much of what I had so far written by way of a synopsis, proved invaluable and inspirational for the ground still to be covered, especially that which related to the eighteenth century, to Venice and to Lorenzo Da Ponte. Likewise, at a somewhat later stage my friend Aijaz Ahmad, in spite of his very different parameters of interest – he has written illuminatingly on Gramsci, however, and in conversation points out parallels between Italy and certain aspects of modern Indian culture – gave his profound philosophical attention to a reading of my study and presented then (and goes on presenting) his brilliant and vivid encouragement. Also with interests mainly in other fields, but full of encouragement and a strong sense of cultural comparisons and strategies for their effective deployment, has been Dennis Walder, of another Department of Literature, that of the Open University. Michael Halliday and Ruqaiya Hasan, the implications of whose own work in linguistics extend to all forms of social and artistic discourse, have talked with me many times about fine details in our shared love of Italy. My friend Jeremy Tambling of the University of Hong Kong has vigorously debated conceptions of Dante and of opera with me over several years, and our differences have helped to sharpen my own ideas considerably. He also included an earlier version of my fifth chapter in a book he edited on media representations of opera, for which I take this opportunity of thanking him again. In the wider world of scholarship I have been inspired by very different writings on Italian subject matter from such eminent figures as Umberto Eco, Lauro Martines, Daniel Waley, William Bowsky, Denis Mack Smith, Giulio and Anna Laura Lepschy, Paul Ginsborg, Peter Bondanella, Giuseppe Mazzotta, Millicent Marcus, Teodolinda Barolini, Catherine Clément, Nicolai Rubinstein, Quentin Skinner, Michael Levey, Alexander Stille, David Forgacs, Robert Lumley, Peter Robb, and many, many others. Edward Said's pioneering culturalist approaches to opera have been a profound influence on my teaching of and writings about that art form, for long the most important genre of public spectacle, and now again significant in renewed ways around the world.

Not all is good tidings, alas. Around me in institutes of learning I see pressures on individuals to abandon wider perspectives in favour of ever more closely focused studies, and a consequent relinquishing of the goal of understanding anything more than brief periods in our cultural history. Under the unremitting need to establish careers, and with the exponential growth of information in the internet age, young scholars are too often forced to specialize to the point of losing touch with the wider world of learning; even though it is scarcely more than fifty years ago that Erich Auerbach in his classic work, *Mimesis*, achieved such global accounts of cultural evolution across centuries – specifically, of how narrative 'realism' in the West had evolved from ancient biblical and classical times through to the modern age. Indeed (if it does not seem immodest to admit to so elevated a model) it was precisely Auerbach's way of coming forward stage by stage in his book, using analyses of selected materials to represent evolutions on the wider scale, that showed me a strategy for dealing in long trajectories with the single culture of Italy – though of course I had to devise and hone scholarly procedures of my own to suit a more contemporary and culturalist agenda of enquiry, in which far more than literature alone needed be taken into account. It should be said also that despite my desire to emulate Auerbach's example, I did not share his faith in the abiding unities of Western culture, and was possibly more driven than he in my own enquiries by factors of disunity, of breakdown and cultural crisis.

Cultural crisis notwithstanding, institutional help of unqualifiedly constructive kinds in my own specific enterprise has not been lacking. The Querini Stampalia Foundation in Venice opened wide its doors during a period when it was otherwise closed, for me to look at its fascinating collection of paintings by Gabriel Bella of everyday Venetian life in the eighteenth century. Several scholars in the Faculty of Letters at the University of Catania who had written on the great modern Sicilian writer, Leonardo Sciascia, virtually constituted an impromtu seminar on my personal behalf to discuss his work, when I turned up unexpectedly to make enquiries there while they were in the process of commemorating another writer of Sicilian origin, Salvatore Quasimodo. The Museo Nazionale del Cinema in Turin kindly supplied me with a copy of the rare 1946 film by Carmine Gallone, *Avanti a lui tremava tutta Roma* (*Before Him All Rome Trembled*), which deserves to be better known, alongside more famous Italian films of the immediate post-war period. Other museums or associations have been generous in furnishing me with photographic reproductions, as listed in my acknowledgements. Above all, my own institution, the University of Essex, and in particular my Department of Literature, have awarded me research grants and study leave at crucial times to pursue this work, always in an enlightened and liberal spirit. In providing me also with stimulating intellectual companionship from colleagues of the high calibre of Gordon Brotherston, Elaine Jordan, David Musselwhite, Gabriel

Pearson, Leon Burnett and others, it has privileged me greatly. I am also grateful for the optimum conditions the department has offered me to teach specialized courses on Dante and on opera and culture, and a general course on Italian literature, art history, opera and film. The feedback from English, American and European students (including several Italians) taking these courses has been highly varied, and incalculably stimulating.

Janet White and our two daughters, Jessica and Kate, shared with me the journeys of imaginative enquiry in Italy which were the origins of the present study, and which I will remember with joy all my life. My brother Nicholas and sister Charlotte, both in Australia, from across the distance of the oceans that separate us have shown a closeness that has moved me greatly, never more than in recent times. Susan and William Oliver have sustained me by their unflagging love and companionship in the difficult finishing phases of producing the book. My deepest regret is for two who did not live quite to the new millennial threshold. My mother Isobel (Sally) White, who so inspired me in my formative years by her own studies in anthropology, and my friend Francis Barker, a colleague of penetrating intellect, personal conviction and great human generosity, both died before I could present them with copies of this book – the latter tragically before time.

# INTRODUCTION
## ITALY IN THE CULTURAL COSMORAMA

This book is a study of dynamic continuities running through different layers of Italian cultural history, but also of surprising *dis*continuities, especially those encountered when some exigency is reached which forces an abandonment of historical roots. Specifically it looks at how Italy has incorporated and continually represents its past, in changing ways to meet changed times. The work consists of a series of enquiries into different events or periods from Dante to the present, asking at every stage what were some of the key elements of specific former configurations of this culture, including their representations of the (still deeper) past – elements, indeed, which perhaps persevere creatively in later times and even into the present? Just how far are such historical moments retained in the present, either as collective memory or, more substantially, as parts of the material fabric of modern existence? Where identifiable aspects of a former Italian culture have gone missing or been forgotten, can we ascribe reasons, and is their disappearance significant? May we, furthermore, think about the likely retention or recuperation patterns of the near future, as the third millennium presents inevitable choices of maintaining or renewing distinctive aspects of Italian culture? Will Italy go on inventively reusing aspects of its past in solving current crises, or resort to modes of social, economic and political self-renewal divorced from its past, and which no degree of familiarity with its long and involved history could allow us to predict? Most pessimistically, might it slide towards some terrible impasse, obliterating the greatnesses of earlier times?

Although this book investigates the case of Italy, many of its large informing questions could apply to other cultures, since it is fundamentally a study in cultural evolution as such. The Italian context provides dramatic illustrations. She led the West in urbanization and in the activities of trade and banking which fostered a post-feudal culture.

My chapters on Dante, Boccaccio and some Renaissance theorists therefore concentrate on perceptions about the nature of cities, on attitudes to their rapid burgeoning and to the commercial activity upon which it was based; first, those found in Dante's and Boccaccio's major writings, and then the changing picture when later theorists such as Alberti and Filarete wrote architectural treatises devising cities to specific blueprints, based on the uses those cities were to serve and the lifestyles they were expected to foster. The principles of design and aesthetics governing these later works influenced urban planning up to the twentieth century and even into this postmodern age.

Many Italians live in cities that grew from their foundations into complex social, economic, political and religious centres in the early centuries of the second millennium. Even cities such as Florence, which had existed in Roman times, rose again almost from nothing, built over the ruins of a former settlement of that very different civilization. Important factors in the eleventh-, twelfth- and thirteenth-century development of cities are a weakening of outright dependency on agriculture, and a corresponding strengthening of activities of trade and commerce, including banking. In contrast with Roman and other ancient civilizations, the new urban culture – crucially the infrastructure of road connections between major centres – was fostered and underpinned more by a logic of commercial rather than military interests.[1] One of the few modern historians to achieve a challenging overview of the entire period, Lauro Martines, has posited the years around 1300 as a moment when 'urban Italy passes from one stage to another': in brief, from the earlier three centuries which had seen 'the physical building of cities and the rise of a new economy, a new society, new states, and a new set of vivid, shaping values', to a second stage, 'extending from about 1300 to the late sixteenth century', and in which ' "high" culture – literature, art, and ideas – pushed forward and became more prominent, more important'. Martines immediately qualifies his dividing line by a recognition that 'the achievement of the second stage was vitally rooted in the resources and values of the first'.[2]

Although there are major problems involved in singling out 'high' culture in the way Martines does, it is nonetheless true that for other historians too the period around 1300 is perceived as a kind of watershed. The centennial year conveniently offers itself as that, both because it was the date of a year-long Papal Jubilee much celebrated at the time (more than faint echoes of which have come down to us), and also because it is very well known to students of literature as the midpoint of Dante Alighieri's life, and as such the year in which his Eastertime pilgrimage through the three realms of the afterlife, the *Commedia*, is set. Dante's work being so compendious and far-reaching a statement about Italy up to and including that moment, any cultural divide based on time before and after its narrative is likely to gain much credence by that factor alone. It may be a combination of all these considerations and more that emboldens one historian, Philip Jones, to signal 1300 as the beginning of the modern era ('l'età moderna').[3]

But is there justification for so grand a formulation? We need the historical long-sightedness of a cultural critic such as Umberto Eco to begin to answer such a question. In an early study by Eco entitled 'The Return of the Middle Ages', which he begins by investigating the contemporary spate of more or less popular-cultural returns to the Middle Ages for fantastical themes and settings, Eco writes persuasively that the Middle Ages have never really gone away – that we still live very largely in cultural constructs, institutions and habits of mind which emerged during this earlier period in the forms from which their present configurations are directly descended. Eco also makes the case that the Middle Ages themselves preserved a heritage of what (from their perspective) was past culture, 'through a constant retranslation and reuse; it was an immense work of bricolage, balanced among nostalgia, hope and despair'.[4] There is a subtle distinction to be made here. By these accounts the activity of 'bricolage' on the part of medieval culture can be interpreted as consciously chosen adaptation, and the 'despair' sometimes felt, as a perceived failure to adapt successfully in some aspect: whereas the sense in which the modern world still lives within constructs of the Middle Ages, while bricolage in part, is more a matter of never having issued forth into some further 'episteme' (as Michel Foucault was in the habit of calling such long cultural ages, in which no radical change in habits of mind has occurred).[5]

Since Eco's overall hypothesis about cultural continuity is so challenging as to require consideration at various stages throughout the present book, its bold outline and a number of the specific matters highlighted in it merit quotation early:

> We are dreaming the Middle Ages, some say. But in fact both Americans and Europeans are inheritors of the Western legacy, and all the problems of the Western world emerged in the Middle Ages: Modern languages,

merchant cities, capitalistic economy (along with banks, checks, and prime rate) are inventions of medieval society. In the Middle Ages we witness the rise of modern armies, of the modern concept of the national state, as well as the idea of a supernational federation . . ., the struggle between the poor and the rich, the concept of heresy or ideological deviation, even our contemporary notion of love as a devastating unhappy happiness. I could add the conflict between church and state, trade unions (albeit in a corporative mode), the technological transformation of labor. . . . The Middle Ages are the root of all our contemporary 'hot' problems, and it is not surprising that we go back to that period every time we ask ourselves about our origin. All the questions debated during the sessions of the Common Market originate from the situation of medieval Europe. . . . In the case of the remains of classical antiquity we reconstruct them but, once we have rebuilt them, we don't dwell in them, we only contemplate them as an ideal model and a masterpiece of faithful restoration. On the contrary, the Middle Ages have never been reconstructed from scratch: We have always mended or patched them up, as something in which we still live. We have cobbled up the bank as well as the cathedral, the state as well as the church . . .[6]

There are several important points to make about this remarkable argument. First, we must immediately renegotiate Eco's term 'Middle Ages'. Admittedly it has its own important lineage, having received its first clear formulation, as Philip Jones has pointed out, by Petrarch and some of his humanistic followers, who saw their own age as a period 'in between' (*media tempestas*), as they looked back nostalgically on the achievements of the classical past, and sought wistfully for signs of a future cultural rebirth.[7] But historians have latterly tired of the term, perhaps in part for the very reason that they share Eco's beliefs and wish by their choice of terminology to signal a cultural continuum. In need of a way of defining the period in question from the point in history where we now stand (and not from where Petrarch felt he stood), it is increasingly called the 'early modern period': early modern precisely because of all the connections back, of the kinds Eco detects, from our world to then. Eco's remarks provide a good working description of an *episteme* – the Foucauldian term referred to earlier – as a lived-in worldview, or set of human circumstances in which similarities prevail from some originary moment onwards. However changed down through history, an episteme cannot be transformed as to essentials, or the rupture in question would by definition have produced the configurations of a new and different episteme. It is Eco's fundamental point that no such rupture has occurred, and that we still live with – or indeed largely with*in* – 'inventions of medieval society'.

As evidence of my intention that this entire book on Italy serve as an example of cultural evolution as such, it is interesting to note that in an altogether earlier period than the one in which Eco was writing, and in describing how a quite different European culture's *legal* institutions had evolved, Walter Scott used terminologies (particularly of architecture) which presage those of the modern Italian thinker:

> I can never sufficiently admire the penetration and clearness of conception which were necessary to the arrangement of the fabric of law, formed originally under the strictest influence of feudal principles, and innovated, altered, and broken in upon by the change of times, of habits, and of manners, until it resembles some ancient castle, partly entire, partly ruinous, partly dilapidated, patched and altered during the succession of ages by a thousand additions and combinations, yet still exhibiting, with the marks of its antiquity, symptoms of the skill and wisdom of its founders, and capable of being analyzed and made the subject of a methodical plan by an architect who can understand the various styles of the different ages in which it was subjected to alteration.[8]

Scott's writing, here and elsewhere, seeks to explore how contemporary Scots culture derived in a process of successive alterations from feudal foundations. Eco's point is really premised on cultural innovations of an immediately *post*-feudal period. Nonetheless, their two senses of change – change which does not make the original form of institutions impossible to distinguish even centuries later – are remarkably similar, and crucial to my argument. The present book aims at some of the 'methodology' that Scott here claims is possible, in an architectural mapping of how cultural institutions (the law in his example) have evolved into their present configurations – and, I would add, interrelations.

Whether or not the cultural fundamentals that both Eco and before him Scott write so well about are still in place, more than a score of years after Eco first formulated his views, the questions to be asked as we turn the corner of a further millennium must be rather pointed, and very much about the *future of the past*. For instance, we need to know the drift of what appear to be fairly dramatic changes in the very recent present (since Eco presented this thesis) from what had gone before. In particular, how much has our still-recent entry into *post*modernity and, most dramatically over recent years, into 'virtual reality' and internet culture turned us, paradoxically, into individuals and societies more like Eco's account of the Middle Ages – restless *bricoleurs*, that is, balanced between nostalgia, hope and despair – than what we may have been right up to and including the period of modernity: namely, direct and all-too-unquestioning inheritors of institutions, cultural formations and habits of mind descending relatively unbroken from an early modern past? If this essay can enter into the space between those two conditions, and prise them somewhat further apart for inspection, it will have helped us to see a little more clearly that which *in ourselves* is most likely to determine our further conditioning at the opening of the third millennium.

Although medieval Europe is the context of Eco's remarks, most of what he points out by way of detail either developed initially in Italy or had states or powers within Italy as key players in the reality described. Indeed, if we consider Italy's cultural history of the last thousand years, as this present essay on different 'moments' seeks to do, then one of our informing questions must be why, at so many critical phases, has it anticipated major changes in Western reality more generally? In recent years, for instance, if we are only half-way alert to what is going on around us, we have been asking ourselves whether Italy (socially, politically and economically) has not been taking a course which other nations might begin to follow – into irretrievable decline – as though it were pied-piping much of the rest of the 'developed' world (the world which Eco conjures into view so well) into the unknown, through cultural breakdown towards whatever unrecognizable conditions may unfold in the third millennium. Or does this apparent decline mask deeper factors of vitality, which are producing positive changes that, because unprecedented, simply have not as yet been generally perceived, let alone interpreted?

Be that as it may (and leaving some of those further questions about *post*modernity temporarily in suspension), it is fundamental to this study that the emergence of phenomena which *turned into* what is recognizably this modern world of ours, in all its manifold complexity, commenced in Italy towards the end of the first millennium, gathering momentum through the course of the eleventh, twelfth and thirteenth centuries. In particular, towns increasingly displaced feudal strongholds as points of population growth, with, as their economic bases, post-feudal modes of existence. Of the many examples Eco mentions, I wrestle with the phenomenon of urbanism itself in the early chapters of the present book, asking what might be meant in the wider sense by naming the 'merchant city', as he does, one of the 'inventions' we have 'mended or patched' – 'cobbled up' – and continued to live in? There are lengthy studies tracing the lineage of the modern city, which the present discussion does not seek to emulate. Instead, the intention is to show that the remarkable strength of the merchant city in Italy – as measured in particular by a contrasting set of attitudes to it from the first half of the fourteenth century – lies largely in the sheer vitality and complexity of its lived conditions, and its own perceptions about itself from that very early period.

In a book which explores a number of themes in Italian culture it is important initially to outline the strands which give shape to the overall enquiry. Our concern is with more than half a millennium. However distinctive the historical layering of Italian culture since Dante, it is only by means of a restless comparativism between ages that the features of any single moment can be best understood. Most important of all are the constant references forward to the present; often, indeed, the pauses to consider the present in its own right. To speak metaphorically, we are positioned in a cultural sense (at this millennial cusp) as though before an optic device such as the portable cosmoramas that were a common sight in piazzas in the second half of the eighteenth century, and that I discuss towards the end of Chapter 4, on the art forms and lifestyles of Venice in that period. (An eighteenth-century line engraving by Zompini of one such cosmorama appears on page 191.) Scenes, events and configurations of the past are presented for our contemplation in a changing succession, challenging us to attain to a higher understanding of how the various aspects of a cultural history interrelate, and also how they correspond to what we see when we raise our heads and seek to read present culture. But when we do look up, we often find that matters of our own times are themselves not free from obscurities, arising in the course of their routes of transmission to us. Reality being always more complex than any single interpretation or 'snapshot', the projections in the 'cultural cosmorama' that we are trying to interpret rarely seem like the full truth of any given moment of our vast inheritance, including even the present. They are simply too 'static', too frozen as single moments in an evolutionary continuum.

Admitting, however, this inevitable partiality of any attempt to understand changing projections in the cosmorama, there is no excuse for not attempting to prise open each angle of interpretion as wide as possible, starting from the earliest. As outlined already, Umberto Eco has claimed that we still live largely in cultural constructs, institutions and habits of mind which emerged in the Middle Ages. My first chapter considers attitudes found in Dante to the rise and growth of the 'merchant city', noting how he always presents us with a dualism of good and bad urban values and lifestyles. In the *Commedia* in particular, the opposition is essentially between a positive myth of an earlier Florence and negative attitudes to the actual commercial dynamic of urban culture in his period. My claim is that such a dualistic vision became recycled in the historiography of cities from at least the time of Dante onwards. It is obvious in the famous Sienese frescoes of Ambrogio Lorenzetti painted in the late 1330s, depicting 'Good and Bad Government in the City and Countryside'. But we also recognize cognate if distant forms of the same dualism much later, in a post–1860s Florence that sought to clear away what were seen as its remnants of 'ancient squalor' and to rebuild itself, after Italian unification, to a programme of late-nineteenth-century ideals. Thinking along the same lines, we arrive at a consideration of modern urban problems of prejudice and exclusion in the light of Eco's theory of the perseverance into the present of medieval habits of mind. Should we infer from Eco's observations that relatively recent social crises, exemplified in Florence by racist attacks on the new immigrant communities in the early 1990s, have their roots in much earlier times? An unexpected and revealing light can be shed on today's social tendency to exclude the so-called *extracomunitari* (from Albania, Senegal, China and elsewhere), by a comparative analysis which sets this alongside Dante's virulent objections to outsiders – *nuova gente* – in the Florence of his day. It is unsettling to note that although there are certain distinctively modern features in the recent outbreaks of prejudice against foreigners, the continuity of which Eco speaks is evident in the economic bases of the objections to their presence, and in the ways in which they are demonized as an extraneous 'other', with habits and lifestyles that are interpreted as rendering them incapable of full assimilation into the Italian community. Paradoxically, in the process some Italians feel excluded from, and utterly unable to grasp, what they see as the interesting lifestyles of the *extracomunitari* who have settled among them.

As difficult a matter as is the global topic of cities, no less challenging are our attempts to understand what goes on in them by way of human interaction. Because of its truly fascinating accounts of social and sexual encounters, not to mention the role money plays throughout, Boccaccio's *Decameron* is the main text studied in Chapter 2. The new commercial activities put paid to rigid feudal class structures, introducing a whole new urban social dynamic of opportunity that, importantly, had repercussions far beyond Italy. The *Decameron* innovates radically by addressing women as its primary readership. It frequently adopts a female perspective on sexuality, or at least a perspective favourable to women. Furthermore, its sheer indulgence in stories relating sexual pleasure contrasts sharply with Dante's treatment of lust and its punishments in hell and purgatory. However, Boccaccio's text is not straightforward in its attitudes, and exhibits multiple internal contradictions that not only participate profoundly in the problematic nature of human sexuality but may also be said to have contributed to it in a lasting way. Some of the great prohibitions of the body named and interpreted by Michel Foucault in his *History of Sexuality*, and identified by him as emerging in the sixteenth and seventeenth centuries, can be shown to be in operation already in Italy at a much earlier date, from the evidence of this seminal text of the mid-fourteenth century. The *Decameron*'s presentation of attitudes to sexuality is interesting not solely from an antiquarian standpoint. Studying certain of Boccaccio's individual narratives we uncover unmistakable blueprints of how behaviour and attitudes go on being culturally encoded, even in our present sexual identities. Working upon the issues raised here may therefore afford us intuitions about the sexual mores of the future.

My third chapter is also about cities, but by now we have moved on to urban ideals and idealizations of the Renaissance. The chapter title comes from Leon Battista Alberti's *De re aedificatoria* (*On the Art of Building in Ten Books*), a Latin treatise of the mid-fifteenth century. Renaissance theorists such as Alberti and Filarete idealized the city. Alberti's very hierarchic notion of class can explain the heavy emphasis in his treatise on the need for methods of surveillance of the people by those in power, in the ways individual buildings are to be constructed and the city laid out. *De re aedificatoria* even contains a blueprint for an 'inner-city' ghetto of artisanal classes, whose trades create smells and congestion best contained, in his opinion, within a walled inner city, a forerunner of modern inner-city slums. Leonardo da Vinci, although in other respects a different kind of thinker from Alberti, shares with him a very class-based notion of city structures. Some of his noted urbanistic plans for remodelling Milan are like nothing so much as Ridley Scott's postmodern film *Blade Runner*, based on a city horizontally layered, reflecting structures of class and power: except that what for the Renaissance planner da Vinci is a pleasant dream has become for the latter-day filmmaker Scott a dystopian nightmare. Another Renaissance urban theorist, Filarete (Antonio Averlino), has more benign ideas for his ideal city of Sforzinda, with taverns and bathhouses and bordellos at the heart of the city, hard by the offices of city government. Very few cities were actually commissioned and built to an Albertian 'ideal city' design; the chapter discusses an 'approximate' example, Pope Pius II's rebuilding in the High Renaissance (around 1460) of the centre of Pienza, as it is now named – originally the village of Corsignano where he was born. The quest for an ideal urbanism remains at the heart of certain utopian thinking. Much later, English writers such as Morris and Lawrence in their different ways still harked back to Italian precedents for inspiration. Even in the heady days of 1960s building, the relationship between architect and patron, as prefigured in Alberti and Filarete, still provided the basis for innovative work, notably in the building of such 'ideal cities' as Britain's new universities, often consciously evoking Italian hill towns. Their 'cityscapes' can be traced back to the Italian lineage of urbanism before the age of the architectural theorists, even if in the built structures they sometimes returned, unintentionally, to the hierarchy of class divisions explicitly aimed for by such as Alberti and da Vinci.

Chapter 4, on the specific city of Venice, explores certain themes of the age of the Enlightenment in an exemplary and fascinating context, weighing antithetical accounts of the city during this period. On the one hand, Venice was enjoying a flourishing age of peace, making possible in the art works, in the material fabric of the culture and in the lifestyles of her citizens a perpetuation of the carnival mode which in any case had come to predominate in each year's calendar. But on the other, Venice's wealth was not limitless, and her global power was shrinking ineluctably throughout the seventeenth and eighteenth centuries, as better-placed nations grasped the opportunity of new trade routes and the possibilities for colonial expansion. The question is, then, to what extent was Venice already moribund when Napoleon finally brought her more than thousand-year history as an independent republic to a close in 1797? Had she become too intent on the carnivalization of almost all aspects of life to read the signs of her own decline, or to show interest in any other reality than her own, or in the wider world's future prospects? In seeking to answer those questions, the closing section of my argument in this chapter suggests that there *was* awareness of decline, but insufficient willpower among those in positions of highest authority to stop the rot. An argument is presented, furthermore, through a discussion of the aforementioned cosmoramas, that far from being mired in communal solipsism, Venice contained persons of creative force – in particular, several artists in a variety of genres – attesting to 'new worlds', and to the possibility that even if Venice as a city did not dominate and 'steal the show' as she had been accustomed to do, at least she might be witness to an unfolding global history, and hence to the birth of futures beyond merely her own.

In Chapter 5 the scope of the Risorgimento movement in Italian politics and its links with modern Italian fissiparous politics serve as context for plotting the key points of Italian opera, and an enquiry into its recent international 'rehyping' for various modern spectaculars, especially on television. For instance, the three tenors' 'Nessun dorma' is a media phenomenon which conveniently provides us with parallels and contrasts between the political significations of Italian operas through-out the nineteenth century and their role in modern representations. A selection of filmed or televised opera is interpreted, with a view to understanding how we have moved from the politics of particular nineteenth-century works at their time of writing, to their modern versions, seen not in the opera house by a select few, but on the small screen by audiences sometimes in the hundreds of millions. The constant, subliminal drive towards unificatory politics within the bel canto tradition, involving individual honour and sacrifice on a heroic scale, has not in fact gone away in these media representations but is instead transformed into an equivalent politics for the modern age. In film and television productions of opera or operatic highlights, these symbolic systems of nineteenth-century heroic individualism modify into a global 'feel-good' politics of unity between disparate peoples, all the more striking in Italy's case considering that its political reality of recent years has been predominantly one of disunity, even disunifica-tion, between regions and specific interest groups. The opera which most undermines unificatory messages, even at the time of its writing, is Puccini's *Tosca*, in which the grand public political stances of Verdian heroism have largely been displaced by personal credos of individualism. And yet in significant media productions of modern times, *Tosca* too has been represented not as a work in which individualism tears apart the social fabric, but as an allegory on the overthrow of fascism or, more recently, as a televisual spectacular, offering Rome to viewers as once again the centre of a 'civilized' world, its focal role no longer imperial or religious as in the past, but cast in terms of the binding secular experience of the modern age, television itself.

Just as the operatic medium for which Italy has been famous provides us with one way of comparing certain nineteenth-century political realities with their late-twentieth-century counterparts, so too in my next chapter exemplary achievements in film and literature of the movement known as 'neorealism' help to focus some of the deepest questions about the interrelated languages of mimesis and montage, and their importance in the modern world. Erich Auerbach and Sergei Eisenstein, great interpretative exponents of each form, are contrasted. There is even at this point a return – which may surprise those not yet attuned to the 'cosmoramic' shifts back and forwards in historical time that are a principle of this book's modes of argumentation – to an interpretation of a key passage in Dante's *Purgatorio*, as an anticipation of the marvel of motion pictures hundreds of years before the fact. The chapter then turns to Giorgio Bassani as a representative instance of what was being attempted in literary neorealism shortly after the Second World War. It closes on a substantial discussion of Gillo Pontecorvo's film *The Battle of Algiers*, which is seen to be as much a great neorealist essay on the nature of film itself as on the French colonial attempt to maintain its power base in the face of the growing struggles for independence on the part of Algeria's indigenous Islamic population. Although not about an Italian reality as such, *The Battle of Algiers* was made with a considerable commercial contribution from Italy, by an Italian filmmaker who had learned his key skills from the movement of cinematic neorealism that by its date of 1966 was essentially over. The film is hence a fine example of creativity within a mode (neorealism) not usually considered when lists are drawn up of typical things Italy has exported to the world.

The seventh chapter concentrates on Sicily, which has long been regarded as a culture abnormally preoccupied by death. An oppressive thematics of death can be studied through art works as well as actual political events. In the twentieth century (which we are only now leaving behind) the island was at times plagued by an organized criminality whereby the reality of death came to dominate the whole of Sicilian society. I attempt to set the mafia killing of Judge Giovanni Falcone in 1992 within a much larger context of death, which includes a reading of the fifteenth-century fresco depicting *The Triumph of Death* (the most important painting in the National Gallery of Sicily in Palermo). But Sicilian attitudes to death also take antithetical forms, distinguishable in different examples from the modern literary period. Two such are Lampedusa's *The Leopard* and Leonardo Sciascia's 'anti-Leopard' set in the same time and place, the novella 'Forty-eight' in his relatively early work *Sicilian Uncles*. Death has a lesser triumph and is even defied in Sciascia's vision of nineteenth-century Sicily, as it is not by Lampedusa, whose internationally famed book published in the same year (1958) represents an eventual coming to peaceful terms with death in the Sicilian context. Giovanni Falcone's own book on the mafia as a culture of death, published in 1991 shortly before he was murdered, acknowledges Sciascia's influence on its interpretations of the intricate characterology of Sicily.[9] Aware as he always was of the constant possibility that he would be killed before completing his life's task of investigating and prosecuting the mafia, Falcone can now symbolize for Sicily and the world the defiance of death found in Sciascia, and hence represents a major turning point, a choice of life and justice for a new millennium, following a century in which death and injustice held too much sway.

My final chapter is a study of the Italian diaspora overseas, done by historical stages and in terms of significant cases. A comic overture to the chapter tells of an exchange in the year 1818 of eighteen kangaroos in the possession of the British Prince Regent for a similar number of papyrus scrolls from Herculaneum belonging to the Bourbon King of Naples, long before mass emigration to the Americas, never mind still later emigration to the continent whence those kangaroos had been brought. The stories of several emigrants of different periods reveal a lot about the exportation of Italian culture and lifestyles. Mozart's librettist Lorenzo Da Ponte, who after his important period in Vienna settled in London for over a decade, and then in the United States for the last three decades of his long life, was the first professor of Italian at Columbia College, later named Columbia University. His *Memoirs* are a fabulous document of late-eighteenth-century Venetian life and of the adventures of exile, written even while he campaigned tirelessly and in the end successfully to have an Italian opera company visit New York. My other case history focuses on the anarchists Sacco and Vanzetti and their famous trial on murder charges in Massachusetts of the 1920s. The lives of a 'fishmonger and poor cobbler' come to symbolize – not least for their extraordinary letters and speeches after conviction, cast in imperfect but nonetheless eloquent and impassioned English – the struggles of the immigrant poor against the might of institutional authority. Liberal America, enlarged and activated as never before by Sacco's and Vanzetti's eventually unsuccessful appeals to have their convictions quashed, keeps vigil outside the jail in which they are executed in 1927. Although the question of their guilt or innocence is still debated today, the case is in fact more important as an intensely heightened drama of the problems of adaptation faced by all New World migrants. Readings of representative novels of Italo-Americans and Italian Australians punctuate and shed further light on these life histories. The questions raised by the famous vitality of 'Italian cultural imperialism', as it has been called by Vittorio Gassmann's character, the Italian visionary architect and urban designer, in Alain Resnais's *La Vie est un roman* (*Life Is a Bed of Roses*, 1983) are: what qualities of Italianness accompany the espresso bars, luxury goods and operas to so many different cultural locations, and what transformations does this Italianness undergo in its new surroundings? Can our reflections on those (often self-exiled) individuals and far-flung Italian communities throw light on the health and survival patterns of Italian culture in Italy itself?

The book began by exploring Italy's pre-eminent role in ushering in early forms of capitalism, this possibly now moribund economic life form. In what respects does the world still see its cultural agenda set by Italy, even perhaps the inauguration of an endgame to capitalism? In the remainder of this Introduction, let us consider that cultural present directly, and first of all in terms of popular perception, within and beyond Italian society itself.

Almost any recent consideration of Italy involves clichés and stereotypes, usually romantic, at least on the part of English-speaking nations. A typical example of this tendency was evident in an *Observer* newspaper survey, that asked where in Europe selected people who had appeared on its features pages would choose to live if Britain were not their home. Most of the many who answered 'Italy' described an identikit country, a mixed cocktail of sunshine and good food, beautiful buildings and architecture, and a happy and welcoming people. The general level of response is well captured in the following representative selection: 'I'd love to have access to those bits of marble, squares and cafés and the sexy language'; and, 'I'd choose to be Italian because the language is beautiful but more importantly because Italian women never seem to suffer from visible panty lines.'[10] The last remark was of course intended as a jest. But whole books on Italy continue to be published on epistemological premises of scarcely less exalted tourist poppycock.[11] I shall have more to say in a moment about national typecasting, not all of it by any means negative.

But first, a caveat about my own position as a non-Italian seeking to define truths about Italy. All essay writing – at any rate since Montaigne long ago gave form to the genre, with an exquisite sense of himself as the fluctuating, divided and restlessly changeable thinking subject – should be undertaken with a keen sense of positionality on the part of the writer. Giacomo Leopardi, Italy's greatest poet of the Romantic period and himself a restless (not to say relentless) essayist, noted two important factors regarding 'point of view' in seeking to specify truths about entire nations, one of them if the people described were other than one's own, the second if they included the writer or speaker. His principle case was a point so general it is really only a truism: namely, that 'it is impossible for a foreigner to know perfectly another nation'. But his second point is somewhat trickier, even a little Byzantine, and was applied specifically to his own culture. 'Italians', he claimed, are 'sensitive above all other peoples about their reputation; a truly strange fact, considering the little or even non-existent national esteem which exists among us, most certainly less than in other countries.'[12] Leopardi was writing this in 1824, still almost half a century before Italy was constituted as a modern nation-state, and possibly its division into multiple political units, many of them foreign dominated, was a prominent factor in the truth of that second remark. On the other hand, the statement would seem to remain largely valid in our own times, though possibly its present veracity is not the result of some continuum of national character from Leopardi's day through to our own, but rather is based on new historical factors, such as (just by way of hypothesis) a late-twentieth-century *dis*unification of Italy every bit as remarkable as the nineteenth-century post-Leopardian history of unification. Interestingly, in much the same period as Leopardi, Stendhal too noted an embarrassment or touchiness in the Italian temper at criticism by others, and bestowed on it the colourful name of *patriotisme d'antichambre.* In evidence, he mentions a particular Italian woman who in his eyes 'united the rarest beauty, the most elevated soul and the most powerful wit', but who was not exempt from this common condition: 'Without petty self-vanity, she was susceptibility itself on behalf of her country: as soon as one criticized some aspect of this dear land, she blushed.'[13]

If it is right to assume that Leopardi's and Stendhal's dicta about the sensitivity of Italians to judgement by outsiders still hold true, then the present enterprise – a set of layered cultural interpretations by one such outsider, and seeking to interrelate nothing less than Italy's past, present and future – is an undertaking fraught with risk. For to recapitulate only these first problems, on the one side lies the Scylla of national stereotyping, on the other the Charybdis of Italian touchiness about being analysed by anyone but themselves. Possibly both dangers can be overcome, however, by taking a course which, rather than seeking to elude them, confronts them head on. As far as Italian touchiness goes, it is something that will have to be braved to a greater or lesser degree throughout the present study. And as everyone with a modicum of sense will attest, there are truths that *only* an outsider can fully register, or at any rate analyse dispassionately. Stereotyping, on the other hand, often reveals quite as much about the mindset of the persons engaged in perpetrating it as about the subject of their descriptions; and furthermore is rarely a total misrepresentation of the latter. In short, it can tell us a lot about both the representer and the represented, and even about connections and relations between them.

An illuminating instance of Italian stereotyping of the English (illuminating, that is, about both Italians and English) appeared in the Italian press within days of the *Observer* article already mentioned, in the *Indipendente* newspaper,[14] which had in any case copied its name from Britain's quality daily. Underneath a photograph of two British bobbies on mountain bikes, one of them wielding a truncheon while riding – much as in previous times cowboys were sometimes imaged galloping ferociously while whirling a lasso – the headline reads, 'Police on mountain bikes against two-wheeled delinquents in London.' There follow four lines of caption, which claim that a wave of crime perpetrated by bicyclists has hit North London, evoking positive response from Britain's flexible police force. With nothing in the photograph to specify what precise provocation one particular bobby had for wielding his truncheon, we can with indemnity imagine it as

**Figure 1** Genial tweaking of a familiar Italian stereotype of the British, published in Italy's daily newspaper, *L'Indipendente*. Study of such clichés can tell us as much about the mindset of those doing the stereotyping as about the subject of their descriptions. Photo: John Stillwell © PA News Photo Library.

being against the very idea of bicycling criminals, of Tottenham or thereabouts.

The instance amuses, no doubt because it concerns a national figure, the British bobby (complete with high helmet and truncheon), who in any case stands out more in Italian than in British minds as somehow quintessentially representative of the culture he 'polices'. The simple stereotype is being updated for Italians by being shown as having real work to do – the cracking of a crime wave – and a new means of transport with which to do it. But therein lies the further comedy. Meeting fire with fire in this case means matching mountain-bicycle-powered delinquency with mountain-bicycle-powered policing. So the pre-existent image of the bobby is brought into the present age, but only by virtue of a means of transport which, although very much an icon of modern times, seems no more likely than the helmet or the truncheon to make all that great a difference in halting real criminality (which the

Italians certainly as a nation know rather more about than the British). The mountain bike hence becomes logged in the unconscious of the nation doing the stereotyping as yet one more quaint appurtenance of the distinctive police force of that (to Italian minds) pleasantly uncriminal nation, the British. Any comparisons with the transport and methods of modern Italian policing will bring home the essential joviality of contemplating the British equivalent (even in its dire moment of mountain-bike-mounted, truncheon-wielding crisis). From the point of view of the Italian mindset I am describing, the crimewave reported in the article is a phenomenon to be appreciated not so much as veritable crime (of any of the varieties all too well known to Italians), but rather as a kind of comic-opera criminality, catalyst of a quintessentially British form of Keystone-coppery by way of response.

The piece in the *Indipendente* was taken from a British newspaper source (PA News), and related to a real policing programme, however flimsily and selectively represented here. But that is hardly the point. The important facts are precisely those of *representation*, for they are what tell us most about modes of perception by members of one culture of another. At the point of representation by Italian journalism, the issuing of mountain bikes to certain North London police units becomes the focus for a pleasant adjustment to an already existing stereotype, but one that only reinforces what that stereotype already represents about the British in the minds of Italians – that they are an essentially peaceful nation, and can thus continue to afford a daffily antiquated and ridiculously equipped police force. The point not to forget is that there is some real truth at the heart of this piece of typecast representation: the kind of truth which only becomes apparent, however, at the level of large-scale comparisons, when considering, for example, the relativities of civil safety, criminality and modes of policing between just such nations as Britain and Italy. Looked at in its own terms by the British, there is no room for the complacency induced by such comparisons, since there is real crime – plenty of it – in Britain. But it simply cannot figure as something for Italians even remotely (or as it were *on behalf of* their British counterparts) to worry about, since the deep crises present in their civil society make British troubles seem enviable.

So far this consideration of national stereotyping has been premised on the logic of there being two parties – two nations in this case – involved in the activity. In point of fact the British themselves – or rather, in this case, the English – are strong on self-stereotyping, but are more likely to interpret their own present post-imperial misfortunes in such terms as their decline as a cricketing nation in relation to the teams of former colonies.[15] Arguments of this kind, however, turn on a set of stereotypes too arcane for the average Italian to grasp (never mind independently produce) without a degree of prior explanation of the intricacies of the game of cricket, which would lack the essential pleasantness of the immediately readable image of bobbies on mountain bikes.

Stereotyping itself, let us not forget, has had a bad press for a very long time – indeed worse than it deserves, since as this argument has indicated, much can be learned about cultures from how they stereotype others, and are in turn stereotyped by them. Admittedly, stereotyping rarely tells the whole story. As an instance of how it may desensitize our perception, consider the terms in which Charles Dickens – himself so noted for brilliant typecasting and caricature – entered a strong note of caution as early as the 1840s in his *Pictures from Italy*, to English travellers in Italy, whom he addressed in droll fashion as 'lovers and hunters of the picturesque'. 'Let us', he appealed to them, after staying for a time in Naples, 'not keep too studiously out of view the miserable depravity, degradation and wretchedness, with which this gay Neapolitan life is inseparably associated!':

> Painting and poetizing for ever, if you will, the beauties of this most beautiful and lovely spot of earth, let us, as our duty, try to associate a new picturesque with some faint recognition of man's destiny and capabilities; more hopeful, I believe, among the ice and snow of the North Pole, than in the sun and bloom of Naples.[16]

Dickens's warning is that by reason of stereotypical appreciation of the Neapolitan sun and picturesque antiquities, we tend to overlook another crucial factor – that there is so much in the living conditions of Naples' inhabitants to be deplored. However, in responding to such a warning it is important not to leap to an opposite extreme. The more seriously we take Dickens here, the more likely it is that we may spout *only* denigration and pessimism, as an antidote to others' enthusiastic twaddle about Italy.

As if the above complexities of interpretation were not enough, there is another possibility we must be vigilant to detect. How far is the Italy of our careful analyses a cultural metonym for something larger – for the West in general? I have already suggested that if we are dealing in something longer than (even very extended) historical periods – something more like Foucault's notion of the episteme – then it has to be granted that Italy had reached, earlier than other places, certain key configurations of the worldviews we still (just about, and however terminally) take for granted in Western life and thought. This notion of Italy as a cultural initiator from at least as early as the Middle Ages is one I have highlighted with the memorable terms of the earlier quotation from Umberto Eco. As a notion it is a huge generalization, mined with exceptions. But it is important to consider ways in which Italy nonetheless certainly has set cultural trends in the past, since they may otherwise remain insufficiently understood; with the further and graver consequence that *present* trends might be neglected or left to sneak up on us unawares, and their significance go all the more uncharted.

So it is important to recognize, amid all the general clamour about Italy in crisis, those few voices which are saying that once again, in these very conditions in which she finds herself, other Western cultures might be wise to see presages of their own future. The experienced political commentator Martin Jacques, for instance, writing of the 'conditions for Italy to become the political laboratory of Europe' – Western Europe that is, since he makes an exception of formerly communist Eastern Europe – admits that 'however acute the crisis of the political class elsewhere, Italy remains the only country in which the political system has experienced meltdown'. But he suggests nonetheless that 'somehow the Italian experience chimes with what is happening in other Western democracies. Everywhere there is a crisis of the political class. . . . People even ask whether it could happen here. From being Europe's odd man out, Italy is rapidly acquiring the status of paradigm.'[17]

There may even be a case for suggesting that the crisis is larger than one of the 'political class' merely: that it has to do with reaching towards new strategies for, or else an endgame to, capitalism itself. But this, like much else in the present part of this discussion, is so huge a topic that no immediate addressing of it can be thoroughgoing, or provide a once-and-for-all settlement of the issues. The following chapters make repeated returns to such a discussion, necessarily in piecemeal ways and from differing angles. For that is the only way that anyone but the most prescient of economists (and I myself am not even an economist, never mind a prescient one) could begin to make sense of the global situation, and hope to carry conviction to others.

Carrying conviction is sometimes a matter of finding the right pointers or analogies for the condition being described. This is not easy in the present Italian context, where the kinds of stereotyping already witnessed may capture eternal verities such as sunlight, the picturesque, or light and carefree lifestyles, but hardly the darker realities of cultural crisis, which, because relatively recent, and prone to alarming and unforeseen worsening processes, have not given rise to fixed and widely recognized stereotyping as yet. Italians themselves are often at a loss for ways to accentuate how dramatically worse is today's reality than yesterday's – when yesterday's bleakness already seemed to exhaust all powers of critical analysis.

However, insofar as in modern times Italy has been through several distinct periods of crisis, it is instructive to look back from the most recent to *previous* 'worst cases'. Comparison between two or more crises is not often achieved by Italian political commentators, except for rare historians capable of standing above the fray. It is undoubtedly easier for outsiders who do not live continuously in Italy to consider the possible lessons of earlier crises, while Italy itself and Italians collectively tend to have their attention monopolized by the present one. One such extreme state crisis, felt and lived through with raw nerves by Italians at large, was the sequestration and murder by the Red Brigades of the prominent Christian Democrat leader Aldo Moro in 1978.

I have already hinted that Italy's modern habit of nurturing its political crises (such that the habitual daily levels of angst about the national situation never diminish) can have the effect in the long run of erasing from clear view the configurations of last year's crisis, never mind an event of decades ago, however momentous at the time. With so many more recent big stories in Italian politics – P2; the maxi-trials of the mafia and eventual killings of the magistrates who had assembled the main evidence, Giovanni Falcone and Paolo Borsellino; the collapse of the post-war party system and rebuilding of another one; *tangentopoli* and *mani pulite*, etc. – the Moro affair of 1978 may seem of little abiding significance nowadays. But to assume it were so would be wrong-headed. There is added value in returning precisely now to some consideration of how the events of Moro's sequestration and murder were viewed at the time, to reacquaint ourselves for comparative purposes with something terrible from the past, by which to measure an actuality which *at any given present moment* may be being experienced as a worst-case scenario. The Sicilian writer Leonardo Sciascia wrote a major book on this case entitled *L'Affaire Moro*,[18] which was largely an attempt to fathom the unspoken – and seemingly at first unspeakable – depths of how bad things had become in Italy as a consequence of that fatal episode. There is no better way of experiencing the particular past of the Moro affair than by returning to consider the substance and manner of Sciascia's investigation. Exactly because of the long and tortuously eventful years since the circumstances the book records, Sciascia's achievement of a kind of distillation of what constitutes conflict in the Italian political framework and his implied views on what, by contrast, might constitute a better Italy, governed by politicians of far greater moral integrity, provide a lesson of enduring relevance.

Sciascia uses his well-honed investigative techniques to trace the hidden (or at any rate least obvious) meanings in the sequence of events, from the moment the Red Brigades first grabbed Moro, through the weeks of his detention and 'trial' at their hands leading to their pronouncing his death sentence, and finally the national aftermath following the discovery of Moro's murdered body in a car boot only metres away from the Christian Democrat headquarters in Rome. These basic facts of the narrative are used as the schema for a far deeper enquiry on Sciascia's part into what he calls, within a page of the book's opening, 'this terrible land which Italy has become' ('questo terribile paese che l'Italia è diventato').[19]

Sciascia engages in a moral study of the plight of Moro himself while in detention, based on a psychological investigation of some of the numerous letters of appeal he made to fellow Christian Democrat leaders. Mounted upon that first study is a related enquiry on the one hand into the bankrupt moralities of the Christian Democrat Movement, as evidenced by the hardened hearts of Moro's 'close friends', and on the other into the still more hardened hearts of the Red Brigade terrorist movement. Moro himself comes in for a moving re-evaluation under Sciascia's scrutiny. No longer the sibylline 'fixer' of Christian Democrat politics, practising an arcane and tortuously manipulative political language, Moro is perceptibly changed in captivity into a mere Christian Democrat militant, existentially speaking a 'figure in-between', a victim of political deals stitched up by a hierarchy of party bosses who seem unmoved by the thought that, until his capture, Moro was himself their overall mastermind, not to mention an intimate friend of each and every one of them.

The book is a study in the reactions of individual power brokers to a political crisis which, analysed and retold as a detective narrative (in Italian the equivalent term is *racconto inchiesta*),[20] paces its revelations to the exact contours of successive events. In Sciascia's narration of the Moro affair, each addition to the store of wisdom about the nature of Italian politics reaches the reader's mind with the same effectiveness that the progressive piecing together of a puzzle in a detective investigation tends to do. Further remarks on this work will be confined to its opening. For what lends extra subtlety to Sciascia's deployment of the techniques of the *racconto inchiesta* is that they are ushered in here only gradually, by an evocative use of a quite different literary genre, that of pastoral. In order to reach for an adequate terminology for understanding 'this terrible country that Italy has become', Sciascia narrates a chance event from his own rural existence in Sicily, which at once evokes memories of another Italy of his childhood and, via that, of a fellow writer, Pier Paolo Pasolini, himself recently murdered by youths 'adorable' but fatal to him, in the terrible beauty (to adopt the Yeatsean term) of this changed Italy.

In brief, Sciascia begins his book about that awful event of 1978 by casting about for an image haunting enough to capture the overall terribleness of the times, one which will register a categorical break between a former, remembered time and the unpalatable present. An isolated firefly encountered during an evening stroll is for him a talisman of the time of his youth, when fireflies were common. Even the memory of Pasolini at this point is not accidental, for it had been that other contemporary writer/filmmaker (born one year after Sciascia himself, in 1922) who had originally drawn a distinction between two post-war epochs in Italian culture – literally, time before and time after the disappearance of fireflies:

Out for a stroll last night, I saw a glow-worm in the cracked plaster of a wall. I hadn't seen a glow-worm in these parts for at least forty years. That's why I took it first for a fragment of schist or a splinter of glass in the plaster and that it was the moonlight threading through the branches which made it glimmer greenly. The idea that glow-worms had come back after all those years didn't occur to me. . . . But it was really a glow-worm on that wall. I experienced an intense pleasure. A double pleasure. Somehow reduplicated. The pleasure of rediscovering a time – my childhood, its memories, this very spot, silent now, echoing then with voices and games – and the pleasure of a time to discover, to invent. With Pasolini. For Pasolini. Pasolini who was now outside time but not yet, in this terrible land which Italy has become.

Ieri sera, uscendo per una passeggiata, ho visto nella crepa di un muro una lucciola. Non ne vedevo, in questa campagna, da almeno quarant'anni: e perciò credetti dapprima si trattasse di uno scisto del gesso con cui erano state murate le pietre o di una scaglia di specchio; e che la luce della luna, ricamandosi tra le fronde, ne traesse quei riflessi verdastri. Non potevo subito pensare a un ritorno delle lucciole, dopo tanti anni che erano scomparse. . . . Era proprio una lucciola, nella crepa del muro. Ne ebbi una gioia intensa. E come doppia. E come sdoppiata. La gioia di un tempo ritrovato – l'infanzia, i ricordi, questo stesso luogo ora silensioso pieno di voci e di giuochi – e di un tempo da trovare, da inventare. Con Pasolini. Per Pasolini. Pasolini ormai fuori del tempo ma non ancora, in questo terribile paese che l'Italia è diventato.[21]

One's first response to the evocative sights and sounds of the earlier Italy of Sciascia's youth may be to wonder what on earth the pastoral description has to do with the subject of this work, Aldo Moro's abduction and killing. We remain in suspense only briefly. Sciascia soon progresses to memories of that other major literary figure, Pasolini, also recently murdered in the vilest of circumstances. Remembering his fraternal fellow writer, now distanced by death, Sciascia recalls that Pasolini had used the noted disappearance of the formerly common sight of fireflies in the evenings as a line of historical demarcation of the post-war years into two distinctive periods, in accounting for the deterioration in Italian public life under the long-running Christian Democrat 'regime'.

At a stroke we understand why Sciascia began his own text with that haunting vision of a firefly, vestige, seemingly, of a prior epoch. In the words he quotes from Pasolini we grasp that the beguiling initial adoption of the genre of pastoral (conjuring up a lost but not as yet forgotten country of earlier years) had been calculated to introduce a subject that is its virtual opposite – the remainder of the book's witness to a newly terrible Italy, which can only be seen for what it has now become by reminders as moving as this pastoral description of what it has once been, *within the living memories* of the writers in question. Pasolini had said:

I shall call that phenomenon which occurred about ten years ago 'the extinction of the glow-worm'. The Christian Democratic regime had two distinct phases. . . . The first phase of this regime (as the radicals have always rightly insisted on calling it) goes from the end of the war to the extinction of the glow-worm. The second goes from the extinction of the glow-worm up to the present.

Quel 'qualcosa' che è accaduto una decina di anni fa lo chiamerò . . . 'scomparsa delle lucciole'. Il regime democristiano ha avuto due fasi assolutamente distinte. . . . La prima fase di tale regime (come giustamente hanno sempre insistito a chiamarlo i radicali) è quella che va dalla fine della guerra alla scomparsa delle lucciole, la seconda fase è quella che va dalla scomparsa delle lucciole a oggi.[22]

Pasolini (Sciascia reminds us) had written some time before his own terrible death of a watershed moment when he and his generation consciously noticed that the fireflies of their youth had disappeared – no longer glowed, no longer existed. Attributable to atmospheric and water pollution, this historical disappearance of the fireflies had by Pasolini's calculations coincided with a distinctive transition in the continuous post-war Christian Democrat rule of Italy: a time, according to Pasolini in the early 1960s, when the public language of those in power had darkened into incomprehensibility, masking, he implied, unfathomable corruption. Pasolini's choice of a correlative – the disappearance of the fireflies – aptly demarcates a rupture in the public political world of Italy between a more benign age and the corrupt and indeed murdersome period which was its sequel, and which eventually proved tragic for Pasolini himself, for Moro and for many others.

Pasolini's correlative works by implying a deterioration in the ecology of natural life, with implications of bad management of the environment on the part of Italians. Sciascia's own chance sighting of a single firefly long after their general disappearance is not a sign of return to a better state, but rather, by its very status as an exception, a further confirmation of the denatured ecological conditions in Italy, as well as the underlying social and political ones which are their cause. The description of the firefly glimpsed by chance has set the stage for the work's overall enquiry into the Italy of the fireflies' disappearance. The pastoral idyll of the opening is thus quickly seen to be serving the overarching genre in which the work is cast, that of the *racconto inchiesta*, Sciascia's characteristic mode, which is concerned not at all with pastoral idylls but with their direct opposite, political evils.

Apart from his adapted demarcation from Pasolini, Sciascia had elsewhere already furnished corollaries from popular culture in attempting to describe the worsening social and political conditions. Some seventeen years earlier, in his most widely read detective novel *The Day of the Owl* (first Italian edition 1961), in suggesting how the rest of Italy is being taken over by the worst forms of Sicilian scandal and corruption, Sciascia focuses the phenomenon in terms of several analogies. One of his characters, in explicating things not easy to be believed – indeed *incredibili* – about Sicily, and subsequently elaborating the proposition that one needs to go to Sicily to take lessons in the larger mystery of Italy itself, suggests that the line of concentrated strong-dark-coffee drinkers moves ever northward, from its Sicilian origins. Likewise, he has heard scientists claiming that the 'palm line' – i.e. the limit of climatic conditions favourable to the growth of palm trees – shifts northward every year by five hundred metres, presumably through global warming due to bad ecological management on the part of those in power. The implication in all these *perceptions read as signs* is that the pandemic malaise of Sicily, itself an 'incredible' reality (if only in the narrow sense that it produces a series of counter-intuitive shocks to normal reasoning processes), is rapidly becoming the condition of Italy more generally.[23] The very instances Sciascia's character furnishes and then generalizes (the northward-moving 'line of the palm, of strong coffee, of scandals') are quaint and comic, and very much in an Italian tradition of drawing attention to something disturbing by means of wry analogies, which help the mind in what might otherwise be its disinclination to look directly at such an unwelcome reality in the first place, or at all.

And yet there is a problem with all of Sciascia's corollaries, whether his own or those borrowed from Pasolini or popular culture. For in providing ways of thinking dualistically about an earlier and purer Italy on the one hand, and then a latter-day corrupt one on the other, they allow us to imagine neither those finer shades of grey between the extremes of purity and corruption – the sheer gradualism or arbitrariness of cultural change, for instance, which is sometimes all the more important for being unseen and hence unattested – nor anything like an endgame to the ever-worsening situation. That may in part be because no 'worst' has proved capable of being imagined. For if the Italian reality – like the Roman imperial one long before it – can be thought of in terms of decline and fall, then the shocking thing to note is how unending is the drama of decline, without as yet any definitive and all-encompassing fall. In these respects the corollaries supplied by Sciascia, though they work imaginatively to register important factors of deterioration in Italian life, leave undefined an important possibility in the national drama – namely, actual collapse. Some different analogy that helps us to imagine a stage beyond mere 'decline' – even if one that has not yet been reached – would seem to be called for. As though on prompt, such an analogy appears as a news item on one of the key icons in Italy's multifarious cultural heritage: 'A long-running Italian restoration farce drew its first act to a conclusion yesterday when the mayor of Pisa threatened to reopen the leaning tower on the second anniversary of its closure, with or without the urgent repair works essential to the tower's survival.'[24]

Pisa's leaning tower was already outstanding for its beauty in the age of the proliferation of towers, quite early in the millennium. Interestingly, it had also begun leaning towards a fall from its earliest days, as a consequence of weak foundations and soft subsoils. The modern Pisan authorities had havered but finally decided. The continued closure for restoration of their ancient and world-renowned tower could no longer be tolerated. Not only because no restoration was in fact taking place, no agreement having been reached on how precisely to restore it (a paradigm if ever there was one for the decisive indecisiveness of modern Italian politics and public life), but also because its continued closure incurred a drastic loss of immediate income to the city – income needed in order to pay accumulated *arrears* on the city's heavily mortgaged *future*.

The first of several proposed restoration projects – to rebuild the leaning tower upright – had been rejected outright. How ridiculous if the formerly leaning tower of Pisa were after restoration to respect the intentions of its first builders, of verticality to the earth. Such rectitude – after so long a history of decline – would not simply be a physical, but a *moral* absurdity, in the Italy which everyone had grown so used to expecting at some stage finally to come crashing down itself. In this country which is something of a byword for corruption, everybody knows that rectitude is no money puller. And plainly it has all along been the leaning tower's very state of incline – and not what should be a still greater magnet, its stunningly original Romanesque beauty – which

**Figure 2** Pisa's twelfth-century Romanesque Leaning Tower, one of an ensemble of breathtakingly beautiful buildings in the Piazza dei Miracoli ('Place of Miracles'). The saga of the piecemeal and stop-go measures taken to prevent the tower's collapse to some extent repeats in miniature the havering and indecisiveness of much public policy-making in modern Italy. Photo: Rik Lee.

has won it attention. Better to revert to the *status quo ante* of impending disaster in this place of miracles (Piazza dei Miracoli) – this ensemble of cathedral, baptistery, burial ground, and ever-more-leaning tower – than for a public Italian body to return something to an original state of upright purity such that it no longer risked falling.

Here in short was the symbol to beat all symbols for a world not yet definitively fallen but so near the end of functioning as it has in the past that no one can say from one moment to another whether this will not be its last. And which, in spite of everything, has been presented with an opportunity of rescue, which after further procrastination it has found the necessary indecisiveness spiced with bravado decisively to turn down.

In slightly more recent times, during the 1990s, discreet holding and corrective solutions to the problem of Pisa's leaning tower (as with social life and the national economy) *have* been effectuated, and the monument is once again *chiuso per restauro* – shut, if not from view, at

**Figure 3** Engineering winch now serving as 'belt and braces' to the Leaning Tower. What a pity it is hidden behind rooftops, since its own twentieth-century design corresponds in attractiveness – across the centuries – with the building it helps to prevent from falling. Photo: Rik Lee.

least from tourists clambering over its various levels, like aspiring Galileos who are nonetheless mostly unaware of the fame of the original's scientific tests of gravity purportedly carried out from this location. Subsoils on the side of the tower opposite to its lean now have massive weights buried in them to lessen its incline, even if only fractionally. And a system of 'belt and braces', attached over nearby rooftops to a hidden mooring winch – so beautiful in its own right that it ought to be more publicly on show, as an instance of modern Italian engineering design at its breathtaking best – seeks discreetly to hold up the show, like breeches that would otherwise fall down with consequent social disgrace redounding upon the nation.

This compulsively courted state of impending disaster – of disaster not yet definitive, partly on account of temporizing corrective measures which are always less than fully adequate to address the problems – *is contemporary Italy*. The message of much of this book is that, as in the past, Italy already lives further into a future which the rest of the world has acquired a millennial passion/malaise for copying. The entire world loves Italy – and, as in the best of marriages, 'for better, for worse'. To say that, however, is to include the proposition that we love those aspects of our own Western culture which first developed long ago in Italy, just as they are today showing some of their worst symptoms of wear and tear in that beloved country. Like many Italians themselves, we perhaps have grounds to be alarmed about inadequately arrested decline. With bated breath we go on fearing some definitive fall.

## Notes

1. Philip Jones, 'La storia economica dalla caduta dell'Impero romano al secolo XIV', in Ruggiero Romano and Corrado Vivanti (eds), *Storia d'Italia* (Turin: Einaudi, 1974), Vol. 2, Tome 2, pp. 1526 and 1530.

2. Lauro Martines, *Power and Imagination: City-States in Renaissance Italy* (1979; Harmondsworth: Peregrine Books, 1983), p. xi.

3. Jones, 'La storia economica', p. 1544, fn. 2.

4. Umberto Eco, *Travels in Hyperreality: Essays*, translated by William Weaver (1986 under title *Faith in Fakes*: this edition London: Pan Books, 1987), p. 84.

5. Michel Foucault, *The Archaeology of Knowledge*, translated by A. M. Sheridan Smith (London: Tavistock Publications, 1972). The essential discussion and definitions of the notion of an episteme occur on pp. 191ff.

6. Eco, *Travels*, pp. 64–8. There is vastly more of interest on these pages than there is room to quote.

7. Jones, 'La storia economica', p. 1470.

8. From 'Memoir of the Early Life of Sir Walter Scott, Written by Himself', in J. G. Lockhart, *Memoirs of the Life of Sir Walter Scott, Bart*, Volume the First (Edinburgh: Robert Cadell, 1837), p. 58.

9. Giovanni Falcone in collaboration with Marcelle Padovani, *Cose di Cosa Nostra* (Milan: Rizzoli, 1991). In English, *Men of Honour: The Truth about the Mafia*, translated by Edward Farrelly (London: Fourth Estate, 1992).

10. *The Observer*, Sunday 29 December 1991.

11. Significant studies of modern Italy in English to have bucked the trend of describing its culture in terms of stereotypes have been Paul Ginsborg's *History of Contemporary Italy: Society and Politics 1943–1988* (Harmondsworth: Penguin, 1990), and the book of essays by various hands edited by Zygmunt G. Baranski and Robert Lumley, *Culture and Conflict in Postwar Italy: Essays on Mass and Popular Culture* (London: Macmillan, 1990). See also the more recent volume of essays edited by David Forgacs and Robert Lumley, *Italian Cultural Studies: An Introduction* (Oxford: Oxford University Press, 1996).

12. Giacomo Leopardi, *Discorso sopra lo stato presente dei costumi degl'italiani*, introduced and edited by Augusto Placanica, (Venice: Marsilio, 1989). The two quotations read in the original Italian: 'impossibile a uno straniero il conoscere perfettamente un'altra nazione' (pp. 121–2), and 'gli italiani, delicatissimi sopra tutti gli altri sul conto loro: cosa veramente strana, considerando il poco o niuno amor nazionale che vive tra noi, e certo minore che non è negli altri paesi' (p. 122).

13. Stendhal, *Rome, Naples et Florence (1826)* (Paris: Éditions Gallimard, 1987), p. 181. The original reads, 'La femme chez qui j'ai vu réunis la plus rare beauté, l'âme la plus haute et le plus d'esprit, Mme M***, n'était point exempte de ce défaut. Sans petite vanité pour elle-même, elle était *susceptible* pour son pays; dès qu'on blâmait quelque chose de ce cher pays, elle rougissait'.

14. *L'Indipendente*, 19 December 1991. The image of bobbies on mountain bikes is a Press Association news photograph by John Stillwell, dated 17 December 1991. The Press Association release accompanying the photo stated that the bobbies were on a test ride 'after Tottenham police purchased two of the bikes to keep up with cycle related crime in the area'.

15. Just such a 'lament for hope and glory' – by that title indeed – appeared in the news review of *The Sunday Times*, 3 April 1994. The ignominy lies not solely in now being a very weak cricketing nation, but in being repeatedly defeated by former colonial peoples, Australians, West Indians *et al.*

16. Charles Dickens, *Pictures from Italy*, in the volume *American Notes, Pictures from Italy, and A Child's History of England* (London: Chapman and Hall, 1891), p. 326.

17. *The Sunday Times*, News Review, 3 April 1994.

18. Leonardo Sciascia, *L'Affaire Moro* (Palermo: Sellerio, 1978); English translation by Sacha Rabinovitch, *The Moro Affair* (Manchester: Carcanet, 1987).

19. *The Moro Affair*, p. 15; *L'Affaire Moro*, p. 12.

20. The term *racconto inchiesta* is used whether the narrative in question relates a real or an imagined event. This was Sciascia's staple genre of writing, which he used in both fiction and non-fiction.

21. *The Moro Affair*, p. 15; *L'Affaire Moro*, pp. 11–12.

22. *The Moro Affair*, p. 16; *L'Affaire Moro*, pp. 13–14.
23. Leonardo Sciascia, *Il giorno della civetta* (Turin: Einaudi, 1961), p. 115.
24. Ed Vulliamy in the *The Guardian*, 7 January 1992.

# CHAPTER 1

# CITIES, DANTESQUE AND OTHER

**Figure 4** Portal to the Piazza della Repubblica in Florence, formerly Piazza Vittorio Emanuele II. This large piazza was created by clearance of the old medieval market area, including towers and houses, the historical Jewish ghetto, together with churches and shops. These medieval and later remains had themselves been built over the site of the ancient Roman forum and central crossroads of the city. Photo from *The Golden Book of Florence: All of the City and Its Masterpieces*, published by Casa Editrice Bonechi, Florence. Reproduced by permission of Casa Editrice Bonechi. The inscription on the late-nineteenth-century gateway reads:

L'ANTICO CENTRO DELLA CITTÀ      [The ancient centre of the city
DA SECOLARE SQUALLORE      from centuries-old squalor
A VITA NUOVA RESTITUITO      to new life restored
MDCCCXCV      1895]

33

Portals and their inscriptions. . . . City walls – what they enclose and what they exclude. . . . A city's 'centre' – literal, metaphorical, or tropological. . . . The life of its citizens. . . . Myths of itself by which it lives. . . . Divided images of the good and the bad city. . . . All these are under scrutiny here.

My topic for much of the present chapter, and the following three as well, is cities and how they are represented. It is a chameleon subject, frequently changing – as cities themselves do – over brief intervals of time, and hence requiring ever-new directions of analysis. Cities are material in form but their social, political and religious realities are constituted in large measure by the lived experience of citizens. Representations and idealizations of cities based on such experience have survived in the form of pictorial or textual records, from ancient times to the present. In this regard the first half of the fourteenth century in Italy, up to and a little beyond the plague of 1348, is crucially important for its consolidation of a mercantile and artistic culture based on independent cities, and fascinating also for the variety of contemporary cultural interpretation it furnishes for study. Two writers who have left us with revealing textual sources – albeit charged with personal attitude and 'spin' – for interpreting both what cities were actually like in this age of the communes and what was most feared and hoped for from them, are Dante Alighieri (1265–1321)and Giovanni Boccaccio (1313–1375). It is writings by these two authors and a great cycle of fresco paintings produced in Siena in the late 1330s by the artist Ambrogio Lorenzetti, depicting good and bad forms of civic life, that are the chief materials for interpretation of cities in this chapter and the next.

Dante was preoccupied by the role of the city for a variety of interconnecting reasons, at once social, political and religious. According to him the city is all-important for the individual, who has free-will, is often mired in sin, but capable of self-salvation. At the other end of the scale the universal empire, of which each particular city is (or at any rate should be) a subsidiary and tributary part, is also in trouble and also capable of being saved.[1] Interpreted by him in a variety of ways, the city – sometimes generic, sometimes particular, occasionally both at once – is also the context from which most of the recently dead and even a few of the classical spirits who interact with his pilgrim self-persona throughout the realms of hell, purgatory or heaven have come. I say realms, but it is clear that although all three are at times denominated

thus (as *regni* that is), two of them, *inferno* and *paradiso*, are also to be
understood as cities in their own right. Indeed, there is a long tradition
from at least as early as Augustine representing the blessed in heaven as
a community which constitutes a city of the good and just, akin to a
paradisal Jerusalem, and the damned in hell as a contrary city of the
wicked, of which Babel, Sodom and Gomorrah (but also Jerusalem
again, under certain of its sinful and earthly characteristics) are the
biblical parallels.[2]

My topic, even in this first chapter, is far more than merely Dante, or
the ways in which as a particular thinker he gave artistic representation
to cities. It is equally, the life of cities in the present moment of
millennial change. Florence is a representative instance. As Dante's
birthplace and also somewhere he was exiled from for the last twenty
years of his life, it was a material and lived reality to which he devoted a
lot of attention in his writings. Furthermore its modern history as one of
Italy's leading artistic and commercial centres, as well as a prime tourist
attraction for its medieval and Renaissance treasures especially, gives it
an importance which is highly revealing of present Italian and indeed
international culture. It must be appreciated, however, that there are
difficulties in presenting so huge a topic as the way in which cities such
as Florence have functioned as living contexts and been conceptualized
in ideological terms from early in the second millennium through to its
close. There is so much to be established that oblique and unexpected
ways into the subject may be just as, if not more, likely to produce
breakthroughs, than any standard attempt at a linear account of what
was certainly nothing so simple as a clear-cut, chronological development.

I have chosen therefore to begin with incidental but nonetheless
highly revealing pieces of writing – two inscriptions on city portals. The
first is on a real portal, visible in the Florence of today. I shall deal with
it independently at the outset, since it helps to introduce a set of
attitudes about the way Florence has long been understood historically
from one age to another. I shall then embark on a larger cultural
analysis of the place and role of Florence – and the concept of the city
more generally – in Dante's writings. Very early in that further
undertaking it becomes necessary to discuss the inscription on another
specific city portal, this time a literary one. Here the inscription is met
suddenly as the unmediated first ten lines of the third canto of *Inferno*,
closing with the almost universally known counsel of despair, 'Abandon

hope, ye who enter.' We are not told till after we have already read those
lines what it is that they constitute: namely, the inscription on a portal
that Dante himself is about to go through into the 'city' they mention,
hell itself.

Indeed, as the chapter proceeds, my analysis concentrates primarily on
a comparison and correlation between the city of hell and that of
Florence, just as Dante himself often did in the *Commedia*. The
particular hell in question is of course Dante's own, the classically named
city of *Dite* (Dis), just as the particular arched portal in present-day
Florence that I want to begin by interpreting, although built hundreds of
years after the *Commedia* was written, bears in its 1895 inscription
(presented as an epigraph to this chapter) interesting verbal echoes from
Dante. Read in conjunction with correlative material from the *Inferno*
and *Paradiso*, it proves rich in hints towards a historiography of the city.
Indeed the inscription on that vast portal in late-nineteenth-century
Florence partakes of an ancient ritual, which Dante himself may have
been almost the first to practise, of seeking to vilify the recent past of the
city – up to and including the present – while praising a long-past age of
glory; one so worthy as to merit at whatever cost being recuperated or
restored (literally *restituito*, as the Italian wording of the inscription has
it), with 'new life' (*vita nuova*) from this time forth, into the future.

A coda to the chapter will require a sharp refocusing, from Dante's
fourteenth-century merchant city, reviled by him for the trading and
banking activities which had led to an influx of what he acrimoniously
called *gente nuova* – newcomers to the city from the surrounding areas
and sometimes further afield, attracted by the fast profits (the *sùbiti
guadagni*) to be made (*Inferno*, XVI, 73) – on to problems of the so-
called *extracomunitari*, or foreign immigrant groups, in the city of
today. For Florence has been the focus in the early 1990s of some of the
worst problems in the whole of Italy between new immigrant
communities and traditional city-dwellers. The city authorities reacted
in tough and (some would say) inhumane ways, which set precedents for
other municipalities and regions. This is one of those issues of the kind
treated in my Introduction. We need to estimate whether xenophobia
has displayed a cultural continuity from Dante's time until our own like
those other institutions, behaviours or beliefs of the Middle Ages that
Umberto Eco lists, within or by means of which he claims 'we still live'.
Or is there instead little connection, historical or typological, between
the two manifestations of the phenomenon so far apart in time?

\* \* \* \* \*

The present Piazza della Repubblica in Florence was created as part of a large widening and modernization programme following the clearing away in 1887 of the city's medieval streets and alleyways, at the heart of which had been the Old Market – a market 'among the more picturesque in Italy' according to a well-known guidebook in Italian.[3] By contrast the nineteenth-century square which replaced the Old Market and its medieval surrounds is, in the words of the writer and art historian Michael Levey, 'a triumph of boastful banality'.[4] This was a recreated space by the reckoning of the 1895 inscription on its main portal, leading into the Via degli Strozzi on the west side of the piazza. The vaunt in that inscription was that 'centuries-old squalor' had been cleared away in order to refashion and bring new vitality to what formerly (it is not clear whether the Roman or medieval period is intended by the adjective 'ancient', 'antico'[5]) had been the historic heart of the city.

There are several points worthy of immediate note. First, this very portal masquerades as a kind of triumphal arch, though it is not free-standing. In its own grandiose way, given the initial name of the refashioned piazza it dominates – the Piazza Vittorio Emanuele II – it registers the triumph of monarchical and unified Italy, one subtext of the inscription being Florence's own importance in that still rather recently constituted unity. (Florence had briefly been the capital city between 1865 and 1870, until the transfer of that status to Rome.)

Second, the refashioning of this central point of the city had gone ahead against the advice of Giuseppi Poggi (1811–1901), the architect and city planner responsible for the main street-widening during the prior years. Poggi's own plans for change had been vast. Most important of all was a ring of avenues (*viali*) around the inner city or *centro storico*. These avenues mainly followed the line of the third set of city walls built between 1284 and 1333. In many places their construction required the dismantling of long stretches of these same walls, a point much regretted by those Florentine traditionalists who resented the 'invading modern spirit' ('invadente spirito moderno')[6] and who would have preferred retaining the intactness of the city represented by its (until then) relatively unbroken outer set of late-medieval walls. The original plans of the so-called Poggi Project (*Progetto Poggi*) had been issued by the printers Litografia Toscana in

April 1865 as an important public poster with numbered explanations. Poggi's avenues were described in this poster as wide carriageways ('stradoni . . . per le vetture'), punctuated at intervals by porticoed piazzas, in the midst of which were to be preserved the ancient gates to the city as monuments of Art and History. The new piazzas with their ornamental fountains were also to have monuments – to illustrious figures of more recent Italian history than those mainly celebrated within the *centro storico* itself. For instance, on the parterre over the Arno near the former Justice Gate to the city was to be built a monument to the eighteenth-century philosopher of human rights and dignities, Cesare Beccaria. Similarly, there was to be a monument to Garibaldi's 'Thousand' ('i Mille'); a Piazza Cavour with two columns, celebrating Italian independence on the one hand and the Battle of San Martino on the other; a Piazza Vittorio Emanuele (not the eventual one in the city centre) with a monument to the king and six grand columns alluding to the great provinces of the kingdom; and a new bridge over the Arno dedicated to Carlo Alberto and connecting the wide avenues of the north to their continuations on the Oltrarno side. Perhaps most impressive of all was to be a Field of Mars for military displays, with alongside it a Great Barracks for Artillery, Cavalry and Infantry. The post–1865 city was to be nothing if not a showpiece of Italian military might and recent grandeur, an admonishment if ever there were one to other nations to show respect and never again interfere in the peninsula's national independence and integrity.

This 1865 Poggi Project for 'amplification, reduction and widening' of streets and spaces in Florence bespeaks an ideology of the new-born nation-state trying to display (or possibly to convince itself of) its importance, even though by no means all of the intended building programme was realized. For the city-central area of the Old Market, by contrast, Poggi had devised a more conservative plan of what we would nowadays call restoration; 'a reordering of the central area of the city, where the present Market for provisions is situated, to consist of two Galleries of four branches apiece, covered over with glass and flanked by shops'.[7] However, the city authorities preferred (and achieved) a more radical clearance, and the creation of a piazza which no doubt expressed what they wished it to say about the Florence of 1895, in the deliberately grandiose rhetoric equally of its buildings as of the portal inscription, but which also, precisely for reasons of this late-nineteenth-century pomposity, scarcely connects in form or content with the greater subtleties of the medieval and Renaissance Florence which surrounded it and key portions of which were destroyed to make way for its construction.

Third, and crucial to the link back to Dante, is the way the inscription on the inner face of the archway in the finished piazza of 1895 makes its point about the restitution of something ancient by giving it 'new life': *vita nuova* being of course also the title term of one of Dante's own major texts. There is no way the city authorities could have been unconscious of this Dantesque echo down through the centuries. Its presence in the overall formulation can therefore be thought of as a subtle reference to the city's most famous writer. A different subtext of this inscription from the one I have earlier specified thus reclaims Dante himself (however subliminally) for the city, from his historical position in a *different* 'squalor', moral rather than physical, of Florence's own creation: namely, his exile by and from the city, which so radically altered the course of his life and made him unremittingly bitter towards his birthplace. In terms of the Florence of 1895, an attempt to lay to rest ghosts of the past is being made by the inscription's high-flown rhetoric of reviling on the one hand – in the verbose alliterative formula of centuries-old squalor, *secolare squallore* – and glorification on the other.

Fourth, however, what is being implicitly passed over by the boastful formulation is that the Old Market and its surrounds that had been cleared away was – if somewhat shabby and dilapidated by the 1880s – an important remnant of the medieval core of the city, the very Florence of Dante in other words, and of at least a century before and after him. In the inscription's covert reference to him we might have supposed it was seeking to conjure up Dante and his age as the city's most glorious past, *before* the squalor set in. Yet it is precisely a prime architectural legacy and centrepiece of his particular age that the authorities had seen fit to knock down and clear away as the offending context. There seems, in other words, to be a certain vagueness to say the least, and maybe even a logical contradiction, at the heart of the grandiose inscription.

Contradictory or not at its more subliminally implied levels of meaning, in brute explicitness the portal's inscription seeks to conjure up a sense of a former, 'ancient' city before the falling off. For Dante too there had been a terrible 'fall', interpretable in the social and economic phenomena of his own lifetime when contrasted with a somewhat earlier period. For him, reaching back to a purer Florence meant conjuring up the city of a crusading age a century and a half earlier. This is done largely through his quasi-invention of a great-great-grandparent and crusader of the mid-twelfth century, Cacciaguida,[8] who reports extensively on that earlier Florence in several cantos that form a centrepiece to *Paradiso*, which I analyse in some detail later. What we have in either case (in Dante and in the nineteenth-century inscription) is a splitting of the presentation of Florence into two quite separate conceptions of the city – one a bad and regrettable city, the other good and to be glorified. The bad city is that of the present or of the recent past. The good city existed further back in time, and can only be recuperated either by having a deceased spirit from the earlier period report on it, as happens in narrative terms in Dante's poem, or else by radical clearance and rebuilding of the kind undertaken in the knocking down of the Old Market in the 1880s and early 1890s, in order to 're-create' what is declared to have been the 'ancient centre of the city' as this late-nineteenth-century extravagance, the Piazza Vittorio Emanuele II.

So, two Florences, one good, the other bad. Similarly, we have in Lorenzetti's Sienese fresco cycle (as I seek to show in greater detail shortly) a city of good rule, with beneficial effects graphically represented, and a city of bad rule under the forces of tyranny, with depredations and robberies, looting and burning. This in turn reminds us of the teleology of good and evil which gives us in the *Commedia* the woeful city (*città dolente*) of *inferno* and the blessed city of *paradiso*, as contrastive states in the afterlife. Our entire discussion is thus marked by a stark separation between good city and bad city – often one and the same place, but under different forms of rule or in succeeding ages. From as early as the age of Dante and of the slightly later Lorenzetti this division between good and bad was a principle of the representation of cities, and thereby often also of the historiography of the Italian city in a wider sense. It was still being drawn on in differing ways as late as the close of the nineteenth century, as we have seen in the specific instance of that 1895 portal inscription.

* * * * *

In the months that had ushered in the centennial date of 1300 Dante had become involved at the highest level in Florentine politics as a member of the bi-annually changed priorate of the city. As such he had to participate in decisions inevitably seen by others as party political, since although a basically Guelf city for many years beforehand, Florence was riven by faction into White Guelfs and Black Guelfs, who sought mercilessly to kill or at very least drive each other from the city. After participating in an unsuccessful mission of Florentine dignitaries to the Pope in Rome a year later in 1301, Dante along with others was prevented from returning to Florence by the overthrow of his own party of White Guelfs by the Black Guelf faction. He was never to set foot in his native city again.[9] His experience of political exile tempers the poem with forms of enduring bitterness and hatred such as no other work worth mentioning in the same breath as the *Comedy* even remotely evinces. Florence is at one and the same time his dearly beloved birthplace, but also a depraved city, 'full of envy' ('piena/d'invidia'), 'divided' ('partita'), and one in which 'pride, envy, and avarice are the three sparks that have inflamed hearts' ('superbia, invidia e avarizia sono/le tre faville c'hanno i cuori accesi') (*Inferno*, VI, 49–75). This definition of her people as 'avaricious, envious and proud' ('avara, invidiosa e superba') (*Inferno*, XV, 68) is a mantra he elsewhere too feels no qualms about repeating, though he tends to put the judgement into the mouths of other spirits met in the afterlife, to give it a greater objective credibility than as a remark simply issuing from his own persona in the poem.

Though for many readers over hundreds of years Dante's bias against the Florence of his own times is part of what gives his poem its valuable savour, the bitterness with which it is invariably vented attracted criticism from no less a commentator than Machiavelli, writing a couple of centuries later. He felt that Dante had displayed more than a little derangement when speaking of his native city. Machiavelli saw Dante's animosity as originating from the 'affront of his banishment', which caused him to indulge in an ongoing defamation of the city by way of revenge. Writing as he was with the benefit of considerable hindsight, Machiavelli had a large enough vision of the workings of history also to note that the stain on Florence's own reputation caused by her having cast off a figure of such enduring fame as Dante's was a grave one. Machiavelli knew what it was to experience both the importance of political office in Florence and then rejection by a new regime. By criticising the earlier Dante for unbalanced judgement, he would seem to be courting a renewal of the city's favours towards himself – as in so many of his other writings, including the most famous of them, *The Prince*. Dante by contrast, in the terms of this account by Machiavelli, 'was unable to stop defaming her; he accused her of every vice, condemned her inhabitants, criticized her situation, slandered her laws and customs, and all this not in a single part of the poem but throughout it, in different passages and in different ways'.[10] Giovanni Villani had already put the point in a milder and less elaborated form in Dante's own century. Summing up Dante's personality in his *Cronica*, Villani acknowledges 'it is true that he in this Comedy delighted to denounce and to cry out after the manner of poets, perhaps in certain places more than was fitting; but maybe his exile was the cause of this'.[11]

But if Machiavelli, in elaborating a tradition ongoing since Villani, was right about Dante on this point, and the animus felt against particular cities (Florence especially, but not exclusively) is pervasive in the *Commedia*, nonetheless a *positive notion of the city* as a social and political entity, well run and well ordered in God's name or even *by* God himself, is of prime importance in Dante's representation of the afterlife, particularly so in the cases of *inferno* and *paradiso*. As already mentioned, in Augustine's most important textual legacy heaven had been represented as a city; the so-called *civitas dei* or City of God. Augustine's text includes several different senses of the heavenly city. On the one hand heaven is literally to be understood as a city: at creation God

> established nothing better than the spirits to whom he gave an intelligence and furnished with the capacity to contemplate God himself. He also bound them together in the single society that we call the holy and heavenly city. In that city, God himself is the reality by which they might be sustained and made happy – their common food and life, as it were.

On the other hand there is, in figural terms, a heavenly city on earth, in the form of a calling of people by act and faith towards God:

> so long as this heavenly city journeys on the earth, it calls forth citizens. . . . While it journeys, the heavenly city possesses this peace in faith, and out of this faith it lives justly when it directs to the attainment of that peace whatever good actions it performs towards God, and also those performed toward the neighbor, since the life of this city is certainly social.[12]

Dante owes a lot to this traditional representation of heaven as the divine city, whether as realized in 'social' existence on earth, or in the afterlife. Thinking about Augustine's notion of a figural heavenly city before death, we are in a better position to understand a major function of the entire *Commedia*. The work exhorts its audience to lead virtuous lives in their earthly journey in order to reach in spirit self that other heavenly city, which is not a figural but an ultimate reality, the contemplation of God himself. We could even say that the poem *transacts* in narrative terms this transit from the figural heavenly city on earth to the real one in the afterlife. But we should always remember that that is not its whole story, because encountered along the way is an infernal city of the wicked, a terrifyingly possible outcome for individuals of their earthly lives, and one also already dealt with by Augustine in the text which was so seminal for Dante.

As for hell, there is never a hint that Dante's representation of *inferno*, in which punishment is being doled out on an almost industrial scale, is anything less than well run under laws and principles established by God. Indeed it is interesting that the punishments of the various circles of Dante's hell are not always far removed from what we meet in contemporary accounts of the actual penalties applied to malefactors. Magistrative bodies of cities meted out horrific punishments, often linked retributively to the specific crime committed, just as occurs in consequence of the well-known law of the *contrapasso* characterizing the punishment of sinners in the *Commedia*.[13]

There are of course some crucial differences between Dante's hell and contemporary Italian cities. In visual terms what is perhaps most striking is that unlike them it is never lit by sunlight. It can therefore be figured not simply as a special category of city, but as a specific institution of punishment *within* the medieval city – a 'sightless prison' ('cieco carcere', see *Inferno*, X, 58–9), typically underground and sunless. In the real cities of Dante's day a variety of other activities filled out urban space and time, as is clear from even the most cursory look at Ambrogio Lorenzetti's fresco representations from the 1330s of good and bad government in the city and countryside. True, Italian cities of the early 1300s dealt with their malefactors by a variety of often quite brutal forms of retributive punishment, as we see in discreet aspects of Lorenzetti's ideological programme. But punishment was only a small part of their method of self-governance, a subcategory, so to speak, of far more extensive techniques of surveillance and control. A complex programme of government by positive example and operation of the virtues fills out Lorenzetti's representation of *good* government, outlined later in the chapter. In Dante's *inferno* however, the entire function of the city in question is punishment, the rationale for this *città dolente* being to visit retribution in eternity – as opposed to the fixed-term sentences of purgatory – on all categories of sinners unrepentant (or unbaptized in the true Christian faith) at the times of their death.

In the sixth book of the *Aeneid*, which treats of the underworld inhabited by shades of the dead, Virgil in the immediately pre-Christian era had included a city – that of Tartarus, ruled over by the severe Rhadamanthus – where those who had sinned in their earthly lives paid dearly in punishment. While being conducted through the underworld by a sibyl from Cumae, Aeneas, the journeying hero of the poem, hears cries from the shades of those in torment: 'sounds of groaning and brutal lashing,/Sounds of clanking iron, of chains being dragged along'. The sibyl tells him of the punishments going on behind the 'enormous portal' and 'columns of adamant' of this city, but 'scared by the din' he does not investigate further.[14] Dante by contrast both hears and directly witnesses the punishments meted out in his infernal city. He passes through the forbidding portal, as Aeneas had not. Some fourteen centuries after the Latin epic, Dante as poet has taken a cue for the elaboration of his own *Inferno* not merely from the more standard format of Aeneas's meeting with the shades of the dead in the underworld, but more specifically from Virgil's notion of a city behind an enormous portal. Not just that, however. Where Virgil's Aeneas had the Cumaen sibyl to conduct him, Dante structures his narrative so as to make Virgil himself – ordinarily a shade in Limbo where among others the spirits of virtuous pagans reside – his special guide to most of the first two realms of the afterlife. Dante's terrifying portal and his onward journeying down through the city with his guide is thus in almost every respect a heuristic use of Virgil.

Throughout *Inferno* the notion of the city as a connecting link between certain of Dante's political and religious preoccupations is paramount. The idea of hell itself as a city begins early, and is the basis for some of the comparisons the present chapter is concerned to spell out. The entry portal at the beginning of the third canto of the poem, like many another in Dante's times, is the gateway to a city, including an inscription naming the place it provides access to – specifically *la città dolente* or 'woeful city'. Inscriptions were a traditional feature of portals, almost invariably as laudatory of and as welcoming to the city as *this* one is a harsh counsel of eternal despair to those entering hell. The city named, although not the City *of* God in an Augustinian sense, is one that the inscription incontrovertibly states was made *by* Him. It has, furthermore, existed from the beginning of time along with all the rest of first-created things of God, who is here defined as the trinity of Divine Power (the Godhead), Supreme Wisdom (the Holy Spirit) and Primal Love (the Incarnation). Only because Dante is alive, and therefore a *visitor* to this city rather than a newly arriving soul who will stay for ever, is he somehow – narrowly – exempt from the portal's general injunction to abandon all hope. From henceforth he will be multiply cast down by bearing witness to the punishments of the damned. Because he is still alive his own destiny is incomplete. In his state of error at the time of the journey in 1300 he risks returning to hell after death if he does not take matters in hand.

Both because of the inscription over it, and because it stands alone, this portal reminds us at first not so much of a city gate as of a Roman triumphal monument such as Trajan's column. Except that this structure, as the inscription makes plain, speaks not to victors but to the defeated. Its anti-triumphalist message is one of despair to sinners. Commentators as early as Dante's own sons Jacopo and Pietro expound its allegorical meaning, the latter explicitly pointing out the city of sorrow it announces as equivalent to a Babylon, to be contrasted with the virtuous and righteous Jerusalem. In this Pietro Alighieri shows an awareness (surely familial in his case) of Augustine's contrasts between an earthly city, peopled by sinners – 'the state of the wicked, that is hell, [which] can properly be called a city' – and the true heavenly city, created according to Augustine 'by the love of God which involves contempt of self'.[15]

Dante's hell is basically a large and varied medieval city, the *raison d'être* of which is to accomplish God's work of punishing sinners. Quite apart from the first gate encountered, many other aspects of its specific topography are related to features of an Italian city of Dante's day. In Canto VIII the veritable outer walls of Dis enclosing its visible and fiery-red mosques (indicative of a citizenry comprised of vast infidel congregations in burning torment) are seen through the hot vapours rising from the marsh of Styx which the pilgrims are traversing in Flegias's boat (*Inferno*, VIII, 70–3). Perhaps most important of all is the fact that this city, like others of the time, has a series of concentric walls, each one enclosing a smaller and smaller space, even if much later what *appear* to be wall turrets turn out to be a ring of manacled giants guarding the lowest (ninth) circle of hell. In most of the flourishing cities of Dante's Italy extant walls were from successive building periods. Indeed, the more flourishing the city, the faster it grew, and the more frequently it had to build new walls of defensive containment. In Florence's case one set of early medieval walls – the 'antica cerchia' of Cacciaguida's speech much later, in *Paradiso*, XV, 97ff. – dates from the ninth century. Another, enlarged circuit is begun shortly after Cacciaguida's period, in 1172, and finished on the Oltrarno side of the river in 1258. And a further wall is under construction but not completed in Dante's lifetime. I have already spoken of this third set of walls, built between 1284 and 1333, which was substantially demolished in the late nineteenth century to make way for the ring of wide avenues around the historic centre of the expanding modern city.[16]

In the case of *Inferno* the various walls enclose significant circles of hell, just as the ten ditches that comprise *malebolge* (XVIII–XXX) resemble defensive moats to a feudal stronghold. That first defensively styled wall of the city of Dis of Canto VIII, closed in the faces of Virgil and Dante (in typical medieval fashion, with its citizenry defending it from above), is only penetrable by the two pilgrims upon the arrival and intervention of a celestial messenger. Medusa and the furies guarding the wall are the very epitome of bad governors in control of a city, destructive figures whose power needs to be overthrown.

What is interesting is that the gate most like a Roman one, and which in real cities of Dante's time would almost certainly have been part of the ancient and *innermost* urban fabric, is this isolated, outer, first-met gate at the beginning of Canto III. There is no wall attaching to it, contrary to what one would expect with ordinary city gates. In a sense we have an inversion of the normal. The gate, so apparently familiar in type – complete with expected civic inscription – operates in fact at one important level as a *de*familiarization device. From its structural form and from the wording of its inscription we recognize the concept 'city'. At the same time we grasp from surrounding sights and sounds of woe, from its complete isolation in the landscape, as well as from what its inscription actually says, that the city about to be entered is an extraordinary instance. As Claire Rose has pointed out, the topography of Dante's hell is *only partially* an urban topography of his day: she sees a 'process of arousing in the reader certain expectations of a "civic" Hell, which are then disappointed by the reality of the infernal landscape' – all possibly with the specific purpose of overturning positive civic expectations.[17] The visual urban forms which would represent civic values are perverted into their opposites, of desert, forest, cliff and frozen lake, just as the specific sins being punished in hell are perversions of Dante's civic ideals, as laid out in his prose treatises and evident, either directly or by inference, throughout the *Comedy*. Those features of the textual landscape of hell which are harsh, wild and least like a city are hence to be understood as menacing; as is the case with real conditions fostering rapine and pillage in a world of *bad* rather than *good* government (as we shall see in Lorenzetti's frescoes of some thirty years later, contrasting those two political conditions). This is so even though as a working city the Dis of *Inferno* must continue to be seen as an instance of *good* government, processing sinners according to the will of God.

We bump into a kind of paradox here. The sinning lives of those who are punished after death, along with the harsh and seemingly *non*-urban landscapes that are the context of many of their punishments, figurally make this city of hell into an *anti-type* of Dante's civic ideal. Yet the certainty that for their sins these people earn such punishment, and that it is efficiently and eternally meted out (all experientially testified by Dante in his narrative report back to the living), ensure that we recognize the city of hell as part of an overall schema of good governance by God in eternity. Hell is hence an essential contribution to the prototype of civic idealism, offered by the three realms of the *Commedia* taken as a whole. A less paradoxical way of making the same logical point is to affirm an indisputable certainty: that each of several elaborations of civic ideals, whether Dante's own, those of the slightly earlier pre-humanist and then Aristotelian political thinkers,[18] or else the ones depicted in Lorenzetti's frescoes of a few years later, relied for a major plank of its efficiency on the punishment of malefactors who are conceived as having attacked or undermined those ideals. For the mainly political thinkers in question, retributive justice belonged to operational mechanisms of the state, usually a city-state. In Dante justice is divine. As the fourth line of the portal inscription makes clear, Justice (Giustizia) is precisely what moved God to his creation of this somewhat 'alternative' city of the afterlife, the City of Woe.

The discussion so far has seen a stark division between notions of the good and of the bad city at the heart of Dante's political and religious epistemology, affecting every aspect of his treatment of individuals and of communities. This dualism has also been shown to be foundational in a historiography of the development of Italian cities, which continued to be drawn upon as late as a post-unification Italy at the end of the nineteenth century. Other properties of this divided vision of cities inform Dante's comparisons in *Paradiso* between an earlier Florence and that of his own day, as the next section will now elaborate. And still further ramifications of an essentially related dualism shape our understanding of Lorenzetti's frescoes of good and bad government – the substance of a further, penultimate section.

* * * * *

In the circle of Mars midway through *Paradiso*, the final *cantica* of his *Commedia*, Dante meets with Cacciaguida, a figure presented in the poem as his great-great-grandfather. Apart from the fascinating if perhaps dubious biographical material it supplies on Dante, the episode comprises a series of comparisons between past and present – and even future, since there is prophecy involved towards its conclusion about Dante's life as a Florentine exile after 1301. (The work having been written after its setting in 1300, the prophecies within it regarding Dante's future can all 'come true'.) It is constructed in the form of a dialogue between Cacciaguida and Dante the character, and we note from the beginning that Cacciaguida is a particular kind of mouthpiece for Dante the poet, since he is constructed as a luminary truthteller about history. In other words, Cacciaguida is not just supplying an account of his own mid-twelfth-century Florence, interpreted as having enshrined a simpler and purer lifestyle and been a place fit for heroes (and incidentally for hero's wives also, though only in their modest and virtuous role *as* wives); he is above all using that account to criticize the Florence of Dante's times, comprehensively rejected as morally debauched by comparison with the earlier age.

The dialogue runs into three separate cantos. In the first phase Cacciaguida eulogizes the Florence of his own times within its first set of medieval walls (XV, 97ff.). What he says about that former and much smaller city establishes the moral measure for everything which follows, for the passage is a fourteenth-century instance of the well-known propensity in some conservative thought to posit the existence of an organic community in the past, by contrast with which everything in the present is a falling off. At its opening the passage even presents that earlier Florence in synecdoche as sober, chaste and physically unadorned – a figure for the women whom he proceeds a little later to extol as the virtuous guarantors of all its other qualities. Indeed, the deeper into this myth that we explore, the more the virtue and probity of its female citizenry make them guardians of the moral hearth; whether coming from their mirrors with 'unpainted face'; or busy at the spindle and distaff; one minding the cradle of the infant generation; another telling her family of still more mythopoeic times; the legendary founding of Rome by the Trojans, and thence of Fiesole – and subsequently Florence – by the Romans.

The time of Cacciaguida's Florence thereby becomes an idealistic intermediary point between a deeper mythology, that of ancient Roman virtue (and before that, the still more distant, magnanimous Trojans), and the moment of explicit corruption and factionalism of Dante's age. The lines that put all this into the most condensed pattern of historical comparison are the following:

> Saría tenuta allor tal maraviglia
> una Cianghella, un Lapo Salterello,
> qual or saría Cincinnato e Corniglia.

Then a Cianghella or a Lapo Salterello would have been as great a marvel as Cincinnatus and Cornelia would be now.

(XV, 127–9)

Read cursorily, it may appear that two main ages are still in focus here – Cacciaguida's and Dante's. But Cincinnatus and Cornelia are, respectively, upstanding male and female models of ancient Roman virtue; and Cianghella and Lapo Salterello corrupt female and male exemplars of modern vice. So the mathematically very eloquent lines that Cacciaguida has uttered can be reformulated in terms of the following *three-way* historical comparison: 'in my day such corrupt people as vitiate your modern Florence would have been as unlikely a marvel, as in your day people as virtuous as the best of the ancients.' The comparison between the two relatively close ages of Dante and Cacciaguida has thus turned into a way of facilitating comparison with an age still more distant in both historical time and moral quality, namely that of the ancient Romans. In other words, the elaboration of details of the pure citizenry of Florence of the mid-twelfth century has been a staging post towards our contemplation of myths of Roman probity, a way of conferring a more easily identifiable 'reality' on them, so that their contrast with the corrupt times of Dante may act the more severely as censure of the latter.

This interweaving of social comment and mythopoeia, which has been the hallmark of the dialogue in the fifteenth canto, turns into a far more searing critique in the next canto. The underpinning of the discourse with elements of myth is largely abandoned, and Cacciaguida focuses undivided attention on the social ills of Dante's times. But this attack on modern customs is only really possible because of the initial construction of a legendary and ideal Florence situated back in an older medieval period, a so-called *buon tempo antico*, itself intricately linked to conceptions of Roman *valor* and *virtù*.

The opening part of the dialogue in the sixteenth canto soon brings Cacciaguida to a condemnation of the influx of latter-day newcomers from outlying towns to the Florence of Dante's day. The descendants of that first migration out of villages and off the land have come up in the world. Their present activities within Florence are that (to Dante) odious twin pair – money-changing (what we now call banking, after the Italian word *banco*, or the bench on which money-changers first did their business) and selling of merchandise (trade). This movement off the land and into the city throughout the course of the thirteenth century is independently attested by demographic history, and mainly attributable to the huge expansion in profitable enterprises of the fast-expanding urban economy. Cacciaguida, however – and via him Dante – is keen to make a class-based point against the *nouveaux riches*, since from his moment in history (the mid-twelfth century) he can attest the poverty of their ancestors. In revealing that the forebears of the bankers-cum-traders of Dante's day were beggars from the back-block communities of Tuscany, Cacciaguida is demonstrating not simply Dante's searing class prejudices, but something a little more positive as well: namely, that Dante could at least see the economic dynamic of his own times with black and white clarity, and furthermore had a shrewd idea of the time span in which it had unfolded from modest beginnings. The fact that he detests it – unlike some of his contemporaries, who saw the flourishing economy as playing a large part in what made Florence the exceptional city that it was in this age[19] – needs to be bracketed off as something else, requiring study and explanation. For Dante was unique in holding what Charles T. Davis has called 'an extended negative theory of thirteenth- and early fourteenth-century Florentine history': 'precisely in the period of the most remarkable growth of his city, celebrated by all the other Florentine writers, he found the seeds of her moral downfall.'[20] This is so even to the extent that in the process of Cacciaguida's great review of the rise and decline of Florentine families, Dante generates the theory that once-great cities may not just decline, but come to nought. 'Udir come le schiatte si disfanno/non ti parrà nova cosa né forte,/poscia che le cittadi termine hanno': 'hearing that families undo themselves will not seem new or striking to you, since cities too have an ending' (*Paradiso*, XVI, 76–8). It is something of a shock to realize, on hearing these words, that Dante seems to have thought that his own Florence – five times the size of Cacciaguida's – was not simply horrifyingly corrupt but in *terminal* decline.

Dante envies the former time of Cacciaguida when Florence was dramatically smaller and when its citizenry were 'pure down to the humblest artisan'. This is *campanilismo* with a vengeance, since in indicating that Florence's populace is now 'mixed' with the blood of outsiders he names places not far beyond its latest (second medieval) set of walls as the origins of the intruders: Galluzzo, Trespiano, Aguglione and Signa (*Paradiso*, XVI, 51, 56).

The general principle is enunciated only several lines later: 'Sempre la confusion de le persone/principio fu del mal de la cittade': 'The intermingling of people was ever the beginning of harm to the city' (XVI, 67–8). This notion, that the integrity of a state and people depended on there being no interbreeding or even social mingling between it and other peoples, was common to medieval jurists and philosophers, having, like so much other political thought of the times, Aristotelian backup (in *Politics*, III, iii and VI, 10).[21] Nonetheless, read from a contemporary perspective it seems shocking, given the terrible history of states based on philosophies of purity of blood that the twentieth century – so recently with us – witnessed.

Dante's idea of the underlying cause of the evil is the political imbalance between Papacy and Monarchy. He may have been suggesting (as a convinced, though independently minded Ghibelline by the time of the writing of *Paradiso*) that the political predominance of the papacy and Roman curia had kept imperial functionaries from their rightful influence over territories such as that of Florence and its surrounds. Dante's views on the necessary separation of church and state powers laid down in his political treatise *De monarchia* would support such a viewpoint. And certainly it chimes with what an early explication of the *Paradiso*, namely *L'Ottimo commento*, implies about the text at this point. Noting that the emperors were 'absent from the imperial seat', this commentary goes on to specify that

there were no censors, provincial prefects, legates, defenders of cities,

lawyers or tax collectors, nor the other officials by whom provinces are
purged of wicked and dangerous persons and by reason of whose rule over
the world wars are averted, and each person rests content within his own
station in life.[22]

L'Ottimo commento is suggesting by that last remark ('infra li suoi
termini') that literally no internal migration between places and no
change of individual station in life is good.

Certainly Dante's own remark on the church acting the part of a
wicked stepmother to the imperial power, rather than that of a benign
mother to her son, posits as one consequence a scale of social migration
and change of lifestyle within two generations at a remarkably local
level in Florentine affairs:

> tal fatto è fiorentino e cambia e merca,
> che si sarebbe vòlto a Simifonti,
> là dove andava l'avolo a la cerca.

there is one who has become a Florentine and who money-changes and
trades, who would [otherwise, if wider corruption in the church and
usurpation by it of imperial power did not abound] have lived on at
Simifonti where his own grandfather went a-begging.

(Paradiso, XVI, 61–3)

Commentaries tell us that Dante may have had in his sights here a
certain Lippo Velluti, a particularly galling member of the class he had
elsewhere in the Commedia scorned as the gente nuova (Inferno, XVI,
73). But particulars are not really relevant to the main point, which
consists in the virulent combination of his resentment of the newcomers
themselves and his resentment of their commercial activities. It is timely
to remember at just this moment that the person in the text actually
uttering these words is his own forebear Cacciaguida, by the reckoning
of the poem a Second Crusader, and patently of old Florentine stock –
all of which is good enough cover for the fact that Dante's own father
may have been a money-lender. Dante's meeting with Cacciaguida again
recalls Virgil, drawing as it does upon the episode of Aeneas's meeting
with his father Anchises in the sixth book of the Aeneid. In this moment
of the Paradiso that so clearly elaborates on the moving encounter in
Virgil's poem, Cacciaguida is quite literally a father substitute: for
Dante never in all his writings alluded – not even indirectly – to his
actual father.[23]

Since we encounter Cacciaguida's representation of a purer twelfth-century Florence in a comparison with Dante's fallen city of 1300 during a narrated journey through a realm which (at any rate in part) is conceived as a heavenly city, Cacciaguida's Florence takes on overtones of the celestial, while Dante's, by contrast, has all the more deeply underscored its infernal aspects, which we have already been hearing about from the first *cantica* onwards. In other words, at the very heart of paradise Dante the poet has narratively constructed for the benefit of Dante the pilgrim – who himself comes from an infernal city on earth, and has passed through an infernal city of the afterlife which is the teleological consequence of the sinning which prevails in the former – a model of an ideal city that is also identified as Florence, even if from an earlier age. We are at the heart of that dualism between the good city and the bad city. In historical terms the good city turns into the bad city, through a process of moral and socio-political decline. In the teleology of the poem both are co-present, as illustrative possibilities of what comes about through lifestyle choices made by individuals and communities.

In the terms of the comparison between Cacciaguida's Florence and Dante's we are being introduced to a choice in lifestyles between virtue and corruption, with dramatically divergent consequences. Scarcely a generation later the governors of Siena were to commission their leading artist Ambrogio Lorenzetti to paint a large fresco cycle in the room where the major decisions of the commune were taken. In effect the ideological programme of the painting is one that contrasts the consequences of good and bad rule. What is essentially one and the same city – as in the case of the two Florences of Cacciaguida and Dante – has to be painted in two different places, on opposite walls, to represent the sharply divergent possibilities of two radically divergent politics: simply speaking a good politics and a bad one.

\*\*\*\*\*

Ambrogio Lorenzetti painted his frescoes in the late 1330s in the council room of the nine governors of Siena (the so-called Sala della Pace or Sala dei Nove) in the relatively recently built Palazzo Pubblico of the city (see Plate 1). The paintings are very well known to art historians, as at once the most explicit medieval representation of the nature of city life and as a complex politico-philosophical statement about what fosters good government and what, on the contrary, leads to bad government. The comparison between the representation of cities in Dante's text and Lorenzetti's frescoes is instructive in a host of ways, sometimes because of similarity, but often for reasons of subtle difference. For example, as I have been stressing, both *inferno* and *paradiso* are figured by Dante's poem as cities in which God's *good* government unfolds in eternity. They were created along with the first things as part of the divine plan for 'the state of souls after death', the subject of the poem being man 'according as by his merits or demerits in the exercise of his free will he is deserving of reward or punishment by justice'.[24] We cannot just say that Lorenzetti's two walls representing good government correspond with Dante's notions of heaven, and his other wall representing bad government with Dante's representation of hell. It is not that simple.

Lorenzetti's, like Dante's, is a complex statement. For one thing, as Nicolai Rubinstein has said in comparing the frescoes with Simone Martini's *Maestà* in the neighbouring room of the Palazzo Pubblico – and the point holds true of any comparison with Dante as well – they have a 'less religious, more secular character', emphasizing not the Virgin, but Justice and the Common Good as ruling principles of public life.[25] In an article seeking to extend Rubinstein's readings into other areas of the painting which he does not closely chart, Una Feldges-Henning agrees on this fundamental point: 'the religious component of Ambrogio's painting is overshadowed by the political; the result of its being commissioned by the civic authorities and its situation in the Palazzo Pubblico.'[26] In Dante by contrast, the justice being dispensed is always divine, even if his work involves a constant *implicit* statement about human government too. His *inferno* may be the city of the lost ('la perduta gente'), as its first gateway's inscription makes clear. But it is where divine justice is being dispensed, rather than human justice under the *inspiration* of Divine Wisdom, or good government in an earthly and civic form *influenced by* the theological virtues, as in Lorenzetti's representation of the complexities of good government. And unlike in the Lorenzetti frescoes of *malgoverno*, Dante's city of woe is emphatically not one of bad government.

Rubinstein's case is chiefly about the way specific traditions of influence – in this case traditions of political thought about rulership – come to a focus in Lorenzetti's work. In an age of the frescoing of town halls these particular paintings by Lorenzetti in the Palazzo Pubblico in Siena embody a vast politico-philosophical programme, linking back to the *specula principum* (or 'Mirror for Princes') tradition, which taught rulers the virtues to inculcate and the vices to avoid in the achieving of good rule on earth. As an influence upon both Lorenzetti and the person or persons who drew up the programme for his frescoes (including their powerful written synopses in the various friezes and scrolls), this tradition had been further tweaked by a more recent set of treatises, reflecting Aristotle's political focus on the common good of all rather than personal advantage for the individual:

> In the early fourteenth century, it becomes a commonplace in political and didactic prose and poetry that only by placing common welfare above private interest can internal peace, economic prosperity and political power be secured and preserved; so does the view that neglect of the common good leads to civic strife and the decline and fall of cities. We find these ideas in 'trattati di virtù', chronicles, rhetorical manuals, sermons and theoretical treatises.[27]

It is mainly this latter, Aristotelian tradition that Rubinstein goes on to explore, in the first major post-war study in English of the 'meaning' of Lorenzetti's fresco programme in the Sala dei Nove, a study so influential that it set certain parameters for later interpretation of the paintings. My only quibble – though it is the groundwork of what I chiefly have to say – is that in following the hunt for textual influences on them (and inspiring others such as Skinner to emulate him, even to the point of fundamental disagreement as to what these prime influences were), Rubinstein neglects the more direct factor of an address to rulers informing the symbolic rhetoric of the paintings and explicit in much of their textual wording. This direct focusing of the message for a specific audience was central to the Mirror for Princes genre in all its forms, so it is a little surprising that having drawn the initial connection with that tradition, Rubinstein does not proceed further to analyse Lorenzetti's discourse of address.

For the paintings and their texts make appeal to us, their audience, as rulers of the earth with a role to play in seeing that Justice and the Common Good prevail over Tyranny and all its attendant vices. Different aspects of the interrelated message converge on us from the separate directions of the three walls across which it is stretched. Somewhat analogous to the modern technology of 'surround sound', the room where the nine governors met in council affects viewers by means of a medieval art of wrap-around imaging. It is an art of grand contrasts, made from adjacent walls designed to be apprehended pictorially as *contrary states* of good and bad rule, even if a host of local details will tease us into further interpretative moves. This impression of being addressed by the paintings from several different angles, and with a plenitude of local micro-detail, certainly amounts to the dominant factor in *how* they make their meaning felt, even if not much reported in the modern scholarly finessing of what that meaning *is*. We are never in doubt that the intention of the paintings is to influence positively our every decision about the city, whose chief authorities we only very temporarily are – for membership of the Nine changed every two months! So the paintings have to function efficiently, and relatively speedily, on us. In keeping with this implicit agenda, I will keep my own discussion of them brief.

Good government is represented on the middle wall, in abstract terms of its structural workings and their attributes. Key figures on this wall of the painting are Sapientia or Divine Wisdom, Justice, Concord and the figure of a Lord in the colours of Siena flanked by the virtues of Peace, Fortitude and Prudence on one side and Magnanimity, Temperance and Justice on the other. Above him hover the three theological virtues, Faith, Hope and (highest of all) Charity. This Lord has traditionally been interpreted as *Ben Commun* or the Common Good. More recently this identification has been contested by Skinner, who interprets him as 'a symbolic representation of the type of *signore* or *signoria* a city needs to elect if the dictates of justice are to be followed and the common good secured'. At this point one can either arbitrate on the debate or turn in a different direction. I choose the latter. The literature of interpretation and identification of the wall of *buongoverno* is already extensive and my own emphasis is in any case on more obvious – but perhaps for that very reason strangely neglected – matters of affect on the onlooker. So I will largely pass over the choice between Rubinstein's and Skinner's readings,[28] to deal speedily with this other issue of contrastive portrayals of good and bad cities.

On the right-hand wall is represented a vast scene of the effects of good government on city and countryside. We see a populous city (easily identifiable as Siena, though probably intended more as the *type* of the good city), with traders, shopkeepers, artisans, builders and dancing women. Beyond the city is the *contado* or countryside, from which it is divided by a defining wall but with which it is equally *connected* by a gate in that same wall. The *contado* clearly provides basic supplies for the city, while being also a context in its own right for pastimes such as hunting and hawking. On the left-hand wall is figured bad government, also in terms of its structural workings and their attributes, with exemplification of its further effects on the city and countryside in the middle and left-hand portions of the wall. Needless to say, the city of bad government is as unproductive as its opposite is productive. It is a place of murder, with habitations in various states of collapse, just as its outlying *contado* is a barren and essentially uncultivated land, in which bands of soldiery engage in factional disputes, and isolated habitations are put to the torch.

Hovering over the fresco of the well-governed city and its *contado* is the winged figure of *Securitas* (Security), holding a scroll which proclaims the fearlessness ensured and the agricultural productivity made possible in a commune governed by Justice; while over the opposite wall, representing *malgoverno*, the dark-cloaked and grimacing figure of *Timor* (Fear) hovers, sword in hand. His scroll proclaims the inverse message: in a world in which 'el ben proprio' (personal good, as opposed to 'ben commun' or common good figured on the adjacent wall) takes the upper hand, 'justice is subjected to tyranny' ('Sommess' è la Giustizia a Tyrannia'), with pillage and fear of death the inevitable effects. And everything specified in the scroll is directly portrayed. Justice with her scales – from the wall of good government – has here been hauled down from her throne, beaten and tied up by malefactors. In her place sits a tusked and horned demon-figure representing tyranny, flanked by six vices, *Crudelitas*, *Proditio*, *Fraus*, *Furor*, *Divisio* and *Guerra*, with three further vices hovering overhead, *Superbia*, *Avaritia* and *Vanagloria* (contraries of the Theological Virtues, as represented over the figure of the Ruler on the adjacent wall).

Each vice in the depiction of *malgoverno* has its chilling attribute. Some of these are easily interpretable without further help from criticism. For instance, Cruelty is about to slay a naked infant whom she holds in one hand, with a knife held poised in the other. But there is one vice, *Divisio*, which is so radical a representation that critical speculation seems not to have fully grasped its message to the city rulers (see Plate 2). The female figure representing this vice has as her attribute a large saw. Like the Ruler figure on the adjacent wall, Division is clad in the black and white colours of Siena. This alone might give us the clue that she represents not division in the abstract, but division as a danger to the *civis*. But Lorenzetti has provided yet more clues. The terms for Yes and No, *si* and *no*, are printed on the two sides of her tunic. The suggestion is that if there is divided opinion on what is best policy – some pulling in one way and some in the opposite – harm will ensue, emphasized by Divisio's act of sawing. The question that has sometimes baffled scholarship is, however, sawing into what? Into some 'object' – unspecified – 'held in her left hand', writes Skinner.[29] I have a different suggestion. The degraded quality of the painting will tend to baffle us, unless or until we consider the most radical solution of all – namely, that Divisio is sawing into herself. Her act of self-dividing makes all the more symbolic sense of the fact that the black and white colours had in any case kept us thinking of her as in part a representation of the city; here the self-divided city, at variance in its votes between yes and no, the very toing and froing threatening to destroy all civic unity.

The double-stranded rope of concord, which in the adjacent portrayal of *buongoverno* had been so eloquent a statement of the connecting link between wisdom, justice, concord, good government and the citizenry, lies here in tangled chaos. As indicated, there is a long-running debate about the portions of the painting which represent the *workings* (as opposed to the mere effects) of good and bad rule. Whole theses have been written on the identification of figures in these portions of the painting, sometimes claimed to be allegorical and sometimes rejected as such. But it is a debate that largely sidelines discussion of the primary *function* of the frescoes in their setting. Indicative of the state of play on this issue is a seemingly throwaway remark, in what is perhaps the most thorough analysis to date of the context of contemporary political theories of government, out of which meaning in the frescoes has recently been determined – Quentin Skinner's 1986 Raleigh Lecture on them. 'Given the setting of the paintings, indeed', Skinner claimed, 'they might even be held to carry the force of a continual reminder to the Nove [the nine governors of Siena] of the civic values they were sworn to uphold.'[30]

In his nonetheless highly convincing pages on these paintings, this is all Skinner really contributes by way of an assessment as to why they were painted in this particular location. His argument that the political programme which they elucidate owes more to a Roman lineage of political thought from Cicero and Seneca – most fully enshrined in the thirteenth-century writer Brunetto Latini – than to a Greek tradition of Aristotelian political theory (in terms of which they had previously been mainly read by Rubinstein), greatly underemphasizes this other context of their meaning: namely, the way they may have been intended to affect the deliberations of successive groupings of the nine governors. In a nutshell, their *siting* is charged with political significance in quite different and possibly more important ways than those pertaining merely to their relation with existing pre-humanist or Aristotelian thinkers. For, sensitive as he is to the varying importance of the two separate traditions of political theory from classical times, which he deftly distinguishes, Skinner's pivotal words 'indeed . . . might even' in the sentence quoted above are a syntactic indication that this other context – of the frescoes' placement – has been given only cursory attention by him, and is seen more as a reinforcement of discoveries already made about their meaning than as the crux of their *intended political affect* on their *intended political audience*. Skinner looks at the frescoes as essentially an extension in painted form of certain *textual* theories of government. My own case is that a large part of their meaning is a factor of their *function*, and goes missing if we lose sight of the fact that their main context is physical rather than textual – a not very large room in which the key deliberations of the nine governors relative to all main decisions about Siena took place.

The paintings act as contrastive exemplifications of the consequences of good rulership or *buongoverno*, and its opposite, *malgoverno*. Crucially, one and the same city – identifiable as Siena – had to be painted twice separately, for simultaneous viewing by the nine governors in council. The two cities represent the opposite outcomes of political action, and are related to each other on their adjacent or opposing walls by thematic polarities: just as there had been two contrastive Florences, a good one and a bad one, in the great middle cantos of *Paradiso*. In both cases the separate representations of the same city are indications of utterly different realities, consequent upon moral choices in politics and lifestyle – good or bad – made by individuals within one and the same context. A city may thrive or it may die. Dante's case is that in the same location as the formerly small but pure community of Florence, represented in Cacciaguida's twelfth-century 'celestial' account of it, by the time of his own mid-life crisis in 1300 not just individuals but families, factions and the entire greatly enlarged city are morally or literally dead or dying as a consequence of pride, avarice and the 'mingling of bloods'.

Lorenzetti's related, but by no means identical, case is that you may have a good city on earth or a bad one; it all depends on how you rule

yourselves. Crucially, if you are a governor of the city, it behoves you to
study carefully what makes for the one and the other. Not surprisingly,
in the only early account we have of the paintings' affect on Sienese
viewers – words from an extant public sermon by the famous fifteenth-
century preacher San Bernardino – this stark division of possibilities into
good and bad rule is what gets most attention. My whole emphasis in
this section has been that the paintings themselves make very clear that
it lies in the hands of the Sienese themselves to determine which of the
two outcomes will prevail. The models to choose between lie always
before and on either side of their governors as they see to issues of the
day. The only direction for their deliberative gazes to turn which is *not*
covered by paint is the window wall, overlooking the very city and its
surrounding *contado* which it lies in their hands to govern, well or ill.

\* \* \* \* \*

I come now to the promised coda to the chapter on matters of today. In
both Dante's and Lorenzetti's idealizations of the city, life is not sullied
by *outsiders*. In the hellish dystopia that Florence had become for Dante
in his own lifetime, it definitely was. What changes in perspective are we
forced into in transferring our gaze to the present?

Nowadays Florence is one of the principal cities in the world for
cultural tourism. This brings in much revenue for the local economy,
although visitors themselves are increasingly disappointed by the sheer
volume of human 'competition' to see the highlights of the tourist
itinerary. For example, to get into the Uffizi queues of two hours and
longer are standard for much of the year. So for the non-Florentine the
main problem with Florence is all the *other* non-Florentine tourists. It is
not a problem with their 'otherness' as such (coming as they do from so
many different and far-flung parts of the globe), but rather the very
*samenesses* of their typical quest, to see and take everything in, and
preferably as fast as possible. For some modern Florentines, however,
from at least as early as a critical moment at the beginning of the 1990s,
a major problem for the city was felt to be 'outsiders' of quite another
kind – the *extracomunitari* from poorer nations, who had gravitated to
the city as to most other sizeable Italian metropolitan centres
throughout the late 1970s and 1980s, and who threatened (at least
according to a certain perception of what was at stake) to turn Florence
from a quintessentially 'Italian' cultural site into just such another multi-

ethnic community as temporary visitors from New York, Paris or Melbourne might have thought they were leaving behind at home.

This is not the place to tell the larger story of how, from being a nation which solved many of its labour crises by widespread emigration and internal migration from south to north, Italy became in the 1970s and 1980s the destination for hundreds of thousands of immigrants from poorer economies, firstly of the Third World, and then, upon the collapse of communism, from the Eastern bloc. The facts and figures, where they can be known, and the general picture of these widescale changes are told well by others.[31] For instance, since unification some twenty-six million persons have emigrated from Italy all over the world[32] (more than seven million alone in the thirty years between 1949 and 1978).[33] But in the space of just thirteen years between 1973 and 1986 for the first time the return migration of Italian nationals outnumbered emigrants (1,324,083 compared with 1,247,284).[34] And these were precisely the years in which (largely clandestine) immigration from other nations – at first relatively unnoticed – was gathering in pace and volume.

Neither am I keen to rehearse here in close historical detail the events in Florence on the last nights of the carnival season in 1990, the 27th and 28th February, which saw youthful racists availing themselves of the opportunities of festivity and disguise for some brutal muggings of north Africans in and near the city centre. The trial of twelve youths accused of the racist attacks was terminated some seven months later for lack of evidence, according to the investigating magistrate, in what struck some commentators at the time as his 'Alabama-style judgement'.[35] From press reports nearer to the events it would seem that the victims were chosen at random and accused by those who mugged them of drug-dealing.[36]

Nor is my present main interest in the subsequent politics of city authorities (much reported at the time well beyond merely the Italian press), who displaced Senegalese and other street hawkers from their pitches on streets and squares in Florence along the main tourist trails and in front of designer-label shops to decentralized areas designated for their 'licensed' trading. Often such street-sellers were only permitted into more central areas after the shops had closed, when many ordinary tourists would have turned in for the night. The common cry was that the *extracomunitari* greatly increased the incidence of drug-dealing, gambling, prostitution, money-laundering and other forms of corruption in the city. Furthermore, their communal living areas were perceived as dirty, noisy and overcrowded. Might we not see this as another echo of Florentine imputation of a present 'squalor' in the public space, requiring clearance? Few organizations apart from the Catholic church's action group Caritas and the Italian labour unions had a record in these years of organizing help to immigrant individuals, families and communities. But this story of their widespread neglect and marginalization is fairly well known.

My own enquiry is essentially into something initially more intangible: namely, the anxieties or prejudices on the part of Florentines (but also of Italians more generally) about accommodating *extracomunitari* at the heart of their ancient communities. Specifically, I want to ask here whether there is long-term historical connection or not between the kinds of passionate objection to outsiders that we detect in Dante's text of the early 1300s and these new manifestations of xenophobia so near to the close of the millennium. The question is of course underpinned by Umberto Eco's proposition, broached in my Introduction, that we are still living the 'hot' problems of the Middle Ages. If one of the factors of cultural continuum from the Middle Ages to the present is rejection of outsiders – whether a local *nuova gente* or people representing a stark cultural 'other' to what was here before – then it is important to distinguish if the specific prejudice takes new forms, unlike anything in Dante. If so, then are we able to imagine what might be required for its overthrow in present conditions? A problem for the interpreter who does not present the sociologist's hard facts and figures on the subject of the *extracomunitari* is what exactly to use as evidence of xenophobia in an attempt to fathom whether there are specifically modern typologies by which it may be recognized?

Since my other dealings are characteristically with texts – often with what they can be made to reveal of *con*text – I shall take as my examples materials from the national and local press, on 'Florence and its Others' as we might for convenience denominate the problem. I have had to be rigorously selective in order to keep analysis within due compass. Therefore, phrases and sentences from only a very few of the many articles that appeared in the early 1990s will have to stand as representative of the local and national discourses that were generated over immigration, and by the troubles that flared up between existing and immigrant communities in the specific case of Florence.

Linking back to other sections of the chapter, it should first be noted that what was most feared in 1990, especially by church authorities when speaking out about racist incidents and tensions, was the possibility of a 'divided city' – simply speaking, a Florence divided by sharp and opposing opinion as to wherein lay its best interests in the matter of the settlement of new ethnic communities within distinct localities of the city. Cardinal Silvano Piovanelli, addressing a rally against racism attended by some thirty thousand people less than a month after the incidents at carnival's end, pronounced that 'The city must not become divided'. 'I have accepted to speak', he declared, 'above all to spread the word that the city must not split open, or become ranged on opposing polemical flanks.' The spectre of *Divisio* with her saw, in updated form, haunts the cardinal's outlook, more it seems than even the evils of racism itself.

At the same rally the president of the Senegalese Florentines, Fallou Faye, pointed out a tripartite division which the city's reactions to the incidents had opened up – with racists in one grouping, another faction sympathetic to immigrants, and a third which was indifferent: 'I want to speak directly to the racists, because they are marginalized exactly as we are, and they must understand that hatred and intolerance serve only to distract us from our real problems.' There is in these pronouncements by Faye the implication that problems can be overcome only in a spirit of togetherness, without the exclusion of anybody, because they apply to the entire community equally, and therefore must be faced in a spirit of unity (yet to be found). It is an interesting olive branch held out by Faye, not so much to distance himself from racists in the city, as to point out the factor of marginalization he and his like *share* with them. In a sense what he is reaching for here is an age-old bargaining chip in Italian politics, that of inclusivity: my inclusion in the *civis* guarantees yours, and yours mine, just as my exclusion by you ensures your exclusion. Or, spelled out with more precise nuancing, the following subtextual implications, it seems to me, flow from Faye's argument addressed to racist Florentines: your acceptance of us, the immigrants you mistakenly perceive as the city's problem, will not only cancel out our marginalized status brought upon us by you but also bring yourselves back from similar societal margins (where you don't yet seem even to realize you have moved) into the inclusive fold of a once-again undivided city.

Always, as in earlier discourses of the city into which this chapter has delved, there is the bogey of disunity and the enticement of unity.[37] But in contradistinction to Dante, the argument is being wielded by a newcomer, an outsider. The 'città partita' or 'divided Florence' is caused, according to Fallou Faye, not by his *in*clusion but by his *ex*clusion, and will only be overcome when all Florentines, new and old, accept one another. It is a striking instance of a member of the modern *gente nuova* having a voice of a positive kind which Dante did not – indeed could not – allow in his textual drama.

Less encouraging than this voice of the new were subtly or not so subtly racist 'discourses' in 1990 and the immediately subsequent years, deploying figures of speech in which immigrants appeared not as communities of human beings with thoughts and feelings of their own, comparable with and understandable by Italians, but rather, more like a shock of nature: typically, a flood or tidal surge. The same articles in which such discourses were couched, often in the national press – and more surprisingly still, even in the columns of left-wing dailies such as *L'Unità* – sought to characterize particular immigrant groups in synecdochal terms of some physically distinguishing characteristic; once again, it seems, so as to avoid dealing at close range with the humanity of the persons being thus grouped. For example, Ernesto Balducci, writing the editorial of *L'Unità* only a little over two weeks after the racist thuggery in Florence of the last carnival days in 1990, compared the influx of immigrants to the city with the flooding of 1966; even if he then went on to say that it was all the fault of inequalities in wealth distribution across the globe.[38] More than five years later in the same paper, Giulia Baldi wrote an article entitled 'Chinese Attack Their Consulate' ('Cinesi assaltano il Consolato'),[39] about the gathering of members from the Chinese community outside their own consulate in the city, in order to get passports and visas stamped according to the *n*th national tweak in legislation with regard to *extracomunitari*. In it she used every form of disaster, natural and man-made, as a means of describing the crowds of immigrant Chinese seeking regularization of their status. From 'bomb with a delayed fuse' to 'exploding chaos' to 'uncontainable tide' to 'flood of the almond-eyed' to 'wave of immigrants', she studiously (or else simply subconsciously) avoided all mention of aspects of their situation which identified them, when all was said and done, as members of the same species as the readers of the newspaper. The assumption all along was that the people written about would not themselves be reading the column.

Herein perhaps lies some of the difference between articles in the Italian press and their counterparts in England and America, in both of which nations multi-ethnicity in the population on an appreciable scale has existed for longer than in Italy. The auto-censorship in operation in major English and American dailies in matters of racial sensitivity cannot simply be attributed to the workings of an Anglo-Saxon 'political correctness'. It presumably has to do also with an assumption on the part of British and American journalists and their editors that the readership of their newspapers and journals is diverse, and will include members of various minorities that make up the social spectrum. In 1990, as still in 1995, the comparable presumption in Italy seems to have been different. To write, as the second article I am taking the trouble to describe in some detail did, in terms of high numbers of the 'almond-eyed community' in Florence by comparison with elsewhere in Tuscany, was apparently not to risk offending the sensibilities of the newspaper's readers. On the one hand, the indelicacy of treating an immigrant community thus in synecdoche seems not to have been a consideration of the author; and on the other, she could safely assume that members of the Chinese community itself would be unlikely to read the paper in the first place. As a category of persons they are 'placed' by Baldi's article in terms that Vanessa Maher has called 'a system of symbolic classification which is little affected by mere information'.[40]

Here, the 'information' that might have been supplied by the article would have included an account of the changes in legislation which had led to the Chinese Consulate opening in this way, specifically to update and regularize the residency qualifications of individual members of its community. But this more sober detail is never engaged, nor any sympathetic investigation of the fears and hopes of those persons gathering at the consulate. Instead, the writer distances the humanity of the immigrant community by means of metaphor, simile and synecdoche, far enough for no protest on their behalf to be felt necessary. At the same time the terminology of natural disasters effectuates a 'symbolic classification' of the Chinese in question: as persons driven not so much by emotions and intellection, but rather by uncontrollable forces of nature. At one level of subtext the message thus purveyed is that persons who are so different are unlikely ever to be sufficiently similar to Florentines to 'fit in'. And nor are they being appreciated for their cultural *difference* as any kind of positive enrichment of the wider Italian community. Most distastefully of all perhaps, in her representations of the Chinese immigrants' plight and behaviour, Giulia Baldi displays the fascination of a voyeur at a scene of disaster, but with self-assured indemnity throughout, as though she had seen fit to represent this scene – so intrinsically distressful for those involved – as somehow, for the rest of us, ineffably funny, and touching our common humanity with the victims not at all.

Not so uninvolved are those Italians whose previous residential or work zones had been progressively taken over by particular immigrant communities. Once again it is the Chinese who are of particular interest. A waggish saying reported in the modern press – 'Florentines don't want gypsies because they have no will to work, and they don't want Chinese because they work too much'[41] – begins to capture the repugnance at perceived new-style 'jobbers' and 'upstart' traders among the Chinese, by humorously contrasting it with the longer historical distaste felt for another minority community (gypsies) equally at variance with an implied Italian norm regarding work.

Even allowing for what one weekly, the *Europeo*, saw in March 1990 as Italy's cultivation of its 'decade-old myth of good-nature' by way of tolerance of others ('l'Italia ha coltivato per decenni il mito della sua bonarietà'),[42] the situation in the San Donnino area of Florence in 1995, a location in which there was one Chinese for every two remaining Italians, had become one of highly strained tension between communities. There is some irony in the fact that the main concentration of this Chinese community in Florence by the mid-1990s stretched as far out in a westerly direction down the Arno from San Donnino as the historic locality of Signa. For this was precisely one of the points of origin of *villani* or rustic peasants in Dante's text. He had claimed they were fast becoming the corrupt forces of new money in the Florence of his day, by moving off the land and coming into the city from such areas in the *contado*, bringing with them their vile stench, at once literal and metaphorical: 'lo puzzo/del villan . . . da Signa,/che già per barattare ha l'occhio aguzzo' ('the stench/of the churl . . . from Signa/who already has his sharp eye out for shady dealing', *Paradiso*, XVI, 55–7).

Although we need to alter our perspectives somewhat in the rapid shift of focus to the present – registering in particular that Signa is no longer a village in the *contado*, but engulfed by the outward sprawl of modern Florence down the Arno valley – in other respects the objections and prejudices on the part of existing Italian communities to the new Chinese inhabitants in such places are often not unlike an updated version of Dante's loathing of the *gente nuova*. In Dante's sense of demographic shifts, the fathers, or at most the grandfathers, of numerous Florentines had come in to the city, from Signa and from other outlying communities which he mentions in the same passage – Aguglione, Montemurlo and Val di Greve – to take up banking and trading activities, often of a sinful nature (namely, 'per barattare' – 'in order to engage in barratry' [political corruption], as stated in the above quotation). By comparison, in the 1980s and 1990s the immigration patterns *to* Signa, and even more notably its neighbouring locality of San Donnino, had been mainly from just one province of China, Zheijang, and indeed from one city, Wenshou. What more can we know about so fascinating a phenomenon as immigration from a specific zone in China to a specific destination in Italy from such press reports?

Sadly, rather little. While certain articles have an objective socio-logical feel to them, and even account analytically for the reasons for and patterns of Chinese settlement in the specific Italian context, others are sensationalist in the manner of a modern Dante, preaching against the lifestyles and the 'corrupt ways' of the outsiders. If, for instance, a certain article tells us with convincing objectivity that 'at San Donnino the Chinese found a productive infrastructure largely in decline, which offered them certain favourable characteristics – autonomous and not dependent work, and the possibility of a contiguity between home and work',[43] others devolve into little more than litanies of objections to the Chinese of the quarter. In the latter articles there is much mention of the *mafia gialla* (the 'yellow' mafia), who purportedly run restaurants and *locali* mainly for undercover operations, in which there is a high turnover in manpower as ever-new illegal immigrants work as birds of passage in operations where the bottom line is purportedly a congeries of money-laundering, gambling and prostitution.

In the earlier years, according to numerous articles written in a style of fulmination, the Chinese penetrated the leather goods industry so rapidly and so pervasively that many Florentines were driven out of the business by competitive pricing. Although leatherworking later became only one line of work in a greatly diversified spectrum, it is interesting to see a report from as early as 1990 when the Chinese still based their lives mainly around this one industry. By this stage, in San Donnino and the surrounding areas they had already reached numbers that inspired counter-reaction and deep-seated prejudice among existing residents. Indeed, the signatories of a petition to the mayor of Campi, complaining of a buyout by the Chinese of an entire leatherworks, state:

'They came to this leather factory in tens, of all ages' to live here, piled one on top of another, and to work here. Day and night. 'There is no longer peace or tranquillity. They work until three in the morning . . . amid the chaos of cars, of machines for leatherworking, din, Chinese music.' And in the daytime the situation doesn't change: the 'going and coming of cars driven at crazy speeds by unskilled persons, indeed mere children', the call of nature satisfied *in* nature, piles of refuse thrown at random.[44]

The litany continues, to the point that the reportage itself apparently shares the residents' gripe. Note for instance in the above translation that some of the words are direct quotations from the residents' petition, but the rest is sympathetic infill on the part of the writer. If one considers that this comes from an article in *La Nazione*, the major national daily published in Florence, and that it is written under a headline that (translated) reads 'Brakes Needed on Chinese immigration' ('Cinesi, occorre frenare'), then any claim that this is unprejudicial reporting falls. We have, in short, the phenomenon of strong antipathy (some would not mince words and simply call it bigoted racism) being both reported on and contributed to in one and the same national journalistic discourse.

There is, however, one vein of writing in this recent era of journalism about immigrant communities which is in no way reminiscent of Dante, and which we therefore cannot, it seems, relate as just a continuation of the 'hot' problem of xenophobia from the Middle Ages to the present. And it is on this point of difference from Dante that I want to close the chapter. The writing I have in mind is when the discourse is a strange blend of objective analysis and subjective bias. Such writing may be laced with a sense of failure on the part of the existing Italian community to relate to the phenomenon of sheer difference met in the immigrant other. I will quote just one sentence and say some closing words about it, since it appears to speak volumes about the race issue as it was to go on exasperating community relations within Italian society. The sentence arises in an article reporting on the development of corruption rackets and a highly and independently organized Chinese community. It reads: 'The Chinese does everything autonomously, organizes himself, speaks a language with thousands of dialectical variants, and has a sort of natural shield which protects him from every kind of contamination.' ('Il cinese fa tutto da sè, si organizza in proprio, parla una lingua che varia in migliaia di dialetti, ha una sorta di scudo naturale che lo protegge da ogni tipo di contaminazione').[45] If I am right, what we have here is an importantly new and stark sense of the divided city. Here the reality being addressed is that of a self-sufficient, fully-fledged community living upon Italian soil in a kind of 'parallel state' to civil society in Italy, but with little or no direct contact of any consequence across the gap between. Most importantly, the sentence seems to report no felt *need* for contact by the Chinese with that other, wider community. The Chinese individual being surveyed by the sentence – a composite figure in any case – is likewise protected from any inroads that the outside world might make on him as if by a 'natural shield'. He does not have need of that other world, because he is entirely autonomous and self-organizing. (It is clear that the Chinese community as a whole is being talked about here, not merely its individual members.) In some ways the factor which adds most to the writer's interest is the one which most nearly replicates an Italian reality, namely the speaking of a language with thousands of dialectical variants. But while on one level this might appear to be a point in common, and therefore one of the realities which most stimulates the Italian's interest in the Chinese he is studying, it is by the same token the very reality which most certainly and profoundly marks the Chinese off as beyond the reach of the Italian's comprehension; as a being, that is, who exists in his own right, within circuits of dynamic and varied communication, all totally impenetrable by the writer of the article or any of his kind.

The pathos in this – for pathos there surely is – arises from the writer being hyper-aware of something interesting going on in an adjacent and visible space, but which he and Italians like him cannot even begin to understand or share. The lives of the Chinese are impenetrable – even to the common instrument of gossip – since what is being said and done by them, while colourfully varied and interesting to an outsider's perception, cannot begin to be fathomed. And note that the 'outsider' figured in this way is the Italian, *within the geographic space of his own city*. For in a sense the writer of the sentence I am analysing, instead of practising some kind of racist exclusion *ex nihilo*, is reporting a state of mild stupefaction at feeling himself excluded – excluded as a 'contamination' – by a (composite) Chinese person, who in his autonomous self-sufficiency has no need of and no 'interest in' him. Given the high levels of mutual genial interest in other people's lives which is one of the glories of Italian society, this sense of being rebuffed by an immigrant *gente nuova*, with its own autonomously interesting language and culture, is problematic to say the least.

A puzzling factor in all this is that Chinese society too is even more well known than Italy for taking an interest in others' affairs, and for a consequent lack of privacy of the kind Westerners take for granted. Nonetheless, the writer feels excluded by the autonomous and seemingly self-absorbed nature of the community he is describing. His point is that the Chinese in Florence are not bringing their self-evidently complex social and economic activities to focus on Italians, out of a spontaneous natural defensiveness against what is understood as 'cultural contamination' (contamination which must include the writer himself). As before, in the case of the speech made by Fallou Faye at the rally against racism in 1990, we seem to witness here a starkly different case of inclusion and exclusion from any in Dante. Here the Chinese community is felt to be operating not so much as outsiders, but as persons who instinctively make *ostensible insiders* – Florentines such as the writer himself – feel *excluded*. Socially, culturally, above all linguistically, that other community has taken up a space within what might previously have figured as the native Florentines' own city, but which can now no longer be experienced as anything so simple. As in Dante the division felt is *internal* to the city, as between newcomers (*gente nuova*) and an older stock: though the power politics, it must be stressed, as to whose terrain this is and what are acceptable forms of social and work practices upon it is so differently configured as no longer to be an easy instance of Eco's case about unchangingness from then till now.

In this coda I have looked at immigration before going at all deeply into the longer historical reality of Italian emigration – the subject of a final chapter. This goes somewhat against the grain of history. But in what is an essentially 'cosmoramic' book, I must often begin with different aspects of where Italy is now, and only then trace specific themes from or back into the past, in ways which subserve an understanding of our own times. The present chapter has in any case identified the main precedents for foreign immigration to have been, not Italian emigration elsewhere, but demographic shifts of peoples within Italy from at least the time of Dante onwards, his own reactions to which figured prominently in the foregoing analyses. We have found that although the fear of the divided city has been a factor throughout, even if somewhat differently configured from one age to another, the forms of reaction on the part of pre-existing Italian communities to the sheer cultural otherness detected in a *gente nuova*, while in part a continuum from Dante's time to our own, have significant inflexions in the present. In other words, civic insularity both endures *and* takes new forms, which is not the least reason for its being so hard to root out.

## Notes

1. A complex ideal of interconnection between (in a descending scale) empire, kingdom, city and finally individual is worked out in its fullest form in Dante's political tract *De monarchia*. We can see its lineaments already in *Il convivio*. See in particular Bk. IV, Ch. 4, which begins by suggesting the individual's need for a community, then the community's need in turn for ascending levels of rule and organization, from neighbourhood to city to kingdom; and eventually, beyond that, for a universal empire of one ruler, 'to eradicate . . . wars and their causes . . . and thereby keep peace'. Dante, *The Banquet*, translated by Christopher Ryan (Saratoga, CA: Anma Libri, 1989), pp. 127–8.

2. See in particular Claire Rose, 'Dante's Hell and the Medieval Idea of Jerusalem', *The Italianist*, Vol. 11 (1991), pp. 7–28. Rose demonstrates how Dante's *inferno* can be seen as 'a mirror image of the medieval view of Jerusalem' (p. 14) or even an 'anti-Jerusalem' (p. 8). But, in keeping with the dualism of 'good' vs. 'bad' in the representation of cities which so much of my own present chapter is concerned to explore, Rose also points out that, although Jerusalem *customarily* had positive values attaching to it, 'the city was far from being simply a positive symbol. There was a strong sense of duality in the symbolism . . . so that it could be at once, heavenly and earthly, holy and sinful, an image of peace and of war'; with, furthermore, plenty of biblical precedent for Jerusalem being 'alternately extolled and condemned' (p. 21). In the Old Testament especially, the split is largely between a theoretical ideal of Jerusalem on the one hand and an opposite and sinful reality on the other. Throughout my own argument attention is paid to positive and negative representations of cities, Florence being the main (but by no means only) example of a real Italian city to have received something like the dualistic treatment which, as Rose so well demonstrates, already characterized the idea of Jerusalem in Dante's time. See also Charles T. Davis, '*Il buon tempo antico* (The Good Old Time)', in *Dante's Italy and Other Essays* (Philadelphia: University of Pennsylvania Press, 1984), pp. 71–93; Joan M. Ferrante, 'City and Empire in the *Comedy*', in *The Political Vision of the Divine Comedy* (Princeton: Princeton University Press, 1984), pp. 44–75; J. K. Hyde, 'Medieval Descriptions of Cities', *Bulletin of the John Rylands Library* (Manchester: Aberdeen University Press), Vol. 48 (1965–6), pp. 308–40; also the same Kenneth [J. K.] Hyde's 'The Social and Political Ideal of the *Comedy*', in Eric Haywood (ed.), *Dante Readings* (Dublin: Irish Academic Press, 1987), pp. 47–71; and Giorgio Bárberi Squarotti, 'La Firenze celeste', in *L'ombra di Argo: studi sulla 'Commedia'*, new enlarged edition (Turin: Genesi, 1992), pp. 361–95. All of the above materials, together with studies of actual communes such as William M. Bowsky's various publications on Siena, have greatly advanced our understanding of medieval representations of cities, in particular in relation to Dante. My own debts to these earlier studies will pervade the two opening chapters

of the present book in ways not always easy or possible to acknowledge adequately.

3. Touring Club Italiano, *Firenze e Dintorni* (Milan: Arti Grafiche Alfieri and Lacroix, 1964), p. 111.

4. Michael Levey, *Florence: A Portrait* (London: Jonathan Cape, 1996), p. 457.

5. The Old Market was itself situated on the former site of the Roman campidoglio of the city. See Guido Carocci, *Firenze scomparsa: ricordi storico-artistici* (1897; facsimile edn, Rome: Multigrafica Editrice, 1979), Chapter X, 'Mercato Vecchio', pp. 91–106. There are in Carocci's book revealing photographic plates of the Old Market and adjacent streets before their clearance. Nicolai Rubinstein in his pioneering article 'The Beginnings of Political Thought in Florence: A Study in Medieval Historiography', *Journal of the Warburg and Courtauld Institutes*, Vol. 5 (1942), pp. 198–227, reminds us that the first known chronicle relating the history of Florence, composed at the end of the twelfth or beginning of the thirteenth century, reports that Caesar ordered a market to be built where one of the two consuls of a Roman army sent to fight the Fiesolans had been killed in a surprise attack. The market was to record the death of this consul, Florinus, and the chronicle goes on to suggest that the city was in part named after him in consequence.

6. Carocci, *Firenze scomparsa*, p. 2.

7. 'Riordinamento della parte centrale della Città, ove trovasi l'attuale Mercato delle Vettovaglie, consistente in due Gallerie in quattro rami ciascuna, coperte a cristalli, fiancheggiate da Magazzini.' *Pianta geometrica della città di Firenze e tipografia de' suoi contorni con i Progetti di Ampliamento delle strade*, Litografia Toscana, April 1865; quoted from the 'Note al Progetto Poggi' in the form of a public poster.

8. 'Only the chance survival of a document relating to the removal of a fig tree from the wall of the church of San Martino proves that Cacciaguida existed at all; whether he was knighted by the emperor Conrad and died on crusade is anybody's guess. But it mattered a lot to Dante.' Hyde, 'The Social and Political Ideal of the *Comedy*', p. 60.

9. A good account of the public events in Florence of the period, and of Dante's own brief time in office followed by his banishment and exile, is given in William Anderson's chapter 'The Taste of Power and the Salt of Exile', in *Dante the Maker* (London: Routledge and Kegan Paul, 1980), pp. 145–64.

10. From *The Literary Works of Machiavelli*, edited and translated by J. R. Hale (London: Oxford University Press, 1961), as quoted in slightly modified form in Michael Caesar (ed.), *Dante, the Critical Heritage* (London: Routledge, 1989), p. 243.

11. *Cronica*, IX, 136. Quoted from *Selections from the First Nine Books of the Chroniche Fiorentine of Giovanni Villani*, translated by Rose E. Selfe, edited by Philip H. Wicksteed (Westminster: Archibald Constable and Co., 1896), p. 450. For Villani's use of and reflections upon Dante see Davis, '*Il buon tempo antico*', pp. 82–6.

12. *City of God*, XXII, 1; XIX, 17, in Augustine, *Political Writings*, translated by Michael W. Tkacz and Douglas Kries (Indianapolis and Cambridge: Hackett Publishing Co., 1994), pp. 184 and 158.

13. See William M. Bowsky, 'The Medieval Commune and Internal Violence: Police Power and Public Safety in Siena, 1287–1355', *American Historical Review*, Vol. 73 (1967), pp. 1–17; in particular for grisly retributive sentences such as hanging by the testicles as a punishment for sodomy. Dante did not invent *ex nihilo* his law of the *contrapasso*.

14. *Aeneid*, VI, 557–8, translated by C. Day Lewis (Oxford: Oxford University Press, 1986).

15. Text translated from *Petri Allegherii super Dantis ipsius genitoris Comoedian Commentarium*, edited by V. Nannucci (Florence, 1845), included in Caesar, *Dante, the Critical Heritage*, p. 146. Maria Picchio Simonelli in *Lectura Dantis Americana: Inferno III* (Philadelphia: University of Pennsylvania Press, 1993), pp. 10–17, deals far more extensively with early commentators' reactions to the portal inscription.

16. Charles S. Singleton provides a good diagram of the successive phases of Florentine walls. See his edition of the *Paradiso* (Princeton: Princeton University Press, 1975), Vol. 2, *Commentary*, p. 261.

17. Rose, 'Dante's Hell', p. 15.

18. The essay which most clearly distinguishes between, on the one hand, pre-humanist political thinkers of the thirteenth century, with their major debt to Roman thought as enshrined in Cicero and Seneca, and the inheritance of the Greek tradition of Aristotelian political thought, on the other, is Quentin Skinner, 'Ambrogio Lorenzetti: The Artist as Political Philosopher', *Proceedings of the British Academy*, Vol. 72 (1986), pp. 1–56. Some of its finer points will be taken up in due course, in the later discussion of Lorenzetti's frescoes.

19. Chroniclers such as Villani and Compagni held positive views on the connection between the city's greatness and its economic prosperity, though like Dante, and before him Brunetto Latini, they viewed civic dissension and faction as a large cause in its undoing. See Davis, '*Il buon tempo antico*', pp. 72–74. Kenneth Hyde further points out (in 'The Social and Political Ideal of the *Comedy*', p. 57) how Latini, Compagni and another figure close to Dante, Remigio de' Girolami, all either praised the wealth of Florence or, even more interestingly, held political theories that included the notion of economic profit as positive, so long as pursued justly and accompanied by acts of charity. Such theories are far more in accord with the actual lives of notable merchants in this tumultuous phase of economic growth and prosperity than is Dante's blanket detestation of someone merely, it seems, because he 'moneychanges and trades', 'cambia e merca' (*Paradiso*, XVI, 61).

20. Davis, '*Il buon tempo antico*', p. 74.

21. *Paradiso*, edited by Natalino Sapegno (Florence: La Nuova Italia, 1957), fn. to XVI, 67, p. 209.

22. *Ibid.*, fn. to XVI, 58, p. 208.

23. For a general account of resentment of the *gente nuova*, see Daniel Waley, *The Italian City-Republics*, 3rd edn (London and New York: Longman, 1988), pp. 26–31. Waley implies that Cacciaguida was a fabrication of Dante. But see fn. 8 above. The slender documentary evidence is of a Cacciaguida in the earlier period of the Eliseo clan who married an Aldighiera, thus giving rise to the branch of the family from which Dante's own surname originates. For the precedent of the *Aeneid*

in relation to Dante's curious omission of all reference to his actual father, see Hyde, 'The Social and Political Ideal of the *Comedy*', p. 60.

24. The epistle to Can Grande della Scala from which these well-known formulations come is thought by most, though not all, scholars to be genuine. It explains the nature and function of the representations in *Paradiso*, and seems for the most part equally relevant to the other two *cantiche*. Quoted in George Holmes, *Dante* (Oxford: Oxford University Press, 1980), pp. 44–5.

25. Nicolai Rubinstein, 'Political Ideas in Sienese Art: The Frescoes by Ambrogio Lorenzetti and Taddeo di Bartolo in the Palazzo Pubblico', *Journal of the Warburg and Courtauld Institutes*, Vol. 21 (1958), p. 189.

26. Una Feldges-Henning, 'The Pictorial Programme of the Sala Della Pace: A New Interpretation', *Journal of the Warburg and Courtauld Institutes*, Vol. 35 (1972), p. 162.

27. Rubinstein, 'Political Ideas', p. 184.

28. I will just say in passing that if there is a weakness in Skinner's attempt to deny that the paintings are strictly speaking allegories, but yet to read the large black and white figure of the Lord in the central fresco as a 'symbolic representation of . . . *signore* or *signoria* . . .' (Skinner, 'Ambrogio Lorenzetti', p. 44), it is that he has thereby steered closer than his argument would seem to allow him to Rubinstein's own case: which (at the risk of simplification) was that since Siena had neither monarchical nor, for a long time previously, strong podestarial rule, in its place had developed a ruling *principle* of state, that of the common good. By the terms of Rubinstein's argument, only if we grasp the Ruler in the painting as *allegorical* may we understand how Lorenzetti has represented 'in one and the same figure the *persona pubblica* of the Sienese city-state and the concept of the common good' (Rubinstein, 'Political Ideas', p. 185). It is hard to see how Skinner's own logic of the Ruler in the painting as 'a symbolic representation of the type of *signore* or *signoria* a city needs to elect if the dictates of justice are to be followed and the common good secured' does not commit him to an almost exactly similar notion as Rubinstein's, of an allegorical principle at work in the figure of the Ruler, allowing us to *identify* him as the Common Good.

29. Skinner, 'Ambrogio Lorenzetti', p. 33.

30. *Ibid.*, p. 45.

31. A series of good articles in English of a fairly synoptic kind documented the changing picture of new immigration in Italy up to the mid–1990s. See, for example, Raimondo Cagiano de Azevedo and Leonardo Musumeci, 'The New Immigration in Italy', *Italian Politics: A Review*, Vol. 3 (London and New York: Pinter, 1989), pp. 66–78; Jacqueline Andall, 'New Migrants, Old Conflicts: The Recent Immigration into Italy', *The Italianist*, Vol. 10 (1990), pp. 151–74; Dwayne Woods, 'The Immigration Question in Italy', *Italian Politics: A Review*, Vol. 7 (1992), pp. 186–98; John Veugelers, 'Recent Immigration Politics in Italy: A Short Story', *Western European Politics*, Vol. 17, No. 2 (April 1994), pp. 33–49; and Vanessa Maher, 'Immigration and Social Identities', in David Forgacs and Robert Lumley (eds), *Italian Cultural Studies: An Introduction* (Oxford and New York: Oxford University Press, 1996), pp. 160–77.

32. Andall, 'New Migrants', p. 151.

33. Cagiano de Azevedo and Musumeci, 'The New Immigration', p. 66.

34. Veugelers, 'Recent Immigration Politics', p. 34.

35. Paolo Vagheggi, 'Raid anti-neri, tutti assolti', *La Repubblica*, 4 October 1990.

36. For example, 'La notte della nuova paura', *La Repubblica*, 1 March 1990.

37. Quotes from Cardinal Piovanelli's and Fallou Faye's speeches at the rally are taken from Paolo Fallai's report in the *Corriere della sera* of 23 March 1990, and translated by myself. The cardinal's reported words were, 'Ho accettato di parlare soprattutto per spendere una parola affinché la città non si spacchi e non si schieri con polemica su fronti contrapposti.' Fallou Faye's argument ran, 'Ai razzisti voglio parlare subito, perché sono emarginati proprio come noi e devono capire che odio e intolleranza servono solo a distrarci dai problemi veri.'

38. *L'Unità*, 13 March 1990.

39. *L'Unità*, 1 December 1995.

40. Maher, 'Immigration and Social Identities', p. 168.

41. 'I fiorentini non vogliono gli zingari perché non hanno voglia di lavorare, non vogliono i cinesi perché lavorano troppo.' Susanna Cressati, 'Non chiamatela Chinatown', *L'Unità* (local section entitled *Firenze Mattina*), 13 October 1995.

42. *L'Europeo*, 13–17 March 1990.

43. Cressati, 'Non chiamatela Chinatown'.

44. Riccardo Corsi, 'Cinesi, occorre frenare', *La Nazione*, 5 September 1990.

45. Alessandro Antico, 'Nidi di rondine, sakè e mafia gialla' ('Nests of swallows, sakè and yellow mafia'), Florence edition of *La Nazione*, 5 November 1995. The subtitle here reads, 'Comprano i locali pagando sempre in contanti. I soldi provengono da estorsioni, gioco d'azzardo, rapimenti' ('They buy *locali* always with cash. The money comes from extortion rackets, gambling and kidnappings').

# CHAPTER 2

# SEXUALITY, CLASS AND ECONOMICS

## THE *DECAMERON* AS ORIGINARY TEXT

There are countless possible ways of discussing the encoding of sexual behaviour in the *Decameron*, particularly in relation to the issues of class and economics that so perceptibly impinge upon and affect sexuality within this text. In what follows several lines of approach will be adopted successively, and where possible interrelated so as to achieve broader and more subtle treatment. I begin briefly with Chaucer, a writer rather more familiar to English readers than the Italian author who most influenced his style and subject matter, and from whom a number of Chaucer's own poems and portions of longer works were drawn.

There is a passage in Gavin Douglas's introduction to his fifteenth-century translation of Virgil in which, reviewing earlier poets, he refers to Chaucer as 'all women's friend'.[1] Douglas clearly saw Chaucer as aligning himself on the side of women in what is sometimes called the *querelle des femmes* (debate about the status of women) of the late Middle Ages. The text which inspired Douglas's comment was Chaucer's *Legend of Good Women* ('hys legend of notabill ladeis'[2]), which sets out programmatically to offset certain prevailing misogynistic prejudices by rehearsing the lives of virtuous women from history and myth. Specifically, Chaucer's persona within the poem is commissioned by the God of Love and his queen, Alceste, to correct the balance of his earlier texts – the translation of the *Roman de la Rose* and his *Troilus and Criseyde* are mentioned – by giving positive accounts of women in place of those texts' defamation of the female gender:

> Thou shalt, whyl that thou livest, yeer by yeere,
> The moste party of thy lyve spende
> In making of a glorious Legende
> Of Gode Women, maidenes and wyves,

That were trewe in lovinge al hir lyves;
And telle of false men that bitrayen,
That al hir lyf ne doon nat but assayen
How many wemen they may doon a shame;
For in your world that is now holde a game.

                                                      471ff.

This seems heady material to start thinking about, especially in the light of its emphasis on a newfangled 'game' of men suborning women (Chaucer's detection of a kind of Don Juanism before the fact). But while such study of gender and sexual mores could be and often is successfully located in Chaucer, his works are not usually originary texts for the debates in question. Rather they form part of a longer tradition, in terms of which his immediate predecessor, Boccaccio, is at once a more innovative and controversial exemplar. Behind Chaucer's *Legend of Good Women* lies Boccaccio's own programmatic tribute to notables of the opposite sex, *De muliebris claris* (*Concerning Famous Women*), in which he had pioneered the viewpoint espoused by Chaucer in the later text: namely, that writers had created a lacuna in history by always conceiving it in terms of prominent men. To Boccaccio the most obvious example of putting notable men on pedestals was Petrarch's *De viris illustribus* (*On Famous Men*), begun before his own treatise, and clearly – from what he says in his preface to *De muliebris claris* – a spur to his writing a companion piece about women.

But already Boccaccio's work of some ten years earlier, the *Decameron*, had been a startling and problematic instance of a text addressed to women, which focuses on their lives, and is largely told by female storytellers. It is this earlier site of the promulgation of legends, prejudices, counter-prejudices and narrative conventions about women's lives and their relations with men that I concentrate on in the present chapter. Indeed, there is no better place for enquiring into the kind of male writer with something like serious claim to Douglas's title, 'all women's friend', than full-scale study of what gets said about and by women in this most radical of Boccaccio's texts on matters of sexuality. A major claim in all that follows is that the *Decameron*, in its attempt to constitute itself as a women-friendly text and to address itself to a specifically female readership, raises at the very threshold of early modernity (*pace* Vittore Branca's well-argued case, discussed later, that this is still a quintessentially medieval text) so much of what still characterizes relations between the sexes in Western societies. Of no other major text in our tradition could Barbara Johnson's claim that 'literature inhabits the very heart of what makes sexuality problematic for us' and is itself an 'incorrigible perpetrator of the problem' be so justly applied.[3] In a sense, therefore, broaching the *Decameron* in this way is not just interesting for what it reveals about the past. It is an imperative delving into how that past has become encoded in our present sexual identities. Dealing with all this may have something – perhaps a great deal – to do with how we manage the sexual mores of the future.

* * * * *

In the nineteenth century the leading Italian Romantic critic Francesco De Sanctis, in pointing towards what he saw as a lack in Boccaccio – 'the emptiness of the author's conscience and his want of moral feeling'[4] – had at least, in laying the charge, put matters of conscience and morality in the text of the *Decameron* on the agenda to be clarified, even if in the form of a muddled generalization. In the middle of this century Erich Auerbach, in a notable chapter of *Mimesis*, takes an almost diametrically opposite approach to that of De Sanctis, seeing in Boccaccio's post-classical treatment of the erotic 'an extremely promising germ of problem and conflict, a practical starting point for the incipient movement against the culture of medieval Christianity'.[5] All this Auerbach saw as *potential*. But on the other hand he regretted Boccaccio's inability actually to dislodge entrenched culture: for by Auerbach's reckoning, when Boccaccio

> undertakes to depict all the multiplex reality of contemporary life, he abandons the unity of the whole: he writes a book of novelle in which a great many things stand side by side, held together only by the common purpose of well-bred entertainment. Political, social, and historical problems which Dante's figuralism penetrated completely and fused into the most everyday reality, fall entirely by the wayside. What happens to erotic and metaphysical problems, and what level of style and human depth they attain in Boccaccio's work, can easily be ascertained from comparisons with Dante.[6]

More than half a century after those formulations of Auerbach, some different perspectives are inevitable. In particular, at the commencement of a new millennium we are more likely to question those notions of cultural 'unity' and artistic 'wholeness' upon which his negative criticism of Boccaccio is mainly premised. Our interest is likely to be arrested (rather than blunted) by cultural fissures running through the text of the *Decameron*, at which Auerbach in part is hinting. For us, ideological faultlines characterize all cultures, and those texts in which these – sometimes very deep-structural – faultlines can readily be studied may be valued the more highly for what they reveal of conflict and difference at the heart of things. In short, we are likely to be more sceptical – even than Auerbach, writing in the shadow of the Second World War – about notions of unity, whether in individual works of art or, still more, in 'culture' understood in the widest senses.

But saying that does not cancel the usefulness of Auerbach's case about Boccaccio for purposes of understanding the emergence of a recognizable early-modern sexuality in the West. Indeed, Auerbach has perceived, here and elsewhere in his chapter, that in terms of 'the erotic' Boccaccio's text had a subject potentially highly disruptive of pre-existent cultural coherence. Auerbach's claim is that Boccaccio simply failed to deliver; specifically, that his deployment of 'the erotic is not yet strong enough to treat reality problematically'.[7] This judgement, although virtually the opposite of my estimation of the *Decameron*, does at least clearly define the issue at stake. Part of Auerbach's case is that there is a lack of *seriousness* in Boccaccio's text – for instance, a making do with 'sentimental forms' in those novelle 'which aim at the tragic'.[8] For all these factors Auerbach's is still the piece of Boccaccio criticism most worth wrestling with, and seeking to answer. Hence, some of the following account adopts a different set of comparisons than Auerbach's between the *Decameron* and Dante's *Commedia*; since curiously, Auerbach, in naming the erotic as the area of principal interest in Boccaccio, did not make comparisons with that factor in Dante's work. When we do so, the *Decameron* is revealed as more disruptive of those cultural certainties that Dante strove to hold to than Auerbach realized.

The 'erotic' as a main theme in the *Decameron* has hardly been neglected since Auerbach formulated his seminal remarks. With a work like the *Decameron*, and in a culture such as our own that delights in the sexually explicit, it seems unlikely that the topic would be avoided. And yet avoided it sometimes was and, strangely, even in criticism that in other respects was marked by clarity of cultural insight. For instance, Robert J. Clements, in an article which first appeared in 1972, claimed that the novella as developed by Boccaccio had been 'a factor in the growth of the Reformation, the modification of feudalism, the reform of courts and professions, and the strengthening of the bourgeoisie and mercantile class who were, as Professor Branca has discovered, the first mass readers of the *Decameron*'.[9] It is rare to see in criticism of Italian literature in English so wide a net of interests being cast. And yet in that list, which Clements makes good in far-reaching analyses, there is a crucial omission, namely the overriding importance in this text of action within the sexual domain. It would not be foolish to claim that a concern with sexual mores throughout the text of the *Decameron* underlay all those other changes and reforms that Clements's analyses investigate.

One recent critic who has written as challengingly of Boccaccio's treatment of the erotic as anyone since Auerbach is Giuseppe Mazzotta, in *The World at Play in Boccaccio's* Decameron (1986). Constantly aware of what he calls 'the lavish heterogeneity of the narrative', Mazzotta's main thesis is that 'in the steady oscillation between surface literal values and the play of the imagination lies the at once delightful and unsettling power of the *Decameron*'.[10] It is not always clear which of two terms in Mazzotta's writing – *the erotic* or *the imagination* – is to be understood as the greater force, and how exactly they are related. In spite of this uncertainty in Mazzotta's terminology, his interpretations have been highly influential in some of my own readings. For where he talks of *imagination* he is in any case dealing with a factor which is always potentially, if not in fact, transgressive – *specific* transgressions being very often sexual acts, of a kind which cannot be accommodated within the configurations of social order as represented by Boccaccio. A key question in most individual instances is whether the transgressive sexual acts are successfully hidden – kept private by the participants, in other words – and if not, how the social order exacts its penalties on those caught infringing its complex (if also inflexible) codes.

*  *  *  *  *

Nowhere in the *Decameron* is Boccaccio quite so radical as in its opening, and in two matters above all. The first is the subtitle of the work, 'Prencipe Galeotto' (Prince Galahalt); the second, the Proem's overtly attempted interpolation of a specifically female readership. So culturally startling – such an inversion of Dante's heavy aspersion cast

upon Galeotto in the fifth canto of the *Inferno* – is Boccaccio's subtitle
that one leading American (and notably Christian) scholar of the
modern epoch has gone to excruciating pains to suggest that it signifies
more or less the opposite of the obvious.[11] Since a lot hinges on these
first words of Boccaccio's lengthy vernacular text, and since in
particular there seems to have been a great shift in sexual emphasis
since Dante's earlier treatment of the lustful in both *Inferno* and
*Purgatorio*, explication is imperative. The question is how books may
function as erotic mediators to sexual desire – clearly an issue that is still
with us.

Boccaccio's text is titled *Comincia il libro chiamato Decameron,
cognominato Prencipe Galeotto, nel quale si contengono cento novelle,
in diece dì dette da sette donne e da tre giovani uomini* ('Here begins the
book called *Decameron* otherwise known as Prince Galahalt, wherein
are contained a hundred stories, told in ten days by seven ladies and
three young men'). Now Prince Galeotto – Gallehault in the Old French
– has had a lot of ink spilled over him. He performs a crucial role in
Arthurian romances concerning Lancelot and Guinevere, as the enabling
go-between in their mutual declaration of love. More importantly, he is
also named in a famous passage in Dante, glossed by Boccaccio some
twenty years after the writing of the *Decameron*, in his teachings on the
earlier author. What does calling a book a 'Galeotto' – either as
Francesca does in the fifth canto of the *Inferno*, or as readapted by
Boccaccio for this subtitle – imply about the erotic functioning of its
text?

We must reconstruct a sense of the context of Boccaccio's subtitle by
stages. In the second circle of the *Inferno* Francesca da Rimini tells how
she and the lover she is still united with in hell (whom we only know
from our notes was her brother-in-law Paolo) were alone reading a
French romance. At the particular point where Lancelot first kisses
Guinevere, made possible by the encouragings of Galeotto, Paolo kissed
Francesca all tremblingly. Even the difference between Dante's passage
at this point and the original French romance is curious. Francesca
implies that Lancelot kissed Guinevere's long-desired lips, whereas in
the Old French manuscript version of *Lancelot du Lac* Guinevere gives
the first kiss, when brought into physical contact with Lancelot by
Prince Galeotto[12] – and *not until then* does the acute shyness of the
courtly lover Lancelot fade away. Although it has sometimes been
conjectured that Dante was working from a version of the story now

lost, he may simply have misremembered which of the two lovers was the more forward, or wished to imply something about the relative roles of Paolo and Francesca. We are left with large general questions about the gendered aspects of initiative-taking within sexuality, whether as originally posited in the Old French manuscript, or as altered in an early fourteenth-century text; or even, as speculated over in modern times by scholars of Romance (themselves subject to the muddied contemporary waters characterizing such matters).

But however in doubt the intertextual matter of initiative-taking between Lancelot and Guinevere, Francesca's last lines to the pilgrim Dante in the *Inferno* are crisply spoken and packed with suggestive meaning:

> Galeotto fu il libro e chi lo scrisse
> quel giorno piú non vi legemmo avante. (V, 137–8)

> A Galeotto was the book and he who wrote it;
> that day we read no further in it.

The last line has traditionally been taken to signify that they left off reading for other activities consequent upon that first kiss. Or perhaps, more darkly, that they were then murdered by Francesca's husband, Paolo's brother, as earlier hinted in the lines with which her first reply to Dante had ended: 'Amor condusse noi ad una morte./Caina attende chi a vita ci spense' ('Love brought us to one death. Caina awaits him who quenched our life') (V, 106–7).

But it is Francesca's penultimate line, 'A Galeotto was the book and he who wrote it,' which merits more attention. We note a multi-layered significance here. Although the book was *about* Galeotto (among other figures of Arthurian Romance), Francesca's remark implies that the text itself has taken on the function of a Galeotto, because it performed for its readers, Paolo and herself, the same function that the figure of Galeotto did for Lancelot and Guinevere in the tale it tells. But Francesca implicates another figure, and calls him a Galeotto also, namely 'chi lo scrisse', he who wrote the book they were reading. Summing up, the Arthurian knight Galeotto figures in a text which in turn can perform for others who read it the same role of go-between that he does, and in such cases the author too falls under the same charge. The text, the figure within the text and the perpetrator of the text are *all* Galeottos, in a world now replete with temptation from that triple-tiered erotic agency to fall, like Paolo and Francesca, into the sin of lust and be damned for ever in consequence. The sexually suggestive power of the written word, by this reckoning, is almost unbounded. Clearly in Dante's world French Romances (*prose di romanzi* as he calls them in *Purgatorio*, XXVI, 118) of the kind referred to have much to answer for. For him these prose Romances – along with the *versi d'amore* with which they are associated in that reference in *Purgatorio* – were the erotically suggestive reading matter of his day.

But what of Boccaccio – writing some forty years later and, we must suppose from his own later commentaries, already conscious of the reputation of Galeotto in Dante's text and especially the idea that books too could be thought of as Galeottos? At face value, it is exactly this function of the written text as erotic mediator that is being conjured up in the subtitle of the *Decameron*, but with this difference from Dante – that here the offer of such a text to his readership seems intended as positive, genuine and generous on Boccaccio's part. Face value is, however, repugnant to the Princeton Augustinian Robert Hollander, one of a line of Christian interpreters from the American school of Charles S. Singleton. Horrified by what he sees as a 'bad hypothesis – that Boccaccio thinks carnal love a perfectly honourable pursuit' – Hollander produces the contrary thesis: that mention of Prince Galeotto in the naming of this work is Boccaccio's way of issuing a warning:

> The subtitle of the Decameron peers out at us like the skull and crossbones on the bottle of dangerous medicament that must be taken in full consciousness and so lead to life and not death: Reader, beware; here is a book that has the power to move you to lust. That does not mean that such is its purpose . . .[13]

Which side of the debate should we take? Hollander musters evidence from the rest of the author's career, of Boccaccio's sense of 'the terrible power of sexual love', and suggests that only an ironic reading of the subtitle of the *Decameron* is possible. He points out that in other texts by Boccaccio both Galeotto's and Pandarus's roles as go-betweens are seen to be those of moral suborners. Now, one of the few times when Galeotto is actually mentioned by name in Boccaccio's writings is in fact in his commentary late in life on Dante's text. There, indeed, Boccaccio concentrates on Galeotto's role as a go-between, 'E così vuol questa donna dire che quello libro, il quale leggevano Polo ed ella, quello ufficio adoperasse tra lor due, che adoperò Galeotto tra Lancillotto e la Reina Ginevra'[14] ('In such a way this woman wishes to say that the book which she and Paolo were reading performed that office between the two of them which Galeotto did between Lancelot and Queen Guinevere.') But there is nothing here that in itself implies condemnation of Galeotto's role. It is possible Hollander is reading his own repugnance at the office of sexual go-between into Boccaccio's neutral definition. Furthermore, in order to produce his thesis Hollander plays down, or neglects downright, two further contexts: the rest of the opening of the *Decameron* itself, which surely supports a reading of the text as erotic mediator; and the rest of Boccaccio's lengthy commentary on Dante's encounter with Paolo and Francesca in Canto V of the *Inferno*, which is the basis of so much of what has subsequently been known and thought about Dante's lovers.

To deal with Boccaccio's *Commentary* first. The present argument is concerned with differences between Dante and Boccaccio in the realm of the sexual (far more, indeed, than in assessing the rights or wrongs of one more scholar's views). But for that we need to hold separate in our minds the moral frisson that can be taken from *Inferno* V *without* the additional knowledge supplied by Boccaccio, and the very different reactions produced by the lovers' acts in the story as told in his *Commentary*. Only thus may we appreciate a possible significant cultural change between Dante's atttitudes to carnal passion and Boccaccio's.

Unglossed by later commentary, in particular Boccaccio's, Dante's interaction with Francesca da Rimini provides harrowing evidence of the power of love to lead its subjects to the *doloroso passo*. Already before Francesca utters the first of her two speeches we are aware, from an atmosphere charged with the terms *love* and *desire*, that these are souls tormented by their very togetherness, blown about as they are in the infernal whirlwind. Earlier in the canto all the souls in this second circle are likened to flights of cranes singing their laments while tossed in the storm winds that punish the sin of lust. At first when called by Dante, the two 'tormented souls' ('anime affanate') are likened in their arrival before the pilgrims to a very different kind of bird, with a host of more tender associations: namely, 'colombe, dal disio chiamate' ('doves called by desire'), 'a noi venendo per l'aere maligno, sí forte fu l'affettuoso grido' ('coming to us through the malignant air, such force had my compassionate cry') (V, 82–7).

But lest we fall deep into the trap from which Dante himself as pilgrim at this stage in the *Commedia* is by no means safe and exempt – of excessive sympathy for persons guilty of this sin – Francesca's first words seem designed to stress the great difference which must be understood as pertaining between souls punished for ever in hell for their sin on earth and persons such as Dante, by definition still subject to the love and salvation of a figure she can only name in circumlocutory terms as 'King of the universe'. Perceived by Francesca as possessing grace and goodness and also pity for the 'perverse ill' the lovers have fallen into, Dante is truly figured as a human made in God's image. Except that he is continuing to exercise those positive attributes in a realm from which the 'King of the universe' has withdrawn them.

Francesca addresses Dante as a 'living creature, gracious and benign', visiting in this 'black air' of the guilty dead the likes of herself and Paolo, who 'stained the world with blood' (V, 88–90). In that latter formulation a strange melding together of their crime of adultery and of their violent death *on account of* that adultery has occurred. Here all Auerbach's teachings on Dante serve to remind us that in such writing the sin, the manner of death and the form of punishment are shot through with profound figural correspondences (that is indeed the basis of the *contrapasso*, or law of retribution, throughout Dante's *Commedia*). For exactly the same reason, when Francesca finally rests her case with the line 'that day we read no further in it', we must understand what follows in consequence – their adultery, their murder by another and their everlasting punishment – not as three separate and consecutive events but as part of one and the same *action and everlasting damnation for it*.

What is so disturbing in the light of that damnation is Francesca's three tercets that spell out the incontrovertible force of Amor which brought them to it. We have already seen that Paolo and Francesca are, even in death, suggestible in both their will and their emotions – 'called by desire' as they are, and 'borne by their will' and by Dante's 'compassionate cry' out of the wind to his side. In a culture which insisted on asking with scholastic pertinacity in what exactly consisted the nature and power of Amor – many of the *dolce stilnovistis'* most elaborate and intellectual poetic productions are attempts to address the subject[15] – Francesca's formulations constitute a fateful answer to the fundamental enquiry. Indeed, it is the shortest and most memorable answer that the world of Scholasticism was to produce. It consists of three parts, each a terzina long, but the links between them are indissoluble, and the end result is death and damnation.

First, 'Love . . . is quickly kindled in a gentle heart.' The example of this first law is Paolo's no sooner seeing Francesca's 'bella persona' than he is 'taken' with it. Francesca qualifies her remark about her 'bella persona' with the syntactic predicate 'che mi fu tolta', 'that was taken from me'. In other words the two acts – Paolo's being taken with her fair person and her loss of that same fair person through death – are presented as virtually coterminous and the same; the power of adulterous Love and its end result (death and the loss of bodily selfhood) are logically and hence syntactically connected in Francesca's very way of putting things.

The second law, formulated in her second tercet, is that 'Love . . . absolves no loved one from loving.' She herself is her own example here. Being loved by Paolo is the cause of her being seized with a love for him 'so strong that . . . it does not leave me even now'. This formulation, which points to their still being united in hell, reinforces the already pronounced togetherness of the lovers. But it does more than that. Once again, what we might tend to understand as three separate temporal zones – life, the moment of death, then afterlife – are connected, shot through by one and the same act of loving, continuous and unabated for eternity. For here, as in traditional medieval sequences, Eternity triumphs over Time – although *unlike* those other sequences, Love itself has not been triumphed over in an earlier phase of the sequence.

The third pronouncement about Love is that it brought them to one death. In this formulation Love is most like a personified Lord. Certainly his command – in this case his leading of them into death – brooks no argument. And although their killer awaits them in a place we hear about now for the first time – Caina – that is supplementary information, which can scarcely be processed at this point in the overall narrative. The killer is not further identified, nor the place he is destined for explained or described. In theory, only when we meet these words again in a second or subsequent reading of the *Inferno* will we know that he must be a blood relation. For it is indeed a brother who has killed a brother (as well as his own wife), and Caina is aptly named by Dante after the first such murderer.

How very different are these many perspectives from the kinds of reaction that Boccaccio's commentary induces in its readership. As Singleton says, 'The story of the two lovers as told by Boccaccio, in his *Comento*, is greatly expanded and embroidered nicely to exculpate Francesca as much as possible.'[16] Furthermore, since no chronicles or documents of Dante's own lifetime tell of the love between Paolo Malatesta and this Francesca da Rimini (daughter of Guido da Polenta the elder, lord of Ravenna and Cervia), Boccaccio's account, along with just a few other earlier commentators such as *L'Ottimo commento* of about 1333, forms the basis of thoughts we are likely to entertain about the lovers, apart from the details in Dante's poem. Whether or not Boccaccio fabricated much of the story in the form that he tells it, as some critics suppose he did, the sheer difference of emphasis from Dante is instructive. If in Dante 'Love' as an all-powerful force with ineluctable laws has been presented as the cause of the tragedy, to the extent that Francesca can even be said to be pleading her own excuse by implying that no choices were possible in view of the fateful laws of Amor, in the story as told by Boccaccio, by contrast, the blame is squarely shifted onto society – the norms and codes that venal persons will employ to gain their ends, at whatever cost to others (even near relations).

In Boccaccio's account, after wars between Francesca's family, the Polenta lords of Ravenna and the Malatestas of Rimini, Francesca was to marry Gianciotto Malatesta, likely future ruler of Rimini on the death of his father, so as to seal a peace treaty between the two families. But because Gianciotto, although a very capable man, was in addition 'ugly and deformed', her father's counsellors advise him to have her married by proxy to one of Gianciotto's brothers – in the event the 'handsome, pleasing, and very courteous' Paolo. Francesca sees Paolo before the marriage, has him pointed out as her real future husband (and not a mere proxy at the wedding ceremony), falls in love with him at first sight and only realizes the deception the morning after the wedding, when the deformed and ugly Gianciotto arises from the bed they have shared! Furious, and still in love with Paolo, she has sexual relations with him during Gianciotto's absence as *podestà* of a nearby town. When Gianciotto's hears of this from a servant he returns secretly to Rimini, surprises the lovers alone together in Francesca's room and, in a macabre and drawn-out description on Boccaccio's part, kills them with his rapier. Amidst general consternation the two lovers are buried on the morrow in the same tomb.

Above all else, what merits attention is that the story in this version, although told by Boccaccio some twenty years after his writing of the *Decameron*, resembles in all important details the other novelle of the fourth day's storytelling of that work – the day on which the *brigata* (company) of seven women and three men tell stories 'di coloro li cui amori ebbero infelice fine', 'of those whose love ended unhappily'. Several factors stand out. First, this is a society in which the lord of a city such as Ravenna will go to great lengths to deceive his own daughter in a matter as important as the choice of her lifelong marriage partner, so as to gain his own political ends of consolidating a treaty of peace with a rival family. Second, he will pursue this strategy of deceit because of her known high-spiritedness ('altiero animo'). In other words, he is sufficiently in awe of her independent willpower that he does not simply force his daughter to marry his own choice of partner, but uses deception to get her to a point from which there is no going back. The further conclusion we must draw from the details at this point in Boccaccio's telling of the story is that a historical cusp has been reached, between the custom of arranged marriages and that of love marriages, wherein highborn offspring will simply no longer comply with the dictates of an arranged marriage in which their own will has not been consulted: 'se ella vede Gianciotto, avanti che il matrimonio sia perfetto, nè voi nè altri potrà mai fare che ella il voglia per marito' ('If she sees Gianciotto before the marriage is concluded, neither you nor anyone else can make her go through with it').

Having cast doubt on the description in *Inferno* as to how Paolo's and Francesca's love for one another became adulterous, Boccaccio gives his own account of the two lovers' meetings while Gianciotto is away, and also the strategy on Gianciotto's part of discovery and bloody revenge on them. Not only has Francesca in her high-spiritedness acted very much according to her own emotional promptings throughout, like such heroines of Day 4 of the *Decameron* as Guiscarda, Lisabetta, Salvestra and the wife of Messer Guiglielmo Rossiglione. In defiance of the society that has deceived her, she has furthermore deliberately and rationally constructed a private sphere in which she and Paolo may together achieve and enjoy the objectives of their desire – most like Guiscarda, Boccaccio's heroine of the first novella of Day 4. The important thing to note is that as in the *Decameron*, Boccaccio does not overtly moralize upon the rights or wrongs of the case. Instead, he allows his readers to understand that Paolo's and Francesca's proceeding to intimate relations was a matter-of-fact consequence of her having originally been tricked, just as her real husband Gianciotto's subsequent revenge was the result of his having made the discovery of his wife's and his brother's intimacy. If our sympathies are engaged predominantly on one side of the story, it is no doubt because Francesca is the first to be deceived: her adultery with Paolo springs logically from the initial idea planted in her innocent mind that *he* was to be her husband, not Gianciotto. The conventional seal of the story – general lamentation throughout the society as the two lovers are buried in the one tomb – is the sign, as it will be in numerous other works drawing upon the novella tradition, including for instance even Shakespeare's *Romeo and Juliet*, that the society in question is admitting the error of its ways, and trying to confirm in the rites of burial a togetherness on the part of lovers in their death which its rigidities have proscribed or made impossible during their lifetimes.

A world of difference separates Boccaccio's conclusion of the story – the rites of a single funeral bier for the two lovers, and general mourning on the part a society whose most powerful figures have wronged them for family-political ends – from the dark implications of Francesca's last words to Dante in Canto V of the *Inferno*. Furthermore, Boccaccio's telling of the story opens up the long-term issues of the relation between the interests of private individuals and those of a clan or larger societal grouping: issues of the *civitas* (human society understood in civil terms). In Dante, by contrast, the moral issues had been resolutely religious in kind, and concerned divine justice as exacted by 'the King of the universe' – however incompletely understood or incorrectly responded to at this stage of his journeying by Dante the pilgrim.

Not only has Boccaccio in his commentary overtly sidelined Dante's emphasis on the incident of the book (the 'unconscious' of Boccaccio's commentary perhaps revealing how little he held with the notion of blame attaching to Prince Galeotto or, more particularly, to books as erotic mediators). He has in addition written up the story of Paolo's and Francesca's love in a way that ends with the funeral bier, not with the afterlife, and hence has forced consideration back onto the actions and values of the society which produced the tragedy in the first place. In doing so he has neither, in Auerbach's sense, failed to 'treat reality problematically', nor furnished 'sentimental forms' in lieu of some fuller tragic vision he might be supposed to have been aiming for. On the contrary, with considerable economy of statement and a total turning aside from the teleological implications of Dante's account (a shift in emphasis surely of major historic significance in its own right), Boccaccio has told a story about a society fundamentally flawed in its cynical use of individuals and of the institution of marriage for ulterior ends of its own.

Very importantly, in the inhibitions imposed on individuals in Boccaccio's version of the story of Paolo and Francesca, it is not possible to trace religious sanctions, only a strong set of secular human interests. We are led by this argument into supposing that Robert Hollander's attempts to see in Boccaccio's subtitle to the *Decameron* all of the negative associations of the figure of Prince Galeotto in Dante's text – someone whose temptations may lead to everlasting hell, as in Francesca's own case – are misplaced. For what Hollander has not appreciated is a great shift in emphasis between the two authors, and one highly significant at a more generalizable cultural level; as simple as a preoccupation in the earlier writer with how earthly self-gratification may lead to damnation, and in the later with those societal norms – some of them rigid interests of clan or larger societal groupings – which inhibit or block off the natural drives of individuals, most particularly in the achievement of their sexual longings.

* * * * *

Our larger concern, it will be recalled, is with what Auerbach first focused on as Boccaccio's post-classical treatment of the erotic. Having spent time saying what it is *not*, by differentiation between Dante and Boccaccio in their separate treatments of the love between Paolo and Francesca, we have only just begun to concentrate on the positive concern in Boccaccio with carnal love. We still need to understand why this concern in the *Decameron* led to an artistically and intellectually fissured text, cleft by faultlines that are not merely those of a single work, but evidence of something more pervasive – 'cultural' in the wider sense. But first of all it is necessary to return to the evidence in the Proem as to why it is not fanciful simplism to take at face value Boccaccio's offer of the *Decameron* as an erotic mediator to a specific readership.

Criticism has not always illuminated – on the contrary has often tended to explain away as best it could – the matter of Boccaccio's consciously invoking a female audience of readers in the Proem to the *Decameron*. From the time of Petrarch's response to Boccaccio in a late letter of 1373 – that 'above all the type of reader it was addressed to would serve as . . . apology' for its being written for 'popular consumption' and with the added offence of 'certain licentious and immoderate passages'[17] – one way of deflecting any of its claims to attention has been to imply that its early textual move to interpolate a female readership was a self-admission that it was light and unserious.

Boccaccio offers the text of the *Decameron* as reading matter for women in his society and is conscious of innovation in so doing. His case in these prefatory remarks about the female sex is that they are confined to home and are diverted by less active leisure pursuits than men, with drastic consequences:

> Esse dentro a' delicati petti, temendo e vergognando, tengono l'amorose fiamme nascoste, le quali quanto più di forza abbian che le palesi coloro il sanno che l'hanno provato e provano; e oltre a ciò, ristrette da' voleri, da' piaceri, da' commandamenti de' padri, delle madri, de' fratelli e de' mariti, il più del tempo nel piccolo circuito delle lore camere racchiuse dimorano, e quasi oziose sedendosi, volendo e non volendo in una medesima ora, seco rivolgono diversi pensieri, li quali non è possibile che sempre sieno allegri. (Vol. 1, p. 5)

> Ladies, out of fear or shame, conceal the flames of passion within their fragile breasts, and a hidden love is far more potent than one which is worn on the sleeve, as everyone knows who has had experience of these matters. Moreover they are forced to follow the whims, fancies and dictates of their fathers, mothers, brothers and husbands, so that they spend most of their time cooped up within the narrow confines of their rooms, where they sit in apparent idleness, wishing one thing and at the same time wishing its opposite, and reflecting on various matters, which cannot possibly always be pleasant to contemplate.[18]

We can hardly fail to be taken aback at how general Boccaccio reckons the repressive social conditioning of women to be. Nor can we ignore the notion – from so many centuries before Freud – that repression of an instinct augments its intensity. We do seem to have from the outset a discourse that is a surprisingly coherent blend of 'sociological' and 'psychological' analysis, if such an anachronistic remark may be allowed. But Boccaccio's all-important conclusion to the problems of gender-conditioning for women in his society is that his text itself may serve a purpose, first as an emotional palliative for the enforced and frustrating states of idleness suffered by women, and second as material instruction in how to achieve the multiple objectives of their desiring. Whether consciously or not, Boccaccio's argument implicitly evokes the neo-Horatian concept of pleasure with instruction. Not surprisingly, some modern criticism of the *Decameron*, inspired above all by Roland Barthes, has tended to highlight the aspect of 'pleasure of the text' in Boccaccio's neo-Horatian formulation, maybe because of what was half-intuited as something still more radical at stake – the dangerous hint at an actual love-lore devised *specifically for women* in that part of Boccaccio's argument which has to do with 'instruction'.

Elizabethan puritan polemicists were not so coy. Roger Ascham, for instance, in *The Scholemaster*, an important manual on training up the youth of a society in the requisite values of citizenship, faces the threat of 'these bookes made in Italie, and translated in England' very much in terms of what they instruct *to*. His conclusion is that such writing, based unquestionably in his opinion on training in 'vice', is to an extreme degree detrimental, above all to a figure who stands in his own text as a model of innocence – the simple, four-square Englishman, who is all too easily confused and therefore misled by such books:

> They open, not fond and common wayes to vice, but such subtle, cunnyng, new, and diverse shiftes, to cary yong willes to vanitie, and yong wittes to mischief, to teach old bawdes new schole poyntes, as the simple head of an Englishman is not hable to invent.[19]

Ascham is writing in 1570 when William Painter's *Palace of Pleasure*, a large Elizabethan compendium of translated novelle from Boccaccio and other subsequent *novellieri* had recently appeared, the First Tome in 1566, the Second in 1567.[20] In it were a number of key tales from the *Decameron*, the source texts of many an Elizabethan or Jacobean play by Shakespeare and his contemporaries. Though Ascham does not mention the *Decameron* itself, Boccaccio was clearly his main target, since he soon suggests that the bad influences lead English youth to 'make more account . . . of a tale in Boccace, than a storie of the Bible'.[21] Clearly Ascham is well aware of the radical nature of Boccaccio's subject matter: he is responding – even if in another age and a different society – to a factor of 'instruction' in love-lore that Boccaccio's own Proem had been at pains to promote. That puritan polemicists of Elizabethan England should see such danger in a book 'made in Italie' over two hundred years earlier is an indication of how far in advance of other parts of Europe were the cultural changes that Boccaccio's text exemplifies – most obviously all the complexities that we intend by the formula 'the decline of feudalism', including the emergence of new urban lifestyles, requiring vast but also subtle adjustments in the sexual mores between old and new classes, and indeed among persons from whatever class.

Boccaccio's actual case in the Proem to the *Decameron* is unmistakably clear in its analysis of the problematic indoor placement of women's urban lifestyles. Indeed, his remarks on their confinement within the domestic space still ring true – in fascinating and mysterious ways – almost a century and a half later, in the Carpaccio painting used on the cover of this book. (See also Plate 3.) There, two women contemporary with the painting (*c.* 1493–1500) sit on an open balcony and stare blankly into space, as though wistful for a world beyond the domestic, even though for us, as viewers from another age half a millennium later, the animals, birds and the small boy in an archway that are in their immediate foreground are actually very charming. The painting is provocatively mysterious, partly because it was cut from a larger panel. We are forced to view this 'portion' as something it was not intended to be, namely a double portrait-in-profile. The other part of the severed painting, now in the Getty Museum in Los Angeles, was originally immediately above, and depicts men actively hunting in boats on the Venetian lagoon.[22] The women in the lower portion are by any reckoning discontented, sharing as they do almost exactly similar expressions, characterized by a bored or at least far-away look in their eyes, and downward-drawn, sad-looking mouths. The mystery is augmented by its being a small white dog (with paw held absent-mindedly by one of the women) whose gaze meets our own, as we study the painting. The dog's own facial expression, especially in the set of its lips and mouth, is not at all dissimilar to the two women's. We wonder at the *wherefore* of such a melancholia, extending as it does from humans even to domestic animals. It is for all the above reasons – of this being an abidingly enigmatic painting, and yet one which (even more pointedly when read in conjunction with the upper portion depicting men hunting) seems in an historical continuum from Boccaccio's mid-fourteenth-century case about women's and men's sharply differing lifestyles – that I have chosen it for the book's cover. If it helps to stress the desirability but also the difficulty of achieving firm cultural interpretation of 'earlier Italies', its present use will have served an important function.

Boccaccio continues his Proem with the claim that women's very confinement to idleness, 'nel piccolo circuito delle loro camere racchiuse' ('shut up in the narrow compass of their rooms'), makes them exemplary recipients of a literature written for them that mediates directly to their condition of suppressed desires. *This* is what the rest of the *Decameron* is being offered as. To convince his intended female readership that they are indeed being addressed relevantly, in terms of an accurate assessment of their social and mental plight, Boccaccio

immediately contrasts it with the free and open-ended condition of
males in society:

> Essi, se alcuna malinconia o gravezza di pensieri gli afflige, hanno molti
> modi da alleggiare o da passar quello; per ciò che a loro, volendo essi, non
> manca l'andare attorno, udire e veder molte cose, uccellare, cacciare,
> pescare, cavalcare, giucare o mercatare. (Vol. 1, pp. 5–6)

> They, whenever they are weighed down by melancholy or ponderous
> thoughts, have many ways of relieving or expelling them. For if they wish,
> they can always walk abroad, see and hear many things, go fowling,
> hunting, fishing, riding and gambling, or attend to their business affairs.
> (pp. 46–7)

Men's spirits are liberated in ways impossible for woman by the
differently gendered organization of their lives. Old feudal forms of
entertainment as well as the new mercantilist pursuits are constantly
releasing men from indoor urban confines and from the need to live in
self-suppressed ways in their own heads. Hence, they are not troubled
by festering, amorous or melancholy thoughts, of the kind faced by
women. Indeed, men are practically forced on exertion by the sheer
variety of non-domestic distractions open to them. Only reading is
notable by its absence from the list of masculine entertainments – the
one activity Boccaccio points toward for women's 'diletto . . . e utile
consiglio', 'pleasure and useful advice'. Whereas the confined urban
room is the locus of frustrated female desiring, the open *contado*, or at
very least the street and marketplace, is the domain of male activity. The
differential 'sociology of gender' thus produced by Boccaccio has as its
context the mixed modes – in part feudal, in part post-feudal – of the
rapidly growing Italian communes of the first three and a half centuries
of the millennium.

The formulation 'forced on exertion' which I employed of Boccaccio's
account of the active lives of men is a conscious reference, not in fact to
earlier centuries of the millennium, but forward across hundreds of
years to an almost uncannily similar case for gender differentiation
made in Jane Austen's last novel *Persuasion*. When towards the end of
that work the heroine, Anne Elliot, says to Captain Harville in a
discussion they are having about differences between men's and
women's daily activities (and hence feelings), 'We live at home, quiet,
confined, and our feelings prey upon us. You are forced on exertion.
You have always a profession, pursuits, business of some sort or other,

to take you back into the world immediately, and continual occupation and change soon weaken impressions,'[23] she might almost be summarizing Boccaccio's remarks in his Proem about the effects of acculturation on sexual difference. It is in the further remarks about literature and education in Austen's text that significant historical differences from the earlier author emerge. For centuries have now passed since Boccaccio had pronounced that women's very housebound status made them exemplary recipients of a literature written for them. Anne Elliot's point is that books as conventionally produced – overwhelmingly by men – disadvantage women in being so biased against them. Indeed, this point is not her own in the form in which it is first made, but Captain Harville's: 'all histories are against you, all stories, prose and verse.' It is as though in terms of literature itself female readers had indeed waited for its mainly male producers to fulfil the terms of Boccaccio's promise – a literature at least made *for* them if not by them, and mediating directly to their conditioning and emotional needs – only to be disappointed time after time to discover the perpetuation of a male gender bias; in Harville's words, productions never lacking in 'something to say upon woman's inconstancy. Songs and proverbs, all talk of woman's fickleness.'

It comes down to sexual politics – namely, who tells the story. For clearly if, as Anne Elliott asserts, 'Men have had every advantage of us in telling their own story. Education has been theirs in so much higher a degree; the pen has been in their hands,' then Boccaccio's central offer to women remains not simply an unfulfilled possibility in the history of literary production, but worse, a promise endlessly ratted on. By this reckoning, men's 'own story' includes female figures, but always seen prejudicially. Hence Anne Elliot's conclusion: 'if you please, no reference to examples in books. . . . I will not allow books to prove anything.'[24] This (at first glance wildly ahistorical) parallel between Boccaccio and Austen is in fact drawn for the purposes of making a large historical generalization. For if Boccaccio stands in some respects at the very forefront of an early modern period in Europe, the kind of optimism with which he sees his text functioning as delight and instruction in the lives of his contemporary female readers is the optimism of a relatively untried approach. The pessimism, on the other hand, of Austen's female protagonist is presented as the result of the sheer weight of unprogressive social history to her point in time, convincing her that education and literary production have remained male-controlled domains, and have notably failed to enlarge the bounds of female freedom or to present the actions of women unprejudicially.

Boccaccio's novel offer to his female readers – of a literature specifically written for them – is itself, upon further inspection, not free from some simple gender biases of a fourteenth-century male author. In the midst of his compelling case about female repression, in which we experience the stifling claustrophobia of actual rooms – indeed, a sense of the crushing mental isolation of women forced to pass their lives within bounded walls – there arises a note of flagrant male bias:

> And if, in the course of their meditations, their minds should be invaded by melancholy arising out of the flames of longing, it will inevitably take root there and make them suffer greatly, unless it be dislodged by new interests. Besides which, their powers of endurance are considerably weaker than those that men possess. (p. 46)

The condescending belittling of women's endurance ('elle sono molto men forti che gli uomini a sostenere' in the original Italian, Vol. 1, p. 5) is a give-away sign on Boccaccio's part, possessing none of the convincing explanatory power of other remarks he makes in nearby sentences. And yet it is these very partialities of a nascent fourteenth-century proto-feminism in Boccaccio – some of them impressively original, some depressingly conventional – that reveal the complexity of attitudes affecting the nature and status of women in his culture.

On that note it is time to start engaging with some of the faultlines regarding gender, as well as other historical fissures and cultural contradictions that add so much to the interest of Boccaccio's text. To do so will involve justifying the detection in it of sexual coding that we may begin to define as recognizably early-modern. At the same time the most immediate question to be resolved is whether this mid-fourteenth-century moment of Boccaccio and of the plague is not still far too early to be talking in terms such as 'repression', in anything like a modern sense.

＊＊＊＊＊

In his chapter on Periodization in *The History of Sexuality*, Michel Foucault descries a first great rupture as 'occurring in the course of the seventeenth century', characterized by 'the advent of the great prohibitions, the exclusive promotion of adult marital sexuality, the imperatives of decency, the obligatory concealment of the body, the reduction to silence and mandatory reticences of language'.[25] And certainly Foucault is very convincing in his readings of seventeenth-century elaborations of these strategies of repression, particularly in such matters as Counter Reformation emphases on confession. He demonstrates why the seventeenth century cannot but figure crucially in his 'history'.

But there is good reason to claim that this 'apparatus of prohibitions', which we tend to associate in any case with the bourgeois epoch, and therefore to imagine as being roughly coextensive in time scale with our definition of it, was already surprisingly operational in the Italy of the mid-fourteenth century – that product of commercial boom, rapid urban expansion and feudal decline, which by 1348, the year of the Black Death, had already seen a vast shake-out in its own economic dynamic, with the collapse of major Florentine banking enterprises from 1340 onwards (a collapse dealt with in more detail later in this chapter). The text of the *Decameron* takes that taboo-laden atmosphere of boom-time mercantilism of the previous centuries and of earlier decades of the present one, but then predicates it upon the advent of the plague, presented so to speak as a climacteric in the lived values of the society. The plague is recounted as an event during which all prior social cohesion dissolves into profoundly disturbing chaos, and from out of which order can only be reconstituted at another level – the pastoral realm of the frame narrative, concerning the ten storytellers who depart Florence together as a *brigata* for their residences in the *contado*.

We are perhaps deceived by what appears to our twenty-first-century minds as the medieval libertinism of the text into assuming that the cultural prohibitions it is clearly sometimes attacking, or more often constructing comic detours around, are of little substantial weight. On the contrary, the very explicitness of a theme such as that of the seventh day's storytelling, 'delle beffe, le quali, o per amore o per salvamento di loro, le donne hanno già fatte a' lor mariti, senza essersene avveduti o no', ('the tricks which, either in the cause of love or for motives of self-preservation, women have played upon their husbands, irrespective of whether or not they were found out') – a theme in no ways unrepresentative of others in the overall work – is the indicator of an already prevalent 'promotion of adult marital sexuality' in society (to revert to Foucault's terminology), which the text goes some way to disrupt. The textual original for 'self-preservation' in that rubric for the seventh day's tales is 'salvamento di loro' – 'saving of themselves' – showing how far expressions originally religious in connotation have been adapted in this text to a secular meaning.

And there are equally explicit factors throughout, which problematize other issues focused in Foucault's words. Take for instance his important notion of a 'reduction to silence and mandatory reticences of language'. In a notable passage the senior female storyteller in the *Decameron*, Pampinea, comments on the way the new age has led to a decline in linguistic adroitness in the female sex, and a commensurate increase in sumptuary expenditure on the body. More shockingly still, Pampinea opines that if women have not been reduced to utter silence by their historical loss of the gift of wit, they ought to be so. Far better, she implies, to adopt a mandatory reticence than to produce stupid replies in good company; or even worse, to chatter only with the lower orders.

Since the passage is one of the most salient accounts of changing patterns of female behaviour in the entire text, with the exception of the introductory description of the great metamorphoses in society produced by the plague, and since it seems shot through with important internal contradictions no less than premised on notions of social fissure, it merits further scrutiny.

> Valorose giovani, come ne' lucidi sereni sono le stelle ornamento del cielo e nella primavera i fiori de' verdi prati, così de' laudevoli costumi e de' ragionamenti piacevoli sono i leggiadri motti. Li quali, per ciò che brievi sono, molto meglio alle donne stanno che agli uomini, in quanto più alle donne che agli uomini il molto parlare e lungo, quando senza esso si possa fare, si disdice, come che oggi poche o niuna donna rimasa ci sia la quale o ne 'ntenda alcuno leggiadro o a quello, se pur lo 'ntendesse, sappia rispondere: general vergogna e di noi e di tutte quelle che vivono. Per ciò che quella virtù che già fu nell'anime delle passate hanno le moderne rivolta in ornamenti del corpo. . . . Io mi vergogno di dirlo, per ciò che contro all'altre non posso dire che io contro a me non dica: queste così fregiate, così dipinte, così screziate, o come statue di marmo mutole e insensibili stanno o sì rispondono, se sono addomandate, che molto sarebbe meglio l'avere taciuto; a fannosi a credere che da purità d'animo proceda il non saper tra le donne e co' valenti uomini favellare, e alla loro milensaggine hanno posto name onestà, quasi niuna donna onesta sia se non colei che con la fante o con la lavandaia o con la sua fornaia favella: il che se la natura avesse voluto, come elle si fanno a credere, per altro modo loro avrebbe limitato il cinguettare. (Vol. 1, pp. 111–12)

Just as the sky, worthy young ladies, is bejewelled with stars on cloudless
nights, and the verdant fields are embellished with flowers in the spring, so
good manners and pleasant converse are enriched by shafts of wit. These,
being brief, are much better suited to women than to men, as it is more
unseemly for a woman to speak at inordinate length, when this can be
avoided, than it is for a man. Yet nowadays, to the universal shame of
ourselves and all living women, few or none of the women who are left can
recognize a shaft of wit when they hear one, or reply to it even if they
recognize it. For this special skill, which once resided in a woman's very
soul, has been replaced in our modern women by the adornment of the
body. . . . I am ashamed to say it, since in condemning others I condemn
myself: but these over-dressed, heavily made-up, excessively ornamented
females either stand around like marble statues in an attitude of dumb
indifference, or else, on being asked a question, they give such stupid
replies that they would have been far better advised to remain silent. And
they delude themselves into thinking that their inability to converse in the
company of gentlemen and ladies proceeds from their purity of mind. They
give the name of honesty to their dull-wittedness, as though the only
honest women are those who speak to no one except their maids, their
washerwomen, or their pastrycooks. Whereas if, as they fondly imagine,
this had been Nature's intention, she would have devised some other
means for restricting their prattle. (pp. 107–8)

Analysis might usefully start with Pampinea's division between a
former age of women and the 'modern women' ('le moderne') who are
her contemporaries. The implication is that even in that former age
women practised mandatory reticences, choosing witty sallies rather
than longer speeches because of a principle which Pampinea states but
for which she gives no reasons in history or culture: namely, that it is
more unseemly for women to speak at inordinate length than for men.
The case about women grows steadily worse as Pampinea proceeds. If
too much female speech is considered by her an outrage to propriety in
any age, the present sees a further defeat in their linguistic prowess –
their loss even of such reputation for succinct and witty sallies as they
formerly possessed. At this point the text produces a terrible irony, its
double-buttressing of women within the mandatory reticences of
speechlessness: 'they give such stupid replies that they would have been
far better advised to remain silent'. The argument gives up on women as
producers of social intercourse, and in despair witnesses their retreat
into purity and honesty as a rationalization for their silences. We might
notice in passing how, though Pampinea is attacking such a move on the

part of her 'modern' (fourteenth-century) women, it too seems to prefigure Foucault's notion of a (seventeenth-century) 'imperative of decency'.

The 'modern' women's last retreat of all – prattle with their own servant class – nearly produces a *treble*-buttressing of the argument against women speaking at all. Nearly but not quite, since prohibiting such domestic intercourse is perceived as unnecessary overkill. Nature hasn't actually bothered to stop off this last, domestic outlet for female self-expression, secure in the knowledge that this is a truly petty realm when it comes to the issue of women's honour.

By this stage of the analysis we are perhaps beginning to feel that on the issue of women and language the text is exhibiting an outright dose of medieval misogyny. To problematize the issue of misogyny still further, there is no avoiding the fact that Boccaccio places the speech in the mouth of a strong female character. And yet a strange segmentation in categories of women has occurred. Pampinea herself seems completely unshackled by the original prohibition she pronounces, of lengthy speech on the part of women, as if at this point in the argument she did not belong to the gender of which she speaks – though it must be pointed out that she reminds us shortly afterwards of how *self*-shamed she feels by her assessment of the diminution in women's linguistic prowess and by their recourse to sumptuary displays. This segmentation into categories of women is most revealing in the sentence which attacks them for deluding themselves 'into thinking that their inability to converse in the company of gentlemen and ladies proceeds from their purity of mind'. I have more to say on the subject of purity later. But let us first concentrate on the phrase 'the company of gentlemen and ladies' – in the Italian, 'tra le donne e co' valenti uomini'. This phrase suggests, at one level at any rate, the existence of an ongoing lifestyle of both sexes together that remains unaffected by this new ethos of reticent purity.

Would it be outlandish to suggest that these *donne* and *valenti uomini* are a kind of vestigial feudal company who have preserved, in the light of new bourgeois strictures of reticence and in the face too of sumptuary displays of new urban wealth, what now looks like an increasingly rare ideal of cultivated discourse, which the text seems to be arguing should be reinstated more generally? Some of the techniques by which it might be reinstated are hinted at in the criticism levelled at associating with one's maid, washerwoman or pastrycook. The implied message seems to be, associate upwards – or at any rate not downwards – and re-hierarchize class levels as effectively as possible.

If such a company exists, in which the honour of the *donne* and *valenti uomini* is not in doubt, nor their tongues hobbled by prohibition or the fear of not cutting a fine enough figure in the realms of language, it is surely the *brigata* of ten storytellers. For the most curious aspect of all about Pampinea's speech is that it could in no way apply to her own most articulate self, nor to any of the other female members of the *brigata*. She has defined a condition of 'modern' womanhood that is compellingly interesting, but that seems to relate more to the post-plague future than to what we note about female comportment in the frame narrative, or in most of the stories for that matter (in which women often display great wit without being 'unseemlily' long-winded).

These stories are set almost exclusively in the preceding two pre-plague centuries, as Vittore Branca has noted in his powerful argument on Boccaccio's medievalism:

> the chronological limits of the narrated actions . . . were almost without exception (only three in a hundred novellas) the period immediately preceding Boccaccio's own time – that is the stormy but splendid age of the last Crusades, the struggles of the communes against the Hohenstaufens, the adventurous events in southern Italy, and the decades of chivalry of the thirteenth and fourteenth centuries which witnessed the apogee of the Italian, but especially of the Florentine, mercantile power.[26]

But the fact that the settings of their stories are pre-plague does not mean that their events transpire in an essentially unfallen world. On the contrary, the overwhelming impression of reading many stories at one sitting is that the crisis which Boccaccio's introduction ascribes to the plague already invested pre-plague Italy. The important distinction is hence not so much between pre-plague and post-plague conditions, as Boccaccio's introduction to the first day's storytelling would have us suppose. Rather it lies in the privileged positioning of the *brigata* at a pastoral remove from the more general crisis. As the next section of this argument elaborates, the plague as textually described is Boccaccio's way of dealing symbolically with this general crisis in the form of a convenient trope; and yet the plague *is* clearly also real and momentous for him at the time of writing.

If the distinction between pre- and post-plague that Boccaccio seeks to sustain largely disintegrates under our inspection, then the conditions of the brigata's or anyone else's purity cannot really be sought for in the past age – that hotchpotch of uncleanliness and urban disorder which not all the frequently noted public measures to police social decorum (notably in cities) had managed to control. Pure the *brigata* nonetheless is. Their elegantly formalized activities place them beyond reproach and furthermore beyond danger, unless – and Boccaccio is most sensitive to this charge and at several points tries to pre-empt it – it is reproach for or danger from these very stories they do indeed narrate. Branca's resolute pointing into the past doesn't help us to come to terms with the fact that the narration itself is *post*-plague and, particularly as regards the ten storytellers, presented textually as a model reordering of life, undertaken *in the face of* plague. Quite how deeply committed therefore is Boccaccio's text to maintaining separate and distinctive levels of purity in the frame group of storytellers? And how are the terms of their exemption from Pampinea's critique of modern women constructed in the *Decameron* in the first place? Does Boccaccio actually manage to preserve their reputations? Or are the storytellers too in jeopardy of a kind that they – and maybe Boccaccio too – are not really fully aware of, or at any rate cannot effectively police and contain?

'Purity' is a topic which has perennially exercised historians and anthropologists, no doubt because so many epochs and cultures have felt compelled to produce distinctions between pure and impure, at levels of the body, the mind, and in codes of interpersonal behaviour. At this point it is valuable to re-inspect and revise one such earlier thesis in the field of social psychology. It comes from Erich Fromm, and was first published in an article in 1932, but brought to the attention of Boccaccio studies by J. Vincenzo Molle in 1982. Molle, writing in French (which I have translated), says:

> The marked attention to purity of the body and of the spirit (if the stories told are often audacious, the morals of the storytellers are by contrast extremely chaste) gives rise to certain observations in social psychology . . . Fromm describes the difference which exists between the feudal age and the ensuing capitalist one in terms of training in matters of purity, spirit of economics, punctuality and a sense of order. These qualities, learned rather late in the medieval period, become very marked with the advent of capitalism.[27]

There is unquestionably a great challenge in Fromm's general thesis. The women who pique themselves on their purity and honesty in the passage from the *Decameron* I have been focusing on would seem, in some sense, portents of the oncoming capitalist epoch and its long-term bourgeois ethos. And that squares too with Foucault's notions about acquisition of an inner dynamic of prohibitions.

But the oddest aspect of all is that the aider and abettor of those prohibitions in our text is the person speaking, Pampinea. And her words have included the vague notion of a vestigial feudal company of *donne* and *valenti uomini*, which the overall text seems to be promoting as an ideal of social association. Furthermore (and very importantly), the model to hand of just such a company is the band of storytellers, whose women have certainly not lost their tongues. It would seen that as far as purity without loss of sophisticated social intercourse is concerned (Boccaccio's model if not Fromm's), the company of *donne* and *valenti uomini* of the frame narrative are a remnant of feudal decorum otherwise laid waste by the plague, rather than, as Molle is suggesting, the portents of a new bourgeois purity. There are portents of that latter in Pampinea's critique, as I have suggested: those women with shrunken linguistic selves whom, in her disgust with them, Pampinea would moralize into still further silence.

But if the company of the *brigata* is *not* the portent of a new bourgeois purity, then why are they (and Boccaccio on their behalf) so preoccupied with chastity, cleanliness and ordered living? Our puzzle seems to know no end. No sooner have we established a division between, on the one hand, 'moderns', who are struck dumb by all the great prohibitions Foucault taught us to look out for, and a distinctive group of storytellers about whom still clings the Romance-charm of high feudal comportment, than we are haunted by this further doubt: that the *brigata* too is invested with many of precisely the same great prohibitions that Foucault and before him Fromm had distinguished in the intertwined histories of sexuality and of the bourgeois epoch.

Is it possible that somewhere in the unconscious of Pampinea – that is to say, in the unconscious of Boccaccio too, and of the text – there is an acutely felt need to distinguish an ideal, which is also a sign of an anxiety at recognizing *identity with* another category that is a decline from that ideal? In this case the latter category is 'modern women' ('le moderne'), who on the one hand infuriate Pampinea, but with whom we have already detected one tell-tale sign of her shame at recognizing herself as identified. If this new hypothesis is true, then we are obliged to say that most of the female storytellers' attempts to keep up social appearances, and to seem like an intact remnant of an integrated pre-plague feudal lifestyle, amount to little more than *produced affect* on their own and their narrator's (i.e. Boccaccio's) part. In truth, we detect from a myriad of details that they are stirred by identical desires to those of the characters they narrate, and are driven by much the same set of prohibitions as the women they seek by means of scorn to distinguish themselves from.

If all this is so, perhaps we can get closest of all to the utter duality of their combination of innocence and experience, by gazing at them bathing in the translucent waters of the 'Valley of Women' at the end of the sixth day:

> E commandato alla lor fante che sopra la via per la quale quivi s'entrava dimorasse e guardasse se alcun venisse e loro il facesse sentire, tutte e sette si spogliarono ed entrarono in esso, il qual non altrimenti li lor corpi candidi nascondeva, che farebbe una vermiglia rosa un sottil vetro. Le quali essendo in quello, né per ciò niuna turbazion d'acqua nascendone, cominciarono come potevano ad andare in qua in là di dietro a' pesci, i quali male avevan dove nascondersi, e a volerne con esso le mani pigliare. (Vol. 2, pp. 192–93)

> Having ordered their maid to go back and keep watch along the path by which they had entered the valley, and bring them warning if anyone should come, all seven of them undressed and took to the water, which concealed their chaste white bodies no better than a thin sheet of glass would conceal a pink rose. And when they were in the water, which remained as crystal-clear as before, they began as best they could to swim hither and thither in pursuit of the fishes, which had nowhere to hide, and tried to seize hold of them with their hands. (p. 517)

A somewhat facetious response might be that this constitutes a fourteenth-century single-sex riposte to naturism. More seriously, it needs to be said that much is revealed by the passage apart from simple nakedness. The seven women have a heavy weight of moral experience determining their action. They take elaborate precautions not to be seen, already historically imbued as they are with what (we yet again recall) Foucault named as another of the great prohibitions – 'obligatory concealment of the body'. Yet having acted thus, in their bathing they display such purity – of bodily form as well as of intent – as seems to constitute the innocence of an age *before* all that weight of prohibitions. And if not to anyone else, then textually to us at least, they are also so extraordinarily visible and beautiful that, taken together with the guileless phallicism of their attempts to grasp the fishes, this must rate as among the most *innocently* erotic descriptions in the entire *Decameron*.

So what is our conclusion about the scene? Perhaps something like the following. The women are neither *exclusively* vestigial remnants of a past age of feudal Romance nor portents of a bourgeois future. They are both at once. They face both past and future in such complicated ways that only the most pertinacious of analyses can begin to separate the one aspect from the other, both being so strong, even if opposites. And just as here, swimming in the translucent waters, the chaste seven remain unseen and yet in another sense – as a rose under thin clear glass – are utterly unconcealed, particularly to readers' gazes, so, in historical terms, they are the essence of complex self-contradiction, fissured in every detail of their natures.

But who, when studied with sufficient historical subtlety and sophistication, is not? It is our good fortune that with the *Decameron* Boccaccio bequeathed posterity a text that, while it goes on tantalizing us to categorize and distinguish, aborts or controverts so many of our conclusions with grand fractures of its own, themselves the stuff of compelling history. It is a world where the morally acceptable and supposedly unacceptable exist in intimate interconnectivity, even interdependence: 'né fu per ciò, quantunque cotal mezzo di nascosto si dicesse, la donna reputata sciocca, che saputo aveva pigliare il bene che Iddio a casa l'aveva mandato' (Vol. 1, p. 146), 'nor, moreover, was the lady considered to have acted foolishly (even though nobody openly said so) for the way she had accepted the blessing that God had left on her doorstep' (p. 127). Above all, as this last instance shows (a wealthy widow has let the robbed and unclad Rinaldo d'Asti via a postern door into her dwelling place at the town wall, and then invited him, once bathed and dressed in her deceased husband's garments, to fulfil the functions of the lover she has been expecting, but who has been called away from his assignation with her), the public façade of morality has become *mere* façade, behind which a private world of fantastical erotic gratification can be textually elaborated. In their reactions to the story the storytellers secretly applaud the lady's action. What is equally important, however, is that 'nobody openly said so'. The storytellers must be above reproach in their public morality within the frame story. And yet we are made party to some of their private thoughts and desires, which are the stuff of an altogether different and *highly* eroticized world. If the word did not have such pejorative overtones, one would be inclined to say that what the text is giving form to is *hypocrisy*: the endemic private flouting of public morality and codes of behaviour, or at very least the willingness inwardly to condone such flouting of them, while outwardly maintaining a show of propriety.

This separation of public morality from private behaviour is pervasive. Both 'good' and 'bad' characters act on the principle of the traditional proverb, 'peccato celato è mezzo perdonato' (Vol. 1, p. 83), 'a sin that's hidden is half forgiven' (p. 91), voiced by the abbot of a monastery in Lunigiana who follows one of his monks into carnal knowledge of a peasant beauty of thereabouts. Put differently, in the more explicit gloss of another character – as she tries to tempt one of the few entirely pure characters in the text, the Count Antwerp, into sin with her – the principle runs thus: 'e come che tal cosa, se saputa fosse, io conosca non essere onesta, nondimeno, essendo e stando nascosa, quasi di niuna cosa esser disonesta la giudichi' (Vol. 1, p. 254), 'if this were to become known, it would be regarded as highly improper; but if it is kept secret I can't really see any harm in it' (p. 194). What is perhaps notable in this widespread separation between public morality and private behaviour is that although many capitalize on it, those who speak out openly, and enshrine their flouting of public morality in words or a verbal principle, are mostly persons of whom the text is in other ways fostering disapproval. By contrast those who follow their private pleasures with an outward show of decorum, like that widow of the walled town of Castel Guglielmo who accepts God's gift of a man in her hour of need, but take pains on the morrow to see that the matter never comes to light, gain textual approval, even though the storytellers themselves have a bit on their tongues preventing their expressing it openly.

We may usefully map the division between public and private in terms of the city wall of Castel Guglielmo itself in the story just mentioned (II, ii). Robbed of his money and clothing, Rinaldo has arrived after its only drawbridge gate has been closed. He has to bed down in a shivering state in some straw by the wall. But this just happens to be near a postern or private entry to the citadel, on the other side of which lies the lady in her bath, able to 'hear the wails and moans being uttered by Rinaldo'. Although he is thence rescued for the night via the clandestine door into her lodgings, for form's sake ('to avoid scandal' as the text says) she sees that he exits the same way early enough the following morning to be at the public gate of the city when it actually opens. He thus has an alibi for his private night of pleasure, being first into the city via its public gate next morning.

The structure of the entire tale therefore, and in particular the significant part played by a city wall – with a clandestine as well as a public entry – neatly diagrammatizes so much of what is going on throughout the text of the *Decameron*. The citadel can be thought of as a figure for public morality, the wall the *cordon sanitaire* protecting it, and the clandestine postern gate the opportunity for private acts which infringe that morality but without coming to notice. In literal terms, with only one known gate to the citadel, all entry by day must be public and licensed. Closed by night, it prevents incursion by malefactors. (This was, incidentally, the real state of affairs in small towns and cities throughout the Italy of Boccaccio's day.) But – unseen and unknown to anybody except the storyteller Filostrato and his audience, including the readers – entry *can* be made at a clandestine point, and figurally speaking this is the access for private pleasure within the city. The only catch is that the night entrant must make a secret exit by the same route before dawn, for public morality not to be seen to have been infringed. For good measure he must also appear at the public city gate at first light, as though (in the figural terms of the text) paying homage to its symbology of the protection of public morality.

A deception has been practised, but in ways that invite the reader to condone – certainly not protest – the gap which the text is opening up, between public appearance and private pleasure. And just to set a further textual seal on public appearances, even the malefactors who have robbed Rinaldo at the story's beginning are caught and hanged at its ending.

\* \* \* \* \*

In condoning the widening breach between a public and a private morality, Boccaccio's *Decameron* could not be more different from Dante's *Commedia*. Boccaccio's account of the Florence of the plague is that of an utterly fallen state. But the vision of fallenness is largely secular; a matter of class-based behaviour succumbing to vice, amid the general scene of death and immorality. Later in the text there are positive visions of redemption from such states of vice, both within the frame and in some of the novelle. And significantly one of the stories involving such a 'redemption' is set partly in Florence, but also imaginatively historicizes for us the developing links between Florence and Britain in Boccaccio's own and the slightly earlier epoch. Before finishing this chapter with a close look at that novella (II, iii), it is important to say something more about the mid-fourteenth-century crisis itself.

The plague and its evasion by the group of storytellers are the key to much else, either literally or symbolically. The feudal remnant of which I have been speaking is very much a reconstituting at another level – in textual terms, the level of pastoral – of upper echelons of society shown otherwise, in the introductory description of plague-infested Florence, to be either dealt their death blow, or brought to an unchaste hybridizing with other social levels that puts paid to the mystique which was formerly a large factor in their power. As a historical event, the plague is seen as hastening the transit from a feudal *plenum* to an utter evacuation of its once glorious lifestyles:

> O quanti gran palagi, quante belle case, quanti nobili abituri, per addietro di famiglie pieni, di signori e di donne, infino al menomo fante rimaser voti! O quante memorabili schiatte, quante amplissime eredità, quante famose ricchezze si videro senza successor debito rimanere! Quanti valorosi uomini, quante belle donne, quanti leggiadri giovani, li quali non che altri, ma Galieno, Ippocrate o Esculapio avrieno giudicati sanissimi, la mattina desinarono co' loro parenti, compagni e amici, che poi la sera vegnente appresso nell'altro mondo cenarono con li loro passati. (Vol. 1, p. 26)

> Ah, how great a number of splendid palaces, fine houses, and noble dwellings, once filled with retainers, with lords and with ladies, were bereft of all who had lived there, down to the tiniest child! How numerous were the famous families, the vast estates, the notable fortunes, that were seen to be left without a rightful successor! How many gallant gentlemen, fair ladies, and sprightly youths, who would have been judged hale and hearty by Galen, Hippocrates and Aesculapius (to say nothing of others), having breakfasted in the morning with their kinsfolk, acquaintances and friends, supped that same evening with their ancestors in the next world! (p. 58)

This is elegiac in the first sentences and ironic in the last. If the opening is clinching proof of Boccaccio's attachment to a feudal world, and seems to show him nowhere more troubled than in his lament for the disappearance (along with all the rest) of 'rightful successors', then the last sentence sees him almost mocking his own elegiac regrets, with the comic fancy that the feudal *plenum* doesn't really disappear but is simply transposed after death to the 'altro mondo' ('next world'), where it goes on with the same sumptuous ancestral feasting. And yet not all the irony he can muster erases the sense of real historical rupture in Boccaccio's descriptions of the vacant habitations and titles of the oldest families. One curious effect of the passage is its vision of the material architectural settings of those former lifestyles, utterly silent now, and depopulated of both high and low in the feudal order – 'infino al menomo fante', 'down to the tiniest child'.

I hope that it will begin to be clear why the plague needs to be understood not just in literal terms, but as an artistic trope for the expression of wider anxieties about social control, and about the breakdown (in particular) of what Foucault in the earlier quote names as 'the imperatives of decency'; decency, we might again notice, being in the present instance not a promise of the new age, but a kind of backward-looking association with notions of a noble past, now threatened with a terrible social goulash of class-intermingling and levelling-down. The all-important passage is the following:

E da questo essere abbandonati gl' infermi da' vicini, da' parenti e dagli amici, e avere scarsità di serventi, discorse un uso quasi davanti mai non udito: che niuna quantunque leggiadra o bella o gentil donna fosse, infermando, non curava d'avere a' suoi servigi uomo, qual che egli si fosse, o giovane o altro, e a lui senza alcuna vergogna ogni parte del suo corpo aprire non altrimenti che ad una femina avrebbe fatto, solo che la necessità della sua infermità il richiedesse: il che, in quelle che ne guarirono, fu forse di minore onestà, nel tempo che succedette, cagione. (Vol. 1, p. 20)

As a result of this wholesale desertion of the sick by neighbours, relatives and friends, and in view of the scarcity of servants, there grew up a practice almost never previously heard of, whereby when a woman fell ill, no matter how gracious or beautiful or gently bred she might be, she raised no objection to being attended by a male servant, whether he was young or not. Nor did she have any scruples about showing him every part of her body as freely as she would have displayed it to a woman, provided that the nature of her infirmity required her to do so; and this explains why those women who recovered were possibly less chaste in the period that followed. (p. 54)

It need hardly be pointed out that what the male servant at such an impasse sees is not just the *naked* body of the gently bred lady, but the *diseased* naked body. It is the perfect trope for indicating not only carnal knowledge across class boundaries, but that the 'nature of her infirmity', if it is not terminal to her as an individual, is so in terms of her class and status. Feudality is seen to have to submit itself *in its infirmity* to its own servant class for inspection and for ministering. In moral terms it is an unchastening process, implying permanent loss of its mystical immunity as a class above and apart.

If we now return to Boccaccio's opening description of the plague, we note that it is much more than an elegiac rendering of the demise of feudal custom. The text specifies quite particularly that other echelons of Florentine society – the 'minuta gente', or common people, and the 'mezzana gente', those most involved in production, trade and banking activities – were brought, if anything, still lower than the nobility:

> Della minuta gente, e forse in gran parte della mezzana, era il ragguardamento di molto maggior miseria pieno: per ciò che essi, il più o da speranza or da povertà ritenuti nelle lor case, nelle lor vicinanze standosi, a migliaia per giorno infermavano, e non essendo né serviti né atati d'alcuna cosa, quasi senza alcuna redenzione tutti morivano. (Vol. 1, p. 22)

> As for the common people and a large proportion of the bourgeoisie, they presented a much more pathetic spectacle, for the majority of them were constrained, either by their poverty or the hope of survival, to remain in their houses. Being confined to their own parts of the city, they fell ill daily in their thousands, and since they had no one to assist them or to attend to their needs, they inevitably perished almost without exception. (p. 55)

This description raises a matter taken for granted by Boccaccio, as part of an everyday and indeed pre-plague reality, though one with power to shock *us* – namely, the apartheid system of life in these fourteenth-century communes, based on regulations controlling where various classes could live.

The plague wreaks havoc on all levels of society. But even more than that, it turns into anarchic chaos the prior ordering of social association between classes and individuals. As an event that sets off decline from pure to impure within the urbanized context, it is a trope for wide-scale detrimental change. If there is an escape to be had from anarchic loss of social control and of civilized mores in times of the plague, it is into the sanctuary of the pastoral sphere, as already mentioned. The decision on

the part of the seven young women and three young men to reconstitute
a dignified social grouping away from the plague-ridden city is presented
as an opportunity for arresting moral decline, without the loss, however,
of social pleasure:

> io giudicherei ottimamente fatto che noi . . . uscissimo, e fuggendo come
> la morte i disonesti essempli degli altri, onestamente a' nostri luoghi in
> contado, de' quali a ciascuna di noi è gran copia, ce ne andassimo a stare, e
> quivi quella festa, quella allegrezza, quello piacere che noi potessimo,
> senza trapassare in alcuno atto il segno della ragione, prendessimo. (Vol. 1,
> p. 33)

> We could go and stay together on one of our various country estates,
> shunning at all costs the lewd practices of our fellow citizens and feasting
> and merrymaking as best we may without in any way overstepping the
> bounds of what is reasonable. (p. 61)

The impulse – which is acted upon – is clearly predicated upon a fine
sense of moral balance between the pleasurable and the reasonable (in
the Italian of this passage, 'piacere' and 'ragione').

But here we come against the great central contradictions of the text,
which more than anything reveal Boccaccio's world divided between
notions of pure and impure – gentle breeding on the one hand, and
acting on the spur of desire irrespective of class levels on the other – and
the constituting of a chaste society of storytellers in the pastoral frame,
many of whose stories act out erotic fantasies located in an urban
culture they have ostensibly left behind.

*＊ ＊ ＊ ＊ ＊*

Importantly, the general crisis of the mid-fourteenth century was not
merely, indeed not even principally, concerned with the demise of
feudalism, however moved Boccaccio himself seems to have been by
that in particular. It was a downturn in the fortune-building dynamic of
the commercial revolution itself. So it is necessary to situate this reading
of Boccaccio's account of the plague – as a trope for wider social and
economic disturbances – in terms of the 'general crisis' in early modern
capitalism much debated by historians of the period. Perry Anderson has
provided a synoptic rehearsal of that debate in his chapter on 'The
General Crisis' in *Passages from Antiquity to Feudalism*, to which the
present analysis is indebted.[28]

The commercial revolution had already elbowed aside or else largely incorporated the major feudal classes. As Martines makes clear, only the really great feudatories – families such as the Guidi counts of Tuscany whose power bases remained firmly in the *contado* – had stood aside and not taken part in the growing communes, often, indeed, obstructing their development by factious wars with them.[29] But Florence's downturn was not principally caused by the old feudal classes, either within or without the city, and although deepened by the plague was also not in principle directly caused by it, since the city's economic wellbeing had already experienced shockwaves for the better part of a decade before the advent of the major plague of 1348. Armando Sapori in his pioneering work in economic history of 1922 provided a compelling account of the crisis suffered by the greatest two Florentine (and indeed Italian) banking houses of the period, the Bardi and the Peruzzi companies.[30] He had tracked their operations in England, in particular from scant evidence of the initial Bardi involvement in England from the 1270s onwards, to the phase when an eventual overstretching of resources by the Peruzzi and themselves brought about their downfall in the 1340s – and with it the downturn in the financial fortunes of Florence itself for a century and more.

There had been banking crashes before among the eighty or so Florentine banking houses in the *arte del cambio*, one of the seven great guilds or so-called *arti maggiori* of the fourteenth century.[31] The business structure of the city had, for instance, already been badly shaken as early as the years between 1308 and 1310, when three sizeable banks, the Mozzi, the Franzesi and the Cerchi had failed.[32] Sapori's great work on the economically powerful Bardi and Peruzzi companies, based as it is in large measure on English records, the Court Patent Rolls, is still the most instructive single narrative of how tied in to its international banking and trading ventures the commune of Florence had become by the time of their major crash. While they had prospered, so did Florence. But now seismic damage had been inflicted on them, deeply affecting the commune's own viability, so soon to be further devastated by the deadliest plague of the entire millennium.

The events of the two prime Florentine families of this economic revolution, as gathered together in Sapori's narrative, can be abridged as follows. Following the initial loans by several Italian banking families to the young King Richard in the late twelfth century for his campaigns in the Holy Land during the Third Crusade, some Italians had crossed the

Channel in the 1190s, not just to extend their purely banking enterprises but for investment in the growing wool industry of England. However, no firm evidence of the Bardi's particular presence there exists until 1277. They were followed by the Peruzzi, whose first presence in England is noted in 1306. There ensues a consolidation of the interests of both companies: for instance, it is their loans above all else which make possible English designs of conquest on the continent.

So strong was the position of the Bardi under Edward II that hatred was fomented on the part of the London populace, leading to the sacking and burning of the family's London storehouses in 1322, which even Villani in distant Florence hears of and records in his gathering Chronicle. Following this the two family companies are put under the special protection of the English crown. With extra privileges such as almost total rights to levies on wool exports from English ports, the Bardi in particular among the Italian banking families seem to be reaching an ever higher level of remunerative operations. Edward III borrows from both the Bardi and the Peruzzi for his war against the Scots, concluded with the victory at Halidon Hill in 1333. In 1338, although the king has all other Italian banking families arrested and their goods sequestered, he makes exception of these two principal financing houses. But their new and larger loans for Edward's French campaigns are devoured by his outstanding payments on other debts, and on 6 May 1339 Edward suspends all repayments to creditors of the state, this time not excluding his favoured Bardi and Peruzzi. Even this exclusion is overturned, however, so that his new French expedition can depart after further borrowing. His special dispensation to the two families promises eventual restitution of all their loans, and even engages his first son Edward, the young Duke of Cornwall (whom we tend to recognize by his later *nom de guerre*, the Black Prince, and whose new dukedom, Cornwall, will figure in an interesting crux of this analysis), to maintain such promises in the event of his own premature death or temporary inability to pay them. Although in 1340 King Edward wreaks havoc on the French navy, destroying all but 24 of its 190 ships and all but some 5,000 of its 35,000 men, he is forced to cut short this second French campaign later in the year. The main losers from his retreat to English shores are the Bardi and Peruzzi, whose enormous loans – 'worth a kingdom' in Villani's estimation – remain unpaid in grand measure. Being themselves debtors to the king for quite separate amounts of money in the mid-1340s, the families are maltreated and variously imprisoned. Meanwhile the situation has darkened for the two companies back in Florence. Hit by a plague in 1340 and by subsequent food shortages in 1341, the commune is reeling economically, and the last thing it wants is a crisis in the international loans of its main banking families. Although the commune has confiscated the goods of some wealthy families, those of the Bardi and Peruzzi are more or less spared, but only because their main holdings are in England by this stage.

Heading already either for liquidation of their assets or at very least retrenchment of their activities, the Bardi attempt, along with other powerful families in Florence, an uprising against the Signoria, in which they are betrayed. The uprising is quashed and the Bardi suffer the traditional punishment of seeing their houses burned to the ground.[33]

From their position as globally important banking houses – far larger in the volume of loans and trade, for instance, than the Medici bank of the succeeding century was ever to become – the two great Florentine families have seen their fortunes collapse to levels from which it is impossible for them ever to recover, in any meaningful sense of the term. But their setbacks are Florence's too, and many individuals are caught up in the fall. Boccaccio himself and his father, who was for many years during Boccaccio's youth and early maturity a factor in the Bardi banking operations in Naples, return to Florence in about 1340, quite possibly because of general retrenchments in the firm's operations. (There is enticingly more to be said shortly about a 'figural' role Boccaccio himself played during the economic crisis, in his novella treatment of Florentine banking connections with England.)

For over a hundred years the volume of trade and banking activities fails throughout Italy to pick up to pre-plague levels. Writing on the continued economic downturn after the plague, Jeffrey Burton Russell has wittily remarked that 'the period from 1349 to 1470 was a golden age only for bacteria'.[34] With that sardonic formulation in mind, if we now return to Boccaccio's treatment of a banking crisis involving both Italy and England, we can appreciate far more the way in which he has projected back recent events, in which he may himself have been caught up, into a more distant and fabled past.

*****

This story of the Agolanti brothers from the second day, concerning early commercial links between Florence and England (II, iii), is fascinating in ways that can now be explored more fully. Read in the light of the Bardi and Peruzzi banking collapse, the degree of inspiration the novella takes from events recent at the time of its writing is highly noteworthy. But far more too seems to be processed in the story. Boccaccio's own self-styled love for a king's daughter in his earlier writings is here transmuted into a fable of fulfilled love, whereby the nephew of mere bankers weds a king's daughter and subsequently becomes a king in his own right. Here also is a story which tackles one of the most sensitive issues of class in contemporary Florence – the question as to whether powerful families are old nobility or *nova gente* (to use Dante's precise term for the *nouveaux riches*) – and which produces a 'solution' that lays the problem to rest. The treatment of the Florentine/English link itself is historically interesting from a host of angles, not least the revealing vision of a trio of brothers living as grandees in Florence, who are quite above sullying their hands in commerce or banking on home ground, but only because of the scale of their banking operations in an entirely different part of Europe. Incidental interests – important for all that – involving a subliminal narratological link between Boccaccio and no less a figure than the Black Prince are discovered when we delve into points of intersection between the historical, the fabulous and the personal in this novella. More than anything else, the story is an account of Florentine 'can-do-ism'. If the Agolanti are in the final analysis *nova gente*, then the story is Boccaccio's positive tribute to the *arrivisme* of this class, and hence runs counter in spirit to the most persistent of his class prejudices in favour of a vestigial feudal aristocracy located in the earlier discussion.

Ostensibly, Boccaccio's story is set deep in time, indeed, contemporary with some of the earliest Florentine banking interests in Britain that we have noted in Sapori's account. But as we shall shortly see, there are aspects of it which seem to foreshorten the century and a half in question, by making narrative capital out of high and low moments in the entire history of commercial connection between the two cultures. Here is a summary of the story as provided by Boccaccio:

Three young men squander their fortunes, reducing themselves to penury. A nephew of theirs, left penniless, is on his way home when he falls in with an abbot, whom he discovers to be the daughter of the King of England.

She later marries him and makes good all the losses suffered by his uncles, restoring them to positions of honour. (p. 127)

Tre giovani, male il loro avere spendendo, impoveriscono; de' quali un nepote con uno abate accontatosi, tornandosi a casa per disperato, lui truova essere la figliuola del re d'Inghilterra, la quale lui per marito prende e de' suoi zii ogni danno ristora, tornandogli in buono stato. (Vol. 1, p. 146)

The novella begins with a sentence about the somewhat unclear origins of the protagonist family, which one might at first be excused for thinking relatively unimportant:

In our city there once lived a nobleman named Messer Tebaldo, who according to some people belonged to the Lamberti family, whilst others maintain he was an Agolanti, perhaps for the simple reason that Tebaldo's son[s] later followed a profession with which the Agolanti family has always been associated and which it practises to this day. (p. 128)

Fu già nella nostra città un cavaliere il cui nome fu messer Tebaldo, il quale, secondo che alcuni vogliono, fu de' Lamberti, e altri affermano lui essere stato degli Agolanti, forse più dal mestiere de' figliuoli di lui poscia fatto, conforme a quello che sempre gli Agolanti hanno fatto e fanno, prendendo argomento, che da altro. (Vol. 1, pp. 147–8).

The issue is quite simply whether the family whose history we are about to follow were from a line of nobles, the Lamberti, or from a far more modest line of money-lenders, the Agolanti.[35] This doubt about 'background' was of importance in Boccaccio's times, as similar class issues tend to be in our own. And it will prove of vital importance to the themes of the story, part of the narrative workings of which will be more exactly to define the brothers in class terms – first of all confirming the shocking ambivalence of the opening sentence, but in conclusion producing a satisfactory resolution to the ambivalence of their social status through a brazen class redefinition on the part of the text.

Whatever their grandparental origins, the three sons of the Tebaldo are wealthy to begin with. But they run through their money 'in an orgy of spending', it being noteworthy that the forms of pleasure they indulge in during this spree are mostly those of the old nobility. Either they are truly of that class or making a fine show of being so by aping its pursuits: 'they employed a veritable army of servants, kept large numbers of thoroughbred horses, hounds and hawks, entertained continuously, gave presents, and entered the lists at jousts and tournaments' (p. 128) ('tenendo grandissima famiglia e molti e buoni cavalli e cani e uccelli e continuamente corte, donando e armeggiando', Vol. 1, p. 148). From time immemorial a besetting worry of old nobility has been how to replenish its coffers once it has converted to a post-agrarian existence and cannot easily engage in productive, wealth-creating activities in its new, urban context. Thus, when the brothers run through their riches they are in a sore quandary.

At this point the story goes through a highly revealing transition, which may not be as 'fabulous' as it at first seems. The brothers quit Florence 'without the slightest attempt at leave-taking' – 'senza commiato chiedere o fare alcuna pompa' – and head for England, where they establish themselves in 'una casetta' ('a small house'), reduce their own spending to a pittance and commence what in time become large-scale money-lending operations, 'to barons on their castles and other properties' ('in prestare a' baroni sopra castella e altre loro entrate', Vol. 1, pp. 149–50). Both sides of the original ambivalence about this family – the question of whether they are old nobility or upstart money-lenders – have by now received one kind of confirmation in the narrative. And already something highly revealing can therefore be noted: namely, that the story is a demonstration that it is perfectly possible to belong to more than one class, not exactly according to one's pursuits or lifestyles – because one has two, and they are mutually contrastive – but based on the separate locations of those pursuits. Indeed, the brothers can and do return to their spendthrift noble lifestyle in Florence, leaving their nephew Alessandro as a factor to run their operation as money-lenders in England.

So, the brothers can live as nobles in Florence, initially because they had the wealth to do so till it ran out, but subsequently because they replenish this wasted inheritance by living as money-lenders in far-off London, even maintaining the valuable operation by proxy when they return to their former lifestyle in Florence. The point is largely in the geographical *dis*connection between the two locations, in spite of there being a hidden (and to the brothers vital) *economic* connection between them. The game is up, however, when the situation in England changes. This is the point where the time scale of Boccaccio's story bears interesting inspection. 'Nacque in Inghilterra una guerra tra il re e un suo figliuolo, per la qual tutta l'isola si divise' (Vol. 1, p. 150) ('a totally unexpected war broke out in England between the King and one of his

sons, splitting the whole of the island into two rival factions', p. 129).
The English king and prince in question are Henry II and his eldest son
Henry, the so-called 'Young King', who along with his brothers rebelled
against his father's refusal to grant him the lands of his inheritance,
initially in 1173 and then sporadically until his death from fever in
1183. Dante had used this history in his canto on sowers of discord.
And, indeed, the telling of these wars in Boccaccio's narrative has a
slightly long-ago and far-away air about it.

But as soon as we witness the negative effect of these wars on the
banking operations overseen by the nephew Alessandro, and the further
knock-on effects in Florence of the English barons' reneging on their
debts and mortgages, the similarity to the period of the Bardi and
Perruzzi companies' collapse of less than a decade before the 1348
plague is apparent. Furthermore, the young Alessandro, after at first
hoping to stay on in England and ride out the political and economic
storm, eventually resolves to return to Florence, where his uncles – who
have all along depended on economic supply from him – have been
imprisoned for mounting debts after such supply has dried up. If this
return of the manager-nephew to Florence following the collapse of his
uncles' overseas venture reminds us of anything, it is surely Boccaccio's
and his own banker/factor/father's similar return to Florence at about
the time of the repercussions of the Bardi company's collapse (brought
about also, it will be recalled, largely on account of English debts). For
Boccaccio, that collapse was still very recent history, and it seems
specifically to have repercussed on his family and himself.

In the tale, there follow at this point the more fabulous events of
Alessandro's meeting – while en route across Europe to Italy – with the
King of England's daughter, in disguise as an abbot (thereby fleeing
from an arranged match with the elderly King of Scotland); Alessandro's
plighting of his troth to her when her reality as a woman is revealed; the
subsequent blessing of their marriage by the Pope in Rome; their
eventual pardon by the King of England; his conferring of a knighthood
plus the Earldom of Cornwall on his son-in-law; and Alessandro's own
conferral of knighthood on one of his uncles. By the end of the story,
Alessandro has not only reconciled the English king to his rebellious
son: the closing sentence reports a belief on the part of some that he
subsequently conquered Scotland and became its king.

In the realm of the sexual there is plenty of interesting detail in the
first encounter between Alessandro and the daughter of the King. But

what is of most interest is how at this point the deeper divide of the story – between notions of nobility on the one hand and banking enterprises on the other – begins to be bridged. The novella turns into a fable of the lowly *arriviste* gaining the heart of a princess on the grounds of merit, even though in the privacy of her own counsel she acknowledges what might be held against him if she had a mind to (which she doesn't): 'The Abbot, on hearing his fine, precise way of talking and observing his manners more closely, judged him to be a gentleman despite the lowly nature of his past occupation, and became even more enraptured with him' (p. 131) ('L'abate, udendo il suo ragionare bello e ordinato, e più partitamente i suoi costumi considerando, e lui seco estimando, come che il suo mestiere fosse stato servile, essere gentile uomo, più del piacer di liu s'accese', Vol. 1, pp. 152–3). This is in keeping with what has been much noted in Boccaccio before (and is the thesis of Branca's major essay on him, 'The Epic of the Italian Merchant') – namely, a bias towards the merchant class. But the point lies not in a levelling-down of values to those of such a 'lowly occupation' ('mestiere umile') as that of money-lending. Rather, this and analogous moments of fabulous class elevation in the *Decameron* suggest that even someone with a money-lending background can look and speak and act with the manners ('costumi') of a prince, and thus win the heart of a princess. As she is later to say in presenting him to the Pope for his approval, 'It may well be that he is less pure-blooded than a person of royal birth, but both in bearing and character he is a worthy match for any great lady' (p. 134), ('li cui costumi e il cui valore son degni di qualunque gran donna, quantunque forse la nobiltà del suo sangue non sia così chiara come è la reale', Vol. 1, p. 157). This readjustment of old feudal discourses proclaims that it is the intrinsic merit of individuals which counts – that is, not their class of origin but their nobility, as evidenced in their personal qualities and actions. The issue will be a contentious one for hundreds of years in Europe, as is witnessed (one among many examples) in Shakespeare's choice, more than two hundred years later, of another novella from the *Decameron* which turns on a similar dilemma (III, ix) as source text for *All's Well That Ends Well*.

Interestingly, in the Boccaccio novella that we are looking at, Alessandro is unaware of the class of the woman he has only just discovered is not an abbot. Two things suffice for him to proceed to a binding marriage – that from 'the size of her retinue he judged her to be a rich noblewoman, and could see for himself that she was very beautiful' (p. 133) ('avendo riguardo alla compagnia che ella avea, lei estimò dovere essere nobile e ricca, e bellissima la vedea', Vol. 1, p. 155). In short, the so-called bias in Boccaccio towards the merchant class is self-evidently not at the same time a bias against the nobility – rather, a wish to see open and flexible negotiation of the existing distance between them. Certain stories like this one put that negotiation in terms of a social transit – out of the negative connotations of having followed a lowly occupation and into the positive connotations of being adopted as a valuable member of the noble class. Here the matter is taken a stage further, as in many such fables. The class one is eventually recognized as enshrining is not simply noble (as in one's self-projections); it is regal (as one had not even aspired to speculate)!

But at this point, further and stranger matters of interest arise. First, on return from Rome via Florence the King's daughter has the three uncles released from prison and sees to it that their debts are paid. In the light of the outstanding debts of the English crown to the Bardi and Peruzzi at the time of the story's writing, this personal intervention to ensure that Florentine bankers languishing from bad English debts are rehabilitated to their former standing is truly a fable most apposite for the Florence of Boccaccio's own day (in which, by the way, no such rehabilitation of the Bardi and the Peruzzi, and certainly not as a result of new moves on the part of the English crown, was forthcoming).

We return to the question as to what had been the 'former standing' of Alessandro's uncles. By their acts they have twice proved themselves wastrels. But they have been redeemed by no less a figure than the King of England's daughter. And their nephew becomes accepted as that same King's son-in-law. The last we hear of them is that 'Agolante recovered all their money down to the last penny, and returned to Florence immensely rich, having first been given a knighthood by Earl Alessandro' (p. 135) ('Agolante ricoverò tutto ciò che aver vi doveano interamente, e ricco oltre modo si tornò a Firenze, avendol prima il conte Alessandro cavalier fatto', Vol. 1, p. 159). They have in conclusion both the benefit of the *nova gente* (wealth beyond measure, 'oltre modo') and that of the nobility (social standing). But interestingly, the confirmation of their social standing in the form of a knighthood has come from England. Whereas earlier in the story public knowledge of one's actions or standing in England would not reach Florence – the reason why the brothers kept quiet their economic distress and travelled so far afield to make it good in the first place – by the story's ending there has been a notable internationalization of information and social class. The original doubt about whether the brothers were true Florentine nobility, descending from the line of the Lamberti, has been annulled by the story's ending. It no longer matters. (Insofar as it is the brother named Agolante who receives the English knighthood, there is a hint of confirmation that, of the two original possibilities, the brothers were probably of a money-lending descent, from the *nova gente* Agolantis.) The brothers have the best of both worlds – the wealth of the *nova gente* and the social standing of nobility; no matter now that the latter is not Florentine in origin, for the 'English connection' has assumed a new and fabulous importance.

It is on that note of an English connection and of fable that the final and strangest point can now be made. As part of Alessandro's elevation into the English royal family he is given 'la contea di Cornovaglia' (the county of Cornwall). Presumably Boccaccio only used this particular idea of a further confirmation of Alessandro's standing because he had heard, some time during the period of actual mid-fourteenth-century crisis we have been considering, that the real English king's first son, Edward the Black Prince, was the *first* such son to have been given the county of Cornwall – a standing bequest of English royalty to this day, the revenues from which are the greatest single source of funds of the present Prince Charles. The Black Prince, remember, had been engaged to absolve the English crown's outstanding debts should Edward III fail to do so in his lifetime. But he died young, predeceasing his father by many years. Which is something of an irrelevance in the present instance, since in the story it is very much because of Alessandro (the substitute figure for the Black Prince in narrative terms, just as in his marriage with a king's daughter he is also a fable substitute for the author, Boccaccio, son of a Bardi factor in love with a regal princess) that the Florentine bankers' problems – created by England – are *absolved* by English regal intervention.

There is in brief, by this (at times tortuous) line of reckoning, a historical link – through fable admittedly: but then it is only *in fable* that intractable historical problems such as those of class and economics are often removed or smoothed over – all the way from the writer Boccaccio to the present Prince of Wales. Boccaccio's novella envisages a substitute-self returning to Florence as a consequence of a banking collapse caused by England; marrying a princess en route; obtaining the lands of Cornwall at the behest of her father the English king; and eventually being crowned King of Scotland. It is a fable of *arrivisme* admittedly, but which happens also to tell us a great deal about how the financial and social map of Europe will be stitched together over succeeding centuries; either in reality, or, when that proves impossible as it often does, at the level of persuasive ideologies of economic and class integration, in the promulgation of which literary fable can play no small a cultural role, as we have seen in the above critique.

## Notes

1. 'For he was evir (God wait) all womanis frend': Gavin Douglas, Bishop of Dunkeld, *Virgil's* Aeneid *Translated into Scottish Verse*, edited by David F. C. Coldwell, 4 vols (Edinburgh and London: William Blackwood and Sons, 1957–64), Vol. 2 (1957), p. 16.

2. *Ibid.*, p. 12.

3. Barbara Johnson, *The Critical Difference: Essays in the Contemporary Rhetoric of Reading* (Baltimore and London: The Johns Hopkins University Press, 1980), p. 13; also quoted in the Introduction to Elizabeth Abel (ed.), *Writing and Sexual Difference* (Brighton: The Harvester Press, 1982), p. 1.

4. Francesco De Sanctis, *History of Italian Literature*, translated by Joan Redfern, 2 vols (New York: Barnes and Noble, 1968), Vol. 1, p. 337. The original Italian speaks of discovering 'nell'autore il vuoto della coscienza ed il difetto di senso morale', *Storia della letteratura italiana* (Milan: Casa Editrice Bietti, 1960), p. 303.

5. Erich Auerbach, *Mimesis: The Representation of Reality in Western Literature*, translated by Willard R. Trask (original Swiss edn, 1946; first edn of this translation, 1953; Princeton: Princeton University Press, 1968), p. 228.

6. *Ibid.*

7. *Ibid.*

8. *Ibid.*, p. 231.

9. Robert J. Clements, 'Anatomy of the Novella', in Mark Musa and Peter E. Bondonella (eds), *The Decameron* (Norton Critical edn, 1977), p. 269. This article was first published in *Comparative Literature Studies*, 9 (1972), pp. 3–16.

10. Giuseppe Mazzotta, *The World at Play in Boccaccio's* Decameron (Princeton: Princeton University Press, 1986), pp. xv–xvi.

11. Robert Hollander, *Boccaccio's Two Venuses* (New York: Columbia University Press, 1977), pp. 102–7.

12. The relevant passage is printed in Paget Toynbee's article on Galeotto in his *Dictionary of Proper Names and Notable Matters in the Works of Dante* (1st edn, 1898), revised by Charles S. Singleton (Oxford: Oxford University Press, 1968), pp. 299–301. See likewise Toynbee's *Dante Studies and Researches* (London: Methuen, 1902), p. 2, fn. 2 and pp. 9–37.

13. Hollander, *Boccaccio's Two Venuses*, pp. 104 and 106.

14. Boccacccio, *Comento*, quoted in Boccaccio, *Decameron*, 2 vols. a cura di

Vittore Branca (Florence: Felice le Monnier, 1960), Vol. 1, p. 1. All Italian quotations from the *Decameron* will henceforth be from this edition, and page references given from it within my main text.

15. In his edition of the *Inferno*, Sapegno reminds us of Guido Guinizelli's 'Al cor gentil ripara sempre Amore' and of Dante's own earlier poem, 'Amore e 'l cor gentil sono una cosa'. *Inferno*, edited by Natalino Sapegno (Florence: La Nuova Italia Editrice, 1955), p. 62.

16. *The Divine Comedy*, translated, with a commentary, by Charles S. Singleton (London: Routledge and Kegan Paul, 1991), *Inferno*, Vol. 2, *Commentary*, p. 84. Teodolinda Barolini, in her recent article, 'Dante and Francesca da Rimini: Realpolitik, Romance, Gender', *Speculum*, 75(1) (January 2000), has written illuminatingly of the episode and of its early commentators, including *L'Ottimo commento* of *c.* 1333, whence Boccaccio takes certain of the historical clarifications of Francesca's story, which he then amplifies and in part varies. Barolini sees the Francesca episode in Dante, together with its early commentators (including Boccaccio), as constituting 'a cultural debate whose coordinates are dynastic marriages on the one hand and romance on the other' (p. 8). In my own analysis I stress that it is Dante who emphasizes the tragic romance element, and that Boccaccio's account, *very much* in debate with what he reads in Dante's text, is not so much a spelling out of what is embryonic there, as a significant departure into a different cultural position: one, indeed, highly critical of such dynastic marriages as Francesca is tricked into, when they are arranged by deception and to the detriment of the individual parties to them.

17. See Thomas G. Bergin, *Boccaccio* (New York: The Viking Press, 1981), p. 63, for the circumstances of this letter to Boccaccio of 1373, included in Petrarch's *Seniles*. Translated, the specific lines relating to the *Decameron* read: 'I would lie if I were to say that I read it; the bulk of the volume and the fact that it is written in prose and for popular consumption were reasons enough not to have it distract me from more important business. . . . But glancing at your book, I was pleased, and although offended by certain licentious and immoderate passages, I felt that your age at the time you wrote it, its language, style, levity of subject matter, and above all the type of reader it was addressed to would serve as your apology.'

18. English translation from Penguin edition, translated by G. H. McWilliam (Harmondsworth, 1972), p. 46. All translation of quotes from the *Decameron* are henceforth from this edition, and page references given from it within my main text.

19. Roger Ascham, *The Scholemaster*, edited by Edward Arber (London: English Reprints, 1870), p. 80. See also Herbert G. Wright, *Boccaccio in England from Chaucer to Tennyson* (London: Athlone Press, 1957), pp. 115–16.

20. William Painter, *The Palace of Pleasure*, 3 vols, edited by William Jacobs (1870; reprinted Hildesheim: George Olms Verlagsbuchhandlung, 1968). Jacobs's original 1870 introduction deals well with Ascham's responses to the kind of Italian material Englished in Painter. See Vol. 1, pp. xix–xxiv.

21. Ascham, *The Scholemaster*, p. 82. Wright, *Boccaccio in England*, p. 116.

22. The evidence was finally put together in a remarkable exhibition in which the painting of the two women was displayed *together with* the upper panel of men hunting on the lagoon, from the J. Paul Getty Museum in Los Angeles, from which it

had been cut in an earlier century. See Bernard Aikema and Beverly Louise Brown (eds), *Renaissance Venice and the North: Crosscurrents in the Time of Bellini, Dürer, and Titian* (Milan: Bompiani, 1999), pp. 236–9. This catalogue of the exhibition in Palazzo Grassi, Venice, also gives a useful synopsis of other speculation about the enigmas surrounding the women in the painting from the Museo Correr in Venice.

23. Jane Austen, *Persuasion* (1818), edited by R. W. Chapman (Oxford and New York: Oxford University Press, 1965), p. 232.

24. *Ibid.*, p. 234.

25. Michel Foucault, *The History of Sexuality*, Vol. 1, *An Introduction*, translated by Robert Hurley (London: Allen Lane, 1979), p. 115.

26. Vittore Branca, from his study 'The Medieval Tradition', included in the collection of his Boccaccio criticism, *Boccaccio: The Man and His Works*, translated by Richard Monges (New York: New York University Press, 1976), p. 212.

27. J. Vincenzo Molle, 'La "Langue" et la "parole": contribution à une analyse des modèles idéologiques dans les nouvelles de Boccace', in François Marotin (ed.), *Frontières du conte* (Paris: CNRS, 1982), p. 125. Molle's original text at this point reads: 'Cette attention très marquée pour la propreté du corps et pour celle de la morale (si les nouvelles sont souvent audacieuses, les moeurs de la brigade sont par contre très chastes) peut donner lieu à quelques observations de la psychologie sociale: dans un article publiée en 1932, Erich Fromm décrit la différence entre l'âge féodal et le capitalisme dans l'apprentissage de la propreté, de l'esprit d'économie, de la ponctualité et du sens de l'ordre. Ces qualités, apprises relativement tard au Moyen Age, deviennent par contre très importantes dès le début du capitalisme.' It will be noted that I have translated 'propreté' as 'purity' throughout, not with the more exact word 'cleanliness'. This is because purity is the more inclusive term, and bodily cleanliness as a form of purity is dealt with in my discussion in any case.

28. Perry Anderson, *Passages from Antiquity to Feudalism* (London: New Left Books, 1974), pp. 197–209.

29. Lauro Martines, *Power and Imagination: City-States in Renaissance Italy* (1979; Harmondsworth: Peregrine Books, 1983), p. 34.

30. Armando Sapori, 'Le compagnie dei Bardi e dei Peruzzi in Inghilterra nei secoli XIII e XIV', *Archivio Storico Italiano*, 80 (1922) (Florence: R. Deputazione di Storia Patria, 1923). Sapori published a separate, expanded account, *La crisi delle compagnie mercantili dei Bardi e dei Peruzzi* (Florence: Leo S. Olschki, 1926).

31. Henry S. Lucas, *The Renaissance and the Reformation* (New York and London: Harper and Brothers, 1934), p. 29.

32. Ferdinand Schevill, *History of Florence from the Founding of the City through the Renaissance* (1936; New York and London: F. Ungar Publishing Co., 1968), p. 186.

33. Main page references for the above abstract from Sapori, *La crisi*, are pp. 5–6, 18, 37, 49–50, 53–5, 57–8, 64–5, 67–8, 73, 84, 87, 115–17.

34. Jeffrey Burton Russell, *Medieval Civilization* (New York: Wiley, 1968), p. 559. Quoted in Charles Muscatine, *Poetry and Crisis in the Age of Chaucer* (Notre Dame: University of Notre Dame Press, 1972), p. 148.

35. See footnotes on these two old Florentine families in *Decameron*, Vol. 1, pp. 147–8.

CHAPTER 3

# 'THE ARCHITECT ACHIEVES HIS VICTORY' [1]

## RENAISSANCE AND LATER IDEAL CITIES

The notion of the architect as an omni-competent designer and builder of total living contexts, master of the arts of peace and of war, comes down to us in its fullest form in Leon Battista Alberti's *De re aedificatoria* (*On the Art of Building in Ten Books*), a Latin treatise of the mid-fifteenth century,[2] which was the first work since a classical treatise by the Augustan architect and theorist Vitruvius to treat the principles of building as matters (the *re* of Alberti's title) requiring comprehensive analysis. Alberti's is a treatise seeking, as he states, 'to be as limpid, clear, and expeditious as possible in dealing with a subject otherwise knotty, awkward, and for the most part thoroughly obscure'.[3] Today many of the topics dealt with by Alberti are no longer obscure: some of them, indeed, are even relatively commonplace and hence overlooked. But to see them tackled from first principles by him is to be drawn into a conscious reconsideration of much that we take for granted about the built environment in which we live and interact, designed as it always is (this is particularly clear in everything Alberti writes) for specific needs and even with specific political forms and outcomes in mind.

In his ten books Alberti follows a scrupulously logical procedure, moving from the whole to various parts of his subject, and never for long leaving his readers without a signpost as to where he is in the overall discourse. He opens, for instance, with a definition of the scope and compass of all that is taken in by the term 'building'. It proves to consist of what we would nowadays include under both architecture and structural engineering. He then divides up the subject into topics and proceeds to devote his ten separate books to addressing these in turn.[4] The logicality has the appeal that intellectual clarity always does, and were it not for certain 'resistances' in the very grain of the subject he treats, we might expect him to deal with the 'things concerning building'

125

(*De re aedificatoria*, which is after all his title) with more despatch than
he does.

Those points of resistance that I allude to prove on closer inspection
to be almost always human beings. Alberti's subject, in other words, is
an irremediably interactive one, in which every attempt to treat the
'things concerning building' *impersonally* perpetually transmutes into a
deeply *personalized* realm of statements about the nature of humans and
their various social contexts. And without doubt it is the assumptions
informing these statements, rather than Alberti's more narrowly
conceived ideas about building, that make for the main interest of this
discourse now more than half a millennium later. One way or another,
Alberti's ideas about building have affected not only Italy but our entire
Western culture of cities. We need to be clear whether this is because his
underlying assumptions about human beings have stood the test of
several centuries of cultural and political development. Or are we
instead, although living largely in the kinds of city described in Alberti's
treatise, behaving in them in ways he did not describe and would not
recognize? If the latter, it might be a costly mismatch.

No claim is being made here that most cities since the fifteenth
century are Albertian in detail. Indeed, very few are, even in Italy. But
the pervasive drive of many of his ideas about town planning, based
as it is upon a reading of the variety of city cultures down to the time of
the writing of the discourse, underlies town planners' ideals through to
the present. Many of the same principles have been at stake – for
example, the need for a well-chosen site, the sensible choice and
preparation of materials, and a view to the established customs and
the actual disposition of political power in the societies being provided
for.

Among Alberti's major preoccupations, the one least in evidence in
modern times is his repeated attention to the need for individual cities to
construct adequate defences. For hundreds of years most warfare has
been at the nation-state level, rather than that of the city-state as it
largely was in his day. In addition the techniques of modern ground and
aerial ballistic bombardment have rendered obsolete many of his ideas
about such things as defensive walls, towers and fortresses. Defence
systems in the form of underground bunkers against some of the worst
effects of nuclear attack were constructed in certain key cities during the
Cold War, but this is a far cry from the forms of military defence system
gone into by Alberti. On the other hand, the fortification of individual

houses or living quarters – a key Albertian motif in the treatise – is a hallmark of our own times, nowhere more so perhaps than in Italy.

The claim that our city cultures have a large Albertian legacy rests on a notion that urban architecture in the West during this millennium is a developing historical continuum, and that Alberti's mid-fifteenth-century treatise is an intelligent slice through a moment in that history, reporting on some of its past or existing urban contexts, and deducing from his studies a host of ideals for the future: ideals which are taken seriously by succeeding theoreticians and practitioners, even if their contact with Alberti's actual document is slender or non-existent. What, more precisely, are some of the determining human values behind the *re aedificatoria*? To answer that question, it is worth assessing Alberti's opening moves in this great treatise, and then some subsequent points in it, most notably from Book Five, where his assumptions about society and the role different types of building play in it are most in evidence.

With a certain inevitability, given Alberti's interests and purposes, his treatise elaborates ideas on architecture that follow two complementary directions. On the one hand there is spelled out the role of the architect, as one who by his knowledges and skills and above all his powers of intellect is the quintessential human figure of the creator:

> Him I consider the architect, who by sure and wonderful reason and method, knows both how to devise through his own mind and energy, and to realize by construction, whatever can be most beautifully fitted out for the noble needs of man, by the movement of weights and the joining and massing of bodies.[5]

On the other hand (and, in terms of the unfolding of his discourse, *consequent upon* this prior establishing of the importance of the architect), Alberti's argument turns to the realm of what the architect actually creates. Although at a local level this consists of a multiplicity of types of edifice or other constructions – public and private buildings, walls with their towers, churches (invariably called temples in this classicizing Latin discourse), theatres, roads, harbours, bridges and squares, most of them meticulously discussed – for Alberti it is axiomatic that to treat of matters of building is to deal in concepts of the city as a whole, as the quintessential context of human habitation and therefore of social community. So in no small sense Alberti's overall subject is cities[6] – where they should be located, how designed and built, and with what overall purposes in mind.

This chapter looks at cities as idealized by Alberti, drawing comparisons with slightly later Renaissance theorists such as Filarete and Leonardo. One actual Renaissance urban context, the small *cittadina* of Pienza in Southern Tuscany, influenced by Albertian principles, figures in the analysis, which closes with a consideration of the later influence of Albertian thinking on some nineteenth- and twentieth-century conceptualizations of the city, and an estimation of how far and with what degrees of success design theories which have their origins in this Renaissance moment have been realized in modern practice.

From its opening, Alberti's treatise extols the architect as a figure incorporating what we would today see as the separate functions of inventor, civil engineer, architect, town planner, arms specialist and site foreman. He is someone deeply versed in what has worked in the past, especially in the classical world (Greece, Rome and Egypt; not to mention such further and well-nigh legendary societies as Babylon and Nineveh), but designing for the present and future. Practicalities are all-important. So the treatise is written at every point in terms of Alberti's interpretations of the way people wish to live and, underpinning those at a still deeper level, his rather ahistorical and all-encompassing readings of human nature itself.

It was not that Alberti did not live his historical moment very intensely and indeed enshrine many of its most ample currents of thinking, as modern scholars since at least the moment of Anthony Blunt's pioneering chapter on him in the publication of 1940, *Artistic Theory in Italy: 1450–1600*, have specified many times.[7] Alberti's is a vision not without the prejudices of its age. Indeed, it begins with one: 'before I go any further . . . I should explain exactly whom I mean by an architect; for it is no carpenter that I would have you compare to the greatest exponents of other disciplines: the carpenter is but an instrument in the hands of the architect.'[8] On Alberti's part, this follows an already largely pre-existing hierarchization of 'mechanical' arts and skills below those of intellectual or conceptual ones. But Alberti doesn't just restate a scholastic hierarchy. He defines the architect in terms wider than have been assigned to any inventor/executor figure in the past, precisely because architects are a composite as never before of all the powers of the 'greatest exponents of other disciplines'. Indeed, Alberti's classicism and his habit of treating everything in terms of first principles often seem to blunt the historical specificity of his writings, his discursive mode implicitly laying claim at almost every moment to being the ongoing utterance of universal truth. For instance, while still establishing the credentials of the architect in his Preface to the ten books proper, Alberti writes of feats which make trade and indeed new discoveries by sea and ocean possible. We as readers may choose to read into his writing at this point certain historically specific factors, such as Alberti's own merchant family origins and the dramatic beginnings in just these years of merchant venturing beyond all bounds of the known world. But Alberti's actual sentences imply a kind of unfixed time-lessness to these particular activities of the architect:

> We are indebted to the architect not only for providing that safe and welcome refuge from the heat of the sun and the frosts of winter . . . but also for his many other innovations, useful to both individuals and the public, which time and time again have so happily satisfied daily needs. . . . What of the methods of drawing up vast quantities of water from hidden depths for so many different and essential purposes? And of memorials, shrines, sanctuaries, temples, and the like, designed by the architect for divine worship and for the benefit of posterity? Finally, need I stress how, by cutting through rock, by tunneling through mountains or filling in valleys, by restraining the waters of the sea and lakes, and by draining marshes, through the building of ships, by altering the course and dredging the mouths of rivers, and through the construction of harbors and bridges, the architect has not only met the temporary needs of man, but also opened up new gateways to all the provinces of the world?[9]

In reordering creation by acts scarcely lesser, if at all, than those of a first creator, and in serving purposes beyond the time-bound, 'temporary needs of man', the architect breaks beyond the fixities of historical time as well as mapped space. And in so doing he acquires an aura – *numen* we could practically call it – as if beyond the human in power and abilities.

Not altogether surprisingly in an age rife with wars, the architect's crowning achievements are reckoned to be military. Consider how, having listed in his 'not only but also' manner of defining all the provinces of skill and practice of an architect, Alberti has reserved till the last his most fulsome and unalloyed praise for his abilities in matters of warfare:

> Nor should you forget ballistic engines and machines of war, fortresses and whatever else may have served to protect and strengthen the liberty of our

country, and the good and honor of the state, to extend and confirm its dominion. . . . The skill and ability of the architect have been responsible for more victories than have the command and foresight of any general; and . . . the enemy were more often overcome by the ingenuity of the first without the other's weapons, than by the latter's sword without the former's good counsel. And what is more important, the architect achieves his victory with but a handful of men and without loss of life.[10]

'The architect achieves his victory . . .' At a local rhetorical level, the victory in question is a matter of actual military campaigns. But Alberti's larger point is that the architect is not only victorious in war but also in other spheres of existence, since he is the being who fashions and maintains the intricate interdependencies of social organization on the one hand with built material context on the other. Furthermore, his tendency to be preoccupied by military notions of defence and offence as by no other is revealed at other levels of social organization, and vastly affects his ideas on urban planning – details of street layout and the design of domestic habitation – as we shall shortly see.

In Alberti's rhetorical build-up to the architect's role in military matters, his definition of this key figure has included everything from what we would nowadays term a structural engineer to a town planner, from a builder of bridges to a master of fluid dynamics and shipbuilding, not to mention an inventor of conveniences for living ('walks, swimming pools, baths and so forth – that help to keep us healthy . . . or even vehicles, mills, timepieces, and other smaller inventions, which none-theless play so vital a role in our everyday lives'[11]). Furthermore, if the passage suggests that the architect's supreme function lies in what he achieves by way of military feat or construction, it had begun quite otherwise – in a listing of the pleasurable and health-preserving pastimes of peace, all made possible by the same being. And the middle portions of the definition had portrayed a complex, interlinked world of trade, not simply in goods but also in ideas and knowledges – in short, the vision of a vast communications network on sea and by land, all dependent on (because only made possible by) the devising mind of Alberti's hero the architect, its necessary prime mover.

This is a toweringly important moment in the Renaissance, for it is the earliest and clearest account of the architect as 'generalist' – no mere dabbler but a creator/inventor figure in whom all skills and knowledges are fused to the highest degree, leading, consequently, to achievements of a quite different order from those of the single arts or sciences. To invoke a notion that has perhaps been overused since Burckhardt first wrote his classic *Civilization of the Renaissance in Italy*, we have in Alberti's unfolding account the clearest version of the so-called *uomo universale*.[12] Given that a manuscript version of this treatise was completed as early as 1452,[13] it is as though Alberti were at one and the same time both begetting a long-running idea and standing as its first exemplar. There is, furthermore, an interesting coincidence in this date. In the same year in the Tuscan village of Vinci was born someone to whom the world has more commonly ascribed the glory of being the all-round artist/inventor/mage figure, and presager of ideas that would in some cases be realized only much later in history (for example, human flight). The more we read the treatises not just of Alberti, but of others in the years following, particularly Filarete and Francesco di Giorgio Martini,[14] the more we realize that that new-born child of Vinci, Leonardo, coming late in a run of figures who approximated to Alberti's generalist description, is no mere isolated instance but a privileged inheritor of the (at first only idealized, but then more and more realized) amalgamation within a single individual of inventiveness and talent across a range of arts and sciences first clearly voiced by Alberti. As though to reinforce this idea of continuity, Alberti and Filarete, the first of these treatise writers, are themselves conscious of the extensive, all-round talents of Filippo Brunelleschi before them.[15] Earlier in his career, for instance, in prefacing the 1436 vernacular version of his *Della pittura*, Alberti had written a dedicatory epistle to Brunelleschi in which the latter's dome of Florence Cathedral, completed in the preceding year, is praised as a key sign of cultural revival: 'vast enough to cover the entire Tuscan population with its shadow, . . . surely a feat of engineering, if I am not mistaken, that people did not believe possible these days and was probably equally unknown and unimaginable among the ancients'.[16] The notion of revival here is actually one of achieving something *un*precedented, even in classical times. For his part, Filarete was to mention Brunelleschi four times in his treatise on architecture, initially in the roll-call of Florentine *maestri* whom he considered for the building of Sforzinda, the city whose construction is the ingenious fiction of Filarete's text: 'I would have sent for another who was an excellent architect, if he had not died some time before; his name was Pippo di ser Brunellescho'. For Filarete, writing in the late 1450s or early 1460s, Brunelleschi is one of the great previous generation now recently deceased, nothing less than the architect 'who revived in our city of Florence the antique way of building', as he will say in his next citation of him.[17]

It should not be imagined from what has been said so far that in this early phase of Alberti's treatise his general ideas are confined to glorifying solely the role of the architect. Already he is considering building from the equally important perspective of the patron. Two points stand out: first, the claim that to build is an instinctive drive of nature – 'you will never find anyone who is not eager to build something, as soon as he has the means to do so' – and second, that to build brings renown: 'not only your own honor and glory, but also that of your family, your descendants, and the whole city'.[18] In such statements Alberti was merely formalizing a belief of his times. In an even more forthright manner, which today might seem vulgar but in its time was almost certainly not, the banker Giovanni Rucellai, one of the richest Florentines in this mid-fifteenth-century moment, was to write in his commonplace book that building came second only to begetting as a primary human urge: 'Due cose principali sono quelle che gl'uomini fanno in questo mondo: la prima lo 'ngienerare: la seconda l'edifichare.'[19] This connection between amorousness and building is extensive in architectural treatises of the period. Only a few years on from Alberti, Filarete will opine that 'building is nothing more than a voluptuous pleasure, like that of a man in love. Anyone who has experienced it knows that there is so much pleasure and desire in building that however much a man does, he wants to do more.' Filarete is indeed quite liberal in his use of this general analogy, for he also proposes that the patron's ideal relationship with his architect should be of the same strength and kind: 'the patron should love and honor him insofar as he wants his building to go well and should show him the same love and devotion as he does to his wife'; the implication being, as Filarete goes on explicitly to spell out, that just as a man begets children by a woman, so he cannot conceive or dedicate a fine building without the architect.[20]

To return to the first of these treatises. By its very modes of address, Alberti's text implies an ideal readership: namely; the class of those with old or acquired wealth sufficient to satisfy this instinctive and glorious creative urge. Crucially therefore, from an early point in his treatise the audience addressed includes architect and patron, both of them dignified in conceptual terms as persons who build. As Filarete was to say in the dedication to Piero de' Medici of one of the manuscript versions of his own slightly later treatise, it contains 'what the architect ought to know as well as . . . he who commissions the building' ('quello che appartiene all'architetto di sapere e cosi acquello che fa edificare . . .').[21] Since both need to know the subject thoroughly, the focus of address can be thus dual. Alberti, in particular, does not use one syntax for the architect who builds and another for the patron who gets things built.[22] Both are seen as active. Unquestionably the feats of building, engineering and warfare in Alberti's day were made possible by the combined forces of multi-talented 'constructors' and their patrons.

And one other factor ensues from a vision such as Alberti's. Such architects will increasingly be recorded by name, and their works interpreted as being stamped with distinctive individuality. Already since the generation of Giotto and a little before that too, the names of the *caput magistri* of prime building projects are recorded in cities' contracts for them or other surviving documents. For instance, though there are few named artists in Vasari's prefatory account of the rise of architecture, painting and sculpture (after its period of slumber consequent upon the demise of Rome), he does name a certain Buschetto as the *caput magister* of the cathedral at Pisa and gives the date of its commencement at the very opening of the millennium – 1016. After that, although he makes mention of rare early examples of architectural achievement, Vasari hesitates to make named attributions to works until he reaches the time of Cimabue, with the single exception of his references to Nicolo Pisano's bas-relief carvings over one of the doors to the church of San Martino in Lucca. With the generation just before Alberti's had arrived the period of more public competition for contracts between individuals with reputations to gain or lose, the most notable such competition – and one also highly important in Vasari's later narrative – being the contest for the commission to sculpt the doors to the Florentine baptistry, in which Ghiberti and Brunelleschi were both entrants. Indeed, as I have already implied, if there is one figure whom Alberti might have had in mind in his account of the multi-talented architect/inventor, it is Filippo Brunelleschi, who had died as recently as 1446, only six years before the first manuscript version of this treatise and probably while it was being written.

Essentially, the city as Alberti variously idealizes it is configured from the viewpoint of those powerful enough and with sufficient wealth to build. Since the treatise is addressed principally to princes or other rulers and the wealthier classes (along with the architect, as previously established), much in it seems designed, not humanistically for the common good of all, but with the interests of those in power uppermost in mind. To a striking degree it therefore reads like a series of blueprints for the kinds of rulership which more than half a century later Machiavelli was to propound in *The Prince*.

In Book Five of *De re* in particular, Alberti develops his most explicit ideas on city structures in relation to social class. Typical of someone who we know from other writings was keen (to the point even of a certain obsession) to promulgate the credentials of his own family – especially in that other Albertian treatise, *Della famiglia*, written in the vernacular – Alberti's greatest antipathies are for the common mass and tradespeople. As he establishes early in this fifth book, his idea of the people *en masse* is a familiar and classical one (known extensively to people of English culture from the somewhat later period of Shakespeare) – that of the 'many-headed monster', unruly and fickle. Writing very much *de haut en bas* when it comes to issues of social class, Alberti naturally inclines to ideas on how to structure a city in such a way as to maintain order among the many for the sake of the few: 'Let us begin with the more exalted. The highest of all are those entrusted with supreme power and judgement: this may be entrusted to several individuals or to just one' (Bk. V, Ch. 1). From this opening move it is only a short jump to the belief that relations between such upper-ranking persons and the classes below them will be largely those of surveillance and control. Euripides is twice quoted to establish a global viewpoint of 'the common people' as potentially dangerous and therefore to be controlled: 'Euripides thought the common people to be a powerful adversary in themselves, but totally invincible when they combine deceit and guile' (Bk. V, Ch. 1). The best protection against the populace, just as against external incursors, is strong fortification in the form of a citadel or fortress. Position is everything. For it must be for defence against attack from both external and internal enemies. Hence, it must normally be built at some peripheral point of the city so as to have 'an unobstructed outlet, by road, river, lake, or sea, through which unimpeded it may seek or admit reinforcements or help from outside, against the enemy or, in the case of treachery or mutiny, against its own citizens and soldiers' (Bk. V, Ch. 4).

We have seen in an earlier chapter on Boccaccio that secret points of breach in the *cordon sanitaire* constituted by a city or castle wall made possible, if not the very birth of early-modern notions of private as opposed to public space, at any rate a significant elaboration of them. Here we have a similar notion of rear entry, essential this time to a concept not of privacy but of defence:

> One might not go wrong in describing it as a well-guarded back door of the town. Call it what you will – pinnacle of the whole work, or lock of the city – the citadel should be threatening, rugged and rocky, stubborn and invincible. A compact citadel is safer than a large one. The former can be entrusted to a few, the latter requires a large garrison; and as a character of Euripides' said, 'never has there been a crowd without some mischievous element' – so here it is safer to put your trust in a few than to risk the perfidy of many. (Bk. V, Ch. 4)

Here is Alberti's essential mistrust in a nutshell. The mathematical logic of making one's fortress smaller and therefore dependent on 'a few', rather than large and hence requiring wide-ranging fidelity in one's subjects, is just one of the numerous ideas in Alberti which we perhaps imagine (until more acquainted with his thought) first meeting in the later and more well-known strategist Machiavelli. Once again it is relevant to ponder how much of the spirit and even the letter of so-called Machiavellian theories of statecraft are already here in embryo in the writings of Alberti, more than half a century earlier.

For Alberti a town's defences are all-important and only 'powerful' cities can afford 'straight and very wide' streets:

> But with a settlement or fortified town the entrances will be made safer if the road does not lead directly to the gate, but runs to the right or left along the wall, and preferably even directly under the battlements. Within the town itself it is better if the roads are not straight, but meandering gently like a river flowing now here, now there, from one bank to the other. For apart from the fact that the longer the roads seem, the greater the apparent size of the town, no doubt it will be of great benefit in terms of appearance. . . . The ancients preferred to give some of their roads within the city awkward exits, and others blind alleys, so that any aggressor or criminal who entered would either hesitate, being in two minds and unsure of himself, or, summoning up the courage to continue, would soon find himself in danger. (Bk. IV, Ch. 5)

This is graphic and self-explanatory. Of real significance is the marriage of aesthetics with defensiveness in one and the same notion of urban structure. On the one hand, visual prospects will be optimized both from without and within: 'it is no trifle that visitors at every step meet yet another façade, or that the entrance to and view from every house should face directly onto the street.' But on the other, when it is 'an aggressor or criminal' who is pursuing such 'awkward exits, and . . . blind alleys', he may be the more easily disadvantaged.

This emphasis on security in Alberti's text extends to details of private existence, almost like an obsession with the perfidy of being taken unawares, or from the rear: 'There are instances of citadels being saved by their own underground waterways, and of towns being lost because of their drains' (Bk. V, Ch. 5). But, *mutatis mutandis*, the fear of being taken unawares by means of tunnels or unsuspected apertures also gets inverted and turned into a policy of aggression; that of doing unto others as you fear being done unto yourself. Hence is justified the idea of furnishing yourself with all such secret passages, entries, exits and built-in 'listening tubes' as you can for surveillance over others; 'Let there be some secret entrance into the center of the citadel, known only to you, through which entry may be forced with armed men, should you ever be shut out' (Bk. V, Ch. 5). Admittedly, the most elaborate suggestions for secret surveillance are reserved for 'the tyrant', but it is noteworthy with what easy empathy Alberti's text enters into the role of devising security measures for such a person. To repeat, the text prefigures Machiavelli, not modern forms of liberalism; 'One matter must not be omitted: a tyrant will find it very useful to have secret listening tubes concealed within the fabric of the wall so as to eavesdrop on the conversation of guests or family' (Bk. V, Ch. 3).

Even sexual relations as revealed by Alberti's domestic building plans are fraught with a sense of personal threat, the text always being male-gendered at such points. This kind of threat can best be controlled by creating personal boundaries within the zones of architected space, and ensuring that one's most private activities can never be scrutinized by others. In accounting for the architectural necessities of a well-to-do villa, for instance, Alberti's ideas for the master and mistress are for ease both of separateness and of congress – by today's sociological reckonings a kind of 'semi-detached' marital state, and one favouring the husband's convenience:

The husband and wife must have separate bedrooms, not only to ensure that the husband be not disturbed by his wife, when she is about to give birth or is ill, but also to allow them, even in summer, an uninterrupted night's sleep, whenever they wish. Each room should have its own door, and in addition a common side door, to enable them to seek each other's company unnoticed. (Bk. V, Ch. 17)

This idea is taken to greater lengths in the case of a prince. Alberti deems fit that princes and their spouses have entirely separate apartments, connected by a common bedchamber; 'The apartments of his wife should be kept entirely separate from those of the prince, except for the most private rooms and the chamber containing the marriage bed, which should be common to both' (Bk. V, Ch. 2). The notion is of dwelling spaces in a kind of Siamese twinship; or, rather, of dwelling spaces in a form of sexual congress in their own right at the point of connection, the bedchamber – since scope for sexual activity is surely what this extravagant idea of entirely separate living spaces (except for the marriage bed as point of contact) is fundamentally about. The arrangement of space itself repeats at a symbological level, in other words, the unseen-by-others copula of the prince and his consort, which it also makes possible.

But the most striking idea put forward by Alberti for containing potential threats from others (referred to before his propositions about the matter of the fortress, or these further refinements of private sexual spaces in villas and princely dwellings) is not so much one that looks forward to Machiavelli, but, rather, a prefiguration of certain urban social developments of a much later age – virtually speaking, our own. This is Alberti's call for an 'inner city' as basically a *no-go zone*, walled in and policed from the commanding heights at or beyond its peripheries:

> The best means of dividing a city is to build a wall through it. This wall, I believe, should not run diametrically across the city but should form a kind of circle within a circle. For the wealthy citizens are happier in more spacious surroundings and would readily accept being excluded by an inner wall, and would not unwillingly leave the stalls and the town-center workshops to the marketplace traders; and that rabble, as Terence Gnatho calls them, of poulterers, butchers, cooks, and so on, will be less of a risk and less of a nuisance if they do not mix with the important citizens.
>
> Nor is what we read in Festus beside the point: Servius Tullius ordered all the patricians to live in a district where any rebellion could be instantly put down from a hilltop.
>
> This internal wall should be planned so as to touch every district of the town. As in other city walls, so especially in this case, the construction

> must be robust and bold in its details, and so high as to dominate the roofs of any private houses. It is best to fortify it with battlements and turrets on both sides, and even perhaps a moat, so as to protect the guards stationed along it from either direction. . . . There must be no projecting balconies, from which missiles could be thrown at soldiers as they patrol the neighborhood. In short, the whole town should be planned to give the one with supreme power sole possession of all the highest structures, and to make it impossible for anyone to restrict movement of his men and prevent them from patrolling the town. (Bk. V, Ch. 1)

There is a curious and complex history behind the phenomenon being described – as so often in Alberti, even if occluded in his manner of developing the idea. From the way the text is written at this point the impression may be taken that the precedents in the past for this inner and walled city are all classical. But in point of fact many cities of Alberti's own day preserved such congested inner 'circles' as their medieval hearts. Or in other words, Alberti is not so much describing the blueprint for a city to be built from scratch, as modifying his ideas as a projector to existing realities.

The fact is that by the time of Alberti many cities in the north of Italy already had two – or if they had been Roman cities first, sometimes the remains of three or even four – walls of containment. What had first been defences against incursion from without could therefore in a later age, in case of need, demarcate what had become essentially the class-based stratifications of different sectors of the city. The innermost circle of walls bound in the oldest part of the city. In most cases by the mid-fifteenth century the parts of the city included in what Dante, speaking of Florence, had already in the early 1300s called 'la cerchia antica' ('the ancient circlet') of walls were the narrow, congested alleyways of the first three and a half centuries of the millennium, which by the time of Alberti probably contained much centuries-old squalor (*secolare squallore*), to revert to the terminology of the late-nineteenth-century portal in Florence analysed in the first chapter. Those earlier centuries had constituted the prime period of urban development, based on new and ever-more far-flung forms of mercantile trade and the companion economic activity of money-changing. We may recall here how heartily Dante despised the *nova gente*, a class that dualistically changes money and trades ('cambia e merca') for its living. (See *Inferno*, XVI, 73 and *Paradiso*, XVI, 61, for the most explicit displays of this prejudice.)

In keeping with the intentionally 'cosmoramic' character of this book, it is necessary to think relativistically back and forth through several centuries at this point. For Dante the *cerchia antica* of walls demarcated an earlier and purer Florence of his great-great-grandfather's times, a crusader age before the decline of social customs into the (to him) despicable forms of his own age. By Alberti's generation a century and a half later, cities had outstripped the *cerchie antiche* still further in their growth. But the ancient walls were often extant, completely or in part. Certainly the cramped streets and dwelling places which they formerly enclosed had rarely been totally razed; hence no *tabula rasa* for a city to be built from scratch had presented itself. On the contrary, just as in the above description from *De re*, the wealthier families (whether old nobility or *nouveaux riches* made little difference in this regard) had tended to build larger palazzi in streets and quarters of the city beyond those first, and by now 'inner', sets of walls. The well-known Medici Palace in Florence is a case in point, built by Michelozzo in an approximate twenty years (1444–64), which include the date of Alberti's treatise in its manuscript form. That palazzo is several hundred metres north of the *cerchia antica* of earlier walls mentioned by Dante.

An essential paradox of Alberti's entire treatise is thus laid bare by the historical relativism of our analysis at this point. As we can see from our vantage point in history, the reality of most Italian cities of any size in Alberti's day was one of concentric circles of walls, marking phases in their historical expansion. So one side of him writes blueprints for 'ideal' cities which are very much an adaptation of what is already coming to pass in physical and political terms – stringent measures of containment of the political underclasses by the wealthy and powerful, the former being mainly labourers and meaner tradespeople living in the most congested (because innermost and earliest built) areas of the older cities. The obverse of the inner-city ghetto (as we would call it today) – remembering, however, that in Alberti's age and for hundreds of years to come ghettos were something else – were the newer, more airy quarters 'for the wealthy citizens . . . happier in more spacious surroundings'. In another vein, however, and especially when he is describing free and independent republics, Alberti presents a blueprint for a far less security-conscious city. When thinking in these terms the 'inner city' is not that of the actual congested lanes of eleventh-, twelfth- and thirteenth-century urbanization, but centralized public spaces or piazzas, flanked by the main public buildings of the city. In the forms in which he imagined these centrepieces, they (and *not* the concentric circles idea, with tradespeople in the innermost and the wealthier classes in the outermost) are what we more readily associate with the term 'ideal cities', much represented in painting and bas-relief sculpting, but little evidenced in reality.

Alberti's ideas for cities – based structurally on prevailing class divisions between rich gentlefolk and the meaner tradespeople – were not isolated or peculiar to himself. Admittedly, there is considerable variance in how social divisions are recognized and planned for in later treatise writers, so that, for instance, someone like Filarete is happy to envisage a central city area in which tradespeople and city officials and dignitaries mix and mingle, as we will see later in brief discussion of his ideas for Sforzinda. But if we imagine that the age of humanism ensures a gathering spirit of proto-liberalism in social arrangements, then a comparative glance half a century onwards from Alberti to some of Leonardo da Vinci's manuscript notebook idealizations for urban structures penned during his first stay in Milan will quickly disabuse us. Already in Leonardo's ideas for a 'river town' his overriding concern, as Lise Bek has succinctly stated, is with 'the socioeconomic basis its appearance should reflect'.[23] When it comes to another idea, this time for a town structured in horizontal layers between high and low, the levels themselves map out and bespeak Leonardo's unwavering categories of high and low in the social scale.

The upper levels of Leonardo's ideally 'layered' city are to be clear of all service traffic. A pen and ink drawing shows colonnaded palazzi at this level which, as Leonardo's accompanying text incontrovertibly states, is reserved for the gentler classes ('per le strade alte no' de' andare carri né altre simili cose: anzi sia solamente per li gientili ômini'). On the lower, essentially 'service', level of the city, move the common people, the *popolo*, carting and hauling their burdens, some for their own survival but others necessarily, as the text goes on to specify, essential provisions – wood, wine and the like – for the rest of the city ('per le basse deono andare le carri o altre some a l'uso e comodità del popolo. . . . E da li usci N si mettino le vettovaglie, come legnie, vino e simili cose'). And there is in Leonardo's layered city a third, cloacal and underground level of drains for both human and animal waste, with its own arterial grid of subterranean passages ('vie socterane'), for named and even unnamed foetidnesses ('simile cose fetide. . .')![24]

Some earlier criticism has not wished to acknowledge the rigidly class-bound nature of Leonardo's thoughts on urbanism, and has chosen to emphasize instead his ethic of concern that all layers of society be catered for in the city structure.[25] But more recently Lise Bek has unprejudicially affirmed that Leonardo's 'division of work- and leisure activities, light and heavy traffic in the urban milieu', when 'seen historically . . . is the acknowledgement of a social structure whose distinction between the privileged upper class of free citizens and the working people, "gientili ômini" and "popolo" . . . is materially symbolised in the two levels, their difference between sun and shadow, breadth and narrowness, silence and noise'.[26]

And there is in Leonardo at this point a still darker vision, of the essential bestiality of the human underclass, or 'poveraggia' as he elsewhere unfeelingly calls them. It comes in his further specifications for communication from upper to lower levels in his hierarchically stratified city. Descent into the sunless lower city, which in any case receives what shafts of light are afforded it only through openings in the higher street levels ('che riceve il lume dalle fessure delle strade di sopra'), is by means of a carefully designed staircasing. This must be spiral in form, because on square staircases, Leonardo with contemptuous certainty asserts, people will piss and open their bowels in the corners ('de' essere una scala a lumaca tonda, perché ne' canton de le quadre si piscia e alarga'). We find him, in other words, seeking to design away the foul habits of the common people by structural features such as the continuous curve of the staircase, which according to him prevents its users from thinking of pausing to relieve themselves, until such exits as open onto purpose-built communal privies and urinals ('e nella prima volta sia un uscio ch'entri in destri e pisciatoi comuni'). The humourless tone of all these suggestions forces us to recognize that in the Leonardo whom we are otherwise so used to praising for futuristic and wide-ranging problem-solving, there persisted the unquestioning class prejudices of the age and cultural context in and for which he was projecting his urbanistic solutions. His staircase has not a hint of 'l'esprit de l'escalier' of a later period (wit, that is, or any of the intellectual flexibilities that such wit might signal). Rather it symbolizes for us a rankly class-bound age and mentality, with no vision of change in the social categories of existence, nor any expectation of basic human decencies in the lowest on the scale.

If there is anything futuristic in all this, it is reminiscent in the surface details of Ridley Scott's dystopian film of 1981, *Blade Runner*, which imagines a Los Angeles of the year 2019 that is also organized hierarchically according to horizontal levels of a fantastical skyscraper city, with corporate bigshots running the world from high atop the sheer walls of dark and imposing buildings. Their lives are passed in a light and sunny atmosphere purged of all the multiple foetidnesses, pollution and incessant rain of street level, where by complete contrast a mixed-race proletariat live out the restrictive conditions of a murderous police state. The essential difference between Leonardo's Renaissance fantasy of urbanization according to social categories and Ridley Scott's postmodern version is that the latter's is a monitory critique of future forms of enslavement of the human race, possibly including a suggestion that the present itself is already tending in these directions by its unthinking use of the unrestrained powers of genetic engineering, symbolized in particular by Scott's vision of a class of artificially created replicants who constitute quite literally a new slave race; whereas Leonardo was not producing a critique at all, and presented his vertically layered city as a valid form of social organization for his day.

Real cities function materially to accommodate the lives and lifestyles of their inhabitants. At the same time they largely express how those lifestyles are being constrained and predetermined. Imagined cities are not so subject to the constraints of what has grown up over historical time thorough complex ages of change. We have seen nonetheless that some of Alberti's imaginings, including in particular his idea for a walled and contained inner city, are adaptations of the material reality of how cities had actually expanded in the earlier centuries of the millennium. Leonardo's high-rise city takes this thinking one stage further. It is an upwards rather than outwards extension in use of space, and remained largely untried till modern times. Nonetheless, the comparison backwards in time, from Leonardo's vertical city of class stratification to Alberti's notion of a city with a congested inner zone for the poor and tradespeople, and more spacious and airy quarters further out for the wealthier and more socially elevated classes, shows surprisingly little change in prevailing social attitudes between mid- and high-Renaissance urbanistic thinking. Class hierarchies and in particular an outrightly pejorative view of the *popolo* surface in both Alberti's and Leonardo's texts, in ways that shock our latter-day sensibilities.

Such public buildings as did exist in Alberti's own period at the heart of the older Italian cities were the cathedrals, baptistries and palaces of the *signoria* or *podestà* of an earlier age, not the more classical buildings of Albertian design and proportion. For the truth is that Alberti's was an age in which rather little building or radical change in city structures took place. Adams and Nussdorfer summarize well the difference between Alberti's and an earlier age:

> The scale of the physical changes to the city in the one hundred years between 1400 and 1500 is relatively small. From the mid-thirteenth until the mid-fourteenth century, the face of the Italian city was radically transformed by the most dramatic changes since antiquity. Massive town halls, vast cathedrals with their giant cupolas, palaces of justice, were planned, constructed or reconstructed to provide new services and a new architectural definition for civil and ecclesiastical protection and the rule of law in the Italian commune.[27]

Such opening up of the town centres and rationalization of their public spaces as had occurred – giving us to this day the major layouts of the *centri storici* of the older cities of Italy – had in other words preceded by a century and more the new and classicizing urge on the part of Alberti. Furthermore, the great cathedrals and palaces and squares of that earlier period had been erected by communes, rarely in the control of single persons: whereas the entire drift of Alberti's discourse is towards the notion of a single patron having the power, and thereby in turn providing a single architect with the opportunity, to build a city from scratch to an *idée maitresse* dominated by the social, economic and political needs of that same patron. In the Latin of Alberti's treatise this figure of the single ruler is often denominated by the term *tyrannos*, which has no intrinsic negative connotations in his discourse: by stark contrast, in that earlier age of the communes the notion of single rule by a 'tyrant' had been a particularly adverse one, as Lorenzetti's fresco of the effects of *malgoverno* on city and country so vividly depicted, with the figure of the horned and tusked tyrant usurping the place of his opposite complement, *buongoverno*, from the contrastive fresco on the adjacent wall treating of good government. Dante too, and slightly earlier than Lorenzetti, had distinguished firmly between *tirannia* ('rule by the one') and *stato franco* (literally 'free state' – that is, any of the numerous communal forms of self-government common in his day: see *Inferno*, XXVII, 54). Lise Bek comments well on Alberti's modifications of the thought of the earlier age when she says that in his proceeding from top-down notions of social hierarchy ('Ordiendum quidem a dignioribus', 'Let us begin with the more exalted', Bk. V, Ch. 1):

[he] indicates an immediate structuring of the treatment of domestic architecture corresponding to the secular hierarchy of contemporary society, an order which was not to be violated. Attention is accordingly called, first to the royal palace and the tyrant's stronghold – the medieval symbolic allegory of 'regnum bonum et malum' transferred to the world of reality – with practical advice on siting, defence, etc.[28]

In this 'transference to a world of reality', the point is that Alberti tends no longer moralistically to distinguish *bonum et malum* in the manner of his medieval predecessors Dante and Lorenzetti, but to theorize 'beyond good and evil' in a pre-Machiavellian, not to say pre-Nietzschean, manner.

We can best perceive an intermediary position between the great building age of the communes, on the one hand, and Alberti's drift towards ideas for the single ruler, on the other, in the civic humanist Leonardi Bruni's 'Panegyric to the City of Florence' of a generation or two earlier than Alberti, that is, the opening years of the fifteenth century. Bruni's panegyric of 1404 is distinctly republican in sympathy, and, speaking only of his own Florence (certainly one of the greatest of the communes to this date), lauds its then government as the achievement of a consummate ideal. The sacredness of justice and the provision of freedom for all are in equipoise, arising from the various levels of its representative government – from the Priorate of nine through several other groupings to the larger bodies, the Council of the People and the Council of the Commune – as well as from the employment, common in these times, of constantly changed foreign magistrates (*podestà*) for judgements and sentences. All these plural and republican forms do not by Bruni's reckoning detract from strong government, but they do make it impossible for a single person to arrogate permanent power into his tyrannical control: 'there is no one in Florence who stands above the law'.[29] 'In this system nothing can be resolved by the caprice of any single man acting in opposition to the judgement of so many men.'[30] Florence's very wars of the period, ending in 1402, have been to ensure her own and other cities' continued freedom from domination by Giangaleazzo Visconti of Milan, who had threatened tyrannical, warlord-style control over north and central Italy until defeated by Florence.

Bruni had in fact begun his panegyric by describing an exemplarily clean city, ideally sited for climate, splendidly laid out and displaying in the magnificence of its public and private buildings the full prosperity of a large and dynamic civic economy. At its focal centre is the Palazzo Vecchio, 'tall and handsome', of 'great beauty and remarkable workmanship', but most of all bespeaking by its sheer size and imposing appearance 'the purposes for which it was constructed', namely rule of the commune by its plural governors:

> In Florence everyone immediately recognizes that this palace is so immense that it must house the men who are appointed to govern the state. Indeed, it was so magnificently conceived and looms so toweringly that it dominates all the buildings nearby and its top stands out above those of the private houses.[31]

This is a signal instance of a political theorist of the early years of the fifteenth century writing of the built city context as an existing reality, and praising a building more than a hundred years old, not in terms of its exact architectural style, but for its overall dimensions and what they bespeak of the greatness of the commune and the importance of its pluralistic (but nonetheless strong) forms of rule.

Our concern is with the striking difference in attitude displayed by the only slightly later theoretician Alberti, writing as he was from the position of the idealist who imagines building cities from scratch to complex blueprints based on use and purpose, but who actually, as we have seen, devised many of his ideal cityscapes in terms of the material structures of the Italian cities of his times, in particular material structures which themselves repeated or reflected class divisions within society. Alberti's text stands for a sharpening of the principles of class hierarchy, by textually mapping such hierarchies firmly onto material differences in building styles for, and locations of, the different classes.

In Alberti's own lifetime, it is true, 'the elite family displaced the communal republican institutions [those so lauded by Bruni in his *Panegyric*], contesting or eviscerating their authority'.[32] But the opportunity to design and build entire new cities to mark their advent to power was rare, and in any case not usually an immediate *desideratum*. A more common way of indicating their social and political dominance was to erect new and impressive family palazzi at key points of an urban structure, as in the case of Cosimo de Medici's commissioning of Michelozzo to design and build the Palazzo Medici on the imposing Via Larga, the (then) main northward artery leading out of old, inner Florence towards Fiesole. Later on, as the Medici consolidated their dominance over Florentine structures of power, Cosimo's grandson Lorenzo would think in terms of an entire *zona medicea* (only very partially realized in the event) along the Via Larga in which Michelozzo's huge edifice stood, a planned area extending through to and including Medicean monuments and chapels in and around the pre-existent parish church of San Lorenzo. As is well known the Medici in the fifteenth century were only ever *de facto* rulers of the city, not *de jure* princes. Actual princely families such as the Montefeltros in Urbino, the Gonzagas of Mantua or the Este of Ferrara and Modena tended to build grandiose ducal palaces as central complexes of their cities, and in the case of the latter family there was, under Ercole d'Este, an extended 'new town' addition to older medieval Ferrara, built to a design which if not Albertian in detail, was so in spirit, a project that 'virtually doubled the size of the previous city and created a zone of elite dwellings uninhibited by the spatial constraints of the old city'.[33]

More outrightly Albertian were certain schemes of church princes, in whose papal employ Alberti himself worked for many years, including the late 1440s, during which he was writing this treatise. For instance, his then employer Nicholas V, humanist pope from 1447 to 1455 (and to whom the first manuscript copy of this treatise seems to have been dedicated), hoped for an architectural amplification and clarification of parts of Rome so as to impress her own citizens (as well as those who made pilgrimage to the holy city) with the power and meaning of the church, and of the Pope as its spiritual prince.[34] His plans never came to full fruition, remaining instead at the level of an ideal only partially realized – in changed terms and circumstances – by later popes, in particular Sixtus IV (1471–84), Julius II (1503–13) and Leo X (1513–21).

During Alberti's lifetime, however, Aeneas Silvius Piccolomini, the first Piccolomini pope (1459–64), had his natal village of Corsignano turned into a miniature version of one such Albertian 'ideal city'. The town was re-christened Pienza after his papal name of Pius II. It figures extensively in the literature on ideal cities of the Renaissance, constituting as it does almost the only instance of such a city built virtually from scratch (admittedly, still only a remodelling of an existing village), on a site chosen on Albertian principles and to a closely Albertian design. Precisely because it has received such extensive scholarly attention, I choose not to dwell at length on this case. As one notable recent study has pointed out,

> the documents relevant to the project have been scrutinized, the urban layout has been accurately recorded, and the building histories of most of the component elements of the project have been clarified. The only important factual question that remains unclear is that of Alberti's participation in the project.[35]

What has been most concentrated on in scholarship are, precisely, details of layout and building, especially the complex aestheticism of the design, as well as speculation on how closely the chosen architect, Bernardo Rossellino, may have been working not just to an approximative realization of his professional associate Alberti's lifelong schemes, but actually under the guidance of Alberti himself as a kind of master spirit of the project. (Alberti too was, after all, in the Pope's employ during the period in question.[36])

Concerned as the present chapter is with social aspects of Alberti's and others' theories of urban planning, it is fair to note that it is precisely the *sociology* of what was involved in changing the far-flung southern Tuscan medieval hamlet over the Orcia valley into a showpiece *cittadina* of architectural humanism of the incumbent church prince Aeneas Silvius and his cardinalate that has not received pride of place in discussions to date. The key document for an understanding of this aspect of the project is Pius's own *Commentaries*.

The first that we hear in the *Commentaries* of Pius's plan to build a new church and palace in Corsignano comes as a direct consequence of his feeling upon a return visit in 1459 (shortly after his election to the papacy) not the 'delight in seeing again his native soil' after many years that he had anticipated, but a keen disappointment that most of his own generation of citizens had already died and the remnant become so bowed down and unrecognizable with age that they appeared like harbingers of death: 'At every step the Pope met with proofs of his own age and could not fail to realize that he was an old man who would soon drop.'[37] It is a short step from here for this prince of the church to feel, not traditional religious resignation to death's inevitability, but the distinctly humanist urge to build something to last beyond death: 'He decided to build there a new church and a palace and he hired architects and workmen at no small expense, that he might leave as lasting as possible a memorial of his birth.' The project, in effect, is not one undertaken for his own long-term delight, since he doesn't expect a plenitude of years in which to experience any such pleasure, but chiefly intended as a consolation for having to die so soon.

The complex is built with astonishing rapidity, its key buildings completed within a space of three years, and ready to be viewed and enjoyed during Pius's visit of 1462. After intricate descriptions of their structures and design layout, and all the advantages for living provided by the amenities of the main palazzo – these latter keenly reminiscent of concerns about site and air and space and visual aesthetics outlined only a few years earlier by Alberti – Pius reverts very much to a concern with the precise social context of the project, in his vignette description of rewarding the architect Rossellino for his labours:

> The Pope had received many insinuations against the architect: that he had cheated; that he had blundered in the construction; that he had spent more than 50,000 ducats when his estimate had been 18,000. The law of the Ephesians, according to Vitruvius, would have obliged him to make up the difference. He was a Florentine named Bernardo, hateful to the Sienese for his mere nationality. In his absence everyone abused him. Pius, when he had inspected the work and examined everything, sent for the man. When he arrived after a few days in some apprehension, since he knew that many charges had been brought against him, Pius said, 'You did well, Bernardo, in lying to us about the expense involved in the work. If you had told the truth, you could never have induced us to spend so much money and neither this splendid palace nor this church, the finest in Italy, would now be standing. Your deceit has built these glorious structures which are praised by all except the few who are consumed with envy. We thank you and think you deserve especial honor among all the architects of our time' – and he ordered full pay to be given him and in addition a present of 100 ducats and a scarlet robe. He bestowed on his son the grace he asked and charged him with new commissions. Bernardo, when he heard the Pope's words, burst into tears of joy.[38]

Here is a graphic instance of the architect of an urban complex being acknowledged in something like the way Alberti had defined as befitting his importance in the commencement of his treatise. But the specific details of Pius as papal humanist abandoning principles of truth and accountability when it comes to paying homage to someone who has designed and completed a work that breaks through the previous bounds of what was considered possible surely tell us more than we could extrapolate from Alberti's vivid but generalized description.

Great building projects are always costly. The incident recounted shows Pius taking a dramatic stand on principles of expense in relation to achievement. Not even the most liberal of patrons, he implies, would approve the full costs of an enterprise *before* seeing it achieved, since no one but the architect has the futuristic vision of the completed work (not just a grasp of its likely stupendous cost, but including even that), before a stone has been laid. It therefore behoves an architect of truly imaginative reach to be deceitful beforehand, simply in order to get the go-ahead at all. Significantly, the implication behind the story is not that Rossellino was simply bad at calculating what the main buildings at Pienza would cost to build. On the contrary, Pius, in one and the same statement, both accuses Rossellino of prior deceit and roundly praises him for it, in the light of what it bought him the time to build. The element of paradox in Pius's rewarding of Rossellino in both financial and social terms for a deceit of such magnitude, when by that dread law of the Ephesians the architect might well have feared having to make up the shortfall himself, would be enough to produce 'tears of joy' – note the continuation of paradoxicality in the *response* to paradox – in any grown man. There are further implications in the humanistic pope Pius, himself Sienese, displaying that he is quite above the *campanilismo* of others, who have watched at close quarters the costly project proceed and with malicious glee looked forward to the Florentine architect receiving his comeuppance. In Pius's naming such regionally inspired ill-will as the traditional sin of *invidia*, while at the same time himself displaying the historical vision to recognize and reward true merit in the 'glorious structures', 'the finest in all Italy', we perhaps witness a form of humanistic pride in the writer at his own generous and large-spirited acts.

That same large-spiritedness was required of other church princes below the Pope himself. If we remember that the whole point and purpose of rebuilding Pienza was as a memorial to Pius's birthplace, and that he expected soon to die, then the action of co-involving in the rebuilding project his cardinalate entourage cannot have been entirely without an element of deceit or at any rate pressure on his part. Pius names several cardinals and also specifies existing unnamed towns-people who 'tore down old houses and built new ones, so that nowhere did the aspect of the town remain unchanged'.[39] Perhaps Pius could not have known with certainty that the idea of Pienza becoming a sort of 'Home from Rome' would die with him. But we may reasonably question his motives in luring other wealthy cardinals and townspeople to fall in with his own commemorative project, if he was aware, as the *Commentaries* seem to imply he acutely was, of his own impending mortality. In the event many fine new palazzi were built by others as well as Pius in this 'ideal city', and at their own expense. But with the death of Pius there died also the cardinals' chief cause for any remove to so remote a haven as Pienza, however ideal it had been in the realization.

Pienza is the prime instance where a self-coherent set of Albertian conditions for the proper functioning of a city were met. And yet the sociology of its continuance was undermined in advance by the imminent mortality of a single individual, its main patron, himself too much its exclusive *raison d'être*. With Pius alive Pienza might have remained important. His death turned it rapidly into a backwater commemoration of his birthplace and, centuries later, the locus of much scholarship on its uniqueness as a Renaissance ideal city built to a plan.

If such was the case when realization of a scheme outstripped the social conditions of context, then what of the more usual case – where conditions may have been ripe, but planning for them so elaborate and monies for them so unforthcoming that nothing came of the designer's grand idealizing impulses?

Consider Filarete's account of Sforzinda. His ideas for an ideal city and its port town are more benign for the common citizen than anything in Alberti, with taverns and bathhouses and bordellos positioned at the heart of the conception, hard by the offices of city government. It is a city only realized on the written page, but described to us in the process of its building with such meticulousness and charm by its designer Filarete that the notion of it as an achieved actuality prevails. Unlike Alberti's treatise on architecture and Vitruvius's long before him, both of which Filarete refers to extensively, his does not deal in general terms with different kinds of cities but constitutes instead a narrative fiction of how just one such ideal context for living was designed and accomplished – the aforementioned Sforzinda, together with its port town of Plusiapolis. The genre of writing is one in which the processes of founding and building a city are recounted event by event, so that what is in fact only a fictional ideal is conjured up textually by Filarete's verbal descriptions as a reality for our mind's eye to contemplate.

Filarete's fictional discovery of the Inda valley as an ideal site provides us with pages of lambent pastoralism. He recounts the 'adventure' of coming across the valley and meeting there a gentleman who subsequently figures as a resident genius of the place, able to show him further sites for the quarrying of the necessary stone and for the hewing of invaluable timbers in the construction of the city. The valley, which quickly becomes the chosen site for Sforzinda, reads in description like an idealized version of the terrain between the Alps and the Po, situated along a south-flowing and deeply channelled river and with small raised hills backed by a high northern mountain chain:

> The river is suited for bringing down wood of every sort from the mountain . . . because it is not too long. I do not think it is more than thirty miles from the foot of the valley to the shore of the sea, so that they can easily come up here. You have seen the site. . . . It is located in the valley in good air, fertile and productive. . . . I will build this city through the power granted me by the aforementioned patron.[40]

Filarete's project is to build a city from scratch, on a scale rarely if ever attempted in the fifteenth century. Nonetheless, in his detailed and practical narrative we do learn a lot about how lesser projects that were actually carried through to fulfilment were accomplished: for example, the numbers of workmen involved, the kinds of material used and where found, the many types of artist subcontracted for work on specific buildings or for particular decorations ('a good painter . . . will not come for less than 200 ducats at the least'[41]), and lastly, the complex set of relations that existed between many persons – the lofty princely patron; next his working agent; then the architect proper, together with the large host of artisans and unskilled workmen employed on the site itself. Filarete's treatise is hence useful to study for two equal and opposite reasons: first, because it was a blueprint which, like many of Alberti's, could not be realized, because it argued from the principle of building an entire city where none previously existed (something of which not even the great Sforzas with all their wealth were capable); but second, because in the description of how individual details of the city were designed and executed we learn a great deal about how large-scale building projects in Filarete's day were in fact accomplished. For instance, if he did not build Sforzinda (though it is the treatise's ongoing fiction to suggest that he *did*, perhaps so as to recommend himself by the multiplicity of practicalities he displays to a prospective patron just such as Sforza himself, or, later on, to Piero de' Medici, for whom another manuscript copy of the treatise was prepared), Filarete nonetheless built one of the largest edifices in Northern Italy, the Ospedale Maggiore in Milan. The treatise describes the astonishing number of people that constituted the labour force of these grand building projects, and the kinds of work the differently skilled artisans were set to accomplish. It is on a scale of operation and at a pace of building that in our own times are perhaps only equalled by those of very rapidly developing economies, such as that of Southern China, in the Pearl River City project:

> First we shall see how many masters and laborers are needed for one braccio of wall. Then we will multiply how many will be needed to complete all the wall in the terms given above. One braccio of this wall from the ground level up to the top will require per day four masters and seven laborers to serve each master, counting in the making of mortar and the carrying of brick. These are necessary so that the master will not lose time. More [important, we] need someone between every two masters to reinforce them, that is to fill up the gap between them. In order to make our computation from this braccio, since there are 375 braccia in a stadio, we will multiply four times 375; this makes 1500. Thus in a stadio we need this number of masters.
>
> You have seen the number of masters needed in a stadio. By multiplying eight stadio to the mile you will see how many masters there will be. I get 12,000. Now we have to determine the laborers and fillers-in. In short we want seven laborers to each master; that will be 84,000, and 6,000 fillers-in. According to this reckoning there will be 90,000 laborers and fillers-in, and with the masters there will be 102,000 persons. These masters, served in the above-stated way, will lay 30 million bricks a day. Our city will thus be completed in ten days.[42]

It is an astonishingly large workforce, and an equally heady work rate for a pre-industrial age. No wonder in a later century Ruskin was to fulminate against the slave element in any post-Gothic architecture that depended on sheer repetition of tasks, as here in Filarete's calculation of how many masters and labourers will be needed to build Sforzinda in the specified time of ten days. As Ruskin saw the matter, the 'signs of the life and liberty of every workman who struck the stone' which are evident in the variety of detail in earlier, Gothic structures, were lost in the classicizing age which followed, and more terribly still in the grimy industrial age in which he was himself living and writing. In his chapter on 'The Nature of Gothic' in *The Stones of Venice*, Ruskin decried all building on the scale of repetition of separate tasks involved here as a falsely named 'division of labour', when what was really involved was a division of men: 'broken into small fragments and crumbs of life; so that all the little piece of intelligence that is left in a man is not enough to make up a pin, or a nail, but exhausts itself in making the point of a pin or the head of a nail . . .'[43] Using the example of Venice, Ruskin had dated the beginning of that city's decline to a time (1423 to be precise, the date of Doge Tomaso Mocenigo's decease) not a full half-century before Filarete's treatise was written. Ruskin neither allowed into his own calculations any sense of how much backbreaking labour had also been required in the great Gothic monuments of Europe, nor how much artisanal skill went on being exerted in those of the *renaissant* classicism.

A reading of Filarete's text affords a thrilling sense of the deployment of masters as well as of men; of incomparably individualistic artistry by the former, equally with the transforming of the latter into an unproblematic, slave-like workforce, all too in keeping with Ruskin's strenuous critique, in order that the millions upon millions of bricks be laid in the required time. 'Do you think that such a number of masters and laborers will respect the overseers, that they will obey them?' Filarete's patron enquires of him. To which the architect replies, 'We can take care of this if you are dubious. Have the army come and draw them up in a battle line. Then give an order, under pain of the gallows, that everyone stay in his place. For anyone who disobeys, the order will be carried out without mercy or remission.'[44] We bridle at the degrees of force exerted to constrain the huge numbers of artisans and their labourers to undertake the building of Sforzinda, and at the fatal accidents recounted in the unfolding narrative of its construction. And yet, for ourselves as readers of another age there is great satisfaction in noting that Filarete's city-in-the-making is being built very definitely for the wellbeing of all of its citizens, undifferentiated in the pleasures it affords between those for a select few and others for an underprivileged many. Indeed, there is a sense throughout Filarete's text of both of Martines's complementary terms – 'imagination' on the one hand at both the grand and the detailed conceptual levels, and 'power' in the form of wealthy and influential patronage on the scale needed to complete so large and widely beneficial a built environment. (It cannot, however, be too firmly repeated that in this instance both the power and

the imagination are entirely a fiction of the text: no such city as
Sforzinda was ever built in reality.)

Perhaps the most appealing pages of all in Filarete's treatise are those
which describe the overall plan of the city. These follow the dedication
of the city by its patron after a series of miraculous episodes, each
interpreted as good omens. Filarete's city of Sforzinda appeals above all
for the attention shown to ensuring aesthetic and civic pleasure to all its
citizens – unlike so much of what we have seen in Alberti's ideas for
cities, based heavily as they had been on felt levels of both external and
internal threat to a single ruler. Filarete's is a city of linked piazzas and
key civic buildings. The piazzas themselves have water canals around
their edges. Each second street being also a canal, the forms of transport
and supply of the city may be as equally by water as by land. (John R.
Spencer explains that 'although it is traditional to associate this use of
canals in the treatise with Filarete's trips to Venice, it is more probable
that he took Milan's Naviglio and its many branches as his model,
which he here regularizes to fit his plan'.[45] However, it seems more
reasonable to say that Filarete's imagination has drawn on both
Venetian *and* Milanese design features in creating a relationship
between land and water in his city of Sforzinda that is new and
distinctive; and hence different in the final analysis from either of the
cities most obviously influencing his thinking at this point.)

Nothing is so altogether appealing in its rich evocation of the lives of
many persons living together harmoniously than Filarete's description of
the city's main piazzas. Even something that might in our latter-day
world seem like an anomalous structure in context, namely the prison, is
clearly as integral as all the rest:

> At the eastern end I will build a cathedral, and the royal court at the
> western. . . . In the northern part of the piazza I will make the merchant's
> piazza. . . . On the southern side of the piazza I will make another piazza
> that will be a sort of market where edibles can be sold, for example meat,
> fruit, vegetables, and other things necessary. . . . At the head of this I will
> make the Palazzo del Capitano on the corner nearest the court, so that only
> the street separates them. In the merchant's market I will make, on one
> end, the Palazzo del Podestà and opposite it the law courts. On the
> northern part I will make the municipal prison. This will be directly behind
> the law courts. On the eastern part, at the corner of the piazza, I will make
> the mint, where money is made and stored, and near it the customshouse.
> In the merchant's piazza, as I said, will be the Palazzo del Capitano and on

the other side the butcher, chicken, and fish shops, the latter in season. Behind this piazza toward the south will be the bordellos, the public baths, and inns, or taverns. . . . Straw and wood will be sold in the two toward the east and the two toward the west. Oil and other things will be sold on the two toward the north. In the southern ones grain and wine will be sold. There will be one or two butcher shops, in each one as you think necessary. The artists will all live around these piazzas.[46]

In terms of human concourse, the central piazzas are a social melting-pot of victuallers and other merchants, of officers of law and order, artists, prostitutes, manufacturers and (even if incarcerated) criminals. What is more, Filarete seems to be designing on the very principle – so alien to the likes of Alberti before him and Leonardo after, as we have seen – that a city works best if persons of utterly different qualities and status live and interact in close proximity. There is convenience and a sense of community generated precisely from the multiplicity of functions that the various adjacent buildings around the central piazzas are designed to serve. The principle seems to be that if something is an important aspect of the city's operation (for example, the mint, to point to only one of the several buildings mentioned) then it merits a central position. The focus of interest of the entire city is hence centripetal, both architecturally and socially.

We have seen in this chapter on ideal cities an important variety in the sociological premises of treatise writers, as well as in some of the later cultural criticism of different periods of building. Most important of all have been questions concerning for whose pleasure and convenience various aspects of a built context are planned. Indubitably, the harshest critic of classical ideals and styles was Ruskin, whose reasons for extolling the form and variety of Gothic architecture were by no means mere aesthetic preferences, but based on a distinction he makes between free and enslaved forms of labour. Whether or not he was correct, Ruskin's notion was that in classical times of Greece and then again in the post-Gothic age, the prevailing aesthetic of the built environment means that 'the kind of labour to which [workmen] are condemned is verily a degrading one, and makes them less than men'.[47] Only Gothic architecture by his reckoning reveals to a later age the creative freedom and inspiration of those who built it. It is a claim that a reading of Filarete's treatise partly supports, but partly controverts.

I would like to conclude the chapter with a consideration of some of the consequences of the Renaissance concern for ideal cities on English thought and its built environment. We can begin with William Morris, whose own judgement of Ruskin's chapter on 'The Nature of Gothic' was that it held 'the truest and the most eloquent words that can possibly be said on the subject'.[48] Interestingly, however, in what he has to say of a utopian kind in his most important piece of prose, *News from Nowhere*, Morris, although in part elaborating an essentially Ruskinian sense of the worth of the Gothic period of building and decoration, seems also not a little indebted to the utopian ideals of Renaissance urbanists in general matters of siting and of the importance of climate and aesthetic effects upon inhabitants. There is the further appeal for him of imagining within an English landscape some of the best of what has moved him from the great past of Italian cities. His vision is of an utter transformation of his own part of London, the (then) outlying village of 'dingy Hammersmith',[49] as he calls it in the 'return to reality', at the close of what the full title of the piece names as a 'utopian romance'.

Morris first describes the houses of this transformed place:

> all pretty in design, and as solid as might be, but countryfied in appearance, like yeomen's dwellings; some of them of red brick like those by the river, but more of timber and plaster, which were by the necessity of their construction so like mediaeval houses of the same materials that I fairly felt as if I were alive in the fourteenth century; a sensation helped out by the costume of the people that we met or passed, in whose dress there was nothing 'modern'.

But it is when he moves on to describe the public buildings enjoyed by the inhabitants (themselves 'so frankly and openly joyous' and characterized by 'great nobility of expression'), that we see the fullness of Morris's imagined integration of the best of southern European and even near-oriental urbanism, with that of northern European Gothic:

> I thought I knew the Broadway by the lie of the roads that still met there. On the north side of the road was a range of buildings and courts, low, but very handsomely built and ornamented, and in that way forming a great contrast to the unpretentiousness of the houses round about; while above this lower building rose the steep lead-covered roof and the buttresses and higher part of the wall of a great hall, of a splendid and exuberant style of architecture, of which one can say little more than that it seemed to me to embrace the best qualities of the Gothic of northern Europe with those of the Saracenic and Byzantine, though there was no copying of any one of these styles. On the other, the south side, of the road was an octagonal

building with a high roof, not unlike the Baptistry at Florence in outline, except that it was surrounded by a lean-to that clearly made an arcade or cloisters to it: it also was most delicately ornamented.[50]

As writing, this is surprisingly close in generic terms to Filarete's equivalent utopian romance, though there is no possibility Morris could have read the former writer's treatise, unavailable as it was in either an Italian edition or English translation during his lifetime. Clearly the hindsight available to Morris from his late-nineteenth-century position-ing allows him to dream of an architectural amalgam, incorporating influences from the best of several different periods and cultures. It is an ideal of a kind simply not possible for Filarete, whose own main stylistic problems were so much more immediate in time and space: namely, how to adapt his Florentine training in visual matters (with all its early Renaissance classical elegances of form) to the north Italian context of Milan (essentially more enduringly Gothic in its building styles), in which he largely worked and for which this particular treatise was first conceived.

Morris here imagines public buildings of varying functions on the north and south side of the Broadway at Hammersmith. Though their stylistic elements are quite unlike those surrounding Filarete's central piazzas of Sforzinda, what Morris goes on to say about the overall human affect of the buildings, in particular upon himself, is entirely in keeping with the mode of narration and principal values of the earlier architectural theorist:

> The whole mass of architecture which we had come upon so suddenly from amidst the pleasant fields was not only exquisitely beautiful in itself, but it bore upon it the expression of such generosity and abundance of life that I was exhilarated to a pitch that I had never yet reached.

Compare this with typical sentences throughout Filarete's treatise, describing the affect of stages in the construction of Sforzinda upon its chief patron: 'When he saw the piazzas and buildings all constructed. . . he was even more surprised, for they were so much more beautiful than they had seemed to him in the drawing. He wanted to see each building one by one.'[51] Uncannily, although the two utopian romances are separated by more than four centuries, there are times when they seem driven along by the same spirit of delight: a glorying in notions of an urban context fit for its inhabitants.

Scarcely a generation on from Morris, another notable English writer,

D. H. Lawrence, would refer even more wistfully to Italian precedent when critiquing urbanistic follies of the industrialized landscape of his upbringing, in a forceful, posthumously published essay from his last years entitled 'Nottingham and the Mining Countryside'.[52] 'What opportunities, what opportunities!' he laments. 'The mining villages *might* have been like the lovely hill-towns of Italy, shapely and fascinating. And what happened?' What happened, according to Lawrence, was that the spirit of the old mining communities was betrayed by a 'tragedy of ugliness': 'The country is so lovely: the man-made England is so vile.' Lawrence condemns the cramp and squalor produced by the nineteenth-century promoters of industry who 'dared to perpetrate the ugliness of my native village':

> These New Buildings consist of two great hollow squares of dwellings planked down on the rough slope of the hill, little four-room houses with the 'front' looking outward into the grim, blank street, and the 'back', with a tiny square brick yard, a low wall, and a w.c. and ash-pit, looking into the desert of the square. . . . The squares were quite big, and absolutely desert, save for the posts for clothes lines, and people passing, children playing on the hard earth. And they were shut in like a barracks enclosure, very strange.

Even without hearing more from Lawrence, we can draw some conclusions of our own in comparing the 'desert' squares of these mining villages with the animated central focus of urban existence as described by Filarete. Lawrence goes on to make a point that reminds us very directly of Filarete's urban centrepiece:

> If the company, instead of building those sordid and hideous Squares, then, when they had that lovely site to play with, there on the hill top: if they had put a tall column in the middle of the small market-place, and run three parts of a circle of arcade round the pleasant space, where people could stroll or sit, and with handsome houses behind!

Essentially, Lawrence condemns the mining barons for not having had enough philanthropic spirit to build with concepts of community and beauty uppermost in mind, instead of their own profit. But the critical charge of his essay is far from merely against the moneyed classes; the writing becomes an attack on the general character of the English people of the industrial age: 'The English are town-birds through and through, today, as the inevitable result of their complete industrialization. Yet they don't know how to build a city, how to think of one, or how to live in one.' Not surprisingly, Lawrence's early contrast in the essay between ugly English mining villages and the beautiful hill towns of Italy is expanded into an entire theory of the lack of urban spirit in the English character, from times long before industrialization even:

> As a matter of fact, till 1800 the English people were strictly a rural people – very rural. England has had towns for centuries, but they have never been real towns, only clusters of village streets. Never the real *urbs*. The English character has failed to develop the real *urban* side of a man, the civic side. Siena is a bit of a place, but it is a real city, with citizens intimately connected with the city. Nottingham is a vast place sprawling towards a million, and it is nothing more than an amorphous agglomeration. There *is* no Nottingham, in the sense that there is Siena.

Lawrence stands in a direct line of descent from Morris and the Arts and Crafts movement in his belief in a people's being inspired to creative expression under conditions of an aesthetically and socially transformed England (that in fact has not come to pass):

> If only they had encouraged some form of beauty in dress, some form of beauty in interior life – furniture, decoration. If they had given prizes for the handsomest chair or table, the loveliest scarf, the most charming room that the men or women could make! If only they had done this, there would never have been an industrial problem.

We may find this theory of 'interior beauty' solving the deepest problems created by industrial capitalism both patronizing and absurd. And the idea of Italian-style hill towns dotted across the mining countryside of Nottinghamshire and Derbyshire is also more than a little far-fetched, considering in particular the very different conditions of climate and of balance between agriculture and industry in the two landscapes. But it is nonetheless interesting to contemplate to what lengths utopian social theorists were driven by their agonized sense, born of comparisons with just such a society as Italy that, in Lawrence's words, 'The Englishman is stupidly undeveloped, as a citizen.'

When conditions were once again ripe for considerable urban building programmes, in the Britain of the 1960s, the example of Italy remained a conscious touchstone of what was to be striven for in the minds of certain planners. Entire New Towns were designed and constructed in the post-war period in Britain, such as Cumbernauld in Scotland and Hook and Milton Keynes in England. The expansionist phase was accompanied by technological developments and by an enlargement of tertiary education, which led to the creation from scratch of seven new universities in England and one in Scotland, three of which at least (East Anglia, Essex and Lancaster) were largely conceived of by their architects as small, self-sufficient 'towns'; hence, they were planned in some respects as a specialized subgenre of the New Town movement itself, and based in their turn on idealizations that frequently had their roots in Italian precedent. These campuses provided the possibility, in Asa Briggs's words, to 'represent for posterity the twentieth century conception of a university'.[53]

More than that. They were, in the words of John Maule McKean, in a notable case study of the material and social principles that went into the making of just one of these ideal campuses, 'for the designers . . . a chance to represent for posterity, their – if not "twentieth century" at least contemporary – idea of a town'.[54] Commentators at the time (largely it must be admitted persons themselves engaged in university education) came to see the chance to build these expressions of their combined urbanistic and educational ideals as possibly the single most important opportunity of influencing the very *Zeitgeist* for the better. In an article significantly entitled 'Universities as Institutional Archetypes of our Age' the architectural critic Joseph Rykwert (later so important in studies and editions of Alberti) announced that 'what makes the British situation particularly interesting is the decision to accommodate the new university population in entirely new complexes of buildings on fresh sites rather than extensions of the old agglomerations'.[55]

Instead of such university conditions as existed in the growth of the oldest of the British universities or else the 'red brick' institutions of the previous century, 'the new universities were being conceived in a changed urban situation. Cambridge and Oxford were concatenations of more or less secularised monasteries . . . in a close and obtrusive relationship to the towns in which they settled.'[56] Red-brick universities were part of the civic expansion of the nineteenth century, sited in and often financed by the industrial towns of which they became a partial expression, in architectural, educational and sociological terms. For the new universities, by contrast, campuses in special and separated locations – sometimes even great parks of an earlier age, which no longer served the leisure functions for which they had been created in the eighteenth century – meant that these idealized urban experiments had greenbelt around them before reaching the larger cities with which they were associated. There hence arose in a number of cases the phenomenon of a 'new university' campus town within a park, which was itself within, or at the boundary of, a larger, pre-existent city. Connection between the 'new' university town and the older city into which it was being integrated and yet, paradoxically, *not* integrated, because protected by a greenbelt buffer zone, could, especially under conditions of crisis in the larger society, become highly fraught by the very factor of difference, so starkly demarcated by spatial separation. Students of the new universities were often inveigled by the offer of plentiful campus accommodation into living their university years largely within an artificially uniform fraction of the larger society, sometimes scarcely in contact with the wider world for months at a time.

The opportunity presenting itself was that of the earlier, Albertian/ Filaretian ideal – for architectural innovation within a previously unbuilt location – but in an essential and modern British form. Unlike in the case of Alberti and Filarete, however, the possibilities for actually building ideal (if small) 'cities' – *cittadine*, to adopt the precise Italian term for tiny cities – were very real and very present, and certainly not merely a matter of textual daydreaming.

Though daydreaming there certainly also was – aplenty! – in the realization of each such new university. So that for any summative judgements on the movement in question there has to be a measuring of the distance between what was dreamed and what was actually achieved. This was precisely what John Maule McKean was attempting in his critical article of 1972 on Essex, the university among the set of new universities which had been most beset by campus 'troubles' in the late 1960s and early 1970s, and therefore the one where, from the position of that moment of early hindsight when McKean was writing, the original dream and the eventual reality seemed to have split most widely apart.

By any reckoning Essex had been, with its bold high-rise residential towers and its pedestrianized concrete-town-pitched-on-podia-over-lower-service-road, the new university that piqued itself most on its design connection with the modernity of great cities, leaning always in intention towards the future. There was to be nothing merely village-like or cosily English in this, 'the most uncompromising of all' the new urban campuses.[57] Curiously too, however, it was also the development where there were the most numerous references back to the Italy of small and manageable hill towns, as well as cities without cars such as Venice. An early university press release defining the intended design speaks of 'platforms each the size of a small Italian town square linked by shallow flights of steps'.[58] For his part Donald Davie, poet and first Professor of Literature at the university, sought to elaborate this combination of ideal Italianate urban context with shock-of-the-new modernity:

> Essex streets may be like Genoa perhaps, or even (since we are sending the cars elsewhere) like Venice. Colchester will be out and around the university in no time at all; and if the university is to assert its identity, among the bypasses, parking lots, power stations, housing 'developments', it needs to make a gesture more imperious than . . . harmony of coppice and swelling turf, rectangular pools and brick arcades. We need Capon's tightly linked piazzas and residential towers.[59]

Many at the time were to remark on the inherent contradiction of attempting to square modernity with medievalism, as well as on another contradiction, which it shared with almost all the other universities built in the same decade, 'of accessibility and remoteness'.[60] (At the beginning of a new millennium, Colchester is still not 'out and around' Essex University, for instance.)

Thirty years later, however, we may be in a better position to see that what the late-modern age saw as contradiction, the postmodern age may more readily be able to think of as combination: the combining, that is, of features profoundly different if we consider them in isolation, but which might, when placed in a single framework, constitute a reality so new that it took a generation or more for many people (other than visionaries such as Davie) to come to terms with, because at first there were so few correlative realities in terms of which to judge it. Even where correlates were initially offered in the 1960s – for example, the residential student towers presented as (however vaguely) reminiscent of the defensive towers of Italian hill towns such as San Giminiano[61] – the shocking dissimilarities of function made the comparison more ridiculous than explanatory. There were simply no existing and adequate explanations for the brutalism of inner-city-type tower blocks being deliberately built as part of a utopian cityscape, in the midst of what was otherwise an extraordinarily beautiful, if largely disused, eighteenth-century great park. 'Like many Londoners and New Yorkers, our students will live in flats or apartments, groups of a dozen or so rooms arranged in towers and forming part of a university town,' the founder Vice Chancellor of Essex, Albert Sloman, had explained in his celebrated Reith Lectures of 1963 entitled 'A University in the Making'.[62] What he failed to acknowledge was that people live in flats and apartments in those great cities precisely because of the particular factors that exist in London and New York, conditions that most signally do not prevail in in Essex's Wivenhoe Park, one of the four parkland campuses with great house attached. (Heslington Park at York, Stanmer Park near Brighton and Earlham Park in Norwich were the other three).

But Sloman's analogy with London and New York was not as silly as it may at first seem, if we recall his grander plan for Essex, shared by one or two others among the more ambitious of the new universities (in particular Warwick, which has in subsequent years come closer to attaining this goal): namely, that it become by means of rapid expansion a powerhouse multiversity of some ten or even twenty thousand students – a kind of MIT of the UK:

> The scale and character of modern research call for such a range of skills and for equipment so complex and so expensive that scientists working independently and alone have given way to teams of specialists, each making his own contribution of information and techniques. As a result, departments and universities will in the future have to be very much bigger.[63]

The frisson of living in flats or apartments like those of the great cities of the West therefore lay in the direct accessibility of a very city-like university, in terms of its contained diversity.

The promise lay in the opportunity to plan so much with relative creative freedom. From the point of view of university education, this moment of the 1960s constituted a kind of Renaissance in its own right: in Sloman's words the 'first chance for seven centuries' to tackle university education on such a scale – 'no one in the future will be bold enough to start from scratch'.[64] We for our part can meaningfully finish by discussing a couple of features of the Capon/Sloman blueprint for a university city, precisely in terms of Renaissance urban theorists such as Alberti, Filarete and Leonardo, the major preoccupations of this chapter.

We may begin with something grim in its conception, still grim in its outcome, and which ought to remind us of nothing so much as Leonardo's lower, non-sunlit 'service' level of the *popolo* or urban poor, going about their lives as labouring drudges, their chief *raison d'être* being to provide for the essential needs of the *gientili ômini*, an upper class of folk, on the higher levels of the built city. Beneath the University of Essex, in the valley bottom over which its podia were raised for the purposes of a marvellous educational and research lifestyle for students and professors, there lies a service road for provisioning the university from beneath, and alongside it many a maintenance store and workshop receiving its light mainly or only from artificial sources. Apart from the parkland, this is still the area where a service personnel of carpenters, electricians, fitters and cleaners live out the majority of their working lives. Already in 1972, less than a decade after the erection of the key buildings of the university, this lower area was described in a book on the building of the new universities. In defining the outcome of Capon's blueprint for how the university town was to be serviced from below, the author, Tony Birks, reminds us of nothing so much as Leonardo's city of differing functional and class layers:

> Enclosed piazzas known in the university as Square 3, Square 4, etc. . . . have effectively created a new ground level, or at least a waterline. Down below, in the cavernous service area, the burly windowless concrete shapes of departmental blocks are identified in stencilled lettering as 'Chemistry Department', etc., like names painted low on the hulls of ships to help the diver about his business in an otherwise undifferentiated gloom.[65]

Even 'service' departments such as that of Language and Linguistics, as originally conceived by Sloman and described in the Reith Lectures, were positioned on the physically lowest educational levels of the university, presumably from the same logic. Such stratification reveals the downside of this creation of the 1960s Renaissance.

The positives on the other hand are too numerous and diverse to be reckoned. But I want, in closing, simply to note a curious parallelism: between on the one hand the way Albert Sloman and his architect, C. K. Capon, are known to have walked the valley in which they were to build their new university town, and, on the other, certain early passages in Filarete's architectural treatise in which he describes surveying the valley named Inda along with a 'gentleman' whom he met there, who was to become his patron's negotiator in the building of the ideal city of Sforzinda:

> About twice a week [Capon] would meet Sloman and they would walk over the site together. 'We hardly exchanged letters at all; we would simply stroll around and talk.' . . . They both remember this period most warmly, and in these terms. Sloman particularly recalls their romantically marching the virgin site – in the knowledge of this 'first chance for centuries' – dreaming of their university.[66]

As Sloman was right to point out, one has to go back centuries for similar chances. Filarete himself was searching for one such commission in the very writing of his utopian romance by way of architectural treatise. And his fiction, designed as it was to entice a noble patron actually to build some such city as the one he describes, has passages that are like a prefiguration exactly half a millennium beforehand (if we remember that Filarete's text is complete by the early 1460s) of Capon's and Sloman's dreaming:

> The more I looked at the site the better I liked it, for I felt that no other place in the world could be more suited and more beautiful for building a city than this one. Then my companion said to me, 'If any city is built here this wood will be cut down.' I told him no, because it was not the sort of wood that was used in building. Moreover, there are many forests of trees used for building in the mountains toward the east and they would be easily transported.[67]

One remembers that Capon and Sloman spared the beautiful Wivenhoe Great Park as far as possible, by confining the building to a lower valley. And one thing that can be said of their initially rather reviled and certainly far from 'ivory' towers is that if they did not afford views over an exciting urban environment such as London or New York, what they did present before the student was at once an extensive view of the past, in the form of one of the more gracious parklands of a former age, and a tiny sliver of the postmodern future, by way of a compact and functional university *cittadina*. The architect Capon and his patron Sloman had achieved their minor, but nonetheless historically highly significant, victory.

## Notes

1. Leon Battista Alberti, *On the Art of Building in Ten Books*, translated by Joseph Rykwert, Neil Leach and Robert Tavernor (Cambridge, MA, and London: The MIT Press, 1988), p. 4.

2. Wittkower accepts Cecil Grayson's arguments that the work was essentially written between 1443 and 1452. See Rudolf Wittkower, *Architectural Principles in the Age of Humanism*, 3rd revised edn (London: Alec Tiranti, 1962), p. 3. It was first disseminated in manuscript versions, including one of 1483 for Federico da Montefeltro's great library of manuscripts in Urbino, before eventually being printed in 1486 with an introduction by Poliziano addressed to Lorenzo de' Medici. See Joseph Rykwert's Introduction to Alberti, *On the Art of Building*, pp. xvi–xviii.

3. Alberti, *On the Art of Building*, p. 7.

4. An account of the logic of Alberti's argument is given in Françoise Choay, *La Règle et le modèle: sur la théorie de l'architecture et de l'urbanisme* (Paris: Éditions du Seuil, 1980), Chapter 2, pp. 86–162.

5. Alberti, *On the Art of Building*, p. 3.

6. The term *city* does not figure in the title of any of the Renaissance treatises on architecture treated here. Filarete does, however, use it in the title of his third 'book': 'Tertius Liber de Aedificatione Urbis'. See Antonio Averlino detto il Filarete, *Trattato di architettura*, 2 vols, edited by Anna Maria Finoli and Liliana Grassi, (Milan: Edizioni il Polifilo, 1972), Vol. 1, p. 65.

7. Anthony Blunt, *Artistic Theory in Italy: 1450–1600* (Oxford: Oxford University Press, 1940), pp. 1–22. Blunt spoke of Alberti's being 'typical of the early Humanists' in his 'width of knowledge, as well as in his rational and scientific approach' (p. 3); of their being 'hardly a trace in him of the theological preoccupations which dominated the thought of medieval writers' (p. 11); and concludes that 'the feature which stands out most is the complete absence of the idea of imagination in his writings. Everything is attributed to reason, to method, to imitation, to measurement; nothing to the creative faculty. And this is quite logical. The artists of the early Quattrocento whose ideas he expresses were entirely occupied with exploring the visible universe which they had so recently discovered' (pp. 21–2). Although a great deal has happened in scholarship on Alberti since Blunt, many of the lines of analysis have not departed in fundamental terms from the parameters he sets here. The present study seeks to read Alberti's text with a view to the cultural mindset revealed in the arguments of *De re*.

8. Alberti, *On the Art of Building*, p. 3.

9. *Ibid.*

10. *Ibid.*, p. 4.

11. *Ibid.*, p. 3.

12. Burckhardt's main ideas on the topic come in the section of his book entitled 'The Development of the Individual'. Addressing the specific subject of the perfecting of the individual, he defines his universal Renaissance man as someone in whom 'the highest individual development was combined with a powerful and varied nature, which had mastered all the elements of the culture of the age'. Apart from then going on to mention Dante as something of a precursor of the legendary type, Burckhardt's first real instance was, interestingly, Alberti himself. But Burckhardt established a trend in remarking that 'Leonardo da Vinci was to Alberti as the finisher to the beginner, as the master to the *dilettante*' (Jacob Burckhardt, *The Civilization of the Renaissance in Italy*, translated by S. G. C. Middlemore from 15th German edn [no place of publication given: Albert and Charles Boni, 1935], pp. 147–50). It is part of the business of the present chapter to show, in direct contrast with Burckhardt's late-romantic and idealizing mystification on the matter of many-sidedness in given talented Renaissance individuals (in particular, his notion that 'the colossal outlines of Leonardo's nature can never be more than dimly and distantly conceived'), that the best way of grasping a lot of what Leonardo as a deviser/inventor is all about is precisely to study the work of some of his immediate precursors among treatise writers. Figures such as Alberti, Filarete and Francesco di Giorgio Martini are by no means dwarfed by Leonardo, since he can best be

understood as an onward development from their talents and preoccupations. This approach to Leonardo via his predecessors, from at least as early as Brunelleschi onwards, is shared by Paolo Galluzzi in his catalogue volume to an exhibition first entitled *Mechanical Marvels: Invention in the Age of Leonardo* (Florence: Giunti, 1996). The exhibition – given slightly differently titles at its various venues – has been to several centres, including the Istituto e Museo di Storia della Scienza, Florence, the Liberty Street Gallery of the World Financial Centre in New York and most latterly (1999) the Science Museum in London.

13. For probable limit dates of composition and for circumstances of early dissemination in manuscript form, see Franco Borsi, *Leon Battista Alberti*, translated by Rudolf G. Carpanini (Oxford: Phaidon Press, 1977), p. 316, fn. 1.

14. Filarete (1400–*c.* 1465); Francesco di Giorgio Martini (1439–1502). In spite of a major recent double exhibition in 1993 devoted to *Francesco di Giorgio architetto* and *Francesco di Giorgio e il Rinascimento a Siena, 1450–1500* (see the two exhibition catalogue volumes with these titles, edited by Luciano Bellosi [Milan: Electa, 1993]), this Sienese artist has still received too little recognition for his architectural and military treatises, not to mention also paintings, sculptures, models and plans of widespread achievements, especially fortresses. Francesco was during his lifetime nothing less than the chief builder of fortresses from Milan to Naples. Revealingly, towards the close of his life he had a great deal of trouble rejecting Neapolitan calls to return and continue his already extensive fortifications there. Not content with putting personal pressure on him, his Neapolitan employers appealed to the state of Siena itself to send its citizen back to them. Francesco was busy about his two bronze angels, his last masterpiece, and would hear none of all this. His manuscript notebooks cover many of the matters of urban planning and fortification for which he was so justly famed in his own lifetime. But to modern scrutiny they are above all fascinating for their pre-Leonardesque inventions: including, significantly, ideas for human flight, but also divers' 'bells' for deep-sea discoveries.

15. Of the magnitude of change from Brunelleschi onwards, Françoise Choay has perceptively expounded on Eugenio Garin's notion of a 'cultural revolution' in the treatment of space by architects, painters and sculptors of the period (the figures she mentions are Brunelleschi, Donatello and Piero della Francesca), leading to a transformation of European man's relations with his own artistic and technological productions (*La Règle et le modèle*, p. 13).

16. Leon Battista Alberti, *On Painting and On Sculpture*, translated and edited by Cecil Grayson (London: Phaidon Press, 1972), p. 33 (Italian original on preceding page). For a recent interpretation of this letter and its own cultural significance, see Christine Smith's *Architecture in the Culture of Early Humanism: Ethics, Aesthetics, and Eloquence 1400–1470* (New York and Oxford: Oxford University Press, 1992), specifically Chapter 2, 'Originality and Cultural Progress: Brunelleschi's Dome and a Letter by Alberti', pp. 19–39.

17. *Filarete's Treatise on Architecture*, 2 vols, translated with introduction and notes by John R. Spencer (New Haven and London: Yale University Press, 1965), Vol. 1, p. 77 and p. 102.

18. Alberti, *On the Art of Building*, p. 4.

19. Quoted in Nicholas Adams and Laurie Nussdorfer, 'The Italian City, 1400–1600', in Henry A. Millon and Vittorio Magnago Lampugnani (eds), *The Renaissance from Brunelleschi to Michelangelo: The Representation of Architecture* (Milan: Bompiani, 1994), p. 206.

20. 'Non è altro lo edificare se none un piacere voluntario, come quando l'uomo è innamorato, e chi l'ha provato il sa, ché nello edificare c'è tanto piacere e desiderio che quanto più l'uomo fa più vorrebbe fare . . .' (Filarete, *Trattato*, Vol. 1, pp. 41–2). For the original manuscript see Florence: Biblioteca Nazionale, Magliabecchianus II, IV, 140. All translated material from this manuscript is taken from *Filarete's Treatise on Architecture*. This quote appears in Vol. 1, p. 16. For the further quote on the analogy between human conception and that of building see Vol. 1, p. 18: the original reads, 'dee essere onorato e amato da chi fa fare non altrimenti che lui desidera che'l suo dificio vadia bene, né con altro amore e diligenza che s'ha inverso di quella sanza la quale generare uomo non si può, neanche sanza l'architetto non si può generare, né dedicare edificio che stia bene' (Filarete, *Trattato*, p. 44).

21. *Filarete's Treatise on Architecture*, Vol. 1, p. 4. *Trattato*, p. 8.

22. As Filarete's treatise is written in a rather more mixed mode, the focus of its address is somewhat more mobile.

23. Lise Bek, *Towards Paradise on Earth: Modern Space Conception in Architecture, a Creation of Renaissance Humanism* (Odense, Denmark: Odense University Press, 1980), p. 140.

24. The relevant page for this material in Leonardo's notebooks is 16r of his MS. B, one of fourteen such manuscripts held in the Institut de France. Transcription of the text is available in *Leonardo architetto e urbanista*, edited by Luigi Firpo (Turin: UTET, 1963), p. 74.

25. See Firpo's defence of Leonardo in *ibid.*, pp. 78ff.

26. Bek, *Towards Paradise on Earth*, p. 140.

27. Adams and Nussdorfer, 'The Italian City', p. 205.

28. Bek, *Towards Paradise on Earth*, p. 73.

29. Leonardo Bruni, 'Panegyric to the City of Florence', translated by Benjamin G. Kohl, in Benjamin G. Kohl and Ronald G. Witt with Elizabeth B. Welles (eds), *The Earthly Republic: Italian Humanists on Government and Society* (Manchester: Manchester University Press, 1978), p. 169.

30. *Ibid.*, p. 170.

31. *Ibid.*, p. 141.

32. Adams and Nussdorfer, 'The Italian City', p. 206.

33. *Ibid.*, p. 216.

34. For this concept see Manfred Tafuri, *Ricerca del rinascimento: principi, città, architetti* (Turin: Einaudi, 1992).

35. Smith, *Architecture in the Culture of Early Humanism*, p. 100.

36. Charles R. Mack informs us that after working for Nicholas V, Alberti left papal service after the election of Calixtus III in 1455, but resumed his Vatican career with the accession of this Piccolomini pope, Pius II. See *Pienza: The Creation of a Renaissance City* (Ithaca and London: Cornell University Press, 1987), p. 36.

37. *Memoirs of a Renaissance Pope: The Commentaries of Pius II*, translated by Florence A. Gragg (New York: Carpricorn Books, 1962), p. 102.

38. *Ibid.*, pp. 288–9.

39. *Ibid.*, p. 289.

40. *Filarete's Treatise on Architecture*, Vol. 1, p. 25; the original reads: 'Di questo non bisogna dubitare, avendo l'attitudine del fiume a condurre il legname della montagna . . . perché non gli è troppo di lunga. . . . Hai veduto il sito. Credo come a me ancora a te debba piacere, e spezialmente sendo posta detta valle sotto buona aire, e fertile e abbondante. . . . Io voglio mediante il potere dell'antedetto edificare questa città' (Filarete, *Trattato*, pp. 59–60).

41. *Filarete's Treatise on Architecture*, Vol. 1, p. 229. This comes in a section on salaries for masters 'in every branch of knowledge and every skill', necessary for a training institution for the young. See pp. 228–9.

42. *Ibid.*, pp. 40–1.

43. John Ruskin, *The Stones of Venice*, 2nd edn (London: Smith, Elder and Co., 1867), Vol. 2, p. 165.

44. *Filarete's Treatise on Architecture*, Vol. 1, pp. 41–2.

45. *Ibid.*, p. 75, fn. 10.

46. *Ibid.*, pp. 74–5.

47. Ruskin, *Stones*, p. 163.

48. William Morris, from a lecture entitled 'The Lesser Arts', G. D. H. Cole (ed.), *Selected Writing: Centenary Edition* (London: Nonesuch Press, 1948), p. 496.

49. William Morris, *News from Nowhere: Or an Epoch of Rest, Being Some Chapters from a Utopian Romance*, 5th edn (London, New York and Bombay: Longmans, Green and Co., 1897), p. 237.

50. *Ibid.*, pp. 24–5.

51. *Filarete's Treatise on Architecture*, Vol. 1, p. 129.

52. D. H. Lawrence, 'Nottingham and the Mining Countryside', in *Phoenix: The Posthumous Papers of D. H. Lawrence* (London: Heinemann, 1936), pp. 133–40. (All quotations from Lawrence given here are taken from this essay.)

53. Asa Briggs, 'The Thinking Behind Britain's New Universities', *Architectural Review*, Vol. 134 (October 1963), p. 233.

54. John Maule McKean, 'University of Essex: Case Study', *Architects' Journal*, 20 September, p. 643.

55. Joseph Rykwert, 'Universities as Institutional Archetypes of Our Age', *Zodiac*, 18 (1968), p. 61.

56. *Ibid.*, pp. 61–2.

57. The judgement comes from Tony Birks, *Building the New Universities* (Newton Abbot, Devon: David and Charles, 1972), p. 26.

58. McKean, 'University of Essex', p. 648.

59. *Colchester Express*, 17 December 1964; quoted in McKean, 'University of Essex', p. 654.

60. McKean, 'University of Essex', p. 640.

61. C. K. Capon, the chief architect of the University of Essex, made this comparison, even if with the caveat that 'the scale is completely different'. Quoted in McKean, 'University of Essex', p. 647.

62. Albert Sloman, *A University in the Making* (London: BBC, 1964), p. 50.

63. *Ibid.*, p. 10.

64. Sloman, quoted in McKean, 'University of Essex', p. 643.
65. Birks, *New Universities*, p. 97.
66. McKean, 'University of Essex', p. 647.
67. *Filarete's Treatise on Architecture*, Vol. 1, p. 25.

# CHAPTER 4

# 'WHEN THE KISSING HAD TO STOP'

## EIGHTEENTH-CENTURY VENICE – APOTHEOSIS OR DECLINE?

As for Venice and its people, merely born to bloom and drop,
Here on earth they bore their fruitage, mirth and folly were the crop:
What of soul was left, I wonder, when the kissing had to stop?
                                    Robert Browning, 'A Toccata of Galuppi's'

Like all living myths, that of eighteenth-century Venice is ambivalent, its waterbound houses functioning alternately in the collective mind as figures of decadence and death, and as signs of life, fulfilment and the birth of the future. Even the historiography of eighteenth-century Venice bears the mark of this ambivalence: an interpretation of a moribund or 'tired' society abandoning its city to the army of Napoleon, who quickly barters it away by treaty to Austria, currently giving way to an analysis of the period as the culmination of a long phase of peace, and a great age not only for art but also for intensely achieved and often fantastical forms of life itself.

If we were to hold exclusively to this latter viewpoint, the earlier 'decadence' theory would have to be discarded, on the grounds that it referred to no inherent reality of the place, but merely to a rationalization projected back in time from the city's easy conquest by the French (a moralistic and moralizing French of a new and violent age at that; not remotely *au fait* with the arts of peace, nor, certainly, its art *forms* – though in the aftermath of conquest they were not above making off with quite a few splendid productions of earlier ages of Venetian painting, as well as the bronze horses of San Marco). After Venice's collapse as a republic, the chief early proponent of the viewpoint that her decay and decadence had been the key contributory factors was Count Paul Daru, one of Napoleon's staff officers. In the years immediately succeeding his hero's fall Daru compiled a compendious history of Venice, highly critical of her eighteenth-century

171

stratagems for remaining a mere spectator of world events, of the kind in which she had previously been a principal player: 'isolated amid her fellow-nations, imperturbable in her indifference, blind to her own interests, insensible to insults, she sacrifices all to the single object of giving no offence to other states, and to preserve a lasting peace'.[1]

What the blaming of Venice for her failure to become more involved in world events tends to underestimate is how far those international power politics had themselves now moved beyond their previous Mediterranean sites into spheres such as the Atlantic, with the New World on its yonder margin, or else transalpine Europe as far as Russia; in both of which a mere Adriatic city republic, no matter what its previous land and sea power when the world itself was smaller, could never seek to be a major player. Venice's former power was by now a quantum that could only be spent, and neither stored for the future nor, certainly, augmented in these changed times, in which the world had grown while she herself had shrunk. 'Venice, like everything else which has a phenomenal existence, is subject to decline,' Goethe had wisely opined ten years before her eventual conquest and subjugation.[2]

With only occasional regret for former glory – and certainly displaying less shame than moralizing outsiders wished upon her – Venice tries one last triumph: to live off inner resources, in a perpetuation of her carnival instinct and mode; in short, nothing less than a carnivalization of her very identity as a place and as a state of reality. More will be said about this turning towards an apotheosis of herself in carnival revelries later in the chapter. Apart from all else, her critics have insufficiently considered that enriching not only the possibilities for an exuberant flourishing of art and, even more importantly, the scope for pleasure and fulfilment in the lives of her own consorted peoples, is a rarer feat in a nation than military achievement or external control over other states or subjects. Venice in this age turns all her vestigial power and reputation into an attempt to perfect (in the sense that works of art are perfected) what is already sparkling and unique in the lifestyles of her citizens, secure in the knowledge that this is no turning away from the world, because the world, as before – but *more* than ever before – is turning up to watch the performance.

In brief, Venice buys time from her funds of former power and glory for turning the arts of pleasure into the pleasures of art. More than in any other place or time, vectors of ancient custom and everyday incident in eighteenth-century Venice *converge on art*, in a host of forms: indeed, Venetian life itself in this period often seems fraught with the 'perfectibility' of narrative, of drama, of design, of colour. Even artists of no great talent such as Gabriel Bella are engrossed in recording holidays and events in the so-called *vita quotidiana* of the city. The list of what he paints seems to know no end: entertainments by the 'zanies' in the Piazza San Marco; tightrope walkers; processions on the feast day of Corpus Domini; the crowning of a doge at the top of the 'Staircase of the Giants' leading into the ducal palace; the chasing of bulls in the courtyard of said palazzo; judgements of malefactors in the Criminal Court of the 'Quaranttia' (Forty); the Counsel of Ten; the Maggior Consiglio (Major Counsel); the newly paved bridgeway over the Riva degli Schiavoni; the women's regatta on the Grand Canal; gondalas bearing courtesans rowed in a water parade along the Rio della Sensa (see Plate 4); bear chases in the Campo Sant'Angelo; the traditional fight with wooden staffs on the bridge of Santa Fosca between Venetians of the Nicolotti district and those of the Castellani; indoor racquet games; outdoor football games; the stage and lighting of the Theatre San Samuele, one of the seven major theatres of the city; the social centre and public gaming house called the Ridotto, larger and more important than the many private ridottos and casinos until it was eventually closed in the year 1774; the drawing of numbers in the public lottery; masquers on the last day of carnival in St Mark's Square; the racing regatta on the Grand Canal of the island of Murano; and tens of other of these 'naive' paintings (sixty-nine in total in the collection, now in the Fondazione Querini Stampalia).[3]

We need, by contrast with both the old or the new theories, to work out how these two main accounts of Venice in the eighteenth century – a city inexorably dying, and yet also never before or since so vividly alive – are only in apparent contradiction: although they may seem to be mutually exclusive hypotheses, they are in fact both true. The trick is to attend equally to the two co-present aspects of a single reality, each located at the heart of the other, even if often in hidden ways. Only by understanding this very strong factor of ambivalence will the Venice which, established deeper even than history, from the realms of myth continues to play so important a role in nineteenth- and twentieth-century European culture begin to make sense to us.

For without a doubt, the vitality of eighteenth-century Venice in our imagination and collective memory pertains precisely to its power to

symbolize life and death in equal measure: in short, to its completeness
as an image of human reality and of the intensity of the great European
turning point, the birth of modernity, consequent upon the decline and
eventual death of the *ancien régime*. Eighteenth-century works of art
and literature have themselves nourished this image so powerfully that
we see the city itself through them to this day, while at the same time
projecting our own fantasies or else our endless questioning back into
the lustrous works. Many of these works are at first unreadable, even
when replete with the characteristics of social documents: we see the
carnival and the famous gaming house, the Ridotto, but the people are
hidden behind masks or seemingly derealized by the backdrop of what
has become, in our mind's eye, the immemorial beauty of the place,
linking melancholy to vitality. Only a form of interpretation able to
penetrate beneath the masked surfaces of faces and social custom, as
though by a process of historical X-ray, will tell some of all that we wish
to know. Although a tall order, such an interpretation is what is
attempted here.

Earlier centuries of the Venetian Republic were undoubtedly its days
of grandeur, but it had only become a permanent 'place of memory'
from the social and historical moment when the beauty of its buildings
and canals served as a backdrop to a human universe which, whether at
work or at play, had relegated its figures of authority in favour of the
principle of pleasure. There is a carnivalization of life forms not
unrelated to Venice's actual carnival season, which lasted half of each
year and sometimes more: from October to Christmas, then from
Twelfth Night to the beginning of Lent; starting again for two weeks on
Ascension Day, another two on St Mark's Day, and always at the
election of a new Doge or Procurator (or even upon other, more minor
pretexts).[4] It is for this reason above all that most mythic representation
of Venice locates it in an eternal eighteenth century. For example, when
Byron in *Childe Harold's Pilgrimage* contemplates 'her palaces . . .
crumbling to the shore', less than a generation after her actual moment
of 'submission' – which, interestingly from the point of view of Byron's
own and his various heroes' vitalistic lifestyle, he saw as wringing from
her 'an infamous repose' – he talks momentously of the passing of
'thirteen hundred years of freedom'. Most of his images and evocations
of her life are not so historically composite or long-sighted, however,
but come straight from the age before Napoleon (and hence himself),
when to Byron's view of things Venice stood alone as 'the pleasant place

of all festivity,/ The revel of the earth, the masque of Italy!'[5] This myth of Venice as the site of masked festivity and revels is elaborated by the likes of Byron not long after the fall of the Republic, and progressively added to until our own times, mainly, I would argue, by means and in terms of eighteenth-century evocations, and largely *in place of* history, which it first simplifies, and then exaggerates.

Even the modern commercial promotion of Venice as 'heritage culture', as a museum of its own past, has for the last two hundred years projected a primarily eighteenth-century image of the place. If Joseph Brodsky was right to critique this terminology somewhat in his claim that the city 'doesn't qualify to be a museum, being itself a work of art, the greatest masterpiece our species produced',[6] then we certainly owe ourselves more by way of interpretation of the period in which the enduring form of the masterpiece was accomplished and a seal set on major further change. Brodsky's own essayistic impressions are one kind of interpretative engagement, in his case so focused on traces from the past operating within the present that there is no room in the Venice thus described for the future: 'If this place is reality (or, as some claim, the past), then the future with all its aliases is excluded from it.'[7]

But maybe the conditions Brodsky is defining here had already been reached in the eighteenth century itself. Venice was after all living its then present so intensively, and was so aware of and formed by rituals from its past that questions of its future may not have been a major consideration. The possibility, indeed, that it might not even have a significant future was perhaps not faced, since the emphasis was on repetition of itself within realms of artistic representation, as if seeking some consummate simulacrum of all that it had been. We are talking here in relative terms, of course, since in some basic senses the immediate future, whatever its current 'aliases', is never wholly excluded from the imagination. This notion that Venetians could not imagine a future, or different worlds than their own, will in any case be returned to at the chapter's close, and some major revisions to it canvassed.

An argument had run throughout the long decades of peace as to how far Venice ought to rearm herself, in particular re-equip and augment her naval strengths. But factors of inertia had won out over the few voices in favour of renewal, thus rather tending to confirm the thesis that the future was for the most part occluded, rendered unimaginable in the long carnivalization of the present. In particular, as Michael Levey pointed out as early as 1955, 'Painting offered one convenient and secure retreat, not so much from the present but from the future.' And he went on to support this idea of a recoil from the future with the revealing detail that 'in the secret instructions drawn up in 1786 for the French ambassador to the Republic there occurred the significant remark that for some years past there had reigned at Venice "une sorte de terreur de l'avenir" '.[8]

By the time of Canaletto, Guardi, Longhi and the younger Tiepolo, the social customs and ceremonies of Venice had a long history, and painters' representations of them showed awareness not only of their antiquity, but sometimes even of a certain creaky antiquarianism about them. Thanks to those artists and to the playwright Goldoni, the sensualist Casanova and the librettist and autobiographer Da Ponte, these dying years of the Venetian Republic set the stage for its new life in the European literature and imagination of the nineteenth and twentieth centuries, as a dominant symbol of eighteenth-century Italy as a whole, and, in fact, of the Europe of the pre-Revolutionary moment and the violently ambivalent events which followed it. It is as if Italy's very marginality in relation to France, combined with its passionate interest and involvement in the great events, gave it a privileged role in embodying the Europe-wide character of that spectacular inauguration of political and social changes which are still occurring today. The gaze of today's egalitarian sensibility does not condemn the luxuriousness of eighteenth-century Venice – that wasteful expenditure of the dying upper classes, which provided the substance from which our collective images are made. The masks and revels, the district pastimes, the street scenes and the pastoral idylls set in the landscape and villas of the Veneto depict close contact between the social classes from a perspective which is often morally and socially critical, but takes for granted the right of all to freedom and pleasure. The resplendent colour of the paintings and the hedonistic brilliance of the literary works seem in league with our collective memory's obstinate selection of the eighteenth century's non-authoritarian aspirations rather than its terrifying, corrupt and sordid aspects.

Furthermore, our modern historical gaze readily sees Venice of the last century of the Republic as 'a seductive maritime playground', a kind of 'eighteenth-century equivalent of Las Vegas' – though admitting intellectual and artistic pursuits which render the latter comparison less apt the more it is reflected upon. (A minor irony of such a comparison is that a recently reopened hotel, casino and shopping mall in Las Vegas itself, called the Venetian, has as its centrepiece a recreated 'Venice', complete with canals, gondolas and replicas of key Venetian locations – all set amidst skyscraper hotels, in a neon-lit landscape of typical American multi-lane highways!) If there is some extraordinary truth in our claiming Venice to have become 'by 1700 . . . the pleasure capital of Europe',[9] and for the next hundred years the prime context for forms of sensual, artistic and intellectual pleasure which massively predetermined their modern Western configurations, then we surely need to understand better this particular place and historical moment. All the more so as contemporary Venetians took great pains to document the pleasures of which they partook.

The notion of lives being quite self-consciously conducted with the panache of drama can be best exemplified in actual incidents from the memoirs of Casanova and, in the following Venetian generation, of his young friend Lorenzo Da Ponte. We might recall here in passing that not only was Casanova a living latter-day example of the Don Juan of legend but he also actually lent a small hand to Mozart and Da Ponte in the devising of the libretto for *Don Giovanni* in 1787 in Prague. The work is hence, although based on legend, conceivably resourced in spirit directly from the lives of those involved in writing the new version of the old story. (There is in consequence a profound appropriacy in Joseph Losey's having situated his film version of the opera not in the Spain of Mozart's hypothetical setting, but in the Veneto of Casanova's and Da Ponte's own early amorous adventures; the same Venice, furthermore, that Mozart himself had visited with his father, and performed in as a young adolescent star.)

Casanova – perhaps the century's most renowned sensualist and pleasure-seeker – was able to meditate astringently on the peculiar dichotomy between state authority on the one hand and individual licence on the other. Crucially, he defines Venice as 'a city where the policy of the government is only too willing to let libertinism serve as a mere sketch of the liberty which ought to reign there' ('une ville où la politique du gouvernement tolère volontiers le libertinage comme esquisse de la liberté individuelle qui devrait y exister').[10] This is an extraordinary notion. Casanova would seem to be suggesting that not only is libertinism like his own morally acceptable, but that it is the first stage (*une esquisse*) towards the realization of a far wider political liberty, which the city's ruling classes ought to promote. In the light of so much Venetian art of the period which concentrates on unbounded pleasure, it is revealing that Casanova used words based on an elemental art form, that of the sketch, in making this point. His analogy would seem to be that libertinage relates to liberty (is no less fundamental to its eventual realization, that is to say) just as the sketch does to an eventual, more fully painted reality.

That the Republic of Venice's echelons of government were highly authoritarian might seem at first to undermine Casanova's claim. But its authority tended to focus almost exclusively on what it interpreted as potentially threatening its overthrow (such as Jacobinism in the final years). Casanova was right to stress that rituals of pleasure were anything but frowned upon by the state, its policy seemingly a classic instance of giving the people their bread and circuses, which, in the case of Venice, meant its carnival. Yet always beneath the visible pleasures was a sense that a grim reality might lurk – much as in an early example from Casanova's own memoirs, where he comes across the awful living quarters of the current woman he has been pursuing and is thereafter forever repulsed by her.[11]

In politics, how grim really was the reality of the Venetian state beneath the façade of its rituals of splendour? Despite the persistence of grisly stories of Venice's State Inquisition, actual instances of political tyranny over its own subjects were now relatively few. Napoleon in his ultimata to the Venetian state threatens to overthrow it if it does not institute principles of liberty along Revolutionary lines. But by this stage only one political prisoner remained in its notorious *pozzi*, and although far from 'free' in anything like a modern (that is, post-Revolutionary) sense, its citizenry had long been living under more relaxed controls, in this *ancien régime* oligarchy, whose very organs of repression had become rusty from lack of use.

Not many years before, in the early maturity of Casanova, the sway of state authority was very real, and much to be feared. Casanova himself gives us some acute insight into its workings. Indeed, our best narrative instance of this earlier period of Venetian state tyranny is the episode of his memoirs in which he escapes from the republic's prisons, known as *i piombi* ('the Leads') for their position directly beneath the sheet-lead roofing of the Ducal Palace. Under duress of imprisonment in the Leads, Casanova's bewildered turn towards philosophy confirms how far Enlightenment thought pervaded the very atmosphere of the Europe which he had already so traversed during the first thirty years of his life (1725–55):

*Plate 1* The Sala dei Nove in the Palazzo Pubblico, Siena, seat of government under the 'Nine', whose rule lasted from 1287 to 1355. The walls were frescoed in the 1330s by Ambrogio Lorenzetti, with representations of good and bad government. These were intended as encouraging and warning instances to the nine governors of the starkly different potential outcomes of their actions. The effect of the frescoes needed to be immediate, since composition of the Nine changed every two months. (See pages 53–60.) Photo: ©Antonio Quattrone, Florence. Reproduced by permission of the Comune di Siena.

*Plate 2* Sala dei Nove, Siena. Wall of *malgoverno* (bad government) by Lorenzetti. Note in particular the vice of 'Division' with her attribute, a saw. Clad in a tunic which is half black and half white, with 'yes' inscribed on one side and 'no' on the other, she is a representation of something much feared by Dante and others of the period – the divided city. (See pages 57–8.) Photo: © Lensini, Siena. Reproduced by permission of the Comune di Siena.

Plate 3  Vittore Carpaccio, *Two Venetian Ladies on a Balcony, c.* 1493/1500, now demonstrated to have been cut from a larger panel, the upper portion of which depicts men hunting in boats on the Venetian lagoon. It is hard to read the two women's facial expressions with any certainty, as they enigmatically stare into a space beyond. However, their melancholy gazes seem to bear out some of Boccaccio's accounts, from a century and a half earlier, of the restricted lifestyles of women. (See pages 92–3.) Reproduced by permission of Museo Correr, Venice.

Plate 4  Gabriel Bella, *Courtesans Rowed in a Water Parade along the Rio della Sensa in Venice.* From a collection of sixty-nine such paintings by Bella of festivals, customs and incidents of everyday Venetian life. (See page 173.) Reproduced by permission of the Fondazione Querini Stampalia, Venice.

*Plate 5* Francesco Guardi, *Launch of Balloon over Giudecca Canal*, Venice 1784. Although this painting is in other respects from the traditional view-painting genre, the balloon signals a truly 'new' world of the future, captured here in the process of being born. (See pages 193–4.) Photo: Jörg P. Anders. Reproduced by permission of the Staatliche Museen zu Berlin – Preußischer Kulturbesitz Gemäldegalerie. Eigentum des Kaiser-Friedrich-Museums-Vereins.

*Plate 6* Giandomenico Tiepolo, *Il Nuovo Mondo (The New World)*, fresco originally painted in 1791 for Tiepolo's family villa at Zianigo. This is perhaps the most important single art work indicating awareness on the part of Venetians of a world beyond their own (quite how extensive it would be hard to estimate), during the very years of the city's decline as an independent republic. (See pages 194–9.) Photo: Osvaldo Böhm. Reproduced by permission of the Museo del Settecento Veneziano.

*Plate 7* *Tosca* as TV. Catherine Malfitano as Tosca, in her suicidal leap, and Placido Domingo as the painter Cavaradossi, savouring his last moments of life before execution. This TV version was beamed live in 1992 to 107 countries, from the real locations in Rome of the opera's three separate acts, and at the actual times of day of its 'Aristotelian' unfolding. The significance of Rome itself, not in religious terms, but as a focus of the binding secular experience of the modern age – television – was enhanced by this operatic production. (See pages 217–21.) Photos: pre-production stills reproduced by permission of Rada Films, Rome.

Within the illuminated image, manuscript text reads:

Patre nostro che nei cieli stai
non circunscripto: ma per piu amore
chai primi effecti di la su tu hai
Laudato sia il tuo nome el tuo ualore
da ogni creatura: come e degno
di render gratie al tuo dolcie uapore
Vegnia uer noi la pace del tuo regno
che noi ad essa non potem da noi
seila non uien contutto nostro ingegno

*Plate 8* Fifteenth-century illumination, attributed to Franco dei Russi, of Dante on the ledge of pride in Purgatory, from Federico Da Montefeltro's copy of Dante's *Commedia*. Dante's explanation of these sculpted depictions of pride and humility is that, because they are produced by God, they surpass the 'limit conditions' of the art form in question. Considered retrospectively, Dante's account of them anticipates the moving and speaking images of cinema – more specifically, Eisenstein's notions about the workings of 'montage' – by hundreds of years. (See pages 232–7.) Reproduced by permission of the Biblioteca Apostolica Vaticana, Rome.

*Plate 9* Anonymous fifteenth-century fresco of the *Triumph of Death*, in the National Gallery of Sicily. The work depicts figures of the powerful (merchants, churchmen, rich youths) lying dead under hoof, or pierced by the arrows of skeletal Death on his equally skeletal horse. What can we surmise about the moral viewpoint of the pair on the left usually identified as the painter and his assistant – the only two figures in the painting watching us, as we look at it? Or the poor, huddled in a corner of the image, and significantly not undone by Death? (See pages 261–4.) Photo: Publifoto, Palermo. Reproduced by permission of the Galleria Nazionale di Sicilia.

*Plate 10*  Lorenzo Da Ponte in old age in the USA. As one of Mozart's librettists in Vienna, Da Ponte had been co-creator of three operatic masterpieces in the 1780s: *The Marriage of Figaro, Don Giovanni* and *Così fan tutte*. After several years in London, he emigrated to America in 1805, where in 1825 he became the first professor of Italian at Columbia College (now University), having also worked as a grocer, bookseller, boarding-house keeper and teacher of Italian. (See pages 298–306.) Photo: Nicholas B. Wood. Reproduced by permission of the owners.

I realized that I was in a place where if the false seemed true, realities must seem dreams; where the understanding must lose half of its privileges; where a distorted imagination must make reason the victim either of chimerical hopes or terrible despair. I at once put myself on guard against anything of that nature; and at the age of thirty years I for the first time in my life turned for help to philosophy, all the germs of which were in my soul and which I had never before had occasion either to value or to employ. I believe that the great majority of men die without ever having thought.

Precipitated thus into an embodiment of the Enlightenment thinker, it is but a short step for this low-born son of an actor and actress (who has always harboured rancorous thoughts against the aristocracy, while also arrogating to himself many of their lifestyle pleasures) to foment in his own mind a scenario of revolution in which he takes a leading role: 'I seemed to be leading the people to exterminate the government and massacre the aristocrats; everything was to be brought to dust; I was not satisfied to leave the slaughter of my oppressors to executioners, it was I myself who should massacre them.'[12] What is important for us to bear in mind is how this particular literary narrative, written, admittedly, much later in the century – Casanova had published incidents of his life in earlier decades, but the full *History* was only begun in the first year of the French Revolution, 1789 – locates imaginary revolution (its details clearly borrowed from recent events in Paris at the time of writing) in his own version of a fustian *opera buffa ancien régime* tyranny of Venice.

If not earlier, Venice's state authorities had indeed become a set of buffos by their fall. They are accused of a kind of monstrous secrecy, in the propaganda and threats against them by Napoleon's revolutionary forces. But the reality by 1796 was considerably less tyrannical. Consider, for instance, how widely available in the Venice of these times was 'secrecy' for the individual citizen – what we should today regard as forms of privacy. In this, Venice is to be distinguished even from its subject territories. One of Lorenzo Da Ponte's earliest amorous intrigues was with a Neapolitan beauty, making escape from the perils waylaying her sex and station in her place of upbringing. She flies northwards through Rome and Florence and eventually reaches Padua. But even here she does not feel safe: only in Venice does it seem possible – importantly, because of social custom – to mask and disguise herself sufficiently to ensure her safety: 'Sembrandomi dunque il soggiorno di Padova pericoloso, risolvemmo d'andare a Venezia, dove l'uso della

maschera era comunissimo, onde m'era più facile nascondermi. Mi
procurai per maggior precauzione un abito da uomo . . .', 'Further stay
in Padua appearing perilous to me, we resolved on Venice, where the use
of masks is so common that it would be easier to hide. As a further
precaution I procured a suit of male garments . . .'[13]

On this specific matter of masks, a curious transposition between art
and life is at work from at least as early as the mid-century. The famous
and widely recognizable character masks of the traditional *commedia
dell'arte* theatre were being discarded, by Goldoni in particular, in
reforms which favoured increasingly realistic situations and progressively less type-casting of character; while at the same time, in the actual
streets and alleys and waterways of Venice the wearing of masks – the
simple bauta for men or the round domino for women – had become
standard apparel, at least among the upper classes. So we have the
phenomenon that whereas the middle- and low-class characters of
comedy have thrown off their masks, and a greater realism ensues, the
dying aristocracy clings to and even increases its use of masks in the
ordinary streets and waterways of Venice.

In spite of Goldoni's reforms of the theatre, his plays set in open
Venetian spaces, such as the tiny domestic square of *Il Campiello*, or in
fishing towns of the lagoon such as the Chioggia of *Le Baruffe
chiozzotte*, are, it must be said, deeply conservative, insofar as they seek
to see the everyday quarrels of common people's lives brought back to
tranquillity; not unlike the passing of squally weather in the lagoon itself
and the return of lapping seas. In the edition of *Le Baruffe chiozzotte* of
1774 we have, for example, an illustration of a *campiello* in Chioggia
filled with men and women in extreme uproar, the men flailing about
with sticks and long daggers. But it seems that in Goldonian comedy of
this kind the remote spectre of social unrest is being raised precisely in
order that its containment at the play's ending may be the more
appreciable for the audience. The very fact that the unrest is so limited
in location – the stage represents a small square around which a mere
handful of people of the same families and class interact (they are all
fisherfolk) – is Goldoni's way of blunting any political potential in the
lives described with the notion that scuffles and imbalances are self-
correcting. The message is that these broils (*baruffe*) arise from the high
spirits of human nature – petty loves and jealousies, envies and domestic
disputes – and not from anything profoundly amiss in the politics or

**Figure 5** Illustration of brawls among townsfolk in Chioggia (across the lagoon from Venice), from a 1774 edition of Goldoni's plays. Goldoni represents Venice and its region with a spirited attention to customs and to the behaviours of differing classes. But his plays, especially those in dialect, in no sense call for radical change, shot through as they are with a conservative love of the world depicted. Even brawls such as represented here are a theatre of catharsis, staving off rather than calling for social reform.

economics of the particular time and place. Neither society in a more generalized sense, nor certainly the state, is ever in question.

And yet in spite of their profound social conservatism – or else because of it, some would no doubt claim – the plays' concern with issues of the happiness and wellbeing of the characters is not only real on Goldoni's part, but a very deep-running vein in the life and language of the dramas. If at a play's ending any slight novelty has come to pass, such as Gasparina's decision in *Il campiello* to leave Venice for ever and go south to the Neapolitan lands of her new husband Count Astolfi (a rise from the status of commoner and of merely aspiring to be a lady at the play's opening, into the actual ranks of the minor nobility), the representation tends not to underscore change as such, but rather continuity, in the way that Venice itself is addressed by Gasparina in dialect verse just before the curtain falls:

> Cara la mia Venezia
> me dezpiazerà certo de lazzarla;
> ma prima de andar via, vôi zaludarla.
> Bondì Venezia cara,
> bondì Venezia mia,
> veneziani zioria.
> Bondì caro campiello:
> no dirò che ti zii brutto, né bello.
> Ze brutto ti zé ztà, mi me dezpiaze:
> no zé bel quel ch'è bel, ma quel che piaze.[14]

Venice, farewell. My dear, dear Venice, fare thee well. Farewell, good Venetians. And you, my campiello – my noisy, beautiful campiello – you I shall never forget. For yours is the only true beauty – the beauty of happy memories – of happy, happy days.[15]

Gasparina's lover's penultimate speech to the assembled company had called for general enjoyment, both because it is in any case carnival time (the play, like so many of Goldoni's, was written to be performed to celebrate the end of carnival), and because by the following morning he and Gasparina will be leaving Venice for good. Goldoni himself was to depart for ever from Venice six years later, to take up a minor sinecure offered him by the French king as director of the Comédie Italienne in Paris, where he died in impoverished circumstances in the early years of the Revolution. Along with so many other unintended errors of those violent times, his pension, royally granted, had been cut off – along with the king's own head, as it were. The error was corrected, but by the time the pension had been restored Goldoni was dead. In the light of this thumbnail sketch of Goldoni's own last years, we cannot help responding to Gasparina's touching farewell as a kind of *aubade* by the dramatist to the Venice he was relatively soon to leave. We might even suppose that there is a suggestion in Gasparina's farewell that it is not only people who are leaving Venice, but Venice itself that is passing from history in these most loved of forms, distilled for ever only in the theatre. The closing speeches of the play suggest that the best times are already over, or at any rate about to be, once the carnival season finishes, and that even the most Venice-loving of Venetians leave for near or far parts of terra firma.

In spite of its chronic conservatism, we cannot help being moved by the deep attachment of this evolving drama to the overall Venetian context that has been the setting and also a kind of beloved character in its own right. What the quoted English translation does not perfectly capture is the complex nature of Gasparina's formulation in her last two lines, which, because it is relevant to the argument in hand, needs to be reformulated. She is trying to say something like the following to the tiny *campiello* or square, which is at once the setting and the subject of the play: 'I cannot say that you are either ugly or beautiful. If you are indeed ugly, it saddens me. But beauty must be defined not by what is beautiful, but what gives pleasure.' Basing our own speculative judgement on a statement such as that, we might hazard the following hypothesis. Although ever-more foreign visitors were flocking to Venice for its renowned beauty (and, incidentally, buying up view paintings of Venice by the likes of Canaletto and his followers on a scale such as the Venetians themselves never did), in the hearts and minds of its resident citizens there was something more profoundly beautiful about Venice than the mere look of the place; something – an essence of its social charms as it were, taken together with the always intimate material settings of this waterbound city – implicit to the happiness of its people. The beauty of a place can only be measured in terms of such happiness: *this* is what his play seems to be implying in those lines about Gasparina's (and Goldoni's) beloved Venice.

Plainly such political conservatism, which rests its case on a quite skilful representation of happiness, and in the process utterly occludes any real consideration of politics or society in more precisely historicized senses, borders on complacency. Goldoni's very defenders have traditionally been in the business of praising him for making dramas in which very little happens. This critical defence of them can even be said to have been set in motion by Goldoni himself. In his brief Introduction to the Reader in the printed edition of *Il campiello*, for instance, he expresses innocent surprise at the widespread success of such works:

> Questa è una di quelle Commedie che soglio preparare per gli ultimi giorni di Carnovale, sendo più atte in tal tempo a divertire il popolo che corre affollatamente al Teatro. L'azione di questa Commedia è semplicissima, l'intreccio è di poco impegno, e la peripezia non è interessante; ma ad onta di tutto ciò, ella è stata fortunatissima sulle scene in Venezia non solo, ma con mia sorpresa in Milano. . . . La mia meraviglia fu grande.

> This is a comedy of the kind I am in the habit of preparing for the last days of Carnival, a time when such works are more liable to amuse the people who flock to the theatre. The action of the play is of the utmost simplicity, its plot of little difficulty, and the conclusion uninteresting. But in spite of that, it was a great success on the stages not only of Venice, but to my great surprise of Milan. . . . I truly marvelled at its success.

If we do not marvel to the same degree, it is because we surmise that the popularity of the play to contemporary Venetians resided precisely in its not threatening them with notions of change or development in the fundamentals of their social existence. Plainly the flip-side of the popularity of this Goldonian drama, in which very little of consequence happens, is that these are essentially stagnant pieces – flattering dramatic mirrors of the essentially static lifestyles of their audience – which baulk at any deeper inspection of endemic social malaise, and do not pursue actions so far or in such a way as to treat the possibility of economic and political abuse of one class by another.

Admittedly, the servant classes in those Goldonian comedies which include a bourgeoisie or minor nobility are abominably ordered about. But the very pettiness of their masters' and mistresses' obsessions suggest that these small-time upper-classes of the local *ancien régime*, though still in positions of command, are no longer able to do real harm to the classes below them. They are more likely on account of their many inanities to injure themselves, possibly by pursuing the over-whelming futility of their lifestyle beyond decline, to fall and eventual extinction as a class. However, even extrapolating conclusions as radical as that from the gentle satire of Goldoni's actions is rather more than they themselves explicitly do. Oddly, criticism of Goldoni along the lines I am pursuing is surprisingly rare. More frequently the plays are admired for much the same reason that the main genre painters such as Pietro Longhi are; for their unthreatening representation of lived realities among the mixture of social classes in Venice.

Such a concentration on achievement, and on the colours of art steeping and hence masking the fallibilities of life, to the exclusion of warnings that Venice was in severe decline, clearly amounts to a falsification. For there *was* decadence aplenty in the last century of the Republic, attested at the time and *not* just projected back as *post hoc* Napoleonic justification for conquest. Venice's long-lasting neutrality, conducted by her still legendary diplomats at key points on the changing map of military campaigns, was a conscious ducking and weaving policy undertaken to preserve her independence from conquest in a Europe some of whose other states had grown vastly more powerful than her, and at a time when her own strength was in steady decline, especially if judged by previous centuries' performance. If we consider, for instance, the public relation of Venice's ambassadors who had attended the coronation in Britain of George III in 1763, it reads like a list of all the benefits this powerful north-west European nation state rejoiced in, and that were now denied Venice:

> Considering what are the causes of the movement and prosperity of so great a volume of trade by that nation, it will be easily seen that its very situation, so opportune for navigation, the nature of its fertile soil and many rich resources, the extent of its crown dominions, and its connections with many fruitful countries of America, Asia and Africa, created the bases of a very extensive and most active trade. Its relations with countries to its north and west prove how well situated it is, and its important holdings of Gibraltar and Minorca facilitate on its part a lively trade in the Mediterranean.[16]

The envy that can be imagined in the Venetian council on hearing such a report (far more extensive than I have quoted here) is almost palpable. If there is some criticism of England's complex economic levers for using its 'sink fund' and for balancing its national debt – 'they have cost the nation a portion of her liberty' – nonetheless the perception is that it is the very use of such a system of national financing which has 'allowed that government to provide in time for the immense expenses of her wars, maintain always the living conditions of those who contribute, and preserve undamaged her commercial activities'.[17] What is impressive here is the intricate and subtle balancing of positives and negatives that these economic analyses of another European nation display, and of precisely the kind of nation which had comprehensively outstripped Venice in political and economic terms, and which had enjoyed vast colonial expansion in the very period of the seventeenth and eighteenth centuries when Venice's sea power had been shrinking inexorably back to the lagoon itself, and, on land, to a notably diminished tract of her former holdings.

Many of Venice's decisions regarding her own policy, conducted in the very same public relations and debates, reveal a desperate clinging to the status quo, for fear of something still worse; or else an internal demonization of one particular minority, the Jews of the Ghetto, for what is perceived to be their dominance in economic affairs to the detriment of others. In the particular debates over the ten-yearly renewal of the Jews' charter of rights (the so-called *Ricondotta degli ebrei*) in 1776, for instance, the 'anti-Semitic' faction of the Maggior Consiglio, led by the rising figure of the Procurator, Andrea Tron, even implies that in spite of hundreds of years of residence the Jews of Venice are not Venetians. It takes another, more 'enlightened', member of the Counsel, Girolamo Ascanio Molin, to assert not simply the duration of the Jewish community's residence in Venice but also their economic importance as investors in arts and industries, and their provision of work and sustenance to many poorer Venetians.[18]

And always there is a return to schemes for neutrality. One small instance of the latter: Venice is declaredly neutral even in a matter as distant as the war between England and her American colonies, explicitly so that she might profit in trade terms from both parties to that war.[19] In the end, however, this comprehensive neutrality in all politics between and affecting other nations, combined as it was with Venice's own by now almost ludicrous military weakness, could not save the Republic:

> Venice was on its last legs; and if most people were convinced of its immortality, the clearsighted were under no illusions. 'We have no power, neither terrestrial nor maritime. We live by chance and accident, clinging to prudence on the part of the Government of the Republic as our sole idea.' Such, already in 1780, was the diagnosis of Doge Paolo Renier: no form of redress was any longer possible. Multiple testimonies speak of a gradual and painless death, such as that of bodies undermined by sheer old age.[20]

In the same speech Doge Renier appealed for unity in tones of desperation not unlike some latter-day party hack – 'If there is a State which ever had need of unity it is this one.'[21] He had beforehand spoken of the many difficulties of the Republic, and detailed them in terms of pervasive sloth, languor and both an intellectual and bodily sluggishness in the nation. But note that in doing so he was speaking against the dangers posed by a reforming group of counsellors trying to sway opinion towards change. How familiar in our own day and age is the cast of his defence, and his sense that the only possible salvation for the state lies in achieving unity around anti-reformist positions. Having himself analysed the status quo in dire terms, in another breath it is essentially the status quo that he entreats the assembled councillors of state to cling to and conserve. It is almost as though in politics he has double-vision: the very matters which in one part of his mind bespeak Venice's dire malaise, from a different mental viewpoint come across in his grand rhetoric as the only grounds of her salvation as an aristocratic Republic. His words, and his party of supporters in council who swayed the day, are a most signal instance of persons whose insight into the ills of the present makes them less rather than more willing to risk changes for the sake of the future. We might call his insights about paralysis in social and political life in the literal sense *stunning*, since they had the effect of paralysing all possibility of effective redressive action. Above all it is interesting to note that it is no longer actions in themselves but instead an 'idea' – that of governmental prudence on the part of the long-surviving aristocratic Republic – which is seen as the rock of salvation. How to go on servicing that ideology is the point and purpose of the Doge's inevitably conservative counsels at this late point of 1780.

External visitors to the city also – by definition involved in the act of comparing what they find with their prior expectations based on its reputation – often noted Venice's decline. Joseph Addison, at the very beginning of the century, speaks of the Venetian state being 'very sensible of . . . decay in their trade'. Offering sophisticated social and economic explanations, Addison incidentally demonstrates an unsentimental English mercantilist sensibility in his ideas as to how and why Venice is losing her place:

> The duties are great that are laid on merchandizes. Their nobles think it below their quality to engage in traffic. The merchants, who are grown rich, and able to manage great dealings, buy their nobility, and generally

give over trade. Their manufactures of cloth, glass, and silk, formerly the best in Europe, are now excelled by those of other countries. They are tenacious of old laws and customs to their great prejudice, whereas a trading nation must be still for new changes and expedients, as different junctures and emergencies arise.[22]

Almost exactly a century earlier Ben Jonson, in his play set in Venice, *Volpone*, had brilliantly sent up the figure of Sir Politic Would-be, the newly arrived Englishman who thinks he has the cure for Venice's every political conundrum (spies and arsonists and the like, seeking to undermine her). Addison might in his overweening self-confidence appear to us like yet another figure of the meddling Englishman abroad. Except that, unlike the overheated imagination of Jonson's Sir Politic, there is a dreadful chill in the tones of Addison's analysis of social parvenus from the merchant class to the nobility, and of the tenacity of custom inhibiting necessary change. If part of the chill is that of the distant outsider, whose own life will not be affected if Venice should prosper or founder, the rest arises from the undeniable accuracy of the account.

Goethe, undertaking an equivalent Grand Tour eighty-five years later, is by no means so smugly superior as Addison had been, nor as persuaded of Venetian inflexibility, pointing out from the outset of his remarks a principle that the earlier Englishman certainly did not hold to: namely, that the uniqueness of Venice means that it 'can only be compared with itself'. For Addison, Venice had appeared simply another state, liable to rise or decline in proportion to the volume and successes of her external trade with others. For Goethe, Venice's uniqueness is something far more – indeed largely other – than economic in kind. Nonetheless, his sense that she can only be compared with herself leads him back in part to economic analysis, in the comparing of past with present Venice. 'This state barge', he says, for instance, of a magnificent bucentaur of an earlier age, 'is a real family heirloom, which reminds us of what the Venetians once believed themselves to be, and were.' His generous, even indulgent approach – indeed, his very tendency to read Venice in personal terms: 'This morning I visited the Arsenal. . . . It was like visiting some old family which, though past its prime, still shows signs of life' – means that a mere ten years before her fall Goethe is still constructing in his mind scenarios in which Venice is saved by the very gifts which made her: 'All that intelligence and hard work created in times past, intelligence and hard work have now to preserve.' But alas, the task was altogether beyond 'this beaver republic', as he had initially defined Venice.[23]

\* \* \* \* \*

While much of what has so far been said confirms Brodsky's notion that in Venice the future goes unreckoned, and that hence, in a sense, it does not even exist for her, the last phase of this argument looks at a curious and, to me, very exciting exception to the predominance of the past and carnivalization of the present. We follow a slender but, it would seem, definite and unbroken thread of evidence that Venice was not totally self-absorbed in its own vivid realities, or parasitically attached to its past, but on the contrary capable of excitement at the prospect of other worlds, even including the possibility that in time it too might evolve another identity.

Particular artists, mostly rather late in the period under consideration, and notably in their representations of a very particular phenomenon in the public life of Venice's squares – a mechanical device called by us a cosmorama, but rejoicing for them in the popular name of the 'new world', *il mondo nuovo* – produce, surely, ideas of a quite different philosophical cast than those so far considered; ones, furthermore, which remind us of how much Enlightenment thought was utopian, and hence *always* potentially about the birth of the future, even in a place such as Venice, otherwise so mired in its past. Here if ever, in the form of the cosmorama, was a specular device of the age of the Enlightenment capable of producing as a consequence of its exotic displays of other states and places considerations of how the present (in this instance, Venice) might be recast in some imagined future. Precisely because of the cosmorama's nature as a device for gazing into, two common terms – *distances* and *prospects* – become of immediate special importance in our discussion, and assume more than their ordinary meaning. From being merely spatial markers, they gradually take on temporal significance as well. This needs explanation.

The two terms are taken directly from the rubric to a line engraving by Gaetano Zompini, among his collection of sixty such engravings executed between 1746 and 1754, representing the common street occupations of Venetians.[24] This particular engraving shows a lantern box, into the peephole of which gazes a young boy, standing on a stool, and steadied by his mother while the owner of the device projects for his delight enlarged relief panoramas within it. As the rubric makes clear, for the cost of one soldo the contraption's owner showed the *Mondo niovo* (Venetian for *mondo nuovo*, or 'new world'), 'con dentro lontananze, e prospetive', 'in which are distances and prospects (or perspectives)'. Several important details need stressing. In discursive terms the new world, and hence the *lontananze* ('distant views') and *prospetive* ('perspectives') which comprise it, are literally *dentro*, 'inside', the device. They are images which we don't see, but which we are encouraged in this image which we *do* see, of the *boy seeing them*, to imagine as an exotic topography. In other words, they enter into *our* imaginary as viewers precisely by being indirectly represented. Already, in this first of several images of cosmoramas under consideration here, the words *lontananze* and *prospetive* take on slightly more than their technical significances, and suggest, romantically, that images of a whole 'new world' really are projected *within the device*. The distances and prospects are internal to the device, in technological terms, but in terms of the imaginary they know almost no bounds. In short, the technology of a relatively small street device mounted on trestles, and which is gazed into, becomes a means of escaping, in geographical terms, far beyond the Venice of the device's present emplacement.

The very term 'new world' has a special resonance of otherness or *différence* in terms of Venice, since the commonly denominated New World of the Americas was precisely one she had not been able to share in the colonization of, as had the Atlantic seaboard nations of Europe. We have already briefly considered how her failure to exploit the New World was one of the long-term causes of Venice's relative economic and political decline. Lacking direct access to it through the transatlantic trade routes of colonization, the reception of the New World second-hand, via just such images as those in a cosmorama, could be seen as both *faute de mieux* and a factor which raised the importance of such representations, because they were all one had. Unable, in short, literally to exploit this New World because of the greater geopolitical distance that separated her from it, its *representation* in Venice has, in consequence, less interrupted routes into the imaginary of Venetians than it might for say, people in London, Lisbon or Amsterdam, so involved as those centres of New World colonization are by now in complex transatlantic extensions of their power. As a toy

**Figure 6** Venetian engraving by Zompini of a portable cosmorama or *mondo nuovo* (new world). Cosmoramas occur in several paintings and poems of the later eighteenth-century Venice, conveying a sense of other, more exotic, past and present worlds. This may seem something of a paradox, since Venice itself – at least to non-Venetians, then as now – seems so distinctly exotic in its own right. Reproduced by permission of Fondazione Querini Stampalia, Venice.

of the Enlightenment, therefore, the cosmorama's compelling images, when deployed in a place like Venice, might well have been all the more directly utopian in kind, certainly in their workings on the mind.

Consider now another example. It is a poem of 1761 by Goldoni entitled, not surprisingly, 'Il Mondo Nuovo', which is an indulgent panegyric on the life of a young daughter of the aristocratic family, the Balbi.[25] The poem formed part of a collection of poems by various hands, which Goldoni put together and published for His Excellency Niccolò Balbi, on the occasion of one of the latter's three daughters taking the veil. The girl's life is recounted in the poem, together with the entire noble context of the Balbi household, explicitly as seen in the projections of one of these cosmoramas. In allegorical terms, the 'new world' in question is, this time, the young woman's brave if also heartrending decision to withdraw permanently from the old and known world of Venice into the convent of the Celestia. Most of the descriptions of the steps towards this decision are presented as part of the standard technology of the cosmorama's representative possibilities. But we are always aware that each scene-projection is also able to point up the element of the marvellous in the person or action represented. More than that, the standard technology of cosmoramas has, of necessity, been extended to incorporate fortune-telling. As the account of the young woman's decisions is developed, we see beyond her present act of taking the veil and into her future reception by the other nuns of the convent into their community. What can we make in historical and philosophical terms of this extension of the *mondo nuovo*'s scene-projection into the future?

Before answering this question directly, let us consider the context just a little more closely. First of all the young damsel and her companions are visited by an old retainer and gondolier of the family, a certain Pasqualin, in the convent where they are cloistered until such time as they choose either a human or a divine spouse. To amuse them he has taken this curious device (the cosmorama) which displays marvels and, 'in virtue of its crystalline optics', is able even to project flies such that they appear as horses. We are told by Goldoni that such devices are commonplace now in the public squares, especially at carnival time, and that their 'inventors' (as he calls them) are able to gather together crowds who are mad for their views of battles and ambassadors, regattas, queens and emperors. The jovial narrative proclaims that Pasqualin had already shown his cosmorama to the author to ensure that it was up to standard. Indeed, much of the poem details how Goldoni had beforehand seen represented in it the glorious past and present life of the lovely Balbi daughter, leading to the moment of her becoming a bride of Christ. In the description we have laid out for us past, present and future glimpses of the entire Balbi clan – one illustrious brother of the current paterfamilias being described as so sweet a figure that he is a 'concoction of sugar and marzipan' no less! The poetry is lightened throughout by Pasqualin's constant need of alcoholic sustenance to keep up the rhetorical flow of his panegyric.

It is my belief that those distances and perspectives discussed already in relation to Zompini's line engraving of a cosmorama have in this poem become projections of time more than of space. What becomes apparent in reading the poem is that historical as well as mythical subject matter had always been a prime realm of treatment in these *mondi nuovi*. And what that in turn makes possible is the very idea of this poem – the notion of a family retainer building one such 'new world' specifically to represent the past, present and a little bit of the future history of distinguished members of his patron's family. (Not surprisingly, Balbi is Goldoni's main patron too.) Fundamental to so crystalline a poetic discourse as Goldoni deploys in this panegyric poem on the Balbi family is the notion of clear historical perspectives opened up by the world of the invention, the *mondo nuovo* itself, locus of projections back and forth in time, and thus a way of recounting a particular story from past into present, and from present into presentiments of a future. It seems to me that we need to be highly aware, philosophically speaking, of the time spectrum which these popular cosmoramas opened up – particularly the notion of the 'new world' as an *unfolding future*. For if we could prove that such a sense of unfolding futurity had become self-reflexive – projected onto Venice itself so to speak – then that would constitute a very important piece of evidence in our enquiry into how open to questions of its own future this society was by the time of its fall.

Let us turn to a painting by Francesco Guardi of 1784, which although not of a *mondo nuovo* (not the optic device as such, that is) is in a sense fit subject matter for the kind of representation of marvels which was the stock in trade of such cosmoramas, being itself a new invention, the aeronautic balloon. This particular balloon was constructed by two brothers of the Zanchi family, able technicians appointed by the Procurator of San Marco in Venice, Francesco Pesaro, to build and launch the vessel at his expense. It was almost certainly an unmanned flight.[26] Looking at Guardi's painting of the balloon's launch (see Plate 5), we witness the marvel of this new invention along with Venice's citizenry, who because of their consuming interest in the event all stand with their backs to us. The portico which frames the painting, and from where some of the people seem to be moving to get a closer view of the balloon, is from the genre that Guardi has been working in, that of view paintings. However, this particular work seems to be moving at a philosophical tangent away from that genre. For what is enframed by the Venetian portico is not some other piece of typical scenery, not even a *capriccio*, but, to repeat, an invention of the present, utterly atypical of what Venice has traditionally signified. In relation to all those older traditions of Venice, and the canals and perspectives which the genre of view painting had continued to evolve new ways of representing – from Carlevaris through the work of Canaletto to Guardi (others have told this history) – the particular painting bespeaks an entirely new world of the future. Indeed, there is a sense in which it would not be fanciful to claim that it represents futurity itself. This might partly explain why we are unable to see any faces in this painting. For faces would imply the present, whereas all our attention must move beyond these people – these contemporary Venetians made anonymous by Guardi's mode of representation – towards the rather small round object that consumes their attention too: the new thing in the firmament, floating above its launch platform at the mouth of the Giudecca Canal.

People with their backs to us. An old world of Venetians in the standard black carnival cloaks and masks, but some of them light on their feet, as though lifted by the painting as they move or gaze towards the sign of a new world that has been spectacularly launched in their otherwise familiar sky (familiar to us too, if only from the view-painting genre which, as I am claiming, this work both uses for its frame, but also goes beyond, in its futuristic subject matter). To repeat. A society now with its backs to us, consumed with interest in something further off than Venice itself. Our words for describing one painting provide the necessary introduction to the last and by far the most haunting work under consideration in this chapter. Another representation of a *mondo nuovo*, the painting is called *Il Mondo Nuovo*, and was executed by Francesco Guardi's nephew and Giambattista Tiepolo's son, Giandome-nico Tiepolo (see Plate 6). This was painted for his private delectation many years after his father's death, indeed a couple of years after the outbreak of the French Revolution,[27] in the modest Tiepolo family villa at Zianigo, nowadays part of Mestre, Venice's twin-city on the mainland. And although, along with other paintings, drawings and etchings of Giandomenico's later years, it is beginning to attract more attention than previously, there has been nothing like a satisfactory interpretation of all that it (perhaps) signifies. Since some of the many things it seems to be aware of pose new and still more challenging questions about concerns at the heart of this chapter, it is fitting to end with it.

Years earlier Giandomenico had painted in the guest rooms of the Villa Valmarana outside Vicenza a smaller version of this large fresco. In the earlier painting far fewer persons are gathered around the small pavilion, in which a showman is presenting what we presume are exotic views of 'otherness', taken from historical or geographical worlds beyond the confines of Venice, and represented in a different kind of cosmorama from the portable wooden ones of Zompini's engraving or Goldoni's poem. Such people as appear in this smaller and earlier painting scarcely make it a crowd scene, far less a statement in paint that might justify our thinking of these onlookers as somehow a cross-sectional representation of Venetian society at large. By contrast, Giandomenico's return to the same unlimited view – an edge where land and sea and sky merge and are scarcely differentiable – in his large private fresco of 1791 allows for and indeed encourages much speculation on our parts.

We look at an extensive line of people gathered around the cosmorama, but again largely with their backs to us. Giandomenico's typical Pulcinella figure is at one end of the crowd, two 'pantomime dames' (as they have sometimes been called) are at the other, while in between all manner of masked and unmasked, bewigged and unwigged persons suggest a complex society of highly differing manners and mannerisms. The art critic Timothy Hyman has well observed that the first impact of this later painting of the new world subject is 'one of mystery'; it is an image 'somehow out of time, linked not to the sophisticated frieze-compositions of contemporary neo-classicism, but to the narrative-strip of Quattrocento fresco'.[28] If we share these first impressions of the painting's being out of time or linked to fresco-painting of a far earlier age, we must nonetheless hold onto the goal of giving it cultural anchorage in its own age, even grasp that the painting may contain some sense of gazing away from Venice towards a possible future, as in the case of his uncle Francesco Guardi in the painting of the balloon launch, but possibly in still more radical ways. Hyman has called the later painting by Giandomenico a 'carnival limbo' and used Bakhtin's interpretations of carnival to make good his case: in particular, the Bakhtinian claim that 'carnival subverts ideology, "its one-sided rhetorical seriousness, its rationality, its dogmatism" '.[29] Certainly, the painting makes impossible any speedy move towards foreclosure of its meaning. To say the least, it stimulates interpretative faculties, rather than aborting or undermining our will to understand.

Take the two gentlemen in profile towards the right-hand side of the painting. These two figures have traditionally been identified as the painter's father Giambattista (closest to the cosmorama) and Giando-menico himself (slightly further back in the line).[30] If this interpretation is correct, we do indeed have a mystification of time on our hands, since the great Giambattista had been dead twenty years by the time of the painting, and even when alive had not figured in the far smaller version in the Villa Valmarana. His presence turns the painting in the direction of allegory, as though it were suggesting that in relation to this 'new world', he in his (now earlier) epoch stood at a four-square and somewhat sceptical remove. His son, the painter, on the other hand has anything but a disinterested air, leaning forward as he is to see everything before him more clearly through the monocle he holds to one eye. His world naturally includes his father in its foreground. Indeed, we might pause to consider how large a distraction the reputation of the father is in our estimating the achievements of the son more truly. Giandomenico's decades of work on commissions for his father are largely what has made his distinction as a fascinating painter in his own right slow to emerge in art history and criticism. (It is not always easy to tell in Giambattista's finished larger-scale pieces in Wurtzburg and Madrid exactly which areas of the paintings are by the son.) And yet nobody could possibly mistake *this* particular painting for work by the father.

The younger and more distant figure of the son looks intently through his monocle at the whole scene before him. Others in that scene are mostly crowding to see what is being displayed in the cosmorama by the showman on his stool. Would it be foolish to suggest at this stage of our unfolding interpretation that if for the rest of the crowd the cosmorama presents mysterious 'other' or new worlds, Giandomenico himself has not ceased to be a human observer of his own society? That society surely figures, at least partially, in his overall sighting of a 'new world', and hence in what we as interpreters of the painting must understand by the term. Several collateral points then need to be established immediately. First of all, it does not really matter to the interpretation if this is not the painter Giandomenico: the main points about what the particular figure sees still hold true. Second, if the man with the monocle sees most (always granting that the showman focuses individual scenes in the cosmorama, and from his position above the others is also the reason why this very crowd scene has gathered in the first place), then the observer – I will call him Giandomenico for convenience – is also an 'observed of all observers', since the dame with the feathered hat looks directly at him. We have in her a minor confirmation that *his* study of all before him is, so to speak, the painting's major key, however much other figures may absorb our partial attention as subjects of speculation in their own right. Harry Matthews has suggested that it is the child in almost full face at the centre of the painting whose viewpoint is a key to the rest.[31] But unlike the figure of 'Giandomenico' with the monocle, the child's field of vision hardly includes much of the crowd itself. He is only one in a grouping of three youngsters whom a man in red frock-coat seems to be helping to see the views presented within the cosmorama: at the moment of the painting, this figure in red is lifting one child in his left arm while turning his attention to the other two. What *is* important, however, is that it is a child that Giandomenico presents to us as looking into the cosmorama, as though the more distantly placed painter wants us to understand that it is the next generation that gazes into the unknown.

The figure of Pulcinella, while important, cannot be said to dominate this painting as he does others of Giandomenico's late period. Not only is he on one side, his face is partially covered by the gold mantle of a woman next to him. If he and the dames opposite him remind us of carnival, and even by their positions seem like inverted commas around the crowd, or a framing device suggesting that all between them must be understood as happening *within* carnival, then the stillness of many of the other figures as they patiently await their turn to peer into the cosmorama, taken together with the subtly emphasized larger-scale observation on the part of the man with the monocle, surely focuses another mode of attention than the carnivalesque. They attest that even if carnival is the social mode and the *time scale* in which the showman's cosmorama goes on general view, it is not the essential *subject* of the painting. Carnival to Venetians of the period was almost the definitive state of being, as I have earlier made clear. It had for long been the focus of social attention, in reality as in artistic representation. What we need to see is that this painting, set during carnival like so much else, is focusing on matters still closer in – or else a great deal further off – than anything so everyday.

'Closer in' than carnival is the sense that this society is no longer in any case the main subject of Venetian genre painting, even if there are vestigial reminders *from* precisely that genre painting to help Giandomenico make the point. Rather, in this portrait of society from behind, the main subject of the painting too must be what they and we are now intent upon – the lure and fascination of an 'unknown' – revealed by peering into an optical device. Our vision includes the fact that most of them are no longer presenting themselves for the social voyeur or each other. Rather, their turned faces draw from us a desire to share in what has captured their attention. The painter himself – whether we understand him to be the man with the monocle or not – seems highly aware that the 'unknown' has now become a social focus of attention more captivating even than society itself. To make that point he has portrayed a plurality of Venetians no longer even remotely self-absorbed. Any greater reminder of carnival would have risked losing the radical novelty at stake, which I would claim involves – as never so markedly before him in the works of Zompini, Goldoni or Guardi studied earlier – a vector into the future.

It is a vector that we must conceive as moving not simply 'closer in' than anything that carnival helps us to focus upon, but also, as I have already said, 'further off'. For if one or two figures are still masked, others beyond those nearest to us look straight before them, not sideways at the local phenomenon of the cosmorama. However much the cosmorama may be a device for focusing unknown scenes and events, there are figures who have as it were bypassed its nearer concentrations, or who, having already looked into them, are now searching in the 'beyond' for the meaning of what it had presented; shadowy figures who steadily gaze out into empty space, unaided now – whether they had been moments earlier or not – by optical illusion.

An alternative reading, of course, might be that these figures are all gazing not into the future but into a lost past, no longer as represented in the material world of Venice's typical genre paintings, but fading into the distance, to the point 'where the Day joins the past Eternity' – as Byron's Childe Harold was to remark in his contemplations from

Venice, when lamenting the 'fall'n states and buried greatness' that seemed to surround him in Italy more generally.[32] Timothy Hyman's reading of the figures in the painting suggests such a possible nostalgia: 'Domenico's tender pearly washes confer on them a kind of love, and some of the wistful glamour of a lost cause.'[33] My own preferred sense of Giandomenico and of this work, however, is that even such qualities of nostalgia or wistfulness as it may evoke do not make it a painting that looks mainly into the past, or that constitutes an exquisite lament in the manner of the slightly later Lord Byron. Even if we were oblivious to the title of the painting, we could not help noting the curiosity of gaze on the part of the persons portrayed, both near and far off, as I have been at pains to point out. That curiosity is certainly not without animation, even if several of the figures appear stilled by their contemplation of the mysteries in question. Neither we nor they are distracted by direct representation of the past in any underlined sense. If one or more of the figures is a reincarnation of the dead, this is not a painting which suggests by any closure of the surroundings (such as many an earlier canal scene from the view-painting genre might have produced) that these are people with nowhere new to go. On the contrary, a few of them are already intent on far horizons, as I have suggested: horizons which we must conceptualize either in terms of time to come or as places as yet undiscovered. In this 'New World', the cosmorama – as it had been for the earlier Zompini and Goldoni – is an object of interest in its own right, but more importantly a sign of the very act of looking beyond the known context of Venice, which it makes possible. We must surely figure this wonderment at novelties no longer intrinsically Venetian as part of a new *Geist* of openness before the unknown of space and time (including the future): a *Geist* which is identifiable – at least in the form of the artistic premonitions I have been discussing in works by Zompini, Goldoni, Guardi and especially Giandomenico Tiepolo – even before the fall of the Republic.

## Notes

1. Quoted in John Julius Norwich, *Venice: The Greatness and the Fall* (London: Allen Lane, 1981), p. 324.

2. J. W. von Goethe, *Italian Journey (1786–88)*, trans. W. H. Auden and Elizabeth Mayer (London: W. M. Collins, 1962), p. 63.

3. See the volume *Cronaca Veneziana: feste e vita quotidiana nella Venezia del*

*Settecento*. View paintings by Gabriel Bella and engravings by Gaetano Zompini in the collection of the Querini Stampalia Foundation in Venice (Venice: Fondazione Scientifica Querini Stampalia, 1991).

4. See Philippe Monnier, *Venice in the Eighteenth Century*, no translator given (London: Chatto and Windus, 1910), pp. 41ff.

5. Lord Byron, *Complete Poetical Works*, ed. Jerome J. McGann, Vol. 2 (Oxford: Oxford University Press, 1980), pp. 125 and 128. Quotes are from *Childe Harold's Pilgrimage*, Canto the Fourth, first published 1818, stanzas iii and xiii.

6. Joseph Brodsky, *Watermark* (London: Hamish Hamilton, 1992), p. 116.

7. *Ibid.*, p. 114.

8. Michael Levey, *Painting in Eighteenth-Century Venice* (original edition 1955; 3rd edn, New Haven and London: Yale University Press, 1994), p. 7.

9. This phrase and the two at the beginning of the paragraph are taken from an article by Bruce Bereford, 'Venice Mythologized: A Seductive Maritime Playground', and another by John Julius Norwich, 'Venice in the Eighteenth Century', which both appeared in *Apollo*, September 1994, pp. 13–16 and 3–6.

10. Giacomo Casanova, Chevalier de Seingalt, *History of My Life*, 6 vols, translated by Willard R. Trask (London: Longmans, Green and Co., 1967), Vol. 2, p. 219. I have used the words 'mere sketch' in place of Trask's term 'simulacrum' in the English translation, as it is a more faithful representation of Casanova's original figure of speech, which I go on to analyse. Casanova, *Mémoires*, ed. Robert Abirached and Elio Zorzi (Paris: Librarie Gallimard, 1958), Vol. 1 (1725–1756), p. 448.

11. Casanova, *History of My Life*, Vol. 1, pp. 194ff.

12. *Ibid.*, Vol. 4, p. 207.

13. Lorenzo Da Ponte, *Memorie*, edited by G. Gambarin and F. Nicolini (Bari: Gius Laterza and Sons, 1918), Vol. 1, p. 20.

14. Carlo Goldoni, *Opere*, edited by Filippo Zampieri (Milan and Naples: Ricciardi, 1954), p. 538.

15. Goldoni, *The Campiello*, translated by Frederick Davies (London: Ginn and Co., 1971), p. 84.

16. S. Romanin, *Storia documentata di Venezia*, 2nd edn, 10 vols, reprinted on the basis of the 1st edn of 1853–61 (Venice: Giusto Fuga Editore, 1915), Tome 8, p. 235. In Romanin's history the original relation of the ambassadors Tommaso Querini and Francesco Morosini at this point reads: 'Considerando quali ragioni promovano, e prosperino a sì gran segno il traffico di quel regno, facilmente si scorge che la situazione del medesimo, opportuna per intraprendere molte navigazioni, la natura del suolo fertile di molti ricchi prodotti, l'estesa del dominio di quella corona, e le connessioni co' molti fruttiferi paesi dell'America, Asia ed Africa, gettarono i fondamenti di un commercio assai esteso, e per la più gran parte attivo. I commerci coi paesi al Nord ed Ovest d'Inghilterra scuoprono quanto ella sia ben situata per li medesimi, e le importanti situazioni di Gibilterra e Minorica facilitano a quella nazione il vivo commercio del Mediterraneo.'

17. *Ibid.*, p. 232. The original text here reads: 'Egli è in conseguenza di questo sistema, che quel governo ha potuto provvedere sollecitamente alle spese immense delle guerre, mantenere in ogni tempo le condizioni alli contribuenti, e non affliggere

il proprio commercio. Ma che questi beni abbiano costata alla nazione una parte della sua libertà, quest' è ciò, che poc' anzi avanzammo . . .'

18. For this debate see *ibid.*, pp. 212–14. There is a highly useful summary of this focus of anti-semitism in Venice, and modern scholarship on it, in Felicity Baker's article, 'Lorenzo da Ponte's Witticisms: The Implication of Jewish Identity in the *Memorie*', in John Lindon (ed.), *Italian Autobiography from Vico to Alfieri (and Beyond)* as a supplement to the *Italianist*, No. 17 (1997), pp. 66–73. Baker's emphasis is on one person who was forced to leave Venice largely as a consequence of new persecutory legislation, namely Da Ponte. See my treatment of Da Ponte as exile and emigré in the final chapter.

19. Romanin, *Storia*, Tome 8, p. 229.

20. 'Venezia era alle ultime battute; e se i più erano convinti della sua immortalità, gli avveduti non si facevano illusioni. "No gavemo forze, non terrestri, non maritime, non alleanze, vivemo a sorte e per accidente e vivemo collo sola idea della prudenza del Governo della Repubblica." Tale, già nel 1780, la diagnosi del doge Paolo Renier; nessuna terapia era ormai possibile. Le testimonianze su un'agonia senza dolori, quale è dei corpi sfiniti dalla vecchiaia, si moltiplicarono.' Adriano Mariuz, *Giandomenico Tiepolo* (Milan: Alfieri, 1971), p. 81.

21. 'Se c'è Stato che abbia bisogno di concordia siamo noi.' Romanin, *Storia*, Tome 8, p. 264.

22. Joseph Addison, from *Remarks on Several Parts of Italy, &c. In the Years 1701, 1702, 1703*, in *Works* (London: Vernor and Hood *et al.*, 1804), Vol. 5, p. 181.

23. Goethe quotes are from his *Italian Journey*, pp. 72, 71, 83 and 58.

24. See examples in *Cronaca Veneziana*.

25. Carlo Goldoni, *Tutte le opere*, edited by Giuseppe Ortolani (Milan: Mondadori, 1943–59), Vol. 13, pp. 689–702.

26. The launch of the balloon flight painted by Guardi took place on 15 April 1784. See the following two publications by Timina Caproni Guasti and Achille Bertarelli for further details: *Francesco Zambeccari Aeronauta (Bologna 1752–1812)* (Milan: Museo Caproni, 1931), p. 8, and *L'Aeronautica italiana nell'immagine: 1487–1875* (Milan: Museo Caproni, 1938), p. 12. I am indebted to my colleague Clive Hart, and to Paul Maravelas, editor of the journal *Annals of Balloon History & Museology*, for tracking down the above sources of information.

27. The painting is dated 1791 in a corner.

28. Timothy Hyman, 'A Carnival Sense of the World', *Royal Academy Magazine*, no. 44, autumn 1994, p. 42.

29. *Ibid.*, p. 44.

30. See Mariuz, *Tiepolo*, p. 83; Hyman's own nice tweaking of this traditional interpretation is that the younger of the two portrait profiles 'peering through an eyeglass (a bit of a fool, or an Andrew Aguecheek) is Domenico's remembered self; the older, his beloved father Giambattista, already 20 years dead'. Hyman, 'Carnival Sense', p. 44.

31. *Ibid.*

32. Byron, *Childe Harold's Pilgrimage*, Canto the Fourth.

33. Hyman, 'Carnival Sense', p. 43.

CHAPTER 5

# OPERA, POLITICS AND
# TELEVISION

## BEL CANTO BY SATELLITE

I daresay that many people who would be hard put to recall who won the 1990 World Cup in Italy have not forgotten an associated musical extravaganza between the so-called 'three tenors' (no need at all to identify *which* three, as they are now household names across the globe). The concert was staged on a balmy summer Saturday night in early July in the Roman ruins of the Baths of Caracalla before a live audience of 6,000, and simultaneously beamed out to a world-wide satellite audience of an estimated 800 million – surely scarcely fewer viewers (if at all) than have ever seen live opera in its entire history.

If ABC television who broadcast the programme live across America had had their way, the concert would have been billed as a 'competition' between the said tenors. According to the head of the audio-visual department of Decca (the recording company who held world rights on the concert), the initial suggestion from the American television network had been 'that the three tenors would each sing "Nessun dorma" ' – the official World Cup theme music – 'and an international panel of judges would give their scores as in Olympic gymnastics – 9.5, 9.75, and so on. . . . Well, we threw that one out of the window pretty damn quick.'[1]

Competition or not – and somewhat inevitably most reporting of the event (including countless private conversations) just couldn't help ranking the singers – the world and its myriad football pitches have never been quite the same since. In choosing that precise anthem in the first place, and then, at the concert's climax, pitching it in medley form from one tenor to the other and so on to the next and back again, the promoters – showing characteristic Italian panache, even if they were not themselves to a man and woman Italian – had exhibited an instinct for the exact historical moment when a redeployment of one of Italy's great artistic traditions, that of bel canto, could achieve maximum impact through being grafted onto another that represents the nearest thing to religion in the secular sphere. I refer of course to *calcio* (football), which for many years has been in its zenith.

Somehow in the grafting process both traditions would be enhanced in status and popularity. Or rather, the high cultural status of football was confirmed (which in Italy has never really been in doubt), and bel canto, we were being reminded, especially when cut loose from its moorings in the fustian of opera – 'Who wants to listen to three hours of warbling in a foreign tongue anyway?', to quote what has been perceived as one of the lowest-common-denominator objections to the medium[2] – and relocated in the same realm as football, could rapidly find the wider public it had once had, or even a popularity it had *never* enjoyed, promulgated in hundreds of lands and indeed millions of homes by the combined modern miracles of television satellite and cathode ray.

The more one contemplates this – at first strange but then very beguiling – collocation of bel canto, football and television, the more quite other matters (essentially political) are seen to be at stake. The stirring tunefulness of the bel canto tradition which, according to many, ends in 1926 with Puccini's last great opera, *Turandot*, had already for at least a century before that date served many political ends, none more important than as a rallying point during the Italian Risorgimento. Specific operas had been linked in their own day with the revolutions of 1848 and had helped to inspire, or were in their turn inspired by, such events as Garibaldi's 1860 campaigns and the eventual unification of the entire Italian peninsula in 1870. The musical name we most associate with this politics is that of Verdi, who in opera after opera had raided earlier moments in Italian history for stories of high ideals combining *gloria*, *patria* and a well-nigh sacred sense of *sacrificio*. Those who already have a sound grasp of operatic history will recall that for a time in the 1850s the cry 'Viva Verdi', launched in the theatre or just as frequently in the streets of Italian cities, was not solely an expression of enthusiasm for a specific composer, but 'code' for a particular unificatory belief which many of his operas served – the initials of his name giving the cry the meaning 'Viva Vittore Emanuele Re D'Italia' – Victor Emmanuel at the time being (until Garibaldi's 1860 successes, that is) only King of Piedmont and Sardinia.[3]

I shall return to Verdi at the chapter's conclusion. But at this early stage someone might already be asking whether that old history is not a far cry from the use of *melos* in the famous 'three tenors' concert? In the first part of my argument, I wish to demonstrate that the potential drive towards unificatory politics inherent in bel canto had never really gone away, even if it had become a somewhat 'underground' stream (however mixed my metaphor at this point). What the Italian cultural establishment (or rather, a set of forces at an international level of cultural promotions) seems to have known was when, and how, and by means of exactly which excerpts, to redeploy the older operatic tradition in such a way that it constituted a modified version of the traditional unificatory message for purposes of the present.

This coup on the part of what I am for convenience implying is a 'cultural establishment' (Italian in part, but more importantly in these times of satellite programme link-up, international) was to become more pronounced two years later. In July 1992 RAI, the Italian national television network, stitched together a gamble of no less impressive proportions, in gaining the support of 107 nations for a production of Puccini's *Tosca*, televised from the actual three Roman locations of the three acts of that opera, and at the same times of day in televisual scheduling as those three acts take place in the unfolding drama (afternoon, evening and the following dawn). It is through this – later award-winning – production of *Tosca* that I want to focus much of my argument concerning the cultural positioning of televised opera, and thereby ask questions about the politics of traditional opera in our culture more generally, particularly in its multiple re-hyped forms, television being but one example. Before proceeding, however, let us pause for a closer look at the memorable climax of the three tenors concert, to see more precisely what it reveals by way of a lead-in to our enquiry into the modern politics of opera.

Interestingly, it too was a *Puccinian* highlight. This little detail of authorship is, paradoxically, only interesting for its utter irrelevance, as it is clear that any sense of this music's origins has been lost in its use as the 1990 World Cup anthem, and indeed its subsequent storming success in the British pop charts for many weeks thereafter. It is a supreme instance of the so-called 'death of the author' *Zeitgeist*, which has been with us from well before Roland Barthe's pronouncement that the author *was indeed* 'dead'. Neither Puccini nor certainly Franco Alfano, who completed *Turandot* after Puccini's death, is of the least consequence in what is revived for popularity in that late-evening medley from the Baths of Caracalla. Not only was the 'author' Puccini truly dead when the 'Nessun dorma' aria he had written was heuristically scored by Alfano as a climactic repeat by orchestra alone for the final bars of *Turandot*; even *Turandot* itself had no consequence whatsoever in the aria's presentation on that warm summer night in 1990.[4]

For the purposes of such a megamedia event all notions of the larger work from which a specific aria is taken – Puccini's *Turandot* as completed by Alfano – are as irrelevant and dead as those authors themselves. To this day the number of people who are aware of the particular aria's provenance and authorship would be extremely small when compared to the figures who listened to the concert or to any of the endlessly repeated 'replays' of this final medley. (Note in passing this coincidence with the language of football.) Its origins simply were not important, and nor was anybody encouraged to become at all curious about them. Significantly, what this made possible – and not for the first time in the bel canto tradition – was the aria's superinscription upon another story (that of the unfolding World Cup itself) and, hence, *another political moment*, in which it could serve new ends. Its very words, insofar as they could be understood, or (if they could not) at the very least its musical fulsomeness, were thus made available for a new and intensely projected message. At the risk of simplification, what in a nutshell was that new political message?

Even someone dead to the Italian language and, furthermore, by no means skilled in the interpretation of musical signification, would not have had too much difficulty recognizing, in the slow, sweeping and increasingly triumphal crescendo of 'Nessun dorma', as offered into the sky by Domingo, Carreras and Pavarotti (and, bounced off spatial satellite, returning into your and my living rooms), a game or mood or politics – its name can be varied almost at will – reaching through increasing ecstasy to its own apotheosis. A game *and* a mood *and* a politics – all in one. But if we step back just for a moment from the strains of uplift, and with a kind of Brechtian detachment (which, by the way, the music itself certainly does not encourage) dare to be hyper-rational for an instant and ask a couple of questions about, for instance, the issue of the last word sung (*vincerò*', I shall win') – namely, *who* will win? and what exactly is it that will *be won*? – then the symbolic system we have been interpreting our way through step by step presents us with an impasse. With, in short, an inbuilt vagueness in the very realms of political signification which most matter.

Unquestionably, winning *is* what any World Cup event (including even this one of the three tenors concert, with what I have suggested was its not entirely subliminal competitive element) is all about. But in politics as in football, if there is a single winner (and the verb form *vincerò* is, let me hasten to repeat, singular – just as it also demarcates the future and hence grows out of a present *will* to win), there must in each case be a loser. And yet what this aria leads us to occlude – and I need hardly point out that all matters of occlusion have political repercussion – is all thought of, and hence any need to sympathize with, a loser.

Importantly, the three tenors' concert was staged the night before the World Cup final. Were we not being led to experience at its climax a sense of victory tainted as little as possible by any sense of defeat? If so, we can generalize the phenomenon in the following way. This producing of an experience resembling victorious apotheosis from the deepest reaches of *melos* must be thought of as having as its political unconscious the purpose of helping its audience – potentially all 800 million of them – overcome the magnitude of any past, present or future defeats (whether figured in terms of this football competition itself, or on the larger stages of national and international politics). The unificatory work of bel canto that I mentioned earlier, and stressed as its ongoing politics, in the present instance consists of the way listeners and onlookers are aroused to respond in only one direction of the political grain of things – that of victory. All the while there is a significant occlusion of any consideration of its necessary opposite (defeat).

In the words of one newspaper review, 'the rollicking 20-minute medley' with which the concert officially closed (before all the planned encores) 'was vulgar, improbable, incongruous and fun'.[5] The chosen adjectives are interesting, if we pause to ponder that each of them could be used extensively (even if not universally) of the Italian operatic tradition in general. What the highlight of the concert was managing to bring to bear on its international televisual audience was thus, perhaps – and I offer this merely as a *hypothesis*, in our search to understand its global politics – a concentrated shot of the same uplifting 'feel-good' factor that much of the operatic tradition had provided down through the nineteenth century and on into ours, as far as the moment of *Turandot*.

Is there not, in any event, some curiosity in the fact that the moment in modern history that most seeks to re-exhume the *bel canto* tradition should climax on virtually the last aria in the last work of that 'great tradition' – as though trying to start up anew from where the tradition had come to a halt, and as if there had been no intervening interval? What, for Italy (to name only one country – though, importantly, the cradle of bel canto, and the context of this particular megamedia event) could possibly be achieved by covering over the traces of the historic interval between 1926 and 1990?

Well, quite a lot. Much of the worst of fascism, together with the drawn-out post-war 'disunification' of Italy, which runs roughly parallel to the previous century's unification of same – a disunification which has steamed ahead at a gathering political pace in the few intervening years since that 1990 'feel-good' event, with only intervals of hope in the dramatic changes produced in every form and structure of the nation's political life. For many years already Italians had felt that all coherence had gone at the national level. By 1990 the nation was about to see an almighty unravelling of its ramshackle party-political machinery, and of the small- and large-scale corruption that had oiled well-nigh all levels of public and corporate existence. 'Cultural promotions' and spectacles were one area which a moribund Italian establishment of politicians, industrialists, financiers and media directors could still use to cloud over harsher truths. At this point in the argument let me make it clear that I am not claiming there was any *conspiracy* to deceive behind the promotions in question. The effects produced by such media extravaganzas (and even, possibly, the urge to stage the World Cup itself) are better understood as a kind of 'political unconscious' of the ruling classes – their own need, quite apart from anyone else's, for larger and larger doses of some feel-good factor or other, as the realities of Italian public existence *for them in particular* grew irreversibly darker.

If I am right pessimistically to claim that this political blurring was the bottom-line agenda of the three tenors concert, at least as far as Italy itself was concerned, then it was even more so in the case of the production of *Tosca* from Rome two years later, when the last figments of respectability of the ageing political and financial classes were finally falling, as the nation's confidence in its leaders snapped beyond all repair. The story of how that production sought to remake Rome into what it had once for so long been in the past – a focus of universal coherence and centre of civilization – is one crucial factor in my present argument. But first we must rehearse those other political purposes that the specific Puccinian opera has been made to serve, in earlier historical conjunctures.

*****

Let us therefore explore some of the history of this opera's original conception by Puccini, and of its interaction with other distinctive political moments than merely our own contemporary one – including those of its setting and first performance. For these are cardinal dates to remember. Set in Rome in the first year of a new century, 1800, it is also premièred in Rome at the Teatro Costanzi in the first year of the next, 1900. If its setting is preceded by a decade of revolutionary politics which has led to Napoleon's rise in France and his present Italian campaign, its première was preceded no less by important political history – an entire intervening century of Risorgimento politics and the subsequent unification of Italy under what had previously been the Piedmontese monarchy. *Tosca* was written during the still highly uncertain phase of consolidation of the Italian state, one generation after its unification under the present King Umberto's father, Victor Emmanuel.

In the action of Puccini's drama a queen of the *ancien régime* (Queen Caroline, the sister of Marie Antoinette) remains offstage throughout, representing the royalist forces of which the villain Scarpia is the police spearhead and henchman. Historically speaking these were forces that had made a comeback in Rome itself and in the Bourbon stronghold of Naples, having been temporarily ousted from both cities in the late 1790s. Between their ousting and comeback, republics had briefly flourished. The opera's opening act sees defeated republicans such as Angelotti, the consul of the overthrown Roman Republic, together with their sympathizers (here represented by the painter Cavaradossi), whose only hope is now focused on Napoleon. Against them are pitted the reactionary forces of royalism, themselves leaning heavily on the church – as witnessed in Scarpia's complete melding of his fiendish plan to arrest Angelotti, outwit Cavaradossi, and ravish Tosca, with the great 'Te Deum' sung by priest and choristers which closes the first Act. (We do well to remember that in the year 1800 Pope Pius VI had been a virtual prisoner of Napoleon.)

But there was a queen present also at the play's première in 1900 – Queen Margherita, wife of the very King Umberto who was to be assassinated by anarchists six months later. This was the Queen who some decades earlier had provided the scholarship for Puccini's Milanese years as a music student. In addition the prime minister of the day, Luigi Pelloux, and several of his cabinet ministers attended the première. We might wonder somewhat, given that this was a work fully engaging the well-noted 'sadism' in respect of individual characters in Puccinian opera – what he himself called his 'neronic instincts'[6] – that its première should have included such royal and political dignitaries in the audience. But then, as William Ashbrook reminds us, close connections between 'high' and 'low' were a crucial element of the age: 'beneath its sometimes lurid surface *Tosca* exists as a fascinatingly representative product of the turn of the century. For all its veneer of elegant leisure, *la belle époque* was a period of deep social unrest, of political prisoners, and of corruption in high places.'[7]

What is most apparent with hindsight is that Puccini's choice of precisely Sardou's political melodrama and thriller, *La Tosca*, was not the act of someone uninterested in politics, or able to escape being the nexus of many vectors of political force; even if what Puccini actually does – and has his librettists do – in adapting the Sardou material is to reduce and blunt its political intricacies to a few essentials, and shift the emphasis away from concerted republicanism and atheism onto a politics of individualism. The opera's sympathies are indeed initially republican, even if less explicitly than in the Sardou play from which it is adapted. There is a popular myth that Puccini was not very interested by the politics of his day, and hence not political by instinct in his art.[8] But this seems to me a confusing of different issues. It is true that grand public political stances in the Verdian manner – the great self-sacrifice of a Rodrigo in *Don Carlo* is a prime example, but there are many others – which even in Sardou's *La Tosca* are still forcible and explicit, have only a vestigial presence in Puccini's drama, and have been largely ousted by a politics of personal credos of individualism (Scarpia's self-delighting commitment to violation, Tosca's 'Vissi d'arte', Cavaradossi's 'E lucevan le stelle').

Indeed, an exception to this politics of individualism is what proves the rule. The act of defiance which leads most immediately to Cavaradossi's condemnation and death is the one truly Verdian moment in the opera – his exultation at the news of Napoleon's secured victory at Marengo, which stirs him to sing his 'Vittoria' aria in the grand old style that would hardly have been out of place in operas of half a century earlier, such as *Nabucco*, *Il corsaro*, *La battaglia di Legnano*. In Verdi, however, that act of political defiance would not have been succeeded and undercut by other, more individualistic credos, such as

Tosca and Cavaradossi himself give voice to as the opera plumbs deeper for underlying reasons why life might be held dear – or, rather, *have been held* dear, since in Tosca's 'Vissi d'arte' aria as, equally, in Cavaradossi's 'E lucevan le stelle', the values registered are given a heart-rending farewell, as qualities banished into the past by the present violence of others. As Catherine Clément aptly reminds us, when Sacco and Vanzetti went to their execution they too sang Cavaradossi's last aria, out of a sense of how much of value it recalls in the life about to be extinguished: 'In the American prison . . . the two convicts were going to die, like the fictional Mario, from police abuse under a racist regime.'[9] (We shall consider Sacco and Vanzetti themselves in greater detail in the final chapter, as surprisingly 'representative' emigrants.)

Puccini pushes his musical adaptation of an otherwise typical instance of what Shaw used to call 'Sardoodledum' towards a rampant individualism that outweighs particular political causes, but which is nonetheless highly political for that, since it elevates the gratifications of art or of personal passion to a plane beyond that of petty worldly concern, even if it is about to be undermined and undone by another individualism, of distinctly baser instincts. In the closing minutes of the opera we are most forcibly reminded of those baser instincts and of their specific location in the dead Scarpia, whose last command while alive still has power to despatch another being, Cavaradossi, to death, and in turn inspire Tosca's suicide leap. On the other hand the final bars of all are an orchestral reiteration of the theme of Cavaradossi's words, 'E non ho mai tanto amato la vita', 'I have never loved life so deeply.' Hence, two stark contrasts in reasons for living at all – one of utter baseness, the other so elevated it is no longer able to hold a place in the world – are juxtaposed acutely in the closing words of the libretto and in the orchestral notes which ring out beyond them.

This much needed to be established before engaging with the political temper of specific subsequent performances of *Tosca* in the century since its time of writing. Initially it seems worth pausing over two rare filmed extracts of the opera, both from the early post-war era, before examining in more detail the full version from our own times.

In 1946 Carmine Gallone, a director already experienced in filming the Italian operatic tradition, and who was to go on making cinematic versions of classic operas in the post-war years, made a film largely in the neorealist style of the day, which deals with a group of singers involved in a production of *Tosca* that is being staged in Rome just before the Germans finally leave the city to the advancing Allies. The cinematic title of Gallone's piece, *Avanti a lui tremava tutta Roma* (*Before Him All Rome Trembled*), is taken from a line sung over the tormentor Scarpia's dead body by his killer Tosca at the close of Puccini's phenomenal second act, in which she has finally stabbed him. At its close, Gallone's film celebrates his characters' opportunity (after their harassment by the Germans) to display their bel canto talents before the unrepressive Allied forces, who have fought their way as far as Rome and are now the toast of the city.

Throughout Gallone's film there unfolds a fascinating parallel between on the one hand the oppressions of Scarpia and his forces, and on the other the brutality of the Nazi occupation of Rome and its region, especially as such brutality impacts on the lives of the singers involved in staging the earlier Puccini work. Clearly the film's title also had been carefully chosen with this parallel in mind. For Italian cinema-going audiences of 1946, the idea of all Rome trembling before one man could not fail to conjure up recent recollections of Mussolini, of his fascist state apparatus and the still worse memories of the German occupation once fascism had collapsed. In the film, the character who sings the role of the painter Cavaradossi is in real life someone who sympathizes with and works in minor ways for the Resistance. In his villa in the countryside just outside Rome he successively harbours both a refugee Polish Jewish musician and an English airman helping co-ordinate the Allied advance with the Resistance forces; just as in the Puccinian opera, the painter-hero succours and hides in his villa the escaped republican, Angelotti. This parallel between Gallone's film and Puccini's opera (long passages of which are staged within it) breaks down at the end of the work, however, since the opera ends tragically, whereas the film culminates in a triumphal *staging of* the opera before the victorious Allies, an event which signals that Italy may now revive and draw new meaning from its deeper artistic traditions, unhindered by the twin tyrannies of fascism and Nazism of the preceding epoch. Indeed, if Gallone's film demonstrates anything in its own deeper parallel structures with *Tosca*, it is that works such as precisely this opera by Puccini – about an earlier tyranny – can help in understanding the more recent past, from which he and his fellow Italians have only just emerged, by no means mentally and physically unscarred.

In Gallone's film, the baritone Tito Gobbi sings the part of the villain Scarpia in the extracts from the opera, a role for which he was already famous and that he was to go on playing in hundreds of further stage and filmed performances (including the next one studied in this chapter), as well as to take master classes in after the eventual decline of his singing career. The role of Tosca, by contrast, was played by the upcoming actress Anna Magnani, someone noted for her lead part in one of the most prominent films of Italy's emergent phase of cinematic neorealism, Rossellini's *Rome Open City* of the previous year, 1945. Not being a singer, those parts of the film in which Magnani is playing the role of Tosca on stage are 'voiced over' by Elizabeta Barbata. The Puccinian extracts are played in period costume of 1800, but the numerous Nazi henchmen in their military uniforms who are seen in the boxes of the opera house in Rome and waiting to waylay its singers in the theatre's back-stage corridors and changing rooms are a chilling reminder – something neorealism repeatedly emphasized in both films and novels of these emergent post-war years – of the dark phase of Italian history just left behind. Left behind, but in order that it be so, *rewritten*, since fascism's account of itself had been an endless glorification, and the real story of its horrors had hardly yet been publicly told. Gallone's film takes its place therefore in this major project of post-war Italian cinema, the rewriting of the history of Italy's recent fascist past and of the Nazi occupation that followed upon fascism's collapse in 1943.

What is so curious is that Carmine Gallone himself, the director of this exemplary cinematic updating of the relevance of a well-loved Puccini opera about tyranny to the period of the Nazi occupation (making his own distinctive use of emergent cinematic neorealism in the process), should have been one of only two filmmakers from the previous epoch to have been banned for six months from all cinematic production, for his implication in the Italian film industry under fascism. This ban of 1944 had been at the hands of the Italian cinema's hastily convened commission for purges (responsible to the High Commission for Purges), which included in its number that other and nowadays better-known director Luchino Visconti, who already had one of the earliest and most important neorealist films to his credit, *Ossessione* (1943), which, whatever else its particular narrative significance, was dedicated to giving the kind of comfortless readings of the Italian reality that fascism had denied the public of its day.

Gallone, in short, was banned for the fairly active part he had taken in the escapist and glorificatory cinema of the 1930s, having been the

**Figure 7** Still from Carmine Gallone's rare 1946 film *Avanti a lui tremava tutta Roma* (*Before Him All Rome Trembled*), with Anna Magnani as Tosca, backstage among occupying Germans. Gallone had been briefly banned from filmmaking after the war for over-implication in cinema under fascism. This 'comeback' piece emulates the political spirit of other neorealist films, while also drawing on an older work, Puccini's opera *Tosca*, for a sense of what it means to collaborate with, or on the contrary act in resistance to an oppressor. Reproduced by permission of the Museo Nazionale del Cinema, Turin.

director, among many other works, of *Scipione l'Africano* in 1937, the kind of epic treatment of Roman history (in this case of the famous military consul of the Second Punic War, Scipio Africanus Major) which was so used by fascism to bolster its own imperial and expansionist policies. We can only surmise that Gallone's first film made at the end of his period of banishment from the industry – this adaptation and updating of some of the essential meanings of *Tosca* to a near-contemporary setting (but one which significantly includes extracts of a period production of Puccini's opera within it) – was *atonement* on his part for the cast of his earlier career.[10]

And thereby hangs a kind of moral. The eras of politics change. But particular individuals' life spans usually include several such eras, which may well be quite antithetical from one to the next. And since the politics of any age are the sum total of complex interrelations between the opinions and actions of individuals living through it, the case of Gallone making atonement in one set of years for his acts of a previous and quite different one seems not, on reflection, to be an exception but, curiously, more like a norm. If this was Gallone's work of expiation, in what sense can we say with utter certainty that the far better known *Roma città aperta* was not Rossellini's?[11] A whole society can only purge its recent fascist past by acts of conscience on the part of its individuals and the consequent evolution of a new morality at the national level. And these in turn will tend to be evident in the art works it produces. Politics is not usually a matter of reaching one set of convictions and remaining true to them for ever. Those few who actually do cling unchangingly to convictions arrived at early are usually either saints or knaves, but in either case living human dinosaurs by our usual ways of reckoning these things. Gallone's *Avanti a lui tremava tutta Roma* was unquestionably his way of guaranteeing, after his brief purge for complicity in the cinema of the previous period, that by 1946 he was as perspicacious an antifascist as any other Italian. (So many others, after all, had swung through an equivalent 180 degrees in their political allegiances in the space of a few short years or in far less time often than that!) At one level the film might even be read as an apologia on Gallone's part and on behalf of the nation. For it shows, especially in the figure of the singer played by Anna Magnani, how easy it was to fall to combinations of blandishment and threat at the hands of the Nazi occupiers: just as in Puccini's opera Tosca herself reveals Angelotti's hiding place to Scarpia, first because of her jealous relation with her lover Cavaradossi (a jealousy carefully played on and heightened by Scarpia at the end of the first act), and second, under the intense torment of being forced to hear Cavaradossi's screams offstage in the second act, as he is being tortured in Scarpia's Roman headquarters, the Villa Farnese. In short, *Avanti a lui tremava tutta Roma* deserves a great deal more attention by students both of opera and of the fall of fascism, and will only be understood fully by analyses that respond to its differing levels of representation of how a dictatorial regime flourishes upon the suppression of individuals. For what seems most important is how flexibly the original structures and content of Puccini's work of 1900 –

particularly its treatment of Scarpia as torturer – lent itself to Gallone's pacey and subtle cinematic representation of the Nazism which had been so recently overthrown in Italy.[12]

The other post-war performance I wish to remark on briefly is Maria Callas's 1958 début at the Paris Opéra. After the initial half of this first performance, during which she had sung arias from a wide operatic repertoire, the whole second half was a staged version of Act II of *Tosca*, with Tito Gobbi once again singing the role of Scarpia, but for the first time opposite Callas. For someone with a known antipathy towards *Tosca* from the earliest years of her time at the Royal Opera House in Athens – to the point of considering it the opera that occupied the 'last place on [her] scale of preferences'[13] – this performance, of which rare black and white footage exists,[14] is a striking testimony that the singer with the so-called 'voice of the century' could lay claim also for consideration in any final adjudication of 'actress of the century'. Possibly by 1958 Callas had herself been so reified in the role of prima donna, with all the journalistic and indeed sexual attention that such a status clearly brought with it, that performing the part of Tosca allowed too little theatrical release into a character that she could play as someone fully 'other' than herself.

For as has elsewhere been remarked of Tosca, in words that can be applied equally to Maria Callas, being the prima donna is her ' "real" profession' in the unfolding drama. 'With her culminates the myth of the prima donna finding its absolute fulfilment. The story turns her life into a stage production.'[15] By the mid-1950s Callas's story too was, sadly, the stuff of world-wide 'operatic' renown. She was beginning to be 'undone' – to deploy a term suggested by the title of Catherine Clément's challenging book, *Opera, or the Undoing of Women* – by the public that had made her. From our vantage point over forty years on, and more than a quarter-century since her premature death (following as it too soon did the sad demise of her voice as the incredible instrument it had once been), it is easier to understand some of the wellsprings of Callas's distaste for playing the part of the sexually harassed and love-torn prima donna Floria Tosca.

But that doesn't mean she couldn't do it. On the contrary, she could play it all the more 'for real', in keeping with what has sometimes been seen as Puccini's thorough exploitation of the themes and styles of *verismo* in this work. Callas's professionalism and perhaps also the increasing levels of personal torment she was facing as a prima donna on

**Figure 8** Maria Callas as Tosca and Tito Gobbi as Scarpia, in the Covent Garden production of 1964. Callas and Gobbi are perhaps still the most famous interpreters of Puccini's work about artistic individualism entrammelled by a politics of oppression. Gobbi sang the role of the oppressor Scarpia many hundreds of times, whereas Callas grew increasingly to dislike playing the figure of the fated diva – possibly for its too close approximation to aspects of her own life. Photo: © Zoë Dominic.

an international scale saw to it that she assumed the narrow but intense role of the *Roman* prima donna of 1800 as perhaps no one before or since has done. T. S. Eliot once said of another artistic achievement sometimes held in low esteem (like *Tosca*) for being two-dimensional and 'of the surface' – Ben Jonson's comedies – that their fineness lay in Jonson's ability 'to deal with the surface of life . . . so deliberately that we too must be deliberate, in order to understand'.[16] Even seeing extant footage of it a full generation and more later, Maria Callas's terrifying 1958 Paris début rendition of Tosca's overthrow of the tyranny that would otherwise ravish her and subject all else to its powers – her killing of Scarpia – was likewise consummately deliberate artistry, which stimulates 'deliberate' attention from the viewer, and repays it in terms of further understanding of the work's own intensities.

\* \* \* \* \*

I now come to the real-time televisual *Tosca* of 1992. With 'disunification' haunting the Italian public at the national level since at least as early as the so-called *anni di piombo* ('years of lead') of the 1970s (years which had produced terrorism from both left and right[17]), and with the international scene looking scarcely brighter, in spite of the absence of global conflicts as we moved into a *fin de siècle*, certain entertainment industries – not just Italian – had vested political interest in producing spectacle which in one way or another represented cohesion, even if it could not really be claimed that they created cohesion of a lasting or permanent kind. A most signal instance of this in the world of opera was, as with the three tenors concert ('the most successful operatic programme ever shown on television'[18]), an important televisual spectacle from Rome. This was the aforementioned production of Puccini's *Tosca*, with Zubin Mehta conducting the RAI Symphony Orchestra, and starring Catherine Malfitano, Placido Domingo and Ruggiero Raimondi in the leading roles (see Plate 7). More important from a novelty point of view, however – and very important for producing the almost subliminal levels of cohesion which in my interpretation of its underlying politics were so crucial – this production was not only set in the real Roman locations of the three acts of the opera, but beamed out by satellite to a world-wide audience in the 107 countries which had become partners in the enterprise, at the three separate times of the day (afternoon, evening and following dawn) that are the times represented by the three phases of the action.

The technical ingenuities that were deployed for this production seem (at any rate to any opera buff used to stage performances) no less than astounding. An account written before the event let us know that there would be

> eight cameras . . . and all the technical paraphernalia for a live show ready for artists on each location. The singers will wear radio microphones in their hair and be able to see and hear the orchestra, the RAI Symphony Orchestra, in its base two miles away, on closed circuit monitors.

The same report had a curious way of discounting any possibility of failure at the operatic level, by claiming beforehand that it could not fail to be a coup in televisual terms: 'If it works, it will be wonderful. If it doesn't work, it will still make the most fascinating television.' A strange new confidence surrounds the art form of opera when it can be underwritten in this manner with a kind of insurance policy that will pay on demand at the very least 'the most fascinating television'.[19]

To form views on whether the production had to fall back on such an 'insurance policy' as TV spectacle, we have to ask questions about how well opera and television have here been merged and made inseparable. That will involve asking also to what extent we are being led by this RAI production's lavish presentation into a kind of televisual tourism of the Roman past or present – the film thus making itself over in part to the 'heritage' industry. If so, what is the significance of those 107 countries *apart* from Italy that were also involved financially? Were they mere financiers of a spectacle that would mainly bring honour to the country of context, Italy? Or were there larger and more global politics at stake?

It would be churlish to suggest that this 1992 production was anything other than a major operatic experience and consummately interesting as television also. For one thing the production took the veristic detail of Puccini's work to further levels, which were only made possible by virtue of that other medium – television itself. Puccini had insisted on exact indications of setting and action in the libretto and, as to the scoring, his preoccupation with actual as opposed to imaginary context is attested in such actions as his much-noted search for information on the notes and timbre of church bells in the vicinity of the Castel Sant'Angelo, so as to achieve mattutinal effects true to the real location of the third act's setting. For all that some commentators speak of his lack of overt political interests, Puccini must have had reasons for putting the Rome of a particular historical moment on the operatic stage an exact century later. I have suggested that these reasons lay in a replacement of the grand self-sacrificial gestures of the slightly earlier political traditions of Verdian opera, and a new harkening to the values of individual experience, which when themselves taken to their limits are almost always at or beyond the margins of social acceptability. Some combination of art and love and sensuality is of supreme importance to all three principal figures in this opera, and although all three die in their attempts to achieve a consummation of their desires, they do so largely because they take their distinctive individualisms beyond sanctioned limits. We have to conclude that if Puccini was not promoting public political causes in the manner of a Verdi – in spite of a few significant republican and Voltairean leftovers from Sardou's stage play – he was by this point in his career highly interested in what one commentator has called 'the ruinous tumult of the instincts in erotic seduction', leading to a destiny and a politics of 'victimism' in his heroes and heroines – itself a politics of the new century, in the first month of which the opera was premièred.[20] The producers of this 1992 television spectacle undoubtedly had certain other ends in view, no less political (in the wider senses of the term). Before speculating on what these were, let us spend some more time exploring *its* evocations.

Consider the credits of the film. They are superimposed over helicopter shots of the course of the Tiber river in Rome – in blurred black and white, the only such use of monochrome in a production which is otherwise sumptuously colourful. There follow further aerial views of the locations of the three acts; the Basilica Sant'Andrea della Valle, the Palazzo Farnese and the Castel Sant'Angelo. The locations are naturally all seen at this early stage from the exterior; whereas apart from one further external shot at the beginning of each separate act the action takes place entirely indoors, until the final execution scene on a rampart of the Castel Sant'Angelo. Likewise, with the exception of a few opening notes from Puccini's score, the soundtrack too, for much of the time that the credits roll, consists only of the noise of the helicopter. Isn't anyone with a modicum of cinema-goer's experience more than faintly reminded of something else in this helicopter introduction to Rome?

Unquestionably, it is the opening to Federico Fellini's film *La dolce vita*. However, the common idea is used to greatly differing effect. Instead of the robust ironies of Fellini's aerial portrayals of a Rome given over to hedonism, the helicopter journey over Rome in this televisual *Tosca* seems bent on another enterprise entirely. In a sense, its aim is to resituate Rome as what it once was, before *La dolce vita*; before, in short, the dissolution or profanation of previously binding factors of common cultural experience – Rome itself, or at any rate the *idea* of Rome, cardinal among them – a dissolution and profanation which Fellini's film of 1960 had been more instrumental than perhaps any other work of art (Italian or otherwise) in signalling.[21] Here in 1992 Rome is once again offered as the centre of a 'civilized' world – its focal role being no longer imperial or religious as in the past, but that of the binding secular experience of the modern age, television itself. The credits emphasize the participation of 107 nations in the production, and some of their names, organized by continent, scroll across the top and bottom of the TV screen in these opening sequences. This underlying ideology of 'civilization' and its resiting with newly reified value around the technological miracles of the modern world's most representative medium, television, was certainly one which all 107 participating countries could – and did – heavily buy into.

For these purposes of promoting Rome as a new kind of (televisual) world capital, it would be hard to imagine a more ideal work than *Tosca*, set as it is in a church, palace and castle of this great city; nor a more captivating 'other' medium (to lend kudos to the televisual) than that of opera, with its cultural profile so recently and successfully relaunched from this very city; and no more attractive a male lead to play the painter and lover of the piece, Mario Cavaradossi, than the only one of the three tenors – so instrumental in that relaunch two years earlier – who could look and act the part, Placido Domingo. (Pavarotti couldn't look it, Carreras cannot really act.)

In my closing comments about this television production I wish to concentrate on just one representative use of the actual setting of Rome used so effectively throughout. This moment happens also to be the production's own final lingering image, after Tosca's suicide leap. It was at once an underlining of her lines about meeting Scarpia again before some final tribunal, as well as a profound *application* of one piece of Rome's vast cultural heritage to those final, musically underlined, aspects of the meaning of Puccini's work. After Tosca has sung her last words and made her leap, and after the final bars of orchestral scoring of Cavaradossi's last aria which stresses never having so loved life as in this moment of losing it, the camera rises to a graceful baroque statue of the figure of Justice, with sword in hand, on high above the Castel Sant'Angelo – as though to stress an eventual justice in the next world if not in this. From a city which down through the centuries of Christianity has so promulgated messages of such a justice, *this* was the kind of underscoring of the work's own leitmotifs which the production could eloquently achieve by having the real Rome as its televisual setting. Too much of the kind would have been tedious. None at all would have been to miss a great opportunity. Fortunately, the producers used the treasures of Rome's remarkable cultural heritage with good taste, and in so doing managed to achieve the effect of global cohesion around images of that 'universal' city.

Let us not delude ourselves, however, about the conservatism of this success. It was a production that aimed for a deep-structural recuperation of a traditional sense of Western cultural cohesion, around edifices and artefacts and beliefs found nowhere in such profusion as in Rome; a recuperation which other countries seemed interested enough in seeing achieved within the binding international medium of television as to pay handsomely for being in on the credit roll. Britain even paid twice, since, in a unique case, the BBC and Channel 4 both screened the production, the first in the real time of the three acts as broadcast live from Rome, the latter all in one programme on the following evening. It was truly in the words of Alan Yentob, then controller of BBC 2, a case of 'stretching the boundaries of television in imaginative ways'.[22]

\* \* \* \* \*

I should like to provide a kind of epilogue to this chapter in the form of some reminders of how opera has always been political (even to the extent that the *absence* or withdrawal of opera from the public scene has been politically important at moments in its history as an art form). A simple way of doing so is by rehearsing just a few cardinal points about one of the great composers in the medium, Verdi, that link clearly with what has already been said about the revitalization of this art form on the part of our contemporary and especially our televisual culture.

Slip back to the year 1848 in imagination, when small revolutions to shake off the fetters of reactionary or foreign overlordship sweep across the face of Europe. Verdi is in Paris at the year's opening, hastily adapting *I Lombardi* as the renamed *Jérusalem* for the Paris Opéra, and completing *Il corsaro* in fulfilment of a contract with the publisher Francesco Lucca. He is thus in that city during the stirring days of February and utterly enthusiastic about the revolutionary turn of events there. But he returns to Italy shortly after news of the Milanese and Venetian uprisings against the Austrian presence, and their declaration as independent republics in the latter days of March. In a famous letter to the librettist Piave in Venice, written from Milan on the 21 April (or in other words, approximately a month after the heroic 'Five Days' of fighting to oust the Austrians), Verdi voices the typical Risorgimento ideal of a 'Republic' that is nothing less than the whole of Italy – a reality that incidentally was not to come to pass until almost exactly a century later, as a result of the eventual plebiscite to abolish the Italian monarchy at the end of the Second World War:

Imagine whether I wished to remain in Paris, hearing of a revolution at Milan. I left immediately I heard the news, but was only able to see these stupendous barricades. Honour to these brave men! Honour to all Italy! Yes, yes, a few more years, perhaps only a few more months, and Italy will be free, united and a republic. What else should she be?

More interestingly still from a musician's point of view, he inverts the notion of politics within music and stresses instead the idea of *no music but that of revolutionary politics*. In times of revolution all other music – all other sound indeed – than that of guns is ludicrous:

> You talk of music to me! What are you thinking of? Do you imagine I want to occupy myself now with notes, with sounds? There is, and should be, only one kind of music pleasing to the ears of the Italians of 1848 – the music of the guns.[23]

This is what I meant a little earlier when I spoke of the politics of opera being important even when opera itself is temporarily *in absentia*. Verdi's notion is in fact not that opera has absented itself from the national stage, but that events on the national stage are the only 'opera' worth attending to, and far more heroical in form than any which has been musically 'composed'.

Let us not forget that this composer, so willing to abandon music in the name of something more important, was the same Verdi who had written operas throughout the 1840s that were progressively more explicit foretastes of the sacrifices and glories to be experienced in any such revolutionary realization of the (so far repressed) political ideals of the times. For one of pronounced Mazzinian tendencies, that inevitably meant the eventual creation of an independent Italian Republic. With the advent of the actual, even if somewhat piecemeal, revolutions of 1848 – making the realization of that ultimate goal more likely – Verdi saw no need for music as such. Music may have helped to unleash the 1848 revolutionary tide sweeping across Europe, but for Verdi personally, writing amidst the fervour of these events, music in itself meant nothing apart from them and, indeed, should no longer be composed as a distraction from them, since *only* they were of any importance. At such a time *only guns comprise music*. It is a highly revolutionary moment when the greatest Italian composer of the century can reduce all meaning in the realms of sound to so unequivocal and concentrated an essence.

The moment passes, both in Europe and in the history of Italian opera. Not before its passing however – later in the same year of 1848, in fact – Verdi had composed and sent to Mazzini a battle hymn, 'Suona la tromba' ('Sound the trumpet'), in response to the latter's hope for something that might become 'the Italian "Marseillaise" '.[24] Interestingly, ever since the composition in 1842 of Verdi's first really successful opera, *Nabucco*, its slave chorus 'Va pensiero' ('Go, my thought . . .') had often served as a musical rallying point of nationalistic ambition, particularly against the foreign oppressor in the north, Austria. Unlike 'Suona la tromba', however, that chorus is a hymn not of direct battle but of yearning for another and freer existence. In other words, Verdi had been better at capturing the feeling of Italian national sentiment in the 'coded' messages of his operas, set in other states and other eras, than in uncoded music written for the overt political struggles of the contemporary moment.

We have in our own times an instance of much the same phenomenon. As instanced earlier in this chapter, 'Nessun dorma' from Puccini's *Turandot* captured the mood of slowly surging triumphalism of the World Cup festivities of 1990, and subsequently became a kind of musical palimpsest for striving and achievement in football. In football, but far more than merely football – in our own age's political *Zeitgeist* more generally, hankering as we must surely confess we mostly do to be surrounded by traditional Western culture, in a kind of apotheosis of the feel-good factors of victory and/or cohesion. Much like 'Va pensiero' from *Nabucco* in the 1840s, 'Nessun dorma' had achieved all this without the general public being aware of, or caring a fig for, its original context and meaning in an 'orientalist' opera of the mid-1920s. Indeed, it is hard to imagine any 'commissioned' piece of music achieving the same level of musical penetration and success.

Returning to Verdi in conclusion. He was scarcely less passionately interested in the detailed course of events in the war against the Austrians of 1859 than he had been in the 1848 revolutions. While buried in the countryside at his rural home of Sant'Agata near Parma he had his friend Mariani keep him posted almost daily during certain of the more eventful periods of fighting. The spirit of excitement and sense of beauty even in the spectacle of battle and sacrifice is well represented in a few sentences of the many hundreds Mariani wrote to the Verdis, husband and wife, in this period:

Oh my Verdi, *sommo Maestro*, why aren't you here, with your kind

Signora Giuseppina, to enjoy this unique spectacle, impossible to describe! Oh! how imposing is the sight of an army and a people, throwing themselves with assurance into battle, in the war between tyranny and justice and civilization! Long live Italy, God's true blessing! Long live those who generously come to shed their blood for her![25]

Any close look at lines like these will demonstrate how much a part of the spirit of the age in question were Verdi's more political operas. Here in the prose of his close friend and correspondent Mariani is the poetic fervour of many a grand gesture by Verdian heroes and heroines, involved in their own battles 'between tyranny and justice'.

If more than a hundred years later new life is being breathed into operas which when originally written gave direction to the politics and vigour to the national struggles of their age, then what precisely is the political agenda they are being used to serve in our present day? This chapter has assumed throughout that the restaging of them is something more than a recuperation of *musical* heritage for its own sake. It has sought plausible hypotheses in answer to the question just posed, in an attempt to stimulate more widespread discussion of the politics of this, our own age. In particular, it has looked at innovatory presentations of the traditional repertoire of opera in film and on television, the underlying agendas of which surely cannot be interpreted except by putting the politics of their moments of production under new forms of scrutiny, such as I hope I have initiated here.

## Notes

1. Mr Herbert Chappell, quoted in *The Times*, 27 June 1990.

2. From the first episode of *Harry Enfield's Guide to Opera* (Ecosse Films for Channel 4, 1993).

3. For a fuller treatment of the connections between Italian politics and the operatic tradition, particularly as developed by Verdi, see George Martin's chapter 'Verdi and the Risorgimento', in William Weaver and Martin Chusid (eds), *The Verdi Companion* (London: Victor Gollancz, 1980), pp. 13–41; also in George Martin's own *Aspects of Verdi* (London: Robson Books, 1988), pp. 3–28.

4. Recontextualization of a not dissimilar kind is to be noted on the new Classic FM radio station in the UK, where Mozart's Piano Concerto No. 21 is no longer given so dry a specification as its Köchel number, but anachronistically referred to as 'Mozart's *Elvira Madigan* Concerto', after the Swedish film in which it was extensively popularized.

5. Nicholas Soames writing in *The Times*, 9 July 1990.

6. See Mosco Carner, *Giacomo Puccini: Tosca* (Cambridge: Cambridge

University Press, 1985), p. 13.

7. William Ashbrook, *The Operas of Puccini* (Oxford: Oxford University Press, 1985), p. 84. See also William Weaver's summary of the unhappy closing years of the nineteenth century for Italy, with the failures of the Abyssinian campaign, and socialist riots as well as urban and rural disorders from Apulia through the central regions to Milan in the north, in *The Golden Century of Italian Opera from Rossini to Puccini* (London: Thames and Hudson, 1980), p. 220. For more detailed accounts of the period see Richard Drake's *Byzantium for Rome: The Politics of Nostalgia in Umbertian Italy 1878–1900* (Chapel Hill: University of North Carolina Press, 1980), and Richard Bosworth's *Italy and the Approach of the First World War* (London: Macmillan, 1983).

8. William Weaver writes of Puccini's having 'little interest in politics' and, for instance, of his writing very casually in letters about such events as riots in Italy, in the years leading up to *Tosca*; in particular, of the offhand way he refers to a truly scandalous event – when the army under the command of General Beva-Beccaris fired upon a civilian crowd in Milan, killing almost a hundred of them and wounding a great many more (*The Golden Century of Italian Opera*, p. 220). This is an indisputable aspect of Puccini's life. But it is a different, and in my view less tenable, argument to proceed as Julian Budden does, to claim in talking of Puccini's works that 'the wider issues, whether of politics or religion, lay outside his grasp' (article on Puccini in *The New Grove Dictionary of Opera*, edited by Stanley Sadie [London: Macmillan, 1992], p. 1171). The evidence of *Tosca* alone interrogates such an opinion forcibly, as I hope the different perspectives on it provided by the present chapter convincingly demonstrate.

9. Catherine Clément, *Opera, or the Undoing of Women*, translated by Betsy Wing, foreword by Susan McClary (London: Virago, 1989), p. 10.

10. Either atonement or, to be more pessimistic still in our hypotheses, a rank opportunism on Gallone's part in projecting the politics of the new era. In support of the first hypothesis, of atonement or expiation on Gallone's part, see Gian Piero Brunetta, *Storia del cinema italiano: dal 1945 agli anni ottanta* (Rome: Editori Riuniti, 1982), p. 476. Brunetta remarks that Gallone 'sought an ideological rehabilitation after the short, formal ban to which he had been subjected'.

11. For a careful assessment of the degree of Rossellini's implication in fascist propaganda in his three war films, *La nave bianca* (1941), *Un pilota ritorna* (1942) and *L'uomo della croce* (1942), and for his tracing of cinematic techniques that were to evolve and flourish in the putting across of quite another politics in *Roma città aperta* and later films, see Gian Piero Brunetta, *Storia del cinema italiano: 1895–1945* (Rome: Editori Riuniti, 1979), pp. 403–6. An account of how he as well as Gallone (see next footnote) and many many others were subject to the investigations of the Commissione per l'Epurazione delle Categorie Registi (Commission for Purges in the Category of Filmmakers) is also given by Brunetta in his subsequent volume of the same work, *Storia del cinema italiano: dal 1945 agli anni ottanta*, pp. 24–5.

12. William Ashbrook makes mention of Gallone's film in *The Operas of Puccini*, p. 84, fn. 51; it is also mentioned along with *Roma città aperta* in Jeremy Tambling, *Opera, Ideology and Film* (Manchester: Manchester University Press,

1987), p. 60. Fuller information on the episode in Gallone's career that I have revisited in this narrative is to be found in Brunetta, *Storia del cinema italiano: dal 1945 agli anni ottanta*. For more on this period of Italian film see Mira Liehm, *Passion and Defiance: Film in Italy from 1942 to the Present* (Berkeley: University of California Press, 1984).

13. From memoirs which originally appeared in the Italian magazine *Oggi* in 1957. Reprinted in David A. Lowe (ed.), *Callas as They Saw Her* (London: Robson Books, 1987), p. 20. There is an interesting consonance to be noted between Callas's distaste for *Tosca* as drama and Catherine Clément's case that the representation of women throughout practically the entire art form of opera is curiously reductive, by being always so interested in their eventual destruction. See Clément, *Opera, or the Undoing of Women, passim*.

14. *Maria Callas: débuts à Paris, 19 décembre 1958*, EMI Classics Video, 1991.

15. Clément, *Opera, or the Undoing of Women*, p. 38.

16. T. S. Eliot, *Selected Essays*, 2nd revised edn (London: Faber and Faber, 1934), p. 148.

17. See Paul Ginsborg's *History of Contemporary Italy: Society and Politics 1943–1988* (Penguin: Harmondsworth, 1990), especially Chapter 10, 'Crisis, Compromise and the "Anni di Piombo", 1973–80', pp. 348–405, for a succinct account of the general fear and malaise of these years.

18. Richard Fawkes, 'Domingo's Authentic *Tosca*', *Opera Now*, July 1992, p. 56.

19. *Ibid*.

20. Lorenzo Bianconi, from his article on Italy in *The New Grove Dictionary of Opera*, Vol. 2, pp. 853–5. Explaining further what he means by the term *victimism*, Bianconi speaks of it as 'the predisposition to a kind of failure that is both actual and (unlike in Verdi) moral' (p. 855). It is highly suggestive to consider the period of the turn of the century (i.e. the period of the composition of *Tosca*) in terms of precisely some such 'failure'; failure, furthermore, at more than just the level of Puccinian heroes and heroines. Thinking along those lines leads us to another reason for saying that although not perhaps interested in every day's political events, Puccini had a deep-structural feel for the political nuances of his times, and could represent such qualities very much *from the inside* in his portrayal of particular characters and their characteristic 'clear but "weary" melodies' (to adopt once again terms used by Bianconi in the article cited).

21. Peter Bondanella's book *The Eternal City: Roman Images in the Modern World* (Chapel Hill: University of North Carolina Press, 1987) deals with Fellini's place in the history of Roman mythology.

22. Reported in *The Times*, Saturday 11 July 1992.

23. Quoted in Frank Walker, *The Man Verdi* (New York: Alfred A. Knopf, 1972), pp. 187–8. I am strongly indebted to Walker's outstanding biography for many of the details about Verdi made use of in this final section of my argument.

24. *Ibid.*, p. 193.

25. Quoted in *ibid.*, p. 305.

# CHAPTER 6

# MIMESIS OR MONTAGE?

## REFLECTIONS ON THE LANGUAGES OF LITERATURE AND CINEMA

The immediate if lesser goal of this chapter is to establish some new lines of approach to neorealism, a phenomenon of early post-war Italian literature and cinema. Neorealism never fully cohered into a programmatic movement but had, nonetheless, a number of distinctive themes and recognizable narrative styles. I shall be seeking to elucidate a few of these *en passant*. But my real subject is larger – namely, a reflection upon the related languages of literature and cinema within the longer history of Western realism. I am not unaware that calculations of real*ism* are themselves only possible in any final analysis by reference to the still more challenging cultural and historical complexities of Western *reality*, in wider senses; and that to attain any (even minimal) purchase on something so difficult, countless factors, forbidding to analysis, of constant change and moment-to-moment difference – difference especially of the kind we must entertain as fissuring specific cultures internally – must be borne in mind.

The core of the implied project of the literary and cinematic movement of neorealism has been defined, in the words of a critic writing about one of the first neorealist films, Luchino Visconti's *Ossessione*, as its attempt to produce an 'X-ray reading of the bone structure of a society'.[1] The neorealist treatment of the preceding fascist epoch strips it of its fake glamour and reveals how impoverished Italy was by the war, materially and spiritually. Italo Calvino in a piece of writing entitled 'Autobiography of a Spectator', which stands as Preface to four film scripts by Fellini, wrote of the stark difference between pre-war and post-war Italian cinema:

> non c'è un mondo dentro lo schermo illuminato nella sala buia, e fuori un altro mondo eterogeneo separato da una discontinuità netta, oceano o abisso. La sala buia scompare, lo schermo è una lente d'ingrandimento

posato sul fuori quotidiano, e obbliga a fissare ciò su cui l'occhio nudo tende a scorrere senza fermarsi.[2]

There is not [as formerly] one world inside the illuminated screen in the darkened cinema and, outside, another heterogeneous world, the two separated by an absolute discontinuity, ocean or abyss. [Rather] the darkened room disappears, and the screen becomes a magnifying lens placed before quotidian reality, which obliges us to stare at what the naked eye tends to pass over without noticing.

A number of the usually small-budget films of the neorealist school have become cinema classics, largely thanks to the intensity of their social criticism. Some of the first and finest, such as Rossellini's *Rome Open City* and his *Paisà*, directly represent the Italian theatre of war. By contrast one of the last of the major neorealist films, and which owes a great deal to those earlier works by Rossellini, treats a different war, contemporary with the last phase of neorealism itself – the French colonial attempt to hang on to Algeria against the independence movement of her peoples. Gillo Pontecorvo's *The Battle of Algiers*, although directed by an Italian and co-produced with Italian money, deals with a politics other than that of Italy itself. This film deepens the achievement of neorealism as a school or artistic principle by pressing it to serve a set of insights concerning a non-Italian phenomenon. The theories of the recently deceased Frantz Fanon on the psychological determinations of late colonialism form its philosophical core. Here we see the strengths of a specifically Italian artistic development exported and deployed in one of the more important statements in any art form about the violent conflict between late colonialism and insurgent independence movements. The film helps us to understand such conflict better and, thereby, to elucidate interrelations between concepts of mimesis and montage. Hence, the exemplary status of my study of certain scenes from it at the end of the chapter.

On the Italian home ground neorealism analysed disquieting realities faced by a large part of the population. It demystified the glorifications that had characterized much artistic representation in the prior fascist epoch. And although this phase of literature and cinema finally gave way to other, often less astringent, styles during the so-called 'economic miracle' in the late 1950s and early 1960s, so distinctive by then had neorealism become that we must ask, today, exactly how and why it was left behind.

Fellini's own career provides a pivotal illustration. His earlier work contributed significantly to neorealism, and it is possible to show that the avant-gardist fabulism of his last two black-and-white films of the great middle period, *La dolce vita* and *Eight and a Half*, still owes much to the achievements of the earlier artistic styles. At the same time those two films testify that neorealism's rigorous gaze into the torments of the past, its attempt to tell exact truths about the way things had been, was finally giving way to more opulent fantasies which, although still intermittently retrospective, presupposed, in the very spaces opened up for dreams and for the contemplation of their symbolic meanings, the alternative possibility of brighter individual and collective futures, certainly more possibilities within a lifestyle still recognizably Italian. Fellini's and other Italian filmmakers' post-neorealist careers, whether predominantly optimistic or pessimistic, pose open questions about what future the ongoing present will turn into, at least as forcibly as they propound a typically neorealist philosophy of the predetermining nature of the past.

An abiding problem of some early neorealist films, and one that rather quickly dated them as works of art, was that in their directors' hopes for, and hence efforts to achieve, a certain simplicity, especially in the contemplation of misery and suffering, they often fell into a self-created trap of mere simpl*ism*. As time goes by, this is what at any rewatching weakens a film like De Sica's *Bicycle Thieves* of 1948, erring starkly as it does in the direction of melodrama with a social message. By contrast, and from the very beginning of his work as a filmmaker in his own right, one of Luchino Visconti's most appealing beliefs was in complexity. As early as 1943 he would declare, 'I was attracted by the cinema because it coordinates so many demands and enthusiasms that lead to a better, *more complex*, work' (my emphasis).[3] This reaching on his part by means of all the many aspects that have to be co-ordinated in filmmaking towards something like the complexity of the world itself as he understood it, led him in the same early article to speak in terms, not utterly unlike Eisenstein's accounts of montage (shortly to be treated in this analysis), of the 'new reality' that comes into being in cinematic art. In Visconti's case the emphasis was not laid upon anything like aesthetic or technical principles of montage as such, as with Eisenstein (whose films and early writings, by the way, Visconti certainly knew well, since they were much studied by the entire group of artists centred on the Centro Sperimentale di Cinematografia in Rome from the 1930s onwards[4]); rather, upon 'working with actors', that is 'with the human material with which we build those living men who give birth to a new reality'.[5]

It will already be apparent that to make sense of the content of the materials for study in this chapter, there is a more fundamental need to engage with certain theoretical considerations of artistic form and process. As always in this book my larger interests remain cultural and historical. But in the present instance formal considerations cannot be conveniently placed to one side. In any case, reflecting precisely upon the *languages* of literature and cinema provides an exciting access route into issues I wish to clarify concerning the cultural moment of neorealism. We can establish some key bearings by referring to statements about montage and mimesis in the writings of Sergei Eisenstein and Erich Auerbach respectively. Another writer who adds to the interest of the discussion immeasurably – particularly in what he implies about the limit conditions of specific art forms (what one medium can reveal where another must remain mute) – is a surprisingly early but nonetheless compelling thinker on matters crucial to the overall subject: Dante Alighieri.

* * * * *

In elucidating how 'the role set itself by every work of art, the need for connected and sequential exposition of the theme, the material, the plot, the action' may be fulfilled, Eisenstein writes of what he sees as a key property of montage in the language of cinema: 'that two film pieces of any kind, placed together, inevitably combine into a new concept, a new quality, arising out of that juxtaposition'.[6] Eisenstein will quickly emphasize that what he is saying about montage is a factor in other art forms also and is by no means merely apparent only in cinematic technique. His main point lies rather in how the juxtapositions involved in *any* representation work to create some 'new concept' or quality; and his argument always rests in a sense of how the 'separate representational elements' reassemble themselves in formal terms within 'the spectator's perception'; 'The strength of montage resides in this, that it includes in the process the emotions and mind of the spectator.'[7]

Erich Auerbach on the other hand, amidst so much else that is spelled out or implied about mimetic processes in the authors he considers in his critical classic, *Mimesis: The Representation of Reality in Western Literature*, sees an important threshold of modernity in the major fiction of Stendhal: 'insofar as the serious realism of modern times cannot represent man otherwise than as embedded in a total reality, political, social, and economic, which is concrete and constantly evolving – as is the case today in any novel or film – Stendhal is its founder'.[8]

On first considering these different positions, one crucial matter stands out: that for Eisenstein the very principle of montage allows for a potential infinitude of expressive and conceptual novelty, whereas for Auerbach any aspiration on the part of art towards a serious realism of modern times, be it in novel or film (the two forms he names, amidst so many other possible ones), always has a yardstick *external* to the art realm in question, against which to measure mimetic achievement: namely, 'a total reality, political, social, and economic, which is concrete and constantly evolving'. We might therefore for simplicity's sake infer that for Eisenstein the marvellous possibilities for something ever new, something 'constantly evolving', lie in the *language of montage itself*, whereas for Auerbach mimesis (realism) is a stricter master because, first and foremost, it is the world *out there* which is ever changing: art works must find ways to represent that other, circumambient order of changing things, so as the more deeply to understand and thence control it – or at the very least know and control one's own place in relation to it.

While it is clear that Eisenstein is concentrating on the expressive possibilities of art and Auerbach on the exigencies of trying to represent a reality that precedes art and which will still be there when artistic representation ceases, it is also clear that there are ample moments in their writings where these roles are reversed – that is, where Eisenstein focuses on the exigencies of capturing on celluloid factors of that total reality about which Auerbach speaks, and where Auerbach dwells by contrast on the powerfully inventive ways that given artists whom he studies have found of representing reality differently from anyone else – nonetheless there *is* a fundamentally different outlook in their two treatments. For Eisenstein, montage really is a realm of artistic possibility so powerful that we are forced to consider it even as a potential tool of propaganda in the changing of reality itself, something that might alter the evolution occurring in the political, the social and the economic (to redeploy Auerbach's terms), a goal which, after all, a number of Eisenstein's own political films certainly had. For Auerbach, by contrast, the subject of discussion is always the *representation* of reality, not the changing of Western reality *by means of* representation.

Additionally, it must be admitted that if one art form has altered reality in our century more than any other it is the one which is the subject of Eisenstein's early and pioneering studies and of his own practice: namely, cinema. This pre-eminent importance of film, and Eisenstein's individual significance as exponent and expounder of its powers – most especially the possibilities of montage – were not lost on the rising generation of neorealist cinematographers in Italy in the closing years of fascism and first decades of emergence from it.

*****

It may seem odd, therefore, that with so pressing a modern art form at the heart of this chapter's interest, I now circle back almost seven centuries to an incident in Dante's *Comedy* and perceptions embedded in it, before proceeding. But I hope the point of seeing the passage in question as a kind of 'shooting script' before the fact will illuminate what is later said about actual cinematic achievements, much as Eisenstein quotes the lengthy notes on the representation of the Deluge from Leonardo da Vinci's *Trattato della Pittura* as an extraordinary 'shooting script', consummate in its montage effects of 'sound and picture coordination'.[9] The material in Dante for discussion at this point is a narrative sequence in which examples of 'montage affects', very much as Eisenstein describes, *as well as* a particularly intense realization of Auerbachian mimesis figure prominently. It comes from a section of *Purgatory*, namely the ledge of pride, where Dante is in any case wrestling long and deeply with the nature of particular art forms. In the course of several cantos (X–XIII) poetry, manuscript illumination, painting and sculpture are all dwelt upon, in a vast critical review of contemporary artists, and of what can, or more appropriately what *should* (given the egregious pride which Dante sees as endemic in individual artists), be considered the highest reaches of their individual achievement.

What is so notable is that Dante himself comments throughout a portion of this incident on the effects of mimesis achieved in stone bas-reliefs, placed here in Purgatory as exempla of humility and pride by the divine artist, God: 'intagli sì, che non pur Policleto,/ma la natura lì avrebbe scorno', ('such carvings that not only Polycletus but Nature herself would be put to shame', X, 32–3). Dante produces in the process of his narrative commentary a kind of spectator-response theory to which we do well to attend. In short, he dwells upon how the bas-relief art works, being the work of no mere human artist but rather the divine sculptor, created uncannily 'realistic' affects upon his own perception as spectator. But even as we hear him comment upon how these particular and utterly novel affects were achieved, we are startled to realize that he is talking in very precise terms of Eisensteinian montage before the fact. Crucial in other words to the drama are what Eisenstein stresses as fundamental, 'the emotions and mind of the spectator' – in this case Dante's own. And ours too, we could claim, since the further affect of this kind of writing is that Dante's account of *his* reactions ventriloquizes a similar set of responses in ourselves;

> Era intagliato lì nel marmo stesso
> lo carro e' buoi, traendo l'arca santa,
> per che si teme officio non commesso.
> Dinanzi parea gente; e tutta quanta,
> partita in sette cori, a' due mie' sensi
> faceva dir l'un 'No,' l'altro 'Sì, canta.'
> Similemente al fummo de li 'ncensi
> che v'era imaginato, li occhi e 'l naso
> e al sì e al no discordi fensi.

(There, carved in the same marble, were the cart and the oxen drawing the holy ark, because of which men fear an office not given in charge. In front appeared people, and all the company, divided into seven choirs, made two of my senses say, the one 'No', the other, 'Yes, they are singing.' In like manner, by the smoke of the incense that was imaged there my eyes and nose were made discordant with *yes* and *no*.)

(X, 55–63)

Here in the bas-relief depiction of the ark of the covenant being removed to Jerusalem, Dante is claiming to witness achievements beyond human art and even beyond nature, such that his senses are disrupted: his sight swearing that he could see the choirs actually singing in spite of his hearing attesting the contrary; and (yet again) his sight leading him to believe he saw the smoke of real incense, whereas his sense of smell remained in denial. As will soon be apparent from further quotation, this passage from Dante rests for its meaning and effect upon the use of the Italian word *pareva*. What we note immediately upon seeking to translate this term is that it covers all the range of meaning in English from 'there appeared' (i.e. what transpired) to 'it seemed' (i.e. what was an impression only, but one strong enough to delude at least one of Dante's senses in any given moment). Largely by means of the range of meaning of the repeated word *parea/pareva*, the effect of the original Italian text is to obfuscate any clear distinction between actuality and seeming.

Since Leonardo's achievements have already been invoked in the larger discussion by Eisenstein, let me recall here in passing how we frequently refer to his dreams in pen and ink of winged contraptions attached to the human form as anticipating by hundreds of years the modern age of flight. In analogous terms, what I am trying to suggest is that we should with no less amazement conceive Dante as having imaginatively anticipated the primary form of 'motion pictures' in these passages from *Purgatory* describing animated bas-relief sculpting. Or rather, perhaps we should say 'motion sculptures', because what is described in movement is a three-dimensional art form. In short, the account is pitched in the zone between virtual and literal reality – just where, indeed, we are now in the habit of stressing that movies themselves reside (or holograms, as a friend has recently put to me). And since we are thinking in such terms, we should emphasize that Dante's account anticipates not the early phase of silent films; rather, his motion sculptures emphasize very particularly an ongoing conversation, such that the analogy we must draw is with the later and technically more amazing 'talkies'.

> Quiv'era storïata l'alta gloria
>     del roman principato, il cui valore
>     mosse Gregorio a la sua gran vittoria;
> i' dico di Troiano imperatore;
>     e una vedovella li era al freno,
>     di lagrime atteggiata e di dolore.
> Intorno a lui parea calcato e pieno
>     di cavalieri, e l'aguglie ne l'oro
>     sovr' essi in vista al vento si movieno.
> La miserella intra tutti costoro
>     pareva dir: 'Segnor, fammi vendetta
>     di mio figliuol ch'è morto, ond' io m'accoro';
> ed elli a lei rispondere: 'Or aspetta
>     tanto ch'i' torni'; e quella: 'Segnor mio',
>     come persona in cui dolor s'affretta,
> 'se tu non torni?'; ed ei: 'Chi fia dov'io,

la ti farà'; ed ella: 'L'altrui bene
a te che fia, se 'l tuo metti in oblio?';
ond' elli: 'Or ti conforta; ch'ei convene
ch'i' solva il mio dovere anzi ch'i' mova:
giustizia vuole e pietà mi ritene.'
Colui che mai non vide cosa nova
produsse esto visibile parlare,
novello a noi perché qui non si trova.

(There storied was the high glory of the Roman prince whose worth moved Gregory to his great victory: I mean the Emperor Trajan. And a poor widow was at his bridle in attitude of weeping and of grief. Round about him appeared a trampling and throng of horsemen, and above them the eagles in gold moved visibly in the wind. Among all these the poor woman seemed to say, 'My lord, do me vengeance for my son who is slain, wherefore my heart is pierced.' And he seemed to answer her, 'Wait now till I return.' And she, 'My lord,' like one whose grief is urgent, 'and if you do not return?' And he, 'He who shall be in my place will do it for you.' And she, 'What shall another's welldoing avail you, if you forget your own?' He then, 'Now take comfort, for I must discharge my duty before I go: justice requires it, and pity bids me stay.' He who never beheld any new thing wrought this visible speech, new to us because here it is not found.)

(X, 73–96)

Let us remind ourselves of the basic situation. On this ledge of purgatory where the proud are punished by being weighed down by vast stone weights which they must carry on their backs, Dante is witnessing, in bas-relief sculpting on the facing of the cornice, representations of pride humbled. The emperor Trajan is one such, delayed in his haste to be off to the wars by a poor widow who is requesting him with arguments that brook no denial to visit justice upon those who have murdered her innocent son. (See Plate 8 for a fifteenth-century manuscript illumination of this scene from *Purgatorio*.) The story is apparently much repeated in medieval compilations of exempla.

We presume that in order to have written up several of these exempla in the way he does, Dante must at some stage have personally responded to the finest contemporary sculpting of the period just prior to his own: work such as that by Nicola and Giovanni Pisano and other lesser-known Pisan craftsmen, examples of which abounded by 1300 in Tuscany and were still being produced. It is hard to conceive of him writing here as he does of sculptings which break the essential limit condition of this art form – its unmoving stillness, whatever the *semblance* of movement carved into the stone – if he had not seen the finest work of mere human artists of the recent period. I say mere human artists, because Dante's whole case is that only because the works he witnessed had come forth from the hand of God could they break beyond the limits of the medium in question ('Round about him appeared a trampling and throng of horsemen, and above them the eagles in gold moved visibly in the wind').

The dramatic conversation between Trajan and the widow is played out with exactly such juxtapositions as are characteristic of Eisenstein-ian montage. From the realm of appearances – 'the poor woman seemed to say . . .' (*pareva dir* – and that is the last we hear that verb of seeming) – the conversation firms in virtual terms through subtle twists and turns, as the widow applies a very scholastic form of argument to detain the reluctant emperor. There is on the part of the poet a registering of actual back-and-forth conversation, in which the very omission of the verb *pareva* now aids and abets the strong impression of passing beyond mere seeming. By the conversation's end Dante is able to commit himself to the oxymoronic notion that what he was witness to was visible speech, *visibile parlare*.

What is extraordinary is that Dante had conceptualized and described an artistry that defies all limits of the given form (in this instance sculpting) in its representation of the protagonists, the emperor and widow: through their intense *conversation in stone* they become not less but more real for him and for us. I have suggested that Dante's sensory responses are themselves analysed in the text in ways that would grace modern, response-based forms of criticism. We might say that while for Dante the extraordinary mimesis lies in the affects of the sculptings on his senses, for us the mimesis is still more all-embracing, by our having Dante's own astonishment represented within the frame of what we witness and are led to think about. And then, at precisely this point of his argument – an argument embedded so far in the emperor's and widow's drama of sculpted retorts (literally visible speech) and of Dante's responses to them – Dante, in a summarizing judgement about God as an artist beyond time and beyond limitation, makes Eisenstein's own point about montage; namely, that the juxtaposition of two utterly different things (here stone and speech) creates something utterly new. ('He who never beheld any new thing wrought this visible speech, new to us because here it is not found'). Historically speaking, nothing like the brave new world of cinematic montage had been even remotely imagined until this point in the *Comedy*, and its actual realization still lay centuries ahead.

After approximately a century of film, we may now have lost some sense of how utterly revolutionary is the ongoing potential of moving images, projected or transmitted with accompanying soundtracks by the complexities of modern screen and televisual technologies. Certainly, the neorealists were not generally in the habit of taking radical changes for granted. I shall later give an example of how, in the midst of his searing film *The Battle of Algiers*, Pontecorvo was able subtly to establish that an inert, documentary presentation of facts is poles apart from the capturing in montage-nuanced sequencing of *meaning behind facts*.

* * * * *

Before tackling the medium of film, however, I should like to dwell on *literary* neorealism. Writers of the neorealist period, to whom we owe many of its finest achievements (a fact too frequently forgotten when neorealism is casually scaled down and thought of as solely a phenomenon of the cinema), were often hypersensitive to how the real enters, or is encapsulated within, a given medium. I shall deal with a single telling instance, indicative of the force of many others.

In one of his earliest stories, 'La passeggiata prima di cena' ('The Walk before Supper'[10]), the Ferrarese writer Giorgio Bassani casually tackles the by then (1950) familiar problem of the modern realist writer or film director: how to penetrate beyond the frozen or unfocused lineaments of mere documents to the inner core of what motivates a life, a group of lives, a region or an entire society. The problem is also the age-old one of how fiction and history may ever merge, instead of being always intrinsically different. How may fiction – mere stories, whether in prose or film – add to our understanding of the actual course of history?

The laconic opening of Bassani's story, telling how mottled yellow postcards almost a century old may still be picked up in the junkshops of Ferrara, gives way to a description of a *particular* postcard of the main city thoroughfare, Corso Giovecca. After describing the non-human artefacts of the old photograph, such as public buildings, shops and tramway rails, the writer proceeds to catalogue the foreground of this picture, teeming with particulars: a barber's apprentice picking his teeth,

a dog snuffling at the footpath in front of the horse-butcher's shop, a
schoolboy almost run over by a hansom cab as he crosses the road, a
gentleman in redingote and bowler hat going into a cafe, and a fine four-
horse vehicle mounting the street towards Ferrara's centrepiece, the Este
Castle. All is orderly and precise in this perspective:

> Senonché, non appena uno tenta di indagare, socchiudendo magari le
> palpebre, l'esiguo spazio centrale della cartolina, corrispondente al fondo
> più remoto della Giovecca, siccome tutto, in quel punto, si fa subito
> confuso (cose e persone non vi hanno più alcun rilievo, dissolte, come
> risultano, dentro una sorta di pulviscolo luminoso), basti questo a spiegare
> perché mai una ragazza di circa vent'anni, che proprio allora, camminando
> sveltamente lungo il marciapiede di sinistra, era arrivata a non più d'un
> centinaio di metri dalla Prospettiva, non sia riuscita a tramandare fino a
> noi, riguardanti odierni, la benché minima testimonianza visiva della sua
> presenza, della sua esistenza.[11]

> Except that no sooner does one attempt with squinting concentration to
> scrutinize the narrow middle distance of the card, corresponding to the
> furthest point of Corso Giovecca, than everything at that moment suddenly
> becomes blurred. Things and people no longer stand out, as before, having
> now dissolved into a kind of luminous mist. All this is sufficient to explain
> how a girl of some twenty years, just then walking briskly down the left-
> hand footpath, and who had come to within a hundred metres of the
> Prospect, might fail to convey to ourselves, onlookers of the present age,
> the least signs of her presence or existence even.

It is a strange narrative moment, this impulse to fill out details in a life
that the photograph failed to record. The mere existence of such
photographs is a sign that the past has not faded beyond recall. They are
documentary proof of former modes of existence, of former lives in this
busy Ferrarese thoroughfare. But there is a corollary point, which is the
inverse of the other. Namely, how poor as documentation of a pre-
existent reality this postcard actually is, both on account of time's
mottling and yellowing processes, but also because the techniques of
photographic recording are themselves only adequate within certain
limits. Beyond those limits are (or rather were) real presences, actual
human existences. The photographs in which all the vast inscape of
personal life cannot be recorded are mere *aides-mémoire*, telling of
context.

For example, in the present instance it is quite hard from the words
Bassani has written to know whether on the old postcard there is any

evidence at all of the 'girl of some twenty years', whose life from this early moment in the story he begins to treat in more than photographic detail. Are we are to understand that she does indeed figure in the middle ground of the postcard, but in a form blurred by the factor of photographic focus, misted over by the ravaging effects of time on the printed image, such that we as modern onlookers will never notice her unless or until she gets singled out by some other procedure of representation such as Bassani's story? Or else that she figures not at all in the nineteenth-century postcard, which can only at best to onlookers of today conjure up a general context from the past, such a context as requires, for the telling of individual lives, a quite other procedure of representation – a logic leading us once again to Bassani's story?

Strangely enough, there is an implied aspersion cast on photography as a recording medium, whether we believe there is some slender evidence of the existence of the girl in the postcard or not. For Bassani's point is that we moderns will miss such evidence in any case – and most certainly know nothing of consequence about particular lives in the foreground, middle ground or background of our old and chanced-upon postcard – unless or until some other measures of representation fill out the lacuna. The aspersion on still photography as a recording medium is to the credit of literature in this instance. As readers we are invited to slip into the middle ground of a particular photograph – one chosen from many and which we only 'see' through Bassani's words, since it too (the postcard that is) in the final analysis is a verbal conjuration. In such a way – the writer with an innocent air insinuates – all that was left unrecorded by the tripod camera of 1888 (a date the story furnishes) may become living detail in the neorealist narrative of 1950. The young woman who does not figure in the old photograph, or at best has only a liminal existence there, is inserted into her place (or brought forth out of the original blurred focus or subsequent mottling) by the writer. And this act of insertion or bringing forth is crucial for the reader. For it is by this literary sleight of hand that we are made to believe in the woman's existence quite as if she *had* figured as a noteworthy presence in the original postcard. The old photograph has served its purpose as documentary validation of lives having being lived. And now, from out of its blur and yellowing the narrative of a particular life develops in the further progress of Bassani's sentences. In a curious way, therefore, the entry into literary narrative via still photography (still photography which in this case is itself really only a conjuration on the part of literary narrative) does actually validate what follows, in spite of the limitations of the photographic medium which have been suggested.

The heightening of effect need not be literary in kind, though it is in the present instance. We can, if we choose, equally imagine the old and blurred postcard as an initial still frame in a neorealist film, which, after several seconds gradually transmutes into the montage effects of cinema, allowing for the singling out of a 'girl of some twenty years, just then walking briskly down the left-hand footpath'. As in the writing, so in the effects of cinematic montage: it does not greatly matter if there were initial traces of the girl's existence there in the original image or not. If there were, they were in any case extremely minimal, and it took the further processes of montage representation to get particular things said about the young woman's life.

Once the entry through the old postcard into a former era has been effectuated – whether in the montage sequences of film, or, as in the present instance, in writing – the subsequent portrayal of the young woman's life (her working-class appearance, her daily cares as an apprentice nurse in the general hospital in Ferrara, her name, even the precise gestures of her ways of moving on the day the photograph was taken) can be recorded as though not a matter of fictional imputation on the writer's part, but a simple documentation of what the camera failed to record. All this counts importantly as a small instance of neorealism's project (that is, not Bassani's alone, and irrespective of how 'consciously' he was rehearsing it in the present example) of *giving a documentary impression*. Neorealism takes an original 'document', the postcard, and elaborates on the basic reality it already records.

Bassani in fact nearly spoils his carefully built effects of a past reality by being a trifle facetious about the unlikelihood of contemporary passers-by noticing Gemma Brondi, any more than the emotionally 'indifferent' camera seems to have done. But he risks this facetiousness in order to imply the further role his neorealist art will play in distinguishing the indistinct.

In una strada del prestigio di corso Giovecca, e, per giunta, nell'ora particolarmente animata, eccitata, che a Ferrara, oggi non meno di ieri, ha sempre preceduto l'intimo rito serale della cena, è da supporre che anche a un occhio meno indifferente d'un obiettivo fotografico il passaggio di una ragazza come questa sarebbe forse sfuggito.[12]

In a street of the prestige of Corso Giovecca, particularly animated and excited furthermore at the hour which in Ferrara, today no less than before, has always preceded the intimate ritual of supper, we may presume that even to an eye less indifferent than a photographic lens, the passing by of a young woman such as this might have gone unnoticed.

Bassani implies here with tongue in cheek that the girl, while not interesting enough for the camera to pick up, and possibly not even noticeable to the 'less indifferent' eyes of her contemporaries (he spends a couple of long sentences describing her un-made-up visage, neither becoming nor unbecoming), is worth *his* while singling out. Worth his while, because she is so everyday and unremarkable in her appearance as to constitute for the neorealist artist an otherwise hidden-from-view norm in that past Ferrarese society he wants to represent more fully. And this too is a crucial aspect of the neorealist project – to take someone on all 'objective' counts (even that of nineteenth-century photography) too ordinary to be noticed, and seek to represent this very ordinariness in a way that does justice to it, in inverse proportion to her absence from all other representations and accounts of the Ferrara of 1888, possibly including even the exemplary postcard.

The process of wresting precise details from the faded anonymity of time past is repeated shortly afterwards in the writer's handling of the man whom Gemma Brondi marries, Dr Elia Corcos. Once again we note Bassani's fascination with the imprecision and gradual blurring of a real context. This time his incidental 'document' is a hospital group photograph in which Gemma and Elia are two small heads among many. The photograph has been preserved by Gemma in a bedside cupboard until her death. It is sold off along with other effects to an antiquary after the presumed death of Elia in a German concentration camp in 1943. And that would seem to be the end of it. It disappears into the anonymizing dust of an antiquary's junkshop, just as the street postcard of Ferrara had emerged from one some years later. Except that Bassani then engages in a curious exercise as he imagines our reaction on rediscovering it:

Ebbene, ammesso che, esplorando le viscere di un polveroso e tarlato mobiluccio venuto fuori da un fondo di magazzino, fosse tuttora possibile recuperare la fotografia in parola, non sarebbe improbabile che, guardando con attenzione il viso smunto, avido e estremamente pallido di Elia Corcos a trent'anni, noi potessimo avere il senso abbastanza esatto dello stupore di Ausilia Brondi, prima, e subito dopo, di sua madre,

> quando i loro occhi alfine si posarono su quella realtà così diversa dall'altra che, a poco a poco, si erano venute costruendo a forza d'immaginazione. Dunque un dottorino di quelli dell'ospedale! – dovettero esclamare, deluse e irritate.[13]

Well, supposing that while exploring the innards of a dusty and worm-eaten chest brought forth from the remote corner of a storehouse, it were possible to retrieve the photograph in question, it is likely that looking attentively at the lean, eager and extremely pale face of the thirty-year-old Elia Corcos, we might experience roughly the same shock as Ausilia Brondi and straight afterwards her mother felt, when their eyes finally lit on the reality, so different from that which little by little they had constructed in imagination. So, just another of those hospital doctors! – they must have exclaimed, disappointed and irritated.

The process of recuperating a past reality is arbitrary and roundabout. First of all, the hospital photograph ('una classica foto-riccordo') is itself a reduction of the doctor's and the young nurse's lives to two scarcely distinguishable heads among rows of others. Its rediscovery more than half a century later is a mere narrative supposition. *We* are the persons imagined as fossicking in these remains of the Brondis' lives, and the writer superimposes our presumed reaction to the photograph onto the sister's and mother's (also presumed) reactions of the previous century, when they realized the identity of Gemma's lover. Once again documentary evidence (however minimal) is used as a peg on which the narrator may hang information of a kind which the document itself never incorporated.

We are on the frontier between historical real*ity* and fictional real*ism*, which neorealist writers like Bassani were concerned to cross in a manner that took their readers with them. The rest of the story, an account of the prosperous Jewish doctor Corcos and his acceptance that his prospects will be limited by marrying a girl of the people (and a gentile, furthermore), depends on the writer's handling of this issue of documentary authenticity. The preoccupation with somehow validating a tale when actual evidence is lacking or drastically insufficient is characteristic of the Italian neorealist movement as a whole, especially in this relatively early phase. In drawing attention to his own piecing together of narrative out of almost nothing – old and faded photographs, which he has even gone to the lengths of imagining being found by a pronominal 'us' – Bassani is virtually exposing his devices of authentication, and pressing the neorealist project towards a *demystification of its own procedures*. Nonetheless, like other writers and film directors of the period, throughout the writing he seems engaged (however 'give-away' his wearing of his philosophy of narration on his sleeve) in an attempt to demonstrate that the gap between documentary-style fiction and actual history really can be minimized, in the interests of telling the fullest truth of these years.

That phrase, the truth of these years, brings me to the most significant point of all about this particular but also representative story. It is very much a 'lest we forget' piece of recuperation. Indeed, Bassani's entire literary project was one haunted by the Holocaust, so recent to the writing of these stories. The longer work for which he is best known, *The Garden of the Finzi Contini*, is in this respect entirely consonant with the key theme of most of his other writings, which record the lives of a major segment of Ferrarese society, that of a centuries-old Jewry, the last generation of which had been decimated by fascist complicity with the Nazi extermination machine. The story I have been treating is itself haunted by the possibility that all these lives may now slip with time into the same relative oblivion as that of the musty, dusty postcards with which it began. We realize with a kind of passion that it is this deeper *philosophy of history* that has been the point of the narration – how arbitrary is our purchase on even the relatively recent past, and yet how all-important it is to hang on to a whole cast of social reality through memory, or at very least seek to re-create it by reference to the rapidly decaying evidence. For Bassani, the imperative was to recapture – before it became too late – the very ordinariness of individual Ferrarese lives, so brutally extinguished by a human machine of annihilation.

\* \* \* \* \*

From a different set of angles, documentation in relation to an obliterating violence is also at the heart of the final stage of this chapter. It comes from virtually the last film we can with confidence still call neorealist, Gillo Pontecorvo's *The Battle of Algiers* (1966). 'Neorealist' in a self-conscious sense since, as Joan Mellen's pioneering and finely detailed 1973 *Filmguide to* The Battle of Algiers[14] makes clear, Pontecorvo traces his own development as a filmmaker back to Rossellini's war film *Paisà* of 1946, and emulates a number of Rossellini's methods in the filming. Like Rossellini working to a tight budget, in classic neorealist fashion Pontecorvo used mainly a hand-held Arriflex camera for the filming. More importantly still, in his direct treatment of a theatre of war he followed Rossellini in the use of an actual historical setting, in this case the city of Algiers.[15]

I have scope here to focus only upon an exemplary segment of the film, which deals memorably with what Pontecorvo as interviewed by Mellen called 'the process by which society, any kind of society, arrives at a point of total crisis'.[16] The crisis in question is that of the Algerian Revolution during the bloodiest of its struggles from 1954 through to 1957. In what follows I study the film's representation of the checkpoints set up between the old casbah of the city and the newer French quarters as revealing sites of that 'total crisis'. In simple terms the main interest of these checkpoints lies in how three Algerian women pass through them unsuspected, on their way to placing bombs at strategic points in the French city. It is important to highlight what Pontecorvo, and before him Frantz Fanon, saw as women's role in the particular revolutionary moment, asking (insofar as the film allows us to) exactly what issues of female identity are raised in this moment of anti-colonial revolution.

The following analysis is mounted upon the strong foundations laid by Mellen, in particular her invaluable interviews with Pontecorvo, which are near enough in time to his making of the film to lay bare other key influences than Rossellini upon it, such as Eisenstein for style and Fanon for some fundamental pointers as to meaning. We now benefit from a further generation's distance from the events represented, with all the added range of possible insight into narrative effects on the one hand and, on the other, the nature of late colonialism in relation to revolutionary independence movements bent on its overthrow. But already in 1973 Mellen had put these matters firmly on the agenda as themes for consideration in any concerted attempt to understand the film. In any case my local study cannot cover all aspects of the film. In a book whose main topic is Italy and Italian culture, to seek to do so might represent too lengthy a diversion away from principal considerations. Nonetheless, there is good reason for dwelling on this loan (as it were) of Italian expertise and thought to the wider world, precisely because it lies outside the realm of what is usually considered when global influences of Italian culture are dwelt upon. As the character of the visionary Italian architect and urban designer played by Vittorio Gassman in Alain Resnais's later film, *La Vie est un roman*, famously put the case, these influences are typically seen as espresso bars, luxury goods and opera.

As a corrective to that kind of conventional account of what gets exported, one of the points of the present argument is that at the end of its useful shelf life in Italy, neorealism as a film style had one more valuable place to go; namely, across the Mediterranean to a newly independent nation which had been born in sorrow out of bloody struggles, after 130 years of colonial domination. In the initial period of neorealism Italy itself had emerged (and been represented precisely by neorealism, in the form of Rossellini's two films *Rome Open City* and *Paisà*, through bloody struggle *as* emerging) from the bonds of the fascist *ventennio*, and from the even worse period of direct Nazi occupation which had followed hard upon the fascist collapse. Mellen informs us that Pontecorvo had originally considered using that biblical term, 'to give birth in sorrow', as the film's title, his intention being, in words used in interview with her, to show that 'the birth of a nation happens with pain on both sides, although one side has cause and the other not'. Mellen's own further point here is that 'Pontecorvo does not agree with Fanon's view that the colonized man finds his freedom, and indeed a positive identity, in and through violence.'[17] We need to ask how Pontecorvo, dependent as he is on Fanon for his ways of representing so much else about the processes of revolutionary action, could have differed with him on so fundamental a point?

In the section dealing with the checkpoints and bombs in the French city, Pontecorvo's film provides its own implied critique on violence. To understand what it is saying we need to attend to the way it records brute historical realities by means of two quite different forms of film documentation. The first one is based on a narration that definitely communicates information and its meaning to its audience. The second, which quickly follows, is a mere dumb recording of the same situation on celluloid, with no clue as to its precise meaning. To do this Pontecorvo needs two films and two audiences. The first film is the frame film, *The Battle of Algiers*, and its audience is of course ourselves. The second is a film within that frame film, taken at a French checkpoint for screening Algerians issuing from the casbah during the period of greatest violence in the city. Its audience is Colonel Mathieu and his French paras, about to 'start again from zero', as Mathieu himself puts it, in getting to the bottom of how those bombs have been placed by the FLN during this bloodiest period of the war.

In the most readable and detailed history in English of the Algerian Revolution, *A Savage War of Peace: Algeria 1954–1962*, Alistair Horne reminds us what a record of honour the French 'paras' (paratroops) held for their combined combat records:

> Before Indo-China most had distinguished themselves in the Liberation and the final battles of the Second World War, and several had been deported to concentration camps for their work in the Resistance. They were to bestride the Algerian scene like demigods until the tragic peripeteia of 1961, and even such a pro-F.L.N. film as the remarkable Pontecorvo–Yacef production *La Battaglia di Algeri* comes reluctantly close to vesting its French para colonel 'Mathieu' with heroic qualities.[18]

Horne is surely right about Pontecorvo's respect for his French colonel, even at this point where Mathieu is about to order that all means be resorted to in the interrogation of suspects, so as to trace the complete command network of the FLN. The film *is* very even-handed in its representation of the sufferings of the civilian French on the one hand and the indigenous population on the other.

But nonetheless, its real interest lies in the nature of Revolution itself. And in this it stays fairly close to Pontecorvo's own distinctly Marxist leanings, inflected as they were by the strong influence of his recent reading of Fanon's vision of late colonialism. A book such as *The Wretched of the Earth* had theorized the distinction under colonialism between the French *ville* and the native casbah or medina as a chasm between two worlds, unbridgeable except by the negative feelings of hatred, fear and envy. This divide between *ville* and casbah is signalled in a grand aerial panning shot at the opening of Pontecorvo's film, and becomes in the process of narration which follows – especially in the French authorities' setting up of checkpoints between the two in their attempt to sift through the Islamic population for the real bombers – as manichaean a division as anything in Pontecorvo's political and psychological master-theorist, Fanon. Indeed, the point of concentration on these checkpoints in Pontecorvo's film is that they highlight what Fanon himself in *The Wretched of the Earth* had called the 'primary Manichaeism' governing colonial society during the bloody period of decolonization: colonizers and colonized in the Algerian situation had never been so clearly each other's 'enemy, . . . opponent, . . . foe that must be overthrown'.[19] The checkpoints are thus chicanes of violent interrogation, harassment, arrest even. Few are those who pass through them unscathed. The film shows us the awesome excitement of three Algerian women doing so undetected, with bombs in their baskets for immediate priming and then placement at strategic points in the French *ville*.

At the heart of these particular scenes in the film lies another and more problematic piece of writing by Fanon on the role of Algerian women in the Revolution: his chapter 'Algeria Unveiled' from the book *Studies in a Dying Colonialism*.[20] Fanon has been criticized by recent commentators for insufficiently understanding the place of the veil in Algerian society.[21] But whether or not he grasped fully the role of women within this traditional Islamic culture, Fanon is certainly convincing in his accounts of the French attempt to persuade Algerian women to unveil themselves, which he interpreted as a key facet in the strategy of colonial domination, and particularly in what he has to say about a subsequent self-transformation by Algerian women under conditions of the Revolution. In unveiling themselves in order to pass unnoticed in the French *quartiers*, they had to learn what he calls a 'new dialect of the body'. Fanon's comments at this point underlie virtually every nuance of Pontecorvo's realizations in the film extract under analysis:

> Carrying revolvers, grenades, hundreds of false identity cards or bombs, the unveiled Algerian woman moves like a fish in the Western waters. The soldiers, the French patrols, smile to her as she passes, compliments on her looks are heard here and there, but no one suspects. . . . We must come back to that young girl, unveiled only yesterday, who walks with sure steps down the streets of the European city teeming with policemen, parachutists, militiamen. She no longer slinks along the walls as she tended to do before the Revolution. . . . The Algerian woman who walks stark naked into the European city relearns her body, re-establishes it in totally revolutionary fashion.[22]

That 'young girl' of Fanon's theoretical description is very much the same young girl of Pontecorvo's representations, whom we have previously seen along with the other two unveiling and making herself up for the bombing mission. The scene at the checkpoint when the youngest of the three women passes through is full of a very solemn humour created by our sheer nervousness about whether she will be detected, since we already know her deadly mission and indeed have just witnessed the no less tragic bombing of the casbah (itself in revenge for the increasing number of killings of French policemen by the FLN) for which it is in reprisal.

Mellen's account of the prior scene of unveiling claims that the three transform themselves 'into French women so that they can pass through the checkpoints',[23] or at the very least, we might add by way of modification, into their darker-skinned *pied-noirs* counterparts; in either case into women at one in spirit with the continuance of French colonial domination of Algiers. It is possible to rest content in that interpretation, which explains better than any other how readily they are accepted into cafe and milk-bar society in the French quarters of the city. But I have been led to doubt if these women in their disguised form are not meant to represent that other and crucial Fanonian category, the indigenous Islamic women who have accepted the French colonial pressure to unveil and adopt Western habits and dress styles – women all the more welcomed in French colonial society, according to Fanon, because their 'coming over' was a sign that the French themselves were successfully stripping the traditional Islamic population of more of its female constituency, so vital for its integrity and continuance. If one thinks of these three women's disguise as transforming them not into Frenchwomen or *pied-noirs*, but into a particular and recognizable (and to the French colonizers highly acceptable) category of Algerian women, namely those who have already put off the veil and 'passed' as more 'evolved' (*évoluées*), because more Western in their customs, then the way in which the particular guards at the checkpoints do not prevent their progress, as they do in the case of all other Arab movements between casbah and French *ville*, takes on a further cultural interest. Indeed, it raises for us more complex questions of 'passing' by means of successful mimicry; or perhaps we need to say, of masquerade, a term more favoured by some within a particular feminist debate on such matters. I shall deal briefly with aspects of this debate.

Fundamentally, it concerns an issue of mimesis itself. As Luce Irigaray famously put the case in writing of 'Subordination of the Feminine', for women operating within a discursive complexity of Western codes and values, mimicry, or the assuming of the 'feminine role deliberately', may be used primarily as a means of converting 'a form of subordination' – that is, 'ideas about herself, that are elaborated in/by a masculine logic' – 'into an affirmation', which can thus 'begin to thwart' that subordination: 'To play with mimesis is thus, for a woman, to try to recover the place of her exploitation by discourse, without allowing

REFLECTIONS ON LITERATURE AND CINEMA

herself to be simply reduced to it.' At this very point in her argument
Irigaray herself talks of *unveiling*: 'if women are such good mimics, it is
because they are not simply resorbed in this function. *They also remain
elsewhere.*'[24] Unveiled only to herself, according to Irigaray, for the
woman who mimes a role defined by masculine 'ideas about herself'
there persists throughout the mimetic performance a different and
specifically 'material' identity, available to herself and in gratifying
forms, but crucially in an *elsewhere* state.

In drawing upon these ideas to help towards a deeper understanding
of Pontecorvo, it must be stressed that in the case of *The Battle of
Algiers* they need to be subtly reformulated for the very different
context. For whatever else may be the similarities with the situation for
women as theorized by Irigaray, the site where mimicry or masquerade
takes place in the film's narrative is not one located internally to the
West. Rather, these checkpoints are where persons, who in our narrative
began as patently non-European women, manage to 'pass' as Western in
all essentials – or at the very least as Western*ized* – as part and parcel of
their being engaged in the revolutionary overthrow of a particular
European colonialism. Certainly, the three women who carry the bombs
into the French *ville* do, in Irigaray's terms, assume a feminine role
deliberately in order to avert detection at the checkpoint. We could even
stay with Irigaray's terminology in calling that possibility of detection a
danger of 'subordination', so long as we supply the caveat that here it is
not really gender subordination which has to be overcome, but the
cultural subordination of one people by another. Issuing forth from the
casbah, as the three women do, the particular 'feminine roles' which
they assume must reassure the French soldiers by appealing to existing
'ideas . . . elaborated in/by a masculine logic'. The three must manage to
set off in the minds of the French checkpoint controllers a set of 'ideas
about themselves' by playing with mimesis. Their disguises must ensure
that they are read by the French soldiers as culturally not different from
but the same as themselves. Overall, therefore, it is not really *gender*
domination that is at issue as in Irigaray's discourse (though the women
in the film do thwart the subordination in question by playing on their
femininity, each in subtly different ways); rather, the particular
masculine logic – if looked at in its fundamental structures – would
be found to be that of *colonial* domination, so widely discussed by
Fanon in writings about this revolution. The women must by their
particular feminine demeanour appeal to this logic and thereby outwit

it, by passing unhindered between Arab and French culture; the point of demarcation between the two being the checkpoint itself, which hence takes on a symbolic as well as a starkly literal significance in the film as a cultural 'border'. The Arab women can only pass such a border undetected through their use of that 'new dialect of the body' of which Fanon spoke. In essence the 'dialect' is understood by the French controllers of the situation as their own. The mimesis goes undetected in all three cases as the *representation* of an evolved European-style femininity, and is mistaken for the real thing.

The three women's *self*-perception at such points of 'total crisis' is the hardest thing of all to understand. Consider what we can know about them from surrounding moments. We are aware in the women's glances of regret before the mirror while effectuating their disguise of Westernized hairstyles and make-up, and then also in the fear displayed by the younger two at the points where they leave their bombs, that whatever the revolutionary identity they put on it is not the 'positive' Fanonian one of finding freedom in and through violence. Indeed, I would risk suggesting that it is instead something more like the gaining of a radically *negative* identity. Adapting for present purposes Keats's wording in defining his concept of negative capability, I should say that the women disguise themselves not with anything like the assurance of an *existence elsewhere* of the kind Irigaray posits, as out of a capacity to go through the uncertainties and self-doubts of violent revolutionary actions without any irritable reaching after gratifications of a recognizable and secure self-identity. That does not mean that they have no need of *apparent* identity, put on as a masquerade for the assuring or even gratification of others. Indeed, implicit in what I am defining as negative identity is the notion that it involves precisely the deployment of an *appearance* for others (in this case the French guards at the checkpoints) to *miss-take*.

The women at this point in the film would seem to be in a *time between* the discarding of their old identities in the unveiling scene and the adoption of new ones which will only become possible with the successful outcome of the Revolution. Only by imagining the situation thus can we understand their acts as a Revolutionary willingness to lose their lives in the cause, and hence even that very possibility of taking up some other and new identity after the Revolution. The deferral of *any and all* identity other than as masquerade for the deception of others is all about sacrifice, about willingness to be sacrificed. Of course, the

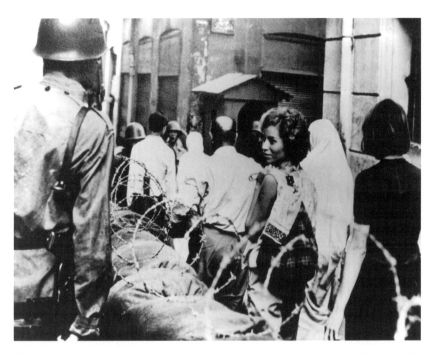

**Figure 9**    Checkpoint between Arab casbah and French *ville*, in Gillo Pontecorvo's film *The Battle of Algiers* (1966). The checkpoints can by thought of as markers of a cultural boundary, between Frantz Fanon's two worlds of the colonizers and the colonized, only able to be passed unsuspected by means of successful 'masquerade' as a member of the dominant, colonizing culture. Such 'passing' is a special instance of colonial mimicry, much discussed in post-colonial studies following a seminal essay by Homi Bhabha. Reproduced by permission of BFI Films: Stills, Posters and Designs.

better their acts of mimesis at the checkpoints, the less likely they are to be caught and hence sacrificed in the cause of Revolution.

The negative or deferred identity of which I am speaking is precisely the condition which facilitates the production of an *apparent* identity by means of a special kind and use of what Homi Bhabha has called 'colonial mimicry'. How may we understand better what the film sees as involved in this assumption of an appearance? Joan Rivière in her elaboration of ideas by Ernest Jones on the early development of female sexuality wrote as early as 1929 on 'Womanliness as Masquerade',[25] anticipating much of the case made by Irigaray that is being modified for the present argument. Rivière says that women may put on 'a mask of womanliness to avert anxiety and the retribution feared from men . . .'

Like Irigaray after her, Rivière was defining acts based on behaviour between individuals of one and the same culture, in their assumption of gender roles and hence culturally characteristic gendered identity. But once again, our example in the film is *cross-cultural*, and that makes a great deal of difference. The three women passing through the checkpoints do indeed assume different forms of womanliness, appropriate to their different ages, and in every sense it is to avert the retribution feared from these men, the French soldiers, should they be caught.

The mask is also a matter of 'make-up', as we see in the preceding unveiling scene. On the relationship between make-up and identity within a Western framework consider the following formulation: 'Cosmetic artifice expresses even more fundamentally a mode of relation to one's own body, a mode of cultivating transience instead of stasis, multiplicity instead of singularity, elaboration instead of simplicity, and extension instead of limitation of one's self-image.'[26] This too has a lot to offer our own present analysis, provided we can see and analyse the difference made by the situation in the film being *cross-cultural*. I spoke before of the women in the unveiling scene taking on, in the process of disguise, a negative identity regarding themselves and an apparent identity for others. The point of framing the case that way lies precisely in its being a transience, elaboration or extension of self-image for the sake of the Revolution. For instance, the particular Algerian woman who puts on lipstick before the mirror in the unveiling scene – with a hardness of look worthy of Lauren Bacall – must surely be imagined as asking herself the equally hard (because life and death) questions, Will this do? Will this pass? 'Pass' as just the kind of transient elaboration of apparent identity by means of cosmetic artifice that will automatically be miss-taken by the soldiers – when she arrives at the cultural divide that they are policing – as the Western or at least Western*ized* woman.

Pontecorvo soon shows us this same scene at the checkpoint as shot on another, hidden camera by the French authorities. And the totality of effect of this film within a film, as well as the important lessons we can draw from it about neorealism (in fact, about montage in larger senses than merely neorealist), constitutes, it seems to me, very great filmmaking. We, the audience of the larger and enframing film, are in a position of total advantage in knowledge over the other audience of the checkpoint recording – Mathieu and his recently arrived 'paras'. But such an advantage hardly feels like a privilege, especially now that we have already seen the devastating effects of the bombs that the young girl and the other two were on their way to place. Having seen the women's revolutionary moves, we are now at the command centre of counter-revolutionary operations. In other words, we began with the scene of 'unveiling', in the sense that we saw the women effectuating the disguises that were to see them through the checkpoints. Unaware as yet of the full horror to follow, we nonetheless saw in their facial responses, backed by the urgency of Morricone's and Pontecorvo's drumbeat soundtrack (itself based on the music of the Gnowa people's blood sacrifices), the transformation at the level of 'dialect of the body' necessary in the assumption of the revolutionary role. We end with the scene of Mathieu showing his paras the inert and unrevealing film record of the checkpoint camera. They know none of all that we do about the identity of the bombers and how their disguises had been achieved.

Instead, as counter-revolutionaries the French start from the point of zero knowledge. This is heavily underlined by Mathieu's comments to his men, which not for nothing *in the montage sequencing of our enframing film* climax in his remark that perhaps the agent of one of these bombs is somewhere – undetected and so far undetectable – just at the very moment that the young woman who is indeed one of the three bombers passes *in their film within our film* through the gauntlet of compliments from members of the army control unit running the checkpoint. She is unquestionably the least suspicious-looking person in the crowd moving through the checkpoint, because, in Fanon's words, she is 'the one radically transformed into a European woman, poised and unconstrained, whom no one would suspect, completely at home in the environment'.[27] Mathieu is in the process of saying in *our* film as she walks across his and his paras' screen in *their* film: 'Et alors parmi tous ces hommes, toutes ces femmes arabes, se trouvent les responsables. Mais quels sont-ils? Comment les reconnaître? Le contrôle des papiers dans ces cas est ridicule' ('So, then, among all these Arab men and women are the persons responsible. But which are they? How are we to recognize them? Inspection of their papers in these cases is ridiculous'). 'Recognize' (*reconnaître*) is the very word he is pronouncing even as this sweet-looking young woman, apparently off to the beach, is trading *badinage* with the troops, totally unrecognized for what in reality she is, Fanon's 'revolutionary woman'.

'Revolutionary woman' is what she is revealed to *us* as being, by the enframing, montage techniques of Pontecorvo's work. At the level of film theory he would seem to be implying that mere dumb documentary celluloid, recording a human world that not one of the French paras knows the elementary life and death secrets of, cannot begin to be cut or spliced into such montage-based narratives of meaning as are the informing principles of our frame film. Even at this point, our outer-frame narrative is giving us knowledge of why, equipped with only their pathetic inner-frame film without narrative, for the present the paras lack the knowledge they need for their counter-revolutionary purposes. Their sense of the personnel of the FLN is so hazy that they must begin from a zero point in rooting out its command network link by link. And crucially, they do not have the narrative key provided by neorealist mimesis to get at the heart of the matter; rather they have only – and this is the full historical tragedy *revealed by* those very structures of narrational montage of the stupendous enframing film which we watch – recourse to torture.

* * * * *

My various examples have concerned, first, montage before the fact in Dante, where the mimetic effects are claimed to have surpassed the limits of nature and art as ordinarily conceived; second, the use by Bassani of documentary motifs in neorealist fiction that subsequently goes far beyond them in its engagement with a recent past, but is happier when building out from the initial touch of authenticity which they offer; and third, Pontecorvo's establishment of the difference between inert documentation by a fixed camera, which can in no way tell the stories that lie beneath the superficial record of people's movements that it reproduces, and a type of mimesis in film narrative which, though also documentary *in feel* – since it records historic events *as though* externally and unjudgementally – shows by contrast and at every point evidence of a controlling hand, with a complex story to tell.

### Notes

1. Pietro Ingrao, quoted in Mira Liehm, *Passion and Defiance: Film in Italy from 1942 to the Present* (Berkeley, Los Angeles and London: University of California Press, 1984), p. 58.
2. Italo Calvino, 'Autobiografia di uno spettatore', prefatory section to

Federico Fellini, *Quattro Film* (Turin: Einaudi, 1974), p. xix.

3. Luchino Visconti, 'Anthropomorphic Cinema', reprinted in David Overbey (ed. and trans.), *Springtime in Italy: A Reader on Neo-Realism* (London: Talisman Books, 1978), p. 83.

4. For the influence of Eisenstein on neorealist filmmakers see Peter Bondanella, *Italian Cinema from Neorealism to the Present*, new expanded edition (New York: Continuum, 1997), p. 24; also Gian Piero Brunetta, *Storia del cinema italiano: dal 1945 agli anni ottanta* (Rome: Editori Riuniti, 1982), pp. 338–40.

5. Visconti, 'Anthropomorphic Cinema', p. 84.

6. Sergei M. Eisenstein, *The Film Sense*, translated and edited by Jay Leyda (London: Faber and Faber, 1948; 1st edn, 1943), pp. 13 and 14.

7. *Ibid.*, p. 34.

8. Erich Auerbach, *Mimesis: The Representation of Reality in Western Literature*, trans. Willard R. Trask (original Swiss edn, 1946; 1st edn of this translation, 1953; Princeton: Princeton University Press, 1968), p. 463.

9. Eisenstein, *The Film Sense*, pp. 29–32.

10. Giorgio Bassani, 'La passeggiata prima di cena', in *Il romanzo di Ferrara* (Milan: Mondadori, 1974); there is an English version in Giorgio Bassani, *A Prospect of Ferrara*, translated by Isabel Quigly (London: Faber and Faber, 1962), but I have furnished my own translations of the passages quoted.

11. Bassani, 'La passeggiata prima di cena', p. 50.

12. *Ibid.*

13. *Ibid.*, p. 56.

14. Joan Mellen, *Filmguide to* The Battle of Algiers (Bloomington and London: Indiana University Press Filmguide Series, 1973).

15. *Ibid.*, pp. 8–9.

16. *Ibid.*, pp. 15, 8–9 and 15.

17. *Ibid.*, p. 5.

18. Alistair Horne, *A Savage War of Peace: Algeria 1954–1962* (1977; Harmondsworth: Penguin, 1985), p.167.

19. Frantz Fanon, *The Wretched of the Earth*, translated by Constance Farrington (Harmondsworth: Penguin, 1967) p. 39. Original French title, *Les Damnés de la terre* (1962).

20. Frantz Fanon, 'Algeria Unveiled', Chapter 1 of *Studies in a Dying Colonialism*, translated by Haakon Chevalier (1965; London: Earthscan Publications, 1989), pp. 35–67. Original French title, *L'An cinq de la révolution algérienne* (Paris: François Maspero, 1959).

21. Anne McClintock has dealt with what she sees as inadequacies in Fanon's account of traditional Islamic society and women's role within it. Her case is that 'a curious rupture opens in Fanon's text over the question of women's agency'. See her *Imperial Leather: Race, Gender and Sexuality in the Colonial Context* (New York and London: Routledge, 1995), pp. 364–8. See also Diana Fuss, *Identification Papers* (New York and London: Routledge, 1995), pp. 149–53, for another critique of Fanon's 'Algeria Unveiled'. Fuss raises her own questions about issues of mimesis and masquerade in Fanon's piece, of relevance to, if angled somewhat differently from, the present discussion.

22. Fanon, 'Algeria Unveiled', pp. 58–9.

23. Mellen, *Filmguide*, p. 37.

24. Luce Irigaray, '*The Powers of Discourse and the Subordination of the Feminine': This Sex Which Is Not One* (1977), extract in Mary Eagleton (ed.), *Feminist Literary Theory: A Reader*, 2nd edn (Oxford: Blackwell, 1996), p. 317.

25. In *International Journal of Psychoanalysis*, 10 (1929); reprinted in Victor Burgin, James Donald and Cora Kaplan (eds), *Formations of Fantasy* (London: Routledge, 1986), pp. 35–44.

26. Katherine Stern, 'What Is Femme? The Phenomenology of the Powder Room', *Women: A Cultural Review*, Vol. 8, No. 2, autumn 1997, p. 186.

27. Fanon, 'Algeria Unveiled', p. 57.

CHAPTER 7

# THE TRIUMPH OF DEATH

## HISTORY IN THE SICILIAN CONTEXT

In May of 1992 I travelled to Sicily, full of premonitions of what to expect, both from my recent reading about resentment felt by northern Italians towards the entire, costly *mezzogiorno*, and from one earlier trip there of 1978, during the so-called *anni di piombo*. ('Years of the bullet' would be a tolerable English translation of that leaden sobriquet, alluding as it does to the widespread political and civilian murders of the decade, and the generalized sense of fear that such terrorism from both the left and the right inculcated in all levels of Italian society.[1]) In 1978 Sicily had been deeply preoccupied like the rest of Italy by the terrorism of the Red Brigades. In local political terms the capital city had been relatively quiet for some years, though from the late 1950s onwards the fabric of the *centro storico* had been stripped of not a few of its architectural treasures in the so-called Sack of Palermo, during which much of the heart of the city, instead of being rebuilt after war damage, was further knocked down for speculation in redevelopment. In the event, rebuilding did not go ahead in central positions on a massive scale, and many spaces remained yawning craters or else fields of rubble, since larger profits were to be made in peripheral high-rise (but low-cost) concrete apartment blocks, run up fast for a rapidly expanding population. The once fabulously beautiful Conca d'oro (literally Golden Shell), or coastal plain ringed by low mountains in which the city sits, was already turning into what it has largely now become, a *conca di cemento*, or urban sprawl of concrete brutalism. But otherwise, as the commentator Alexander Stille has written, 'At the time, a general Pax Mafiosa reigned in the city. There had been virtually no major mafia killings in recent years, which led some people (in good faith as well as bad) to declare that the mafia no longer existed.'[2]

By a law of inversions, the period of relative lack of mafia violence actually meant that Cosa Nostra was rapidly consolidating after a

257

notably unsettled period in the early 1960s. This was what Stille elsewhere calls 'the lost decade of the 1970s, when government inertia or outright collusion allowed the mafia to grow to unheard-of levels of power'.[3] Internal ructions were not to break out in publicly visible ways until a new mafia war of the early 1980s. With it began not only a series of killings between feuding *cosche* or 'clans' for hegemonic control over all the island's 'families' (a war that was virtually over by 1983 with the victory of the chief clan of Corleone, under its boss Salvatore 'Totò' Riina) but also external hits against anyone – judiciary, police force, city or regional politicians – who threatened to curtail the otherwise ever-extending activities of illegal profit-making. For these were years of 'illustrious corpses', of public figures who had taken part in the battle to curb the increasingly successful activities of Cosa Nostra, but paid with their lives.

In March 1982, for instance, a new Prefect of Palermo, the national hero and general of the *carabinieri*, Carlo Alberto Dalla Chiesa, was appointed to wage war on terrorism in Sicily. Just before he took up his appointment in April, the mafia killed the leader of the main communist opposition party, Pio La Torre. Dalla Chiesa, who spent his first day as Prefect attending La Torre's funeral, was himself cut down along with his young wife and their bodyguard scarcely four months later, on 3 September 1982. As Stille points out in his closely detailed account:

> In just four years, Cosa Nostra had killed some of the most important public officials in Sicily: the head of the main governing party in Sicily (Michele Reina), the head of the main opposition party (Pio La Torre), the president of the Region (Piersanti Mattarella), two chief prosecutors (Cesare Terranova and Gaetano Costa) and two leading police investigators (Boris Giuliano and Emanuele Basile). Now they had killed Dalla Chiesa.[4]

Stille's subsequent chapters in his book *Excellent Cadavers*, which I shall be drawing on further for some of the grist of detail needed to sustain my own commentaries on Sicily in this chapter, are an account of the swaying fortunes of Cosa Nostra on the one hand, and the fight to contain it on the other. A restricted 'pool' of expert magistrates, of increasing national and international fame, largely waged the role of law enforcement, as breakthroughs led to prosecutions of literally hundreds of both 'big-fish' and 'small-fry' mafiosi in huge purpose-built bunker-style courtrooms.

Stretched over my own intervening memories of Sicily's troubled 1980s was a sense, from reading and from subsequent visits to continental Italy, of concerted attempts to extirpate the *mala pianta* ('rooted evil') of organized crime. I harboured confused images of maxi-trials in reinforced concrete courtrooms, ringed (as an opera house is by boxes) with multiple cages, for defendants already divided by conflicting loyalties, and who were made even more enraged among themselves during the course of these strange proceedings by some of the more important informers (*pentiti*) ever to breach the ancient code of *omertà*. As the informers 'sang' from witness stands of the *platea*, those they incriminated bellowed in fury from their 'boxes' – operatic indeed. My impression was, however, that the state had at best only kept on level terms with organized crime in the Sicilian context, and that, measured internationally, Cosa Nostra had gone from strength to strength, increasingly basing its overseas networks on the lucrative drug trade, though still largely controlling its complex operations from bases within Sicily. And over Cosa Nostra within not only this Sicilian context, but in many an international arena as well, ruled the ruthless *Corleonesi* – men of Corleone who had weakened much of the remaining effective opposition from rival families by killing their heads one by one, and thereby frightening the lesser 'soldiers' into compliance with their ongoing demands.

As I travelled by overnight train from Naples my purpose in the first instance was to see and study a large fifteenth-century fresco called the *Triumph of Death*, which in a cloudy sort of way I felt underwrote the fixation upon death on the part of Sicilian culture, a fixation which has endured from at least the epoch of that great painting through to our own. The fresco I was journeying towards and which I did eventually stand before (even if in a rather different frame of mind than I had anticipated) was painted probably in Sicily itself, possibly by a north Italian or Spanish or even northern European artist, and almost certainly in the 1430s. It represents one of the great tropes of late-medieval belief – Death's triumph over the living. I did not know how unavoidably I would find myself asking questions about whether art that laid claim to understanding in the past could also become a guide to momentous events in the present, or even, perhaps, a good place to dig for prognosis as to the future. In short, I did not anticipate – no one but the perpetrators of such a slaughter could have – that on the morning of my own arrival in the island's second city, Catania, the chief Italian prosecutor of the mafia throughout the 1980s and early 1990s, Judge Giovanni Falcone, would be killed, along with his wife and three police guards, in one of the most skilfully timed detonations of a moving vehicle in the entire annals of modern terrorism, on the road from the airport at Punta Raisi to Palermo.

Quite apart from this painting, in the particular cultural context of Sicily death is such an insistent and recurrent theme that a large part of my purpose in going there at all had been specifically to penetrate beyond mere platitudes on the matter. I wanted to understand the motif of death in Sicilian culture far more exactly; in particular, whether it was unitary and unchanging, or on the contrary multiple in configuration, stretching down through a history indubitably cross-hatched with complexities, themselves not easy for an outsider to fathom. I chose to do so by means of what I was trained to analyse, namely visual art and literature. From the moment I first heard news on the radio of Falcone's murder, I had a whole set of supplementary reasons for trying to fathom the Sicilian culture of death. Why, for instance, did Falcone, engaged in the precise work he was, come out with the following remarks scarcely a year before his murder?

> The culture of death does not belong solely to the Mafia; all of Sicily is impregnated with it. Here the day of the dead is a huge celebration: we offer cakes called 'skulls', made of rock-hard sugar. Solitude, pessimism, and death are the themes of our literature, from Pirandello to Sciascia. It is almost as though we are a people who have lived too long and suddenly feel tired, weary, emptied, like Tomasi di Lampedusa's Don Fabrizio.[5]

My instinct from prior reading was that the culture in question was *not* uniform on these matters, and that on closer inspection writers of Lampedusa's and Leonardo Sciascia's stature were to be found in rather different political and social camps, which in turn differentially affected their ways of understanding Sicily's obsession with death. But I felt I needed a prior point of purchase, far back in pre-modern time, since the 'impregnation' of the culture with death of which Falcone had written was clearly of long standing. The late-medieval painting remained the best starting point for an enquiry.

The murder of Falcone and his wife and bodyguards had made my investigation horrifyingly 'for real'. I felt the need to interrelate medieval and modern understandings of the culture in question because, at least superficially, the terrorist event which had so stunned the Italian nation seemed graphically to re-enact something akin to the awful reckoning with death of the centuries-old painting. On my quest to comprehend this particular painting of the universal *Triumph of Death*, I had been profoundly shaken before even standing in front of it by one of those recurrences in reality of what one expected to be questioning only on the artistic plane. In short, I was plunged into the midst of an island in grief, following a shocking new instance of the triumph of death over life.

As indicated, I had all along intended – even before the massacre of Judge Falcone and the four others – to dwell upon this frescoed *Triumph* as a prelude to any further thinking about the place of death in Sicilian culture. The huge painting (see Plate 9) is very much within a pan-European late-medieval constellation of moral teachings on the vanity of earthly existence, and on the pointlessness of amassing wealth or pre-eminence in any earthly sphere, in view of all-triumphing Death – in this case a skeletal horseman on a skeletal horse, trampling down the living or piercing them with arrows shot at a gallop. Presenting the work to a Sicilian public upon its return after many years *in restauro* in Rome, the scholar Maria Grazia Paolini had pointed out how, in the tradition of which the painting is very much part,

> the theme of Triumph . . . as many extant literary texts also bear witness . . . apart from its purpose of edifying and admonishing, added the consoling and reassuring demonstration of how death strikes more swiftly the powerful and the happy, and pleasureful youth, than it does those who invoke it as a release. It brought to bear an altogether explicit sense of the comeuppance of oppressors, of usurers, the proud, and all those who in the pursuit of lucre or of power, dealt in or enjoyed every sort of privilege, whether in the context of the church or that of civil society.[6]

If we are *not* consoled or reassured in every detail by such a 'demonstration' – what is wrong exactly with 'pleasureful youth', except for its being a highly enviable state for those who don't possess it? – Paulini's points about the judgemental intent of the painting are undeniable. Originally from the wall of a Palermo poorhouse hospital, as Peter Robb in his moving and at the same time sardonic modern classic *Midnight in Sicily* reminds us,[7] the painting almost certainly was meant to provide consolation to the poor for what might otherwise have been unendurable states of envy of the lifestyles of their 'betters'. We look into the field of the fresco and witness figures of powerful churchmen, of rich and handsome noblemen and women, of merchants,

Figure 10 Remains of the vehicle of Judge Giovanni Falcone, in which along with his wife and three bodyguards he was blown up by the mafia in May 1992. This and the subsequent mafia killing only weeks later of Falcone's colleague, Judge Paolo Borsellino, galvanized the nation into a renewed spirit of protest against mafia terror. But the danger persists. Photo: Publifoto, Palermo.

rulers and all those capable of sumptuous displays of wealth fall dead under hoof, or being pierced to the quick by archery which, given the gallop of the archer's steed, would not be disgraced by comparison with the skills of one of Kurosawa's seven samurai.

Exempt from Death's trampling and from his arrows, for the meantime, are a group of suppliants and onlookers, including a pair usually identified as the painter and his assistant. These last are the only two figures in the painting watching us, as though to monitor how we watch it. And what we watch is a spectacle of death that is not universal but specific. Put simply, Death triumphs over persons of either gender who might be thought to be having too good a time in this life, even if the 'fault' that has caused their enjoyments, such as being rich, or beautiful, well-born, powerful or simply young, is not always one that can be avoided by moral choice. The vision of such people being triumphed over by Death for belonging to categories of person favoured in this world is, for the painting (as also for a great deal of European thought of the late-medieval period) unexplained, and yet, within the implicit righteousness of the representation, it apparently requires no justification. Hence, the triumph on the part of Death becomes a licence for outright, moralising *shadenfreude* on the part of the poor and unprivileged. By the standards of today, there is thus an additional cruelty about Death than just its inevitable universality; namely, its partiality (as represented in the fresco) for taking certain *categories* of people into its eternal realm, over and above its eventual taking of *everybody*.

In spite of the painting's ongoing capacity to shock, we do not forget who we are and where we are in history. We are moderns, on the cusp of a new millennium. And this fresco before us is a chance vestige from the deep cultural past of Sicily. Apart from all else in the more than half a millennium since it was painted, it has survived a near-direct hit by Allied bombing in 1943. It is now the prime treasure of the Palazzo Abatellis, which houses the National Gallery of Sicily, the most important art collection of Sicily, and arguably of Italy south of Naples. Whether because of or despite its age and rarity, the painting refuses to countenance *our* refusal of its terms. People in the depiction are killed by categories. And however that may outrage our latter-day liberal consciences (as a kind of supreme assault upon our notion that individuals may *transcend* their mere categories as statesmen, church-men, nobility or rich burghers), the work unremittingly preaches to us that success and happiness in this world are a temptation to Death to strike before time. As moderns, by contrast, we probably tend to sidle up mentally to the inevitable powers of the Grim Reaper far differently: as in the wry colloquialism of a Woody Allen, 'it gets you in the end'.

What is certain for us is that however the painting may seem to take the stance of a poor person's delight in Death's triumph over the rich and powerful, that delight neither alters the material wellbeing of the poor for the better, nor manages to demonize every one of those grandees and *grande dames* who are being felled or trampled by the skeletal horse and rider. Death may triumph in their overthrow. But we cannot. If the painting is meant to stir a sense of justice in the viewer, in our age that affective function fails in the very terms of its presentation. For although a sense of the *in*justices done by some of these folk is manifest – their privileges and high-handed dealings over others are a part of what the painting narrates, simply by the contrast between their sumptuous habits and the far more plain-clothed onlookers, including the painter and his assistant – for a modern conscience this is not adequate reason for their being placed under sentence of death by the painting, and executed within it. Clearly, for a work of art to condemn and execute by category, it had to rely on an original audience of viewers complicit in the overall terms of the sentence it passes and carries out. With a change in *Geist*, the complicity between painter and spectator is broken.

Broken, if only because in modern times (and sticking with the specific Sicilian context) a different kind of hope had come slenderly to prevail – a hope peculiarly evidenced in the career successes of one contemporary Palermitan, Judge Giovanni Falcone. This was a hope more and more widely felt by Sicilians, not to mention Italians generally, because of Falcone's successes in the fight against organized crime. In recent Sicilian culture – despite the centuries of misrule by others; despite the internal dissensions and civilian carnages wrought by mafia rivalry; despite endemic poverty, and the consequent fragility of every betterment in living conditions – out of the very gulf of despair had been born an infant historic optimism, a hope that Death might not triumph so terribly in the future Sicilian context as it had in the past.

But if, as suggested, that optimism had found a focus in the work of Judge Falcone, philosophically speaking it had already been anticipated by several decades. Nowhere more than in early pieces of writing by Leonardo Sciascia about the conditions and temperament of the Sicilian people. Most notably, it resides in Sciascia's sweeping but serious judgement from one of his earliest stories:

> I believe in the Sicilians who speak little, in the Sicilians who worry deep inside and suffer: the poor who wave to us with a weary gesture, as if from the distance of centuries, and Colonel Carini, always silent and distant like that, full of melancholy and worry, but ready for action at any moment, a man who seems to have not many hopes, and yet he's the very heart of hope, the fragile, silent hope of the best Sicilians.[8]

Interestingly, this remark is attributed in the fiction in question (the novella 'Forty-eight', from *Sicilian Uncles* of 1958) to the historical figure of Ippolito Nievo, an actual writer on the Italian condition in his own right and, importantly for Sciascia's piece set in mid-nineteenth-century Sicily in which Nievo figures momentarily as a speaking character, a member of Garibaldi's original Thousand.[9] (I shall have more to say later about Sciascia's particular version of historical positivism within the prevailing despair of Sicilian death-consciousness in a contrast between it and Giuseppe Tomasi di Lampedusa's stoic pessimism, evidenced in the much-better-known fiction *The Leopard*, written in the same years of the mid-1950s.)

Unquestionably, if anyone in modern Sicilian history were to be graced with Sciascia's epithet, 'a man who seems to have not many hopes, and yet he's the very heart of hope', it would be Giovanni Falcone. Until the tragic day of his murder, he had progressively become the focus of that wider change in the temper or *Geist* of Sicilian thought at which I have been hinting. From the time of his own birth in central Palermo in the late 1930s, Falcone, like many another Palermitan, had grown up aware of endemic poverty, of weak regional government and insufficient concern with Sicily at national level, all of which, taken together, fostered the conditions for the mafia to fill the power vacuum with its own alternative to the state.

As an investigating magistrate working to overcome the mafia's grip on society, Falcone had achieved an almost impossible combination of passionate commitment to the activity of enquiry ('I have always known that to fight you have to work as hard as possible . . .'), with great methodological caution ('I concluded that I had. . . to verify at every step the border between what is known and what is not').[10] Falcone's successes in *moving* that border, such that what was known of the mafia began at last to encroach significantly on the vast realm of the *un*known, seems in large measure to have derived from the human warmth with which he treated a string of individual informers. His very reputation for candour with them earned their respect and added to their number, with many a potential informer specifying before 'coming over' that he would treat with Falcone and no other.

Even as Falcone held onto his firm convictions as to the global evil of Cosa Nostra, he worked from a perception that the behaviour of its members and their very code of honour were based in traditional Sicilian values, and that the distortions of those values were the consequence of a long historical process, not the sole fault of individual mafiosi:

I was born in the same neighbourhood as many of them. . . . My *pentiti* know that I know that the Mafia is nothing more than a distortion, an exaggeration, an extreme and aberrant version of the traditional Sicilian way of life. So I have become a defender of the supergrasses because, in one way or another, I respect them all. . . . I have learned that, whatever happens, you have to behave decently – to show real respect . . . and not just make meaningless gestures. . . . The categorical imperative of the Mafia is 'to tell the truth' [to other 'men of honour'], and it has become a cardinal principle of my own personal ethics, at least as far as the really important relationships in my life are concerned. However strange it may seem, the Mafia have taught me a lesson in morality.[11]

Falcone's belief was that Sicily's ills derived from a lack of a sense of the state – the state as a producer of social morality interiorized by its citizens, that is – and that this lack was itself a consequence of the Italian state's own past failings, present weaknesses and essential inability to inculcate in people this apprehension of its worth. But there is another and more striking sense, perhaps only fully appreciated by most Italians *after* his death, in which Falcone himself, by his unwillingness to flinch from his enormous and ever-growing task of tracking down and putting pressure on Cosa Nostra, and by his personal bravery under repeated death threats and throughout years of an enforced life of armoured vehicles and constant heavy police protection, came heroically to embody his own vision of the (otherwise all too absent) state, as a positive force for good in the lives and morality of its citizens.

Consider his largest achievement, the depositing of the first maxi-indictment in September 1985, after years of painstaking work. It was a work of 8,607 pages in forty volumes, plus approximately 4,000 further pages of appendices. Finishing and handing it in was the precondition for the maxi-trial to begin in February of the following year, at which, before more than six hundred members of the world's press, evidence was presented against 475 defendants. Written mostly by Falcone himself, the indictment, in the words of Alexander Stille, constitutes 'a great historical saga with the sweep of a Tolstoian novel'. Stille rightly points to its magisterial opening words – 'This is the trial of the mafia organization called "Cosa Nostra", . . . which, with violence and intimidation, has sowed, and continues to sow, death and terror' – as evidence of the importance of Falcone's 'lucid diagnosis of a diseased society', on a par with Giuseppe di Lampedusa's *The Leopard* in his opinion.[12]

But if one man had become the incarnation of change in a culture, we cannot attribute the *causes* solely to him. Change must have come about through more general historical influences. How, therefore, may we trace the fundamental turnaround in attitudes, and particularly the abiding presence, even alongside new rhythms of life in Sicily, of older, unforgotten rhythms of death? The question arises as a natural consequence of our critical contemplation of the frescoed fifteenth-century *Triumph of Death*, all the more so as we are forced to bear witness at another level than that of art to a horrendous actual triumph of Death over a figure in modern civilian life of such towering eminence as Falcone.

Let us premise the jump in time scales from late-medieval fresco to late-modern terrorism (a jump which is in itself a kind of intellectual violence, even if one which, at the specific moment of my arrival in Sicily, was forced upon me) with more by way of general context. Importantly, the preceding weeks of early 1992 had seen a more profound collapse in coalition government in Italy than for many years, accompanied in the end by the premature resignation by the state president only months before the completion of his statutory term. The nation saw itself in crisis, obviously not for the first time, but far more gravely than habitually. Recent elections had shown the north of Italy harbouring millions who resented with a vehemence as never before the subvention of taxes to state welfare programmes in the *mezzogiorno*, especially Sicily.

As far as prosecution of the mafia was concerned, after the first maxi-trial there had been three more, each painstakingly prepared by Falcone with the help of others, but each one also a smaller affair in terms of numbers prosecuted and popular support. Falcone seemed to be losing some of the battles for the hearts and minds of the Italian people and losing support too from its vacillating and usually compromised governments. Often lacking the state support and protection he called for, and several times passed over in promotion by others (persons either less astute in their understanding of the mafia, or else far less committed to the task of maintaining a prosecutorial advantage over it), Falcone in his scepticism and despair produced his own interpretation of death by violence in the Sicilian context, in the year before his murder:

> One usually dies because one is alone, or because one has got into something over one's head. One often dies because one does not have the right alliances, because one is not given support.
> In Sicily the Mafia kills the servants of the State that the State has not been able to protect.[13]

Staying alive depends on alliances, on power. The remark is pure realpolitik, its first sentences as applicable to individual members of Cosa Nostra itself, and to internal wars within it, as they are to the mafia's external enemies, the servants of the state. Looked at in one way, nothing could be further than this from the interpretation of Death in the late-medieval fresco, where it was precisely the strong and powerful who were taken before time, in their pride of life. Evidently Sicily, by this modern reckoning, was a world in which the strong survive and the weak perish, *punto e basta*.

In support of this pessimistic view of cultural overdeterminations, Falcone would elsewhere quote from the confession of the earliest modern mafia informer of consequence, Leonardo Vitale, a killer who underwent a religious crisis as early as 1973 and hence broke the code of silence well before there was any state apparatus ready to give credence to or make full use of the extensive and vital information he made available. 'I have been made a fool of by life', Vitale had said, 'by the evil that rained on me from the time I was a child. . . . My sin is having been born into a mafia family and of having lived in a society where everyone is a *mafioso* and is respected for it, while those who are not are treated with contempt.'[14] In Falcone's sense of things, Vitale had certainly got into things 'over his head'. The 'contempt' with which the state treated him is displayed by the Palermo Court of Appeals overturning the convictions of the many mafiosi initially found guilty on his evidence. At the same time as it ratified their innocence, Vitale himself was placed in an insane asylum, and thereby taken out of circulation for an entire decade by a form of arrest in its own right, so unable was Sicilian officialdom at that stage to believe a self-incriminating mafia witness, let alone provide protection for him in anything like the way Falcone was some years later calling for. Italy was never in fact to provide a 'Witness Protection Programme' of anything like the safety and support of the American scheme of that name. And all too predictably, when in 1984 Leonardo Vitale was eventually released from the imprisoning conditions of the asylum, eleven years after he had freely walked into a Palermo police station to make full confession, Cosa Nostra was waiting for him one Sunday morning after he had taken his mother to Mass. It was as though (to alter the terms of the ancient fresco) several of the powerful in the painting were to be found killing one of its indigent and poorly dressed 'witnesses', instead of themselves providing a spectacle of the overweeningly strong being laid low.

And yet there is a narrower sense in which Falcone's bleak sense of the matter is not a turning on its head of the message of the frescoed late-medieval *Triumph of Death*, but subtly in consonance with it. Each of the strong and rich and powerful being killed in the painting by Death the skeletal archer is dazed and alone. Although many are being killed at the same time, in the total field of the fresco each is dying an individual death and provides a separate instance for study. The painting hence seems to proclaim that riches and power are at best only an *apparent* defence, and that the reality is that *even* such people are utterly isolated, without adequate protection or the 'right alliances', when it comes to something so universal as death. In particular, their institutional role as churchmen, rich merchants or civic officials is no defence: they too are let down, like Falcone was to be, by their particular institutional equivalent of the modern state. For this was that Sicily which, even as I journeyed towards the anciently frescoed *Triumph*, harboured persons readying themselves to end judge Falcone's record-breaking – but for the present not universally valued – fight against organized crime. Either from revenge, or so as to pre-empt his being promoted head of a new arm of law which he was devising – a *superprocura*, or sort of Italian FBI, designed to incorporate powers equivalent to that American institution in its prime – they coolly and successfully blew him up.

Any contemplation of Falcone's death produces a sense not just of finality but of futility. The Italian state and people, stunned initially into silence and sorrow, in fact reacted quickly to the meaningfulness of his long fight against organized crime. Too late for Falcone, and for his colleague Paolo Borsellino, also blown up by Cosa Nostra a few short months later, Italians did in fact emerge from differing levels of complacency or *anomie*, and bring to fruition many of the measures against organized crime which such magistrates had long been calling for from the Italian citizens and state.

\* \* \* \* \*

Falcone's and Borsellino's deaths in one sense provided so great a sense of closure that nothing further might have been expected to happen in the space left vacant by their absence. Since a similar stasis might also be expected to befall any analysis seeking to move on from such historically significant killings into new material, in what remains of the chapter I wish to reframe the discussion entirely, in terms of distinctive *literary* accounts of Sicily as a culture preoccupied with mortality. So much of Sicily's modern literature has sought to come to grips with the theme that there is a difficulty in choosing works sufficiently representative of the totality. The following analysis therefore focuses on writings which, precisely by their very differences, help us to chart how variously death is viewed. As in the cross-comparison between the painted late-medieval *Triumph* and an act of modern terrorism, understanding calls for great subtlety.

The historian Denis Mack Smith has suggested that Sicily's troubles caused during successive phases of colonization by others had come, by the time of the unification of Italy in 1860, to constitute a complex general stoicism of temperament: 'the legacy of these episodes was an abiding consciousness of defeat and the conviction that more wars and conquests would be likely to follow every change in the Mediterranean balance of power.'[15] Mack Smith had in fact been taking his cue for such a judgement from a memorable piece of writing by Sicily's most famous author of the post-war years, Giuseppe Tomasi di Lampedusa. In point of fact, not only Lampedusa but other modern Sicilian writers have had much to say on the character of the island's people. We do well to concentrate here, however, on only two: Lampedusa himself, and the aforementioned Leonardo Sciascia. At very much the same moment in the 1950s both had written texts on Sicily which related, if they did not actually attribute, the island's ongoing malaise to earlier instances of great human wrongs, or to a perennially fallen or defeated condition of her peoples. On this score Verga too had earlier called his series of novels (of which only two were completed) *I vinti* (*The Defeated*). And going back still further, to a point just before that watershed moment of 1860 in Italian history, even the composer Verdi, when searching for a formative moment in the island's long series of domination by outsiders, had fastened on the occasion of the so-called Sicilian Vespers and, in writing his opera of that name, concentrated on an event from the island's long ago but far from forgotten past: a terrible massacre by the people of their foreign overlords. Of this event Sciascia was to write later with sardonic pessimism:

> The only times when the Sicilian has acted decisively and been resigned to making his own history, he has made disgraceful mistakes, as for instance

happened in the case of the Sicilian Vespers, which closed the door on France only to open it wide to Spain.[16]

Lampedusa's novel *Il Gattopardo* (henceforth referred to by its English title, *The Leopard*) is internationally famous, and the subject of one of Luchino Visconti's important films. Sciascia's story 'Il quarantotto' (henceforth 'Forty-eight'), published in the same year as Lampedusa's novel, 1958, is scarcely known within Italy, never mind beyond. And yet the different accounts of nineteenth-century Sicily in the two historical fictions make for an interesting comparison, and one which perhaps helps us question more rigorously what occurs when any novelist seeks to clarify how the present and future have been overdetermined by the past. The analysis which follows seeks to understand contrasts between the two writers' attitudes to Sicily: in particular, why Sciascia's piece has been figured by some past criticism as his *anti-Leopard*, in terms of the philosophy of history on offer.[17]

Of utmost importance in the overall comparison are questions regarding what Friedrich Nietzsche called 'critical history'. The term is one of three categories of history defined for us in his 'Untimely Meditation' entitled 'Of the Uses and Disadvantages of History for Life'. It was Nietzsche's strong view that all cultures need to reckon their past 'critically'. Especially important at moments of potential new development (just such cases as the ousting of the Bourbons and the unification of Italy, of which Lampedusa and Sciascia write so differently), critical history is a culture's instinct to 'possess and from time to time employ the strength to break up and dissolve a part of the past',[18] not simply contenting itself, in other words, with the emulation of former heroes and their deeds involved in 'monumental' history, nor with seeking to relive the past through the treasure-storing activities of 'antiquarian' history (Nietzsche's other two historical categories in the particular Meditation). It is worth pausing a moment longer with Nietzsche, before proceeding to the substantive comparison. By the criteria of Nietzsche's definition of the term, *both* Lampedusa and Sciascia promote critical histories of what lies behind or beneath the Sicilian reality: accounts so unlike, however, that we cannot but qualify them as opposing representations of the same phenomena. The question is then, must we not *choose between* critical histories when they run counter to one another? The issue is a large one, since it raises further questions of how we use literature's many histories in establishing values and seeking solutions within the present.

Consider the following passage from Nietzsche's 'Meditation', which encompasses some of the problems involved in inheriting any particular and given history:

> Since we are the outcome of earlier generations, we are also the outcome of their aberrations, passions and errors, and indeed of their crimes; it is not possible wholly to free oneself from this chain. If we condemn these aberrations and regard ourselves as free of them, this does not alter the fact that we originate in them. The best we can do is confront our inherited and hereditary nature with our knowledge of it, and through a new, stern discipline combat our inborn heritage and implant in ourselves a new habit, a new instinct, a second nature, so that our first nature withers away. It is an attempt to give oneself, as it were *a posteriori*, a past in which one would like to originate in opposition to that in which one did originate: – always a dangerous attempt because it is so hard to know the limit to denial of the past and because second natures are usually weaker than first.[19]

The primary notion here is that of confronting a historically accreted inheritance *knowingly*, as a first act of trying to work out our place in relation to it. Even in this primary activity Lampedusa and Sciascia are, as writers, about as different as any two tackling essentially the same history could well be. Lampedusa's only and posthumous novel constitutes an aristocratic *aubade* to Sicily's Bourbon past, in which feudal rank counted for almost everything. Set mainly at the time of Garibaldi's sweep with his small army first through Sicily, then up through peninsular Italy in his 1860 campaign of national unification, *The Leopard* bears witness, during the half-century it documents (up to a final chapter set in 1910), to a gradual fading away of the twin hegemonies of Bourbon and of feudal Sicily, and even an eventual crumbling of vestigial remnants of them into dust. This said, however, there is a deeper sense in which Lampedusa contemplates the possibility that despite, or indeed because of all the changes that came to pass as a consequence of Garibaldi's revolution, things in essence 'remain the same', because in Sicily, according to Prince Salina (the protagonist of *The Leopard*), the fundamental reality of her peoples, whatever their class, is one of unbroken 'sleep', from which they most particularly do not wish to be awoken. The paradox enunciated here is the claim that total change is the only viable precondition for things remaining as they are.

Whatever else we may say, the leopard's evocations are in stark contrast with the Sicily that we perceive in Sciascia's many writings. In any comparison with Lampedusa's old-world code of values, Sciascia must figure as a radical, if not indeed, considering his humble origins as the grandson of a worker in Sicily's dreadful sulphur mines, something of an upstart. For him – and the insistent plangency with which he writes is perhaps one of the few points Sciascia shares with Lampedusa – the past injustices of Bourbon and other rule (especially, in modern times, mafia rule) over the peoples of Sicily's far-flung towns, *feudi* and cities must forever be scrutinized and countered. The hallmark of his writing is that of a supremely rational, reproachful, even censorious Sicilian sensibility. Above all, his every act of writing implies the vigilance of being wide awake, not the moral lassitude implied in Lampedusa's account of a proclivity on the part of Sicilians to sleep through their unfolding history. Reading Sciascia, one is aware of a critical mind investigating actual, or constructing fictional instances of, overlordism of the weak by the strong, down through Sicilian history. A reader may be inclined to wonder whether the confronting of this particular cultural inheritance of oppression with revelatory knowledge of it might not release a force indeed capable of withering away what Nietzsche had named as inherited 'aberrations, passions and errors'.

Such a force, if it existed, would be an especially valuable power operating within writing, ideally one which ensured that age-old crimes against humanity committed by people with power or authority would finally be redressed. But here we stray onto the ground of Nietzsche's original warning. To what extent must we say that so pertinacious a seeking on Sciascia's part after a radical redress to historically embedded wrongs constitutes a dangerous attempt to rejig reality towards 'a past in which one would like to originate in opposition to that in which one did originate' (to re-quote Nietzsche)? Literature's attempts to restructure reality are a factor of its enormous challenge. What we have to ask is whether narrations no less critical, such as that offered to us in fictional form by Lampedusa – narrations that do not project back into the past any radical reformism, but instead realize just as fully the pains as well as the happinesses of lives dead and gone, without in the same act wishing them other than they were – do not in the long run provide a greater, and certainly a more 'tragic', sense of history?

In the act of posing these alternatives, which simplify down to a choice between a *reformist* or a *tragic* critical stance in relation to history, I certainly mean to be provocative, since the issue is one which seems to divide students of literature very starkly, and yet for all that not to receive nearly enough discussion. Partly so that it may gain the fairest hearing possible, the present analysis locates the debate on ground which for most readers will be relatively neutral, or at any rate unbiased – a comparison between two writers of the post-war Italian period, both using their native Sicily as a crucible of reckonings which go far beyond Sicily in philosophical and historical import. Comparing the two works encourages us vigorously to investigate what Nietzsche called (in his title for the chapter from which I have been quoting) the 'uses and disadvantages of history for life'. Plainly, one implication of Nietzsche's account of being pulled towards a critical activity of history is that it commits us to asking where we stand, as beings who have evolved out of the past while being, also, endlessly projected into an unforeseen future? How far can we or should we seek by present intervention to influence the outcome of that future?

In the mere asking of such questions we perhaps also surmise that all history is essentially 'of the present', since it is a processing – under pressure from the impending future – of what has produced the realities being lived in the here and now. How does Leonardo Sciascia, for example, even when he is investigating the past, produce this feeling that the critical history at issue in the period of unification is very much a constituent of the present? The question is perhaps best answered by continuing with our contrastive comparison between his novella 'Forty-Eight' and key philosophical positions on Sicilian history outlined in *The Leopard*.

One caveat: in proceeding with a consideration of Lampedusa's far better known account of Sicily, we must be cautious in the face of its seemingly definitive grasp of both contemporary and perennial realities, to grant it the status of an hypothesis only, one to be tested against the counter-strengths of Sciascia's representations.

From first to last Lampedusa's *Leopard* is about death – the portrayal of a dying class within a sleeping and possibly also moribund culture. If it shows nostalgia for the feudal past, it also has the perspicacity to see that the productions and the pastimes of the Sicilian aristocracy under laissez-faire Bourbon rule amounted only, at best, to shadow fruit. The novel begins with a sentence in Latin from the communal prayers of the particular aristocratic family whose fortunes it will follow. Significantly the supplication, 'Nunc et in hora mortis nostrae. Amen' ('Now and in the hour of our death', p. 5), refers forward, as the novel in its entirety will do, to the death of those present, including the person speaking, the Prince of Salina, or 'Leopard' of the novel's title.

The rest of the novel comprises a series of chapters that represent significant stages in the passage towards death, either on the part of the Prince or of those around him – his family and retinue. The book is concerned with a feudal lifestyle which, because vestigial, is already a lived paradox on the grand scale. In turn, at the level of minutiae, this means small paradoxes in almost every detail. Still on the first page, for instance, family prayers once over we read, 'everything dropped back into its usual order or disorder'.[20] The original Italian text here implies that things went back to their normal orderly, *that is* disorderly, state ('nell'ordine, nel disordine, consueto'), with the implication that order and disorder in minute events, as in much larger realms of history, cannot really be philosophically differentiated. The very walls surrounding these family prayers are covered with paintings more representative of a pagan world of polytheism than of the Christian beliefs of the religious ritual which has just taken place within them. What we are presented with is an infidel Sicilian world, more ancient and more all-pervading than the narrowly based Christian one that has sought unsuccessfully through the ages to supplant it. The latter has at best only nested precariously within that larger and historically much older context. Only in the last chapter, set in 1910, many years after the Prince's death, will his surviving daughters and daughter-in-law witness the triumph of Catholic priestcraft, as their carefully amassed collection of purported Christian relics is mostly adjudged by a delegation of the church to be a heap of profane bagatelles, and the very chapel that is adorned with them to stand in need of reconsecration.

Lampedusa was here making a case about Sicilian culture that other modern students of it – partly, it must be admitted, because of the very forcefulness of his representation – have been powerfully persuaded is a truth: namely, that the more distant past is a larger determinant upon the nature of things in Sicily than anything which happened only yesterday or which might happen tomorrow, however momentous (and temporarily obscuring of longer-term realities) any such modern occurrences may seem. For instance, Garibaldi's campaign to unify Italy, commencing, as the novel's own narrative does in the spring of

1860 with the wresting of Sicily from Bourbon domination – a monarchy which in Salina's eyes for a long time already 'bore the marks of death upon its face' (p. 12)[21] – is presented as merely the latest event to ruffle the surface of what Lampedusa would have us see as this ageless (and in terms of its deeper structures *unchanging*) Sicilian condition of order/disorder.

The essence of Lampedusa's position is outlined on several pages of the novel describing how the 'Leopard' Prince refuses an invitation made by the envoy of the Piedmontese monarchy to join the processes of Italian unification by accepting a seat in the new Senate being established in Turin. Extracts from these crucial pages have been much quoted in other writers' or critics' discussions of Sicily since the publication of the novel in 1958, but all too often for effect, and seldom with genuine critical intent. The 'truth' of these pages is accepted without questioning, and the philosophical position which they map out with regard to Sicily's history and its place in the world is hence not opened up to further discussion, let alone submitted to any rigorous comparison with alternative positions, such as Sciascia's.

Lampedusa at the commencement of the discussion between the Prince and the envoy Chevalley presents the former as an immensely proud member of the older order and the latter as a rather ingenuous newcomer. In particular, Chevalley is not above making verbal faux pas, like calling Garibaldi's successes in Sicily a 'happy annexation', before correcting himself and naming it as 'the glorious union of Sicily and the Kingdom of Sardinia' (p. 120).[22] This initial mistake plays into the Prince's hands, insofar as it underlines his ensuing assertions that Sicily has always been colonized, and never on equal terms with the colonizing power:

> We Sicilians have become accustomed, by a long, a very long hegemony of rulers who were not of our religion and did not speak our language, to split hairs. If we had not done so we'd never have coped with Byzantine tax gatherers, with Berber Emirs, with Spanish Viceroys. Now the bent is endemic, we're made like that. . . . We are old, Chevalley, very old. For over twenty-five centuries we've been bearing the weight of superb and heterogeneous civilisations, all from outside, none made by ourselves, none that we could call our own. We're as white as you are, Chevalley, and as the Queen of England; and yet for two thousand five hundred years we've been a colony. I don't say that in complaint; it's our fault. But even so we're worn out and exhausted. (p. 122)[23]

At first we may feel we are listening to an apology on behalf of a colonized people for their being second-rate (Lampedusa's equivalent to Naipaul's notion of colonies as 'mimic' cultures, incapable of originality). But the drift of the argument is more subtle than any such supposition on our or Chevalley's parts.

Just when we may be thinking that this ascription of a defeated tiredness to the human character of Sicily might constitute a mere excuse for its people feeling like perpetual underdogs, Lampedusa has the Prince produce a new twist to the argument (and not the last one), whereby the great sleep that Sicilians are deemed to desire is not seen primarily in its negative aspects, as a result of the aforementioned history of colonization, but positively, as a more erotic form of escapism altogether, a recurring death wish, inherent in Sicily's native population, and in large measure a 'given' of the extreme climate and landscape of the island.

> All Sicilian self-expression, even the most violent, is really wish-fulfilment; our sensuality is a hankering for oblivion, our shooting and knifing a hankering for death; our languor, our exotic ices, a hankering for voluptuous immobility, that is for death again; our meditative air is that of a void wanting to scrutinise the enigmas of Nirvana. (p. 123)[24]

A triumph of death indeed, and one accompanied by what the Prince is willing to admit is a 'terrifying insularity of mind' on the part of the perpetually defeated and sunstruck peoples of Sicily (p. 124). By such a reckoning, it is not the best Sicilians whom the Prince sees as in any way overcoming this sleep-and-defeat-and-heat-induced insularity of mind, but rather those 'half-awake' exceptions to the rule; persons whom he actually rather disdains, like the politician Crispi, already in Turin, and who he predicts will in old age 'fall back into our voluptuous torpor; they all do' (p. 123).[25] (Writing with almost a century of historical hindsight regarding the career of Francesco Crispi, Lampedusa can lend his protagonist Salina this wry *fore*sight: that is one of the advantages offered by the genre of the historical novel.)

The greatest and bitterest irony of all is reserved for late in the argument, when Prince Salina recommends instead of himself (in cultural terms the moribund leopard of the piece) the *nouveau riche* (and aptly characterized jackal) antagonist of the novel, Don Calogero Sedara, to a seat in the reconstituted Senate in Turin: 'his family, I am told, is an old one or soon will be' (p. 125).[26] This is supremely nihilistic humour, coming as it does from someone who has worked hard to see his own beloved nephew Tancredi married to Sedara's beautiful daughter Angelica, and in so doing had to fight hard at every point against his repulsion at swallowing whole this social 'toad' – the novel's other animal figuration (apart from jackal) of the unscrupulous, up-and-coming mayor of Donnafugata.

It is not as though Prince Salina's sounding board for these bitter, death-directed views on Sicily has nothing to say or think in his own right. As a Northerner, the envoy Chevalley has an outsider's compassion for the squalor caused by social inequalities in Sicilian society: 'he found himself pitying this prince without hopes as much as the children without shoes, the malaria-ridden women, the guilty victims whose names reached his office every morning; all were equal fundamentally, all were comrades in misfortune segregated in the same well' (p. 126).[27] *Compagni di sventura segregati nel medesimo pozzo*: the verbal intensities of Lampedusa's definitions of Sicilian conditions, even when, as here, coming in novelistic terms from the mind of a North Italian outsider, seem to brook no argument. If it were not for other Sicilian writers such as Sciascia, who have sought to gainsay the inevitability and timelessness of such things as class segregation within the 'single well' that Sicily is figured here as being, we should surrender immediately, as many commentators have done, to Lampedusa's overall tragic interpretation.

Before turning to Sciascia's contrastive and contestatory vision, however, we need to recognize the last twist of all in Prince Salina's argument about Sicily is actually the hardest to overthrow: namely, the view that Sicilians resist interference in their destiny from outsiders or indeed from insiders, because they believe themselves gods in perfection. The Prince confesses that this is the argument he used with some British navel officers who had admired the panorama from the rooftop of his aristocratic palazzo while visiting him in Palermo, but who had at the same time been horrified at the filth and decay of the surrounding streets. Listing again at the end of the conversation, as at the beginning, all the many foreign conquerors who had sought unsuccessfully 'to canalise Sicily into the flow of universal history' (p. 127),[28] the Prince implies that Chevelley too, even in speaking for a newly uniting Italy, represents merely the latest in a line of interfering colonial powers that were not obeyed before and will not be this time: 'Sicily wanted to sleep in spite of their invocations; for why should she listen to them if she herself is rich, if she's wise, if she's civilised, if she's honest, if she's admired and envied by all, if, in a word, she is perfect?' (p. 127).[29]

Prince Salina, in short, even while throughout his argument admitting faults and a 'terrifying insularity of mind' (p. 124)[30] on the part of Sicilians – most particularly, 'this sense of superiority that dazzles every Sicilian eye, and which we ourselves call pride while in reality it's blindness' (p. 127)[31] – has not only himself refused to step outside of the pride and blindness and insularity which he magnificently analyses, to join in the new Italian cause seeking to ameliorate these faults of the past, but resolutely insisted that they are realities of the present and of the future too. 'For the moment, for a long time to come, there's nothing to be done' (p. 127).[32]

Overall, the Prince's is a cultural analysis that stubbornly allows no point of attack. Presented *by* a Sicilian, it is claimed as being unrepeatable to other Sicilians. And there is a final admission that even had it been presented by the outsider Chevalley to the Prince himself, who so passionately holds to this tragic set of beliefs, it would have been resented.[33] We are reminded of Giacomo Leopardi's dictum about Italians more generally, that they say evil of themselves that they would never allow if it were delivered as criticism by someone who was an outsider: 'Italians are sensitive above all other peoples about their reputation; a truly strange fact considering the little or even non-existent national esteem which exists among us, most certainly less than in other countries.'[34] I have suggested in my Introduction that these factors of cultural sensitivity to criticism are far from unique to one nation or people.

With Lampedusa, the trap for the reader is great. We are caught either way we turn. To agree with his Prince is to be critical of Sicilian culture in such fundamental ways that, by the Prince's own admission, one would court resentment by Sicilians themselves. (So only Sicilians are allowed the luxury of anything like full agreement.) To *disagree* with him, however, is to acknowledge not merely that one may never be able to fathom so different a culture – Leopardi's second dictum that it is 'impossible for a foreigner to know perfectly another nation' is clearly relevant here[35] – but also that one does not choose to sustain the burden of so tragic a vision, and must cling instead to ameliorative notions of history. There may be nothing morally wrong – on the contrary, everything morally right – in insisting that the future *can* be made better than the past. But we should not forget Nietzsche's sense that in doing so one risks stepping beyond proper limits in one's denial of the overdetermining factors in a specific cultural or individual history. In this case the specific culture is Sicily, and Lampedusa's analysis from the mouthpiece of his Prince proclaims that historical and climatic overdetermination is overwhelming and will remain so. Furthermore (he is convinced), an individual such as himself does right to refuse the blandishing offers of a say in future rule from Turin that will make no essential difference.

In 1958 and indeed until his death some thirty years later, Leonardo Sciascia for the most part thought very differently, even though in his later work he was himself often accused of tragic pessimism, a charge which in discussion he always resolutely refuted. In the early novella 'Forty-eight', Sciascia too portrays in great detail a member of the old landed aristocracy of Sicily, Baron Garziano: like Lampedusa's Prince, someone linked to the Bourbon past that confers on him his title and his power. But whereas in the 'Leopard's' case those links are indissoluble, even though the Bourbons are clearly seen for the feudal oppressors of Sicily they have always been, Sciascia's Baron by contrast is himself the very essence of a jackal in human form, as demonstrated at the end of the story when he dissolves in a trice his loyalties to his Bourbon masters and sucks up to the new man, Garibaldi. The worst of it is that in Sciascia's narrative Garibaldi cannot even see through the Baron's duplicity. It takes another kind of intelligence – that of Ippolito Nievo – both to penetrate the Baron's fear of offending the new power in the land, and to understand that the real strength of Sicily lies in the courage and determination of another and altogether more silent type of Sicilian, oppressed for centuries but still not defeated.

Just as in *The Leopard*, where much of the action takes place in the small village of Donnafugata, run on semi-feudal principles and dominated by its aristocratic pre-eminence (even if Lampedusa's *nouveau riche* mayor is a man on his way up in power), in Sciascia's 'Forty-eight' the situation takes place almost entirely in the medium-sized town of Castro in Western Sicily. The Baron is a foul-mouthed and adulterous boor, not above having the husband of his peasant lover wrongfully imprisoned for years in the Bourbon system's deadly labour camps. Semi-illiterate himself, he behaves with feudal absolutism to all around him. Although not all-powerful, he makes 'arrangements' with the local bishop and sub-intendant, and even uses a local bandit, Vito Lacruna, to kill one of his enemies. Along with the bishop, the sub-intendant and the King's judge, he ensures the imprisonment of eleven liberals in the period between the uprising of 1848 and the advent of Garibaldi in 1860.

Sciascia's sympathies are entirely with the common citizen under the heels of Bourbon oppression:

> The citizen on whom the arm of the law landed had very little likelihood of proving his innocence. If he succeeded in doing so. . . and was declared innocent, he still had to reckon with the police, who could keep him in prison at their discretion, even for years at a time. Because of this, arrest was feared almost more than death itself, and the peasants sang about it in those terms in the words of a lament. (p. 104)[36]

We might note here that, for Sciascia, a sense of lament for death's triumphs over life in the Sicilian context is trumped by his perception of a still deeper fear among the peasants – the fear of social injustice, and their consequent lament, *not* for inevitable death, but for the worse miseries of their lives beforehand. It is a subtle but significant departure in spirit from that other Sicilian tradition of all-pervasive consciousness of death; and one at root positivistic, since the existence of social injustice, however lamentable, always includes, in Sciascia's very ways of putting the case, the possibility of its opposite – a new time of social justice for those presently oppressed. From this early point of his career onwards, Sciascia's social conscience never wavers from that goal. In his writings concerning social oppression he seeks models whereby the oppressors may be better known, and thereby unmasked, at the very least *by the reader*, even if their powers should prove too strong in specific historical contexts for their immediate overthrow.

Being a scrupulous economic and social historian in everything he writes, Sciascia in this early narrative of 'Forty-eight' portrays a situation on the land in which 'through the Monastery of St Michael and the Bishop's Revenue, the Bishop had a good third of Castro's landed property in his hands; the Baron had another third; and the remaining land was divided into small estates and State demesnes which, slowly but surely, the Baron was usurping' (p. 104).[37] We thus are presented with a knavish hierarchy of power in which the petty aristocrats such as the Baron are at once the meanest and the most unscrupulous persons in the entire society, and in the event, when power at the top does eventually change, also the most chameleon. Not for them such refusals of opportunity to grasp power and influence in the new Italy as Prince

Fabrizio Salina displays in *The Leopard*. When Garibaldi's troops do eventually enter Castro, Baron Garziano vexes the proto-revolutionary who narrates the story (the son of the Baron's gardener) by managing to avoid exposure as the petty feudal dictator of the district that he has been to this point in the story. Worse than that. Through his readiness to supply victuals and lodgings and to fly the tricolour, the Baron appears as the most pro-Garibaldian man in town – that is, to all except the perceptive soldier Nievo, who at this point, along with the young narrator himself, must be thought of by the reader as (on one level) a mouthpiece for Sciascia's own views on the underlying class realities of Sicily in this revolutionary matter of overthrowing Bourbon hegemony.

Which brings us to the not unnatural question as to how Sciascia reacted to his recently deceased compatriot Lampedusa's much larger and relatively pro-aristocratic, if not exactly pro-Bourbon, canvas. Within a year of the publication of both *The Leopard* and his own 'Forty-eight', Sciascia was to be found wrestling with an extended idea about the representation of class in Sicilian fiction from the late nineteenth century onwards. Before he could adequately define why in Lampedusa's novel the aristocracy is the most substantial class presence, and to his mind the only one spoken for as if from within, he felt he needed to point to what he saw as an entirely honourable *absence* of treatment of the aristocracy in the most important writer of the great period of *verismo*, Giovanni Verga (1840–1922). Verga had finished nothing beyond his second novel in the sequence of *I vinti*. When it came to moving up the social ladder, after depicting the tragic fisherfolk of *I malavoglia* and the equally doomed rising peasant-landholder class of *Mastro Don Gesualdo*, to a representation of Gesualdo's daughter's marriage into the Sicilian aristocracy, as the eponymous heroine of the intended but never completed novel *La duchessa di Leyra*, Verga felt he did not have the literary skills to make the persons of the *gran mondo* in his novels speak with what he reckoned to be the forked duplicity of that class's every utterance. According to Sciascia, Lampedusa supplies Verga's gap in representation half a century later. Indeed, Lampedusa, if anything, has Verga's problem in reverse: 'He is an author', writes Sciascia in 1959, 'who knows how to make persons of the *gran mondo* speak, but cannot do the like for the poorer classes.'[38] But if Sciascia is right, it was only because Prince Giuseppe Tomasi di Lampedusa was himself of the aristocratic class in question and, furthermore, did not even remotely believe, along with Verga and Sciascia, that it was a class perennially mired in mendacity. On the contrary, in such figures as Prince Fabrizio Salina, it was if anything *au dessus de la mêlée*.

Two great differences stand out. First, Lampedusa writes from the point of view of a declining aristocracy who feel that after their demise will come only hyenas and jackals; whereas Sciascia from the first is a writer with, in the words of Joseph Farrell's interesting coverage of some of these same issues, a 'social and democratic passion for the peasantry and the subaltern classes'.[39] And second, Lampedusa fundamentally believes that no change (in particular, no amelioration) of human conditions in Sicily can be envisaged; whereas Sciascia, with his grounding in the Enlightenment, is a committed if at times crafty and hesitant positivist. In a sense the debate comes down to a matter of Sciascia's denial of Nietzsche's sense of overdetermination.

Both Nietzsche and Sciascia employ the notion of a chain in speaking of history, but with fundamental differences. For Nietzsche the chain is what ties one generation to the 'aberrations, passions and errors, and indeed . . . crimes' of earlier generations. The past is hence, first and foremost, a realm of overdetermining bondage for the living. At best, change can result from an act of dangerous 'denial', but only when the past that is being denied has firstly been thoroughly faced up to and 'known'. The processes of *both* fully knowing *and* denying the fully known, and replacing it with something entirely new, are part of the complex operation of 'critical history' as Nietzsche presents it. But even this idea of change never quite erases the original force of the past as a chain of overdetermining bondage, of which we are the 'outcome'. For Sciascia a rather different idea of the 'chain' of history appears in that same first 1959 meditation on Lampedusa, in relation to views on Sicily. Sciascia takes great exception to Lampedusa implying that Moslim imams, King Roger's knights, Swabian scribes, Angevin barons, jurists of the Most Catholic King, Spanish viceroys and Charles III's reforming functionaries *all* 'conceived the same fine folly', of changing Sicily from what it already and immutably was as a culture – as if it had an essence, so to speak, which existed outside of and unaffected by historical time. Rather, in Sciascia's view of the matter, each one of those conquerors – a single Arab governor is the example he focuses on – took on Sicily as a living context ('una dimora vitale'), which for him may have been absolute and unique, but which for us is relative, and *similar to just one link in a longer chain* in our notion of Sicily. On this fundamental principle of the philosophy of history Sciascia seems to have held firm.

His belief in 'a continuum of links, each dependent on the other', as Farrell aptly puts the crux of Sciascia's idea of history,

> involves the dynamism of flux, conflict and change and its essence is choice, the assertion of certain ideas and the rejection of others, the triumph of certain interests and the discomfiture of others. The fact of living, and writing, in history carries with it the need to reject all determinisms, all absolutisms, all finalities.[40]

Because so different from Nietzsche's idea of the chain of history as a bondage of which we are the 'outcome', Sciascia's case about rejecting determinisms, absolutisms and finalities has implications above all for any final consideration in this chapter of Sicily as a culture of death. In the interval since the terrible murders of Judge Falcone and Judge Borsellino in 1992, arrests and trials of tens of high-ranking mafiosi led in September 1997 to life sentences on twenty-four for the killing of Falcone, and in December 1999 on seventeen for the bombing of Borsellino and his five bodyguards. This certainly represented that principle of the triumph of certain interests – in this case those of justice – and the discomfiture of others which have been traditionally based upon the ethic of killing anyone inimical or simply inconvenient to the mafia's aims.

But against that must be set the acquittal of the seven-times prime minister of Italy in the 1970s and 1980s, Giulio Andreotti: in one trial for ordering the murder of an investigative journalist who had written critically of him and uncovered evidence allegedly linking him with the mafia; and in another for alleged collusion with the mafia, in particular by providing them with political and judicial protection. These two trials had dragged on for several years. Eventually, in the first it was decided there was 'no' evidence to connect Andreotti with the killing, and in the second that there was 'insufficient' evidence of guilt on the collusion charge. To large sectors of the Italian community who wished for some sign that political corruption in the very highest places really was being successfully relegated to the past – corruption of the kind Sciascia himself had pointed to with such prescience in his most famous novel, *The Day of the Owl*, as early as 1961 – these acquittals came as a heavy disappointment. Not surprisingly – as though to illustrate the obverse of Falcone's law, that one is most in jeopardy in the absence of powerful friends – two important fellow politicians of the present times, the (then) prime minister Romano Prodi and foreign minister Lamberto

Dini, had expressed in 1997 their inability to credit that Andreotti might be guilty, some while before he was exonerated in the two unrelated trials:

> Prodi, in an interview in the German *Welt am Sonntag* newspaper, stated that he could not believe that a person such as Andreotti, who had led seven governments, was 'a friend of the Mafiosi and someone who ordered homicides'. Andreotti welcomed Prodi's intervention, and later claimed in the *La Repubblica* newspaper that 'a lot of people were now in agreement' that his was a 'political trial'. Foreign Minister Lamberto Dini was amongst a growing number of influential figures and commentators who had also recently questioned the basis of the trial.[41]

It all seemed to be a case of the claim made by the great modern Sicilian painter Renato Guttuso about the status of truth in the Sicilian context: 'you can find dramas, pastorals, idylls, politics, gastronomy, geography, history, literature . . . in the end you can find anything and everything, but you can't find truth.'[42] Or rather, put more cynically, it was a case once again in Sicily of truth being decided by a form of suffrage in which the powerful and prominent – far from being reaped before time by Death, the skeletal rider on his equally skeletal horse, as in our anonymous fifteenth-century fresco – had vastly disproportionate voting rights. If Giuseppe Tomasi, Prince of Lampedusa, could have slept easily with that latter historical reality of the abiding influence of the powerful, even though his own moribund aristocratic class had finally succumbed in its attempts to stave off death (in the process choosing to enfold its fears of *thanatos* in the longed-for embraces of *eros*), the project by contrast of the 'anti-leopard' Leonard Sciascia's entire writing career can be said to have been to overthrow it.

## Notes

1. The best historical account of this period is in Paul Ginsborg's excellent *A History of Contemporary Italy: Society and Politics 1943–1988* (Harmondsworth: Penguin, 1990). See in particular Chapter 10, 'Crisis, Compromise and the "Anni di Piombo", 1973–80', pp. 348–405. For the mafia's rise to prominence world-wide in post-war years, Claire Sterling's *The Mafia: The Long Reach of the International Sicilian Mafia* (London: Hamish Hamilton, 1990) is still the most comprehensive account, though of course it cannot inform us about evolutions in the narrative since its date of publication.

2. Alexander Stille, *Excellent Cadavers* (London: Jonathan Cape, 1995), p. 28. For the 'Sack of Palermo' see also the memorable description in Peter Robb's

*Midnight in Sicily* (Potts Point, NSW: Duffy and Snellgrove, 1996), pp. 22–3.

3. Stille, *Excellent Cadavers*, p. 175.

4. *Ibid.*, p. 66.

5. Giovanni Falcone with Marcelle Padovani, *Men of Honour: The Truth about the Mafia*, translated by Edward Farrelly (London: Fourth Estate, 1992), p. 73. The original reads: 'La cultura della morte non appartiene solamente alla mafia: tutta la Sicilia ne è impregnata. Da noi il giorno dei morti è festa grande: offriamo dolci che si chiamano teste di morto, fatti di zucchero duro come pietra. Solitudine, pessimismo, morte sono i temi della nostra letteratura, da Pirandello a Sciascia. Quasi fossimo un popolo che ha vissuto troppo e di colpo si sente stanco, spossato, svuotato, come il Don Fabrizio di Tomasi di Lampedusa.' Giovanni Falcone in collaboration with Marcelle Padovani, *Cose di Cosa Nostra* (Milan: Rizzoli, 1991), p. 86.

6. Maria Grazia Paolini, 'Il "Trionfo" oggi', in *Il 'Trionfo della Morte' di Palermo: l'opera, le vicende conservative, il restauro* (Palermo: Sellerio, 1989), pp. 21–2. The original reads: 'Il tema del Trionfo . . . come comprovono i superstiti testi letterari . . . univa al fine di edificazione e di ammaestramento quello consolatorio e rassicurante nel mostrare come la morte più rapidamente colpisce i potenti e i felici, i giovani gaudenti che non coloro che la implorano come liberatrice, e recava, tutt'altro che sotteso, un significato di rivalsa nei confronti dei sopraffattori, degli usurai, dei superbi, di tutti coloro che a fini di lucro e di potere godevano, e facevano commercio nell'ambito della chiesa come nella società civile, di ogni sorta di privilegi.'

7. Robb, *Midnight in Sicily*, p. 192.

8. Leonardo Sciascia, 'Forty-eight', in *Sicilian Uncles*, translated by N. S. Thompson (Manchester: Carcanet, 1986), pp. 144–5. The original reads: 'io credo nei siciliani che parlano poco, nei siciliani che non si agitano, nei siciliani che si rodano dentro e soffrono: i poveri che ci salutano con un gesto stanco, come da una lontananza di secoli; e il colonnello Carini sempre cosí silenzioso e lontano, impastato di malinconia e di noia ma ad ogni momento pronto all'azione: un uomo che pare non abbia molte speranze, eppure è il cuore stesso della speranza, la silenziosa fragile speranza dei siciliani migliori.' From 'Il quarantotto', in *Gli zii di Sicilia* (1958: Turin: Einaudi, 1975), p. 161. Henceforth page numbers in the English translation will be given in brackets after quotations.

9. Sciascia, *Gli zii di Sicilia*, p. 161.

10. Falcone, *Men of Honour*, pp. 22 and 25. The original reads: 'Ho sempre saputo che per dare battaglia bisogna lavorare a più non posso . . .' and 'Ne ho tratto la conclusione che occorre procedere con la massima cautela e che bisogna verificare a ogni passo il confine tra il noto e l'ignoto' (Falcone, *Cose di Cosa Nostra*, pp. 40 and 43).

11. Falcone, *Men of Honour*, pp. 52–5. The original reads: 'Sono nato nello stesso quartiere di molti di loro. . . . Sono dunque diventato una sorta di difensore di tutti i pentiti perché, in un modo o nell'altro, li rispetto tutti. . . . Ho imparato a riconoscere l'umanità anche nell'essere apparentemente peggiore; ad avere un rispetto reale, e non solo formale, per le altrui opinioni. . . . L'imperativo categorico dei mafiosi, di "dire la verità", è diventato un principio cardine della

mia etica personale, almeno riguardo ai rapporti veramente importanti della vita. Per quanto possa sembrare strano, la mafia mi ha impartito una lezione di moralità' (Falcone, *Cose di Cosa Nostra*, pp. 68–71).

12. Stille, *Excellent Cadavers*, p. 174.

13. Falcone, *Men of Honour*, p. 162. The original reads: 'Si muore generalmente perché si è soli o perché si è entrati in un gioco troppo grande. Si muore spesso perché non si dispone delle necessarie alleanze, perché si è privi di sostegno. In Sicilia la mafia colpisce i servitori dello Stato che lo Stato non è riuscito a proteggere' (Falcone, *Cose di Cosa Nostra*, p. 171).

14. Quoted in Stille, *Excellent Cadavers*, p. 176.

15. Dennis Mack Smith, *A History of Sicily*, 2 vols (New York: Dorset Press, 1968), Vol. 1, *Medieval Sicily: 800–1713*, p. xiii.

16. My own translation of Leonardo Sciascia, *La Sicilia come Metafora: intervista di Marcelle Padovani* (Milan: Mondadori, 1979), p. 46. The original reads: 'Le sole volte che il siciliano ha deciso da solo e si è rassegnato a far da solo la storia, disgraziatamente si è sbagliato, ed è così che hanno avuto luogo i Vespri siciliani che hanno chiuso la porta alla Francia per aprirla alla Spagna.'

17. See, for instance, Ian Thomson's use of the term in this connection, in his 'Conversation in Palermo with Leonardo Sciascia', included in the volume by Leonardo Sciascia, *1912 + 1: A Novel*, translated by Sacha Rabinovitch (Manchester: Carcanet, 1989), p. 111. Joseph Farrell points out that Giancarlo Vigorelli and others had also applied the term to Sciascia's substantial historical novel of 1963, *Il consiglio d'Egitto* (see Farrell's *Leonardo Sciascia* [Edinburgh: Edinburgh University Press, 1995], p. 105). I have preferred in the following to compare Sciascia's shorter work of 1958 with *The Leopard*, because of the coincidence in the period and events being dealt with in the two works.

18. Friedrich Nietzsche, *Untimely Meditations*, trans. R. J. Hollingdale, introduction by J. P. Stern (Cambridge: Cambridge University Press, 1983), p. 75. (The second Meditation, 'Of the Uses and Disadvantages of History for Life', from which this and subsequent quotations from Nietzsche are taken, first appeared separately in the original German in Leipzig, in February 1874.)

19. Nietzsche, *Untimely Meditations*, p. 76.

20. Giuseppe Tomasi di Lampedusa, *The Leopard*, translated by Archibald Colquhoun (London: Collins Harvill, 1960), p. 5. The original reads: 'tutto rientrava nell'ordine, nel disordine, consueto' (*Il Gattopardo* [Milan: Feltrinelli, 1958], p. 17). Henceforth, page numbers in the English translation will be given in brackets after quotations, and the Italian original in the notes from this Feltrinelli edition.

21. 'questa monarchia che aveva i segni della morte sul volto' (p. 28).

22. 'Dopo la felice annessione, volevo dire dopo la fausta unione della Sicilia al Regno di Sardegna . . .' (p. 205).

23. 'Noi siciliani siamo stati avvezzi da una lunga, lunghissima egemonia di governanti che non erano della nostra religione, che non parlavano la nostra lingua, a spaccare i capelli in quattro. Se non si faceva così non si scampava dagli esattori bizantini, dagli emiri berberi, dai viceré spagnoli. Adesso la piega è presa, siamo fatto così. . . . Siamo vecchi, Chevalley, vecchissimi. Sono venticinque secoli almeno

che portiamo sulle spalle il peso di magnifiche civiltà eterogenee, tutte venute da fuori, nessuna germogliata da noi stessi, nessuna a cui abbiamo dato il *la*; noi siamo dei bianchi quanto lo è lei, Chevalley, e quanto la regina d'Inghilterra; eppure da duemilacinquecento anni siamo colonia. Non lo dico per lagnarmi: è colpa nostra. Ma siamo stanchi e svuotati lo stesso' (pp. 209–10).

24. 'Tutte le manifestazioni siciliane sono manifestazioni oniriche, anche le più violente: la nostra sensualità è desiderio di oblio, le schioppettate e le coltellate nostre, desiderio di morte; desiderio di immobilità voluttuosa, cioè ancora di morte, la nostra pigrizia, i nostri sorbetti di scorsonera o di cannella; il nostro aspetto meditativo è quello del nulla che volesse scrutare gli enigmi del nirvana' (pp. 210–11).

25. 'ricadrà nel nostro voluttuoso torpore: lo fanno tutti' (p. 211).

26. 'il casato, mi è stato detto, è antico o finirà con esserlo' (p. 214).

27. 'ebbe pietà tanto del Principe senza speranze come dei bimbi scalzi, delle donne malariche, delle non innocenti vittime i cui elenchi giungevano ogni mattina al suo ufficio: tutti eguali, in fondo, compagni di sventura segregati nel medesimo pozzo' (p. 215).

28. 'incanalare la Sicilia nel flusso della storia universale' (p. 217).

29. 'La Sicilia ha voluto dormire, a dispetto delle loro invocazioni; perché avrebbe dovuto ascoltarli se è ricca, se è saggia, se è civile, se è onesta, se è da tutti ammirata e invidiata, se è perfetta in una parola?' (p. 217).

30. 'una terrificante insularità d'animo' (p. 213).

31. 'quel senso di superiorità che barbaglia in ogni occhio siciliano, che noi stessi chiamiamo fierezza, che in realtà è cecità' (pp. 217–18).

32. 'Per ora, per molto tempo, non c'è niente da fare' (p. 218).

33. 'Questi sono discorsi che non si possono fare ai Siciliani: ed io stesso, del resto, se queste cose le avesse dette lei, me ne sarei avuto a male' (p. 218).

34. Giacomo Leopardi, *Discorso sopra lo stato presente dei costumi degl' italiani*, introduced and edited by Augusto Placanica (Venice: Marsilio, 1989), p. 7. The original reads: 'gli italiani, delicatissimi sopra tutti gli altri sul conto loro: cosa veramente strana, considerando il poco o niuno amor nazionale che vive tra noi, e certo minore che non è negli altri paesi' (p. 122).

35. *Ibid.* The original reads: 'impossibile a uno straniero il conoscere perfettamente un'altra nazione'.

36. 'il cittadino su cui il braccio della polizia si abbatteva, aveva ben poche probabilità di poter dimostrare la propria innocenza; e se davanti al giudice ci riusciva, se il giudice. . . lo mandava assolto, doveva ancora e sempre fare i conti con la polizia, che a discrezione poteva trattenerlo in carcere, anche per molti anni; perciò l'arresto era temuto più della morte e così, in strofe di lamento, ne canta il popolo contadino' ('Il quarantotto', p. 116).

37. 'Il vescovo, attraverso il monastero di san Michele e la mensa vescovile, aveva in mano un buon terzo della proprietà terriera di Castro; altrettanta ne aveva il barone; il rimanente territorio era diviso in piccole proprietà e in terre demaniali: e le terre demaniali il barone lentamente ma sicuramente veniva usurpando' (p. 116).

38. My own translation of Leonardo Sciascia, *Pirandello e la Sicilia*, 2nd edn (Caltanisetta and Rome: Salvatore Sciasci, 1968), p. 154. The original reads: 'è un autore che sa far parlare la gente del gran mondo, ma non sa far parlare la povera gente'.

39. Farrell, *Sciascia*, p. 105.
40. *Ibid.*, p. 104.
41. *Keesing's Record of World Events*, News Digest for August 1997, p. 41783.
42. Robb, *Midnight in Sicily*, p. 275.

CHAPTER 8

# 'A FINE FUNERAL OF OUR IDENTITIES'?

## THE ITALIAN DIASPORA OF THE MODERN EPOCH

In a coda to Chapter 1 I dealt with the relatively new factor in Italian society of immigration on a significant scale. This final chapter returns to an older phenomenon, that of emigration to other lands and continents, in particular the problems faced, and the forms of Italianness that took root or else evolved by mutation, in the new conditions. As before, the study undertaken is not a sociology of emigration based upon figures and graphs. It aims rather at as canny an interpretation as possible of exemplary persons and texts, in an attempt through analysis of particular emigrant experiences to produce understanding of a more generalized kind.

The quotation in my chapter title comes from the early pages of a chaotic novel of modern Italian migrant experience in Sydney, Rosa Cappiello's *Oh Lucky Country*, winner in its original Italian version of the Calabria prize for literature in 1981.[1] This is a work which can be used as an initial marker for one extreme of migrant experience of the modern epoch – that of being down and out, with little prospect of either a return to one's homeland or any improvement of one's existential lot in the new country. Before further exploration of the Italian diaspora, I wish to consider aspects of this one disturbing novel. Although Cappiello's representation cannot be taken as a globally valid blueprint for migrant experience, the extremism of her case is nonetheless an instructive worst-case scenario, which on that basis alone merits an exemplary status at the start of this chapter.

The sentences from which the title quotation comes are characteristic of the bleak perspectives offered by Cappiello of emigrant experience:

Once we had arrived here the past was all played out, aimless, senseless. Memories were quickly sucked up by the present and withered, drained away through the torn pages of the calendar. . . . With the act of migration we had ordered ourselves a fine funeral of our identities, to be reincarnated in sewers, as factory workers, in machinery, in knots, as tender morsels for despotic men.[2]

Practically the entire book is gendered female. It is not only not a work which claims to represent the angst that may be felt by migrant males, it positively demonizes the male sex for the most part, whether in the persons of Anglo-, or Italo-, or otherwise 'New' Australians. That said, the kinds of dilemma Cappiello narrates, and many of the horrors of immigrant lives she describes (when not actually committed by men against women), need not be accepted by the individual reader as so inevitably gender-specific as the text makes out.

Later in this chapter, analysis is undertaken of a selection of histories or portrayals of migration – complex interweaves of positive and negative experience. But this beginning – with Cappiello's depictions of lost female identity in the rootless slum conditions of a sub-Bohemian Sydney – encourages us to find a language for other negative aspects of migrant experience. No amount of sociological or economic statistics on the extent to which migration often involves a forsaking of lifestyles and skills of a prior existence manages to represent adequately the desolation involved in such changes. For instance, carefully pieced together tables showing, among other things, that 'most of the women in the artisan class (seamstresses/lace-makers) were unable to continue their craft in Australia' and that 'the majority went from craft and home duties in Italy to factory work in Australia',[3] constitute only the outer shell of a story of which Cappiello's descriptions in her novel provide the harrowing inner substance. The following passage from the novel is representative:

This is the female factory worker, wife of the modern coolie and coolie herself, who has got down to a fine art the act of tying her baby to the bed or to the downpipe of the kitchen sink so as not to forego the happy hour on Friday which is pay day. Slave of the dollar, she sends her newly-born babe to relatives in Egypt, Yugoslavia, Spain, Greece, and after a few years back it comes like a postal package by sea or by air. That little boy, that little girl, sometimes two, deprived of their weaning, guaranteed the deposit for buying a house or a re-entry visa to the home country with riches without regrets. Bitter details. Structure of modern society. You have to adapt. Go along with it.[4]

Adapting means facing the main jeopardy of such a lifestyle – the possibility of losing one's job, with all the consequent uncertainties:

> What's it like to find yourself unemployed and in a strange land to boot? I didn't know. Like I didn't know that there was the NSW family assistance, unemployment benefit, sickness benefit, special benefit, which allowed extra earnings for the enterprising types. All I knew then was that there wouldn't be any bread, or security, or fun.[5]

What is so interesting about Cappiello's way of representing the female migrant labourer's fears subjectively is that at another level of the writing there is knowledge of an extensive social welfare system in the host nation for catching and looking after the victims of unemployment. Here, that knowledge is used precisely to help define the fears experienced during the earlier phase of ignorance. Not only does that other level of knowledge not mitigate the situation of the migrant woman who is represented as lacking it: if anything she is rendered more abject to the reader, precisely by the fact that hers is ignorance of the very things that would ease her state of mind were she already to know them. In other words, the early migrant experience is defined by relation to other experiences or knowledges that are being registered acutely by their lack. Meagre material comforts are all the more compulsively and pathetically enjoyed for their being perpetually in danger of disappearing – for example, the triad of bread, security and fun.

This extreme case about migration naturally turns the host nation – in this instance Australia – into a caricature of inhospitality: 'this country will never be home. It will never be a refuge for anyone who isn't a sheep.'[6] There is little point in disputing this subjective account with some 'objective' facts about Australia's receptiveness to outsiders, enshrined even in its modern constitution, especially since 1972 legislation which saw the abandonment of a 'White Australia' policy that had remained on the statute books continuously since 1901, when, under workers' union pressure, the so-called Fathers of Federation had passed the Immigration Restriction Act. Little point, because the force of Cappiello's case is precisely that hers is the *subjective* migrant's-eye view of life in the new country. The possible benefits of the host country's as yet unknown opportunities are null and void, since at this stage they are just that – unknown – and hence, existentially speaking, *non*-existent for the migrant in question. This is important, because it represents a common migrant experience across the globe. All that is said in the rest of this chapter must be measured in terms of this worst-case scenario – of emigration producing a 'fine funeral' of past identities from the sender nation, and no compensating Phoenix-like rebirth from their ashes of *new* selves to be enjoyed in the host nation. Only reincarnation as 'slave' selves of the dollar.

Under such terrible conditions as Cappiello's text represents, the migrant subject herself disappears beneath the threshold of self-recognition: 'All this will not have happened, because what has happened and continues to happen belongs to too many people and to recognize oneself in all of this is impossible.'[7] Having documented the chaos and anomie of life for groups of migrants in Sydney, the novel's last words suggest a grim dualism: that on the one hand the experiences represented are pervasive, but on the other that their very all-pervasiveness renders any sense of individual destiny – hence control over one's own life and future – impossible. Migration by this reckoning becomes a Jungian nightmare, suffered so generally that the pain felt is unindividuated. Under such conditions there is simply no constituting of the single self that experiences: 'to recognize oneself in all of this is impossible'.

This existential black hole must be borne constantly in mind during the following accounts of an Italian diaspora. It must be understood as one possible fate haunting the innumerable mutant forms of 'Italianness' created by more than a century and a half of migration overseas from communities of peninsular and island Italy. In short, Italianness, like selfhood, may simply prove evanescent in the bleak lived conditions of emigration.

* * * * *

Despite the foregoing, emigration did not usually involve the extinction of all prior identity. Whether as an extreme expedient to economic hardship in Italy or simply undertaken in a spirit of adventure, emigrant experience took as many different configurations as there were emigrants, much of it highly positive in kind. Sometimes it fell into patterns from which we can formulate generalizations, sometimes not.

What follows is a reflection upon certain histories of Italian emigration, or texts dealing with emigrant communities. Through what is (of necessity) an arbitrary set of examples, ridiculously small in number, the intention is nonetheless an ambitious one: to reveal representative as well as unique and bizarre aspects of the Italian diaspora, and hopefully with a freshness of insight not always possible in more conventional historical or sociological approaches.

Inevitably, some fundamental questions need to be asked. Not all of them are answered in the following study, but it seemed important that they be at least formulated. Questions such as: What do mutant forms of 'Italianness' abroad tell us about the Italy that was left behind, during the more than hundred and fifty years that emigration was a major demographic factor? Are there not some respects in which 'Little Italies' – whether in New York, Buenos Aires, Melbourne or elsewhere – developed long-term patterns of cultural renewal greater than those of the nation from which they took their origins and sometimes their names too? If so, what accounts for such revitalizations? And if, as seems likely, the answer to the last question lies in the hybridizing of old-world Italian customs, patterns of work, cultural assumptions and technical expertise, with emergent or already defined varieties of New-World experience and know-how, then beyond what thresholds did Italianness as something recognizable in its own right disappear, under the combined pressures and seductions of the dominant host culture? Richard D. Alba, for instance, has written convincingly of 'the twilight of ethnicity' – 'a stage when ethnic differences remain visible but only faintly so'. In this twilight phase people hang on to a sense of their own or their ancestral origins, and to 'ethnicity as a leisure-time activity, rather than as a life-organizing force'.[8] We need to test this kind of sociological notion against literary texts that witness ethnicity still very much as a life-organizing force: for instance, in the enduring Sicilian clan mentalities of the American mafia – even if, in the vision provided by writers such as Mario Puzo, the dream of a specific 'godfather' may well be that his children 'grow up to be All-American kids, real All-American, the whole works'.[9]

Multiplying questions still further, are there important differences to be noted in cases where the country of adoption was not of the New World (whether in the Americas, or still more distant Australasia) but another old-world European nation, such as Britain, with long-term malaises and demographic factors of its own that, apart from all else, produced emigration in their turn? In what follows, for instance, we have an opportunity to consider the case of an early Italian emigrant: someone richly cultivated and historically prominent, who largely made his money from a traditional form of writing (that of the opera libretto), and for whom settling first in Vienna, then in London – in each case for quite some years – did not provide a sufficient livelihood for the kind of egregious wastrel he seems partially to have been, and who therefore continued his migrations across the Atlantic to the United States, never to return. What are the interconnections between the *economic* migration of persons and the *cultural* migrations of musical or literary or art forms: in particular, when specific and sometimes renowned artists (such as the one mentioned) are themselves economic migrants? Is it possible to arrive in a new country long before some aspect of one's former culture takes hold – and hence to be in the position of welcoming, perhaps even facilitating, its advent? Are not emigrants constantly having to suppress forms of disturbance, including even anger, that a host community or nation sees little reason for their feeling – so much are they, *when figured as immigrants*, presumed to have much to be grateful for in what they have found; rather than as persons who have lost others dear to them, a home maybe, a cultural context certainly, all perhaps sorely missed?

The above are just some of the questions and issues. Others emerge *en passant*. The chapter closes with a concerted attempt at answers pitched at a more general level. But first a prelude about early forms of contact between Italy and the farthest-flung of continents, from times long before mass migration.

\* \* \* \* \*

By a delightful irony of history almost the first 'Australians' (if we may name them thus, particularly in a period when Australia was a number of separate colonies of the British crown) that made the reverse transit to Italy were not humans but a small number of kangaroos, exchanged for an equivalent tally of papyrus scrolls from Herculaneum in the course of 1818 and 1819. The parties to the exchange were, on the one hand, the Bourbon King Ferdinand III of Sicily (and IV of Naples) – or as he styled himself when the union of these two crowns had been recognized by the Congress of Vienna, Ferdinand I of the Two Sicilies – and on the other the British Prince Regent, acted for by Sir William A'Court, Lord William Bentinck's successor as Commander in Chief of the British Forces in Sicily and Plenipotentiary and Envoy Extraordinary. The papyri went to England rather than to Australia. The kangaroos were obtained for a menagerie of the Villa Floridiana on the Vomero hill above Naples, which Ferdinand had had done up for his morganatic wife, the Duchess of Floridia. A later English visitor, Lady Blessington, does not mention the kangaroos specifically, but found the menagerie itself 'the only drawback to this charming place', which also contained fabulous gardens, grottoes, greenhouses, tempietti and artificial ruins. For her, 'the roaring of lions, and screams of the other wild beast, are little in harmony with so Arcadian a spot'.[10] General Pietro Colletta by contrast, who published a *History of the Kingdom of Naples, 1734– 1825* almost thirty years after the exchange,[11] remembers of the menagerie only the kangaroos, 'kept . . . there as a luxury, animals from Australia, which, by a singular deformity, walk on their paws and long twisted tails'.[12] He remarks on the exchange of eighteen papyrus scrolls for an equivalent number of these exotic beasts, but concludes that the kangaroos were 'obscene'.

Does this mean Colletta had seen the kangaroos or their progeny? Probably so. The description of their mode of movement and his subsequent disgust with them seem first-hand reactions. The exchange testifies to Europe's dual fascination with classical antiquities on the one hand and exotic fauna on the other. Both Ferdinand I, the Bourbon king, and the Prince Regent were excited by the finds at Herculaneum. The latter called on Sir Humphry Davy, 'the most eminent of our Professors in various branches of natural Science', to help out after 'attempts pursued by Dr Sickler under His Royal Highness's Patronage to unroll some of those manuscripts presented by His Sicilian Majesty entirely failed'. As Lord Castlereagh writes to A'Court, 'The Prince Regent is so impressed with the importance of leaving nothing untried to open to the Public these valuable stores of ancient Literature.'[13]

What more can we discover about the kangaroos? Oddly, after initial plans for the exchange were laid in 1818, five of the marsupials due to be taken to Naples were overlooked by Castlereagh in England over the subsequent winter. Their keeper in the King's Mews in London is forced to remind others of 'these unfortunate kangaroos'. Plans are thence laid to take them out in 'the first Ship of War or Store Ship destined for the Mediterranean'. But when a boat is found, they are unable to sail a direct passage. They are to be transported to Malta in one vessel and then forwarded at the next available opportunity, making sure 'to feed them during the Passage to Malta at a Rate of five guineas for each'. Sir William Hamilton writes that 'directions have been given to the Clerk of the King's Stables at the Royal Mews, to cause the five Kangaroos to be put into the proper Cages and sent aboard the Ann'.[14]

Overall, the exchange – even its touchingly comic hitches (the kangaroos forgotten for a winter, some of the papyrus scrolls damaged or destroyed in the attempt by the Prince Regent's first appointed expert to unroll them) – is an instance of Old-World courtly diplomacy. One European realm in 1818 is newly possessed of a fine example of an art treasure from a rich site of Roman remains, another of exotic animals from its faraway penal colony in the southern oceans. The rarities of each can be measured in the courtly balances of the exchange: for each papyrus, one kangaroo. Possibly King Ferdinand knew he could lay hands on plenty more of those Herculaneum scrolls. And perhaps too, William A'Court had some idea of the plentifulness of kangaroos in New South Wales. What is interesting is that the place from which the kangaroos had come in no way figures yet as somewhere for humans to migrate – not at any rate the subjects under Ferdinand's rule, from Naples southward, including Calabria and Sicily (i.e. notably the areas of mass migration of later periods). Australia, even thirty years later, in General Colletta's text, is still seen merely as the provenance of these strange animals. And equally, so far as we can tell, no one with Australian interests was involved in the diplomacy between King Ferdinand and Sir William A'Court. The circulation of goods is confined to Old-World protagonists.

More research is necessary. The event merits study in its own right, not (as here) as a prelude to further discussion of Italian emigration. It would of course be fascinating to find out how the kangaroos had been brought from Australia in the first place. Were they part of a larger number of specimens, or brought from Australia specifically for this deal? Going backwards in time from the period of actual exchange, at what point would we begin to encounter persons in the NSW colony, or on vessels, actually involved in the catching of the animals or their shipment to Europe? And with what initial purpose or purposes? The overall curiosity of the exchange, the range of persons involved in the correspondence and the fascinating light shed on the interconnectivity between the Bourbon court of Naples and the Regency court in Britain, not to mention the farther shores of provenance of the marsupial specimens, are worthy of a playwright's hand.

One last historical irony of rediscovering this exchange of 1818 and 1819 between a Neapolitan king and an English plenipotentiary acting for the Prince Regent (in which, from the evidence of research to date, no Australian interests as such were involved) is that Italian emigrants making a return from Australia to Italy in modern times are sometimes called *canguri*.[15]

\* \* \* \* \*

Some years *before* those kangaroos were placed on the Vomero in Naples – on the 4th of June 1805 to be precise – there stepped off the packet boat *Columbia* in Philadelphia one of Italy's and Europe's most colourful characters. He was emigrating to the United States in an almost Micawberish hope that something would turn up, after multiple financial imbroglios of gain and loss in Venice, Vienna and London over many years. Born a Jew in Venetian territory at the end of the first half of the previous century, in 1749, he had converted to Christianity along with his father and the rest of the family, for what seem to have been typical reasons of expediency. Furnished with this new Christian identity, including a new name, he even took minor orders, but after a series of political and amorous intrigues in Venice had to flee, by stages to Vienna, under pursuit by the Venetian Inquisition and more than one jealous husband, according to a legend largely disseminated by himself. (Recent scholarship has seen the virulent anti-Semitism of the party in Venice led by the Riformatore, Andrea Tron, as the more deep-seated cause of his leaving the city.[16]) Apart from artistic achievements, his eventual most successful and lasting enterprise was a somewhat improbable marriage to a beautiful young English woman half his age – a marriage possibly never solemnized, given his status (even if in another country and earlier existence) as an abbot of the church. His Nancy – that was the young woman's name – seems to have been almost the only stable point of reference in the life of someone of classically unstable artistic temperament.

Here was a person who, once finally arrived in America, and although past his fifty-sixth birthday, was to open and close numerous trading enterprises (today we would call them grocery stores) in New York, Philadelphia and Sunbury in Pennsylvania, as well as educational establishments for cultivating young American men and women in the refinements of the Italian language and literature, and sundry other elements of good breeding – not to mention running boarding houses and whiskey distilleries. Under the influence of cultural contacts he became in time a foreign bookseller, essentially of classical Italian texts. This he had done before, in London, and here too, as there, he published and sold pamphlets, poems, libretti and some longer works. He was in time (twenty years after arrival, in 1825) made first Professor of Italian at Columbia College (forerunner of the University of that name) – although, somewhat characteristically for the person in question, this honorific post, held in name till his death in 1838, never paid him a stipend. And he was to be keenly instrumental in the promotion of Italian opera in America, his involvement in the genre in the Old World of Europe having not been inconsequential.

Here was a man whose American years by his own reckoning were as crossed as his European ones before them, according to a passage in his *Memoirs* written many years after his arrival in America: 'a continued series of calamities, afflicting a man by now arrived at his very old age, unfavoured of fortune, incapable of a base act, and sole supporter of a family of dependants'.[17] Indeed, already within two years of arriving on American shores he had sought to pull every heartstring with characteristically ham rhetoric about how friends had disappointed him; rhetoric so pathetic that its effect is surely unintentionally comic: 'One absconded, one failed, one went to jail, one laughed at him, one tried to make people believe that I had defrauded him.'[18] This constitutional grumbler and egotist, whose family – especially his industrious, all-suffering, but uncomplaining wife – contrary to his protestations about martyring himself for their sakes, supported him through countless hare-brained, get-rich-quick schemes,[19] had been in quite another European age the intimate of Casanova. Still more importantly, he had a hand in some of the greatest operas ever written. Indeed one of them, *Don Giovanni*, was to receive its New York première only now, in 1826, thirty-nine years after its original opening night in Prague in 1787, during the death throes of the ancien régime (about which, as a work of art, it reflects not a little), and fully twenty-one years after the poet's own arrival in America. He could thus receive and attend that work of another age (and, in his particular case, of an earlier self) which, in a kind of belated *cultural migration*, had followed his personal transatlantic move to the United States. For this was none other than Mozart's librettist, Lorenzo Da Ponte (see Plate 10).

*Cultural* migration as a specific factor within the larger histories of the movements of people is very much our subject here. But Da Ponte's own was a treble *economic* migration (as we would now call it) – first to

Vienna, thence onwards some years later to London, and, only when utterly washed up there, from Old to New World. Da Ponte's Viennese years need little introduction. But no account of the eventual American years will be adequately focused without establishing something about the kind of Italian abroad that Da Ponte was, even during his less-well-documented years in London, from 1793 to 1805.

In 1792, his Viennese years now behind him and newly attached to someone who was to prove to be his partner as long as she lived, Da Ponte is restless to turn his hand to the Italian opera in some new but important city. It is an art form which sells well, and in every burgeoning opera house of Europe there is a need for librettists to cut, expand, adapt and translate old works, and even (more occasionally) to devise entirely new ones. He and Nancy avoid heading for Paris, their first choice of city, both on a suggestion from the fast-ageing Casanova, whom they have seen at Dux on a stage of their north-west post-nuptial journeying through Germany, and also because on travelling further they hear of the imprisonment of the French queen Marie Antoinette, to whom Da Ponte bears a (now useless) letter of recommendation. Frightened by the advances of the French revolutionary armies upon Maintz, the Da Pontes take an evasive course. London seems a safer bet. Nancy spent her early years in England and even has a married sister living there. The Italian opera is relatively well established, even if the principle theatre in which of late it has been housed – the Kings Theatre in Haymarket – has recently burned down. That particular theatre will shortly be rebuilt on the old site by investments from opera impresarios with whom, in succeeding years, Da Ponte is to become involved in speculations and endless financial wranglings. For Da Ponte will never follow Casanova's two other pieces of advice to him concerning London – first, never to waste time in the Caffé degli Italiani, and second, never to sign his name to financial transactions. How can we put in a nutshell these twelve or thirteen years the Da Pontes spent in London? Perhaps best of all by concentrating on one early moment that Da Ponte regarded as a success – even, indeed, as victory over his rivals – after several crushing initial months of relative failure.

Da Ponte had arrived in London – where he already had contacts in the opera business – with hopes (founded on his reputation from his time in Vienna) of filling the soon-to-be-vacant post of established and paid librettist. Upon seeing another Italian of many years standing in London – a certain Badini – preferred in his stead, he complains bitterly to all and sundry. But within a little while he is to be found journeying into Holland, harbouring the still larger idea of becoming both impresario and librettist in Rotterdam, Brussels, the Hague or anywhere else that he can secure the post. As so often, his plans come unstuck, this time when the singers he has counted upon now ask, as their price for joining his venture, for exorbitant moneys up front which he doesn't remotely possess.

At his wits' end, sending begging letters to Casanova and via him appeals to the latter's own patron at Dux, Count Waldstein, all to no avail (the European smart set had by now learned not to lend money to this man), Da Ponte and Nancy are eventually saved from starvation in the Low Countries only by a letter from her sister Louisa in London. This missive brings the amazing news that Badini has been dismissed in scandalous circumstances in London, and that Da Ponte's presence is urgently requested for the post, with its annual stipend of 120 guineas plus added rights to profits from all sales of librettos.

This is revealing in three respects: the spirit in which Da Ponte responds to this offer; the ongoing feud between himself and Badini; and the reasons for his own subsequent loss of the official post in question some five years later. He crows in a letter to Casanova of his success:

> This victory of mine is all the better for being unlooked for. In my case too, as with other friends my dear Casanova, you have proved a Prophet. . . . Remember too, my reputation has seen me preferred (even though far away, and without stirring on my part) to ten poetasters long established in London, who have many protectors, and did their all to bag the post. What a deal of envy I shall therefore have to put up with. But let those others go hang, I shall laugh.[20]

It reads like the triumphalism of a diabolically unstable temperament – someone in whom flourished what an earlier operatic associate in Vienna, the impresario Zaguri, had defined as Da Ponte's 'destructive canker'.[21]

If Da Ponte had such a canker, so too did other expatriate Italians, including Badini. The dismissed librettist, who had already written a scurrilous pamphlet against Da Ponte's ode on the death of the French king ('The Heart's Tribute'), which without much inventive wit he called 'The Balls' Tribute' – I am translating rather liberally at this point – was to strike again within a year and a half, before finally heading back to the continent himself, and disappearing from history. One of Da

Ponte's early successes on the London stage was a comic opera in 1795 entitled *School for Husbands* (*La scuola de' maritati*). Badini published his torrid attack on it:

> Brief notice of an Opera Buffa entitled School for Husbands, or How to come by Horns; written by the renowned Lorenzo da Ponte, who having been Jew, Christian, Priest and Poet, in Italy and Germany, is to be found Self-Unfrocked, Married and an Ass in London.[22]

Remember that these attacks, though typical of literary dog-fighting of this Regency period in England, were between rival Italian émigrés librettists, and conducted in Italian. One begins to appreciate Casanova's wise earlier advice not to haunt the Caffé degli Italiani, suggesting as it does familiarity on the great adventurer's part with a danger Da Ponte was quite unable to avoid in the event: that of becoming entrammelled in webs of scheming, rivalry and bitterness, within a hothouse community of mainly Italian artists. For this was a swirling world of singers, composers, librettists, impresarios and others, who together constituted the collective force behind that extraordinary and Europe-wide phenomenon: the mounting of Italian opera *in Italian* in the opera houses of all the major cultural centres, from Dublin to St Petersburg and beyond.

So how does Da Ponte finally come to grief in London as he had previously in Vienna? To cut a long story short, by being trusted too far: specifically, with the duty of a return trip to Italy after many years absence, to search out and engage new singers for the London impresario Taylor, in order to supply a gap left by some sudden resignations. Da Ponte and Nancy invest in a modest carriage of their own, and set out for a spree of fun in the old country, omitting till very late in the piece to spend time in Bologna, which is at the time a kind of marketplace for Italian singing talent. Both the prima donna and the male lead whom Da Ponte does eventually engage are singularly unsuccessful in London, the woman after a few performances, the male singer because he reneges on the terms of contract before fulfilling a single engagement. While the Da Pontes had been gallivanting about the drawing rooms of artistic Italy – Da Ponte had even gone ahead alone across the Apennines to Florence, which he had never before seen, and settled for weeks on end in the artistic community there – Taylor had been fretting in London, and was forced to publish notices of delays in performance:

The accident of the first comic woman not being arrived is not to be imparted to the direction of the Opera, whose interest suffers by her absence, but to the deranged circumstances of that part of the Continent from which she is to come, and where there has been an agent, at a considerable expense, some months ago, sent expressly to bring her over.[23]

That 'agent' and his wife seem to have been very little incommoded by 'the deranged circumstances of that part of the Continent', though Da Ponte does provide us many years later in his *Memoirs* with a description of the ruinate state in which he had found Venice on this return visit of 1798, so soon after the fall of the Republic and the vast depredations of the invading French troops.

Da Ponte eventually returns to London only to find himself dismissed from his position by the exasperated Taylor. With his typical entrepreneurial zeal, having lost one gainful employ, he diversifies his money-making operations by opening a printing and publishing business, and in addition an Italian bookshop. At first this position as bookseller in London must have been closely allied with his other operatic activities, since the first (1803) address of 'L. Daponte, Foreign Bookseller' is at 28, Haymarket, within a stone's throw of the site of the Italian Opera in the same thoroughfare. Successive addresses of the business, carried on by his brother Paolo even after Lorenzo's and his family's departure for America in 1805, were also in the heart of theatrical London of the day: in Jermyn Street, St James's, and Poland Street in Mayfair. He publishes principally opera libretti, but the bookshop holds a comprehensive range of Italian classics in the best editions of the day, as is evidenced by the sale catalogue when, Da Ponte once again in financial straits, the stock is finally sold at auction in April of 1804, in the year before he sails definitively for America. Arthur Livingston's synopsis of the Da Pontes' family fortunes over the entire duration of their marriage (and therefore including both the English and the American years) is that 'the Da Pontes were prosperous all in all, Da Ponte spending, Mrs Da Ponte, saving. Da Ponte, always beset by the dream of easy money and big money, suddenly discovers a new opening . . .'[24] In the end he seems to have wearied of new schemes in England, desiring an entirely new context in which to seek to achieve his various dreams.

We move now to the long-drawn-out final three decades and slightly more of Da Ponte's life in America, the broad outlines of which have already been summarized. How may we best recover for examination all the conflicting elements of Da Ponte's American years? His luxuriating in realms of exilic melancholia; his re-creating within his family unit, as well as in the more extended circle of his devoted young American pupils, a kind of Idyllic Italy of great literary classics; yet all the while not neglecting his other money-making ventures – collecting the boarders' rent, selling the special hooch, and suing old friends who had turned into new enemies? One particular literary enterprise he undertook in the American years seems, not just as a work in itself but in terms of the other literary paraphernalia with which he enframed it, most nearly to represent the gamut of experience of Da Ponte's multiple cultural migrancy – namely, his 1821 translation of Byron's *Prophesy of Dante*.

This poem was composed by Byron as part of his own reaction to exile from England after his broken marriage and scandals of an incestuous relationship with his half-sister. It is important also that Byron is spending these years in Italy. If we are keen on author-based criticism, there seems no doubting that Byron's poem, though it is an elaboration on Dante's august bitterness in years of exile from Florence after 1301, is in fact forged on the anvil of his own resentment at his recent treatment in England. (Byron apparently wrote the poem while residing very near to Dante's tomb in Ravenna.) Ignoring – if, indeed, he knew of it – the bitter taste of Byron's particular exile, Da Ponte appropriates the poem by the act of translating it as an expression of his own destiny. His opening dedication to Lord Byron, written in a florid Italian, relatively quickly establishes the groundwork of several important personal identifications on Da Ponte's part:

> I, separated by more than forty years from my homeland, and having reached the seventy-third year of a forever uncertain and unhappy life, the last seventeen of them passed in America, where few speak or read the Italian tongue, have been unable to resist the temptation of translating your *Prophesy of Dante*, and, however mediocre the outcome, of publishing it.

Da Ponte proceeds from this rather ornate launchpad to ascend through realms of adulation to the all-important self-revelations:

> The beauties I have discovered in it (and I well know, Milord, that I discovered but a fraction of all there are), the noble truths which you so justly and eloquently have issued forth as utterances of the greatest poet of

eighteen centuries, and the desire that these truths be heard by a People so dear to you, by whom your own tongue is slenderly known, but above all a certain analogy which (saving due proportions) I felt existed between the circumstances of Dante's life and my own, all prompted and inclined me to a work which, not without great trepidation, I dare to present to you.

We may note in passing that (so far) Da Ponte has made two important and matching points about language communities that bear very directly on the two emigrants he sees himself and Byron as being. In America the Italian tongue is 'slenderly known', a melancholic string that he never tires of harping upon in other works and statements. Conversely in Italy, where Byron is, utterances written by him and placed in the mouth of Dante, 'the greatest poet of eighteen centuries', *but framed in English*, will be equally unappreciated by an Italian people which does not know that language. Essentially then, for Da Ponte, it is this problem of living to the full the language and creations of a great heritage, but in an entirely other linguistic and cultural context, that is the sorest trial of the émigré – one that never heals, as this very poem by Byron, *The Prophesy of Dante*, also understood.

What is excruciating for Da Ponte is to know the Latin and Italian cultural heritage extremely well, and yet, for all his foreign engagements down the decades as a librettist and teacher, to have only slender means of living or re-creating that inheritance within another context than Italy. In the well-known case of Dante, the bitterness was against the Florentines for placing him in unending exile. In Byron's case, as interpreted by Da Ponte, the problem lies in the matter of writing from within an English tradition of letters about an Italian subject, and even within an Italian context, and yet knowing that what is expressed will be essentially unavailable to an Italian understanding. This palimpsest of exilic conditioning in one artist after another gives rise to a vast venting of romantic frustration on Da Ponte's part.

'Yes Milord', he writes – and at this point, as high as a kite, he breaks from prose into terza rima, translated elsewhere in the document by his daughter Fanny into still more tumid English terza rima:

> Yes, from a land ingrate too fondly loved
> I, too, by jealous scorn and hatred driven,
> In life's best days, an exile's sorrows proved;
> Fond ties of love and kindred then were riven,
> And o'er the cragged rocks, the billows foam,

I pass'd unheeding, all to misery given.
Thus doom'd in foreign climes, unknown, to roam,
I sought the desart's solitary shade,
And midst the rocks and wild woods made my home.[25]

(p. 65)

It is time to leave Da Ponte, but on the reassuring note that he wasn't entirely 'doom'd' in those 'foreign climes' where he spent more than five decades of his life. In the garland of literary addenda with which he enframes the second edition of this translation of Byron's poem, there is an endearing initial dedication of the work to Madamigella Giulia Livingston (Mademoiselle Julia Livingston, daughter of a deeply supportive family of friends of the Da Pontes), in which the point is made that she above all others had made distinguished progress under Da Ponte's guidance in the acquiring and appreciating of the Italian tongue and its literary works – a point similar to ones he was to make in his *Memoirs* and elsewhere about many another of his (clearly devoted) American pupils. And there is something else – a delicate poem to another *madamigella*, distinguished only by the initials N. N. and an alias, *Rosa d'amore* ('Rose of love'), in which he expresses exquisite thanks for – of all things – a delicious tart baked by and received from her hands as a Christmas gift. Clearly, the Da Ponte of seventy-three years of age was not an entirely different being from the librettist who could preface Leporello's catalogue aria of Giovanni's conquests, sung to the disappointed Donna Anna, with that brilliantly interjected term of *mock – and at the same time real – endearment* to the lady: 'Madamina . . .'

His express wish that the name of Mozart be forever 'entwined with that of Da Ponte, as the ivy with the oak'[26] has long been fulfilled. I have spent my own time entwining the name of Da Ponte with other matters in his life – the places and circumstances of his exile, in London and America – and with a younger contemporary whom he was not alone in judging to be the most sublime English poet of the century, Lord Byron.[27]

\* \* \* \* \*

Track forward just less than one hundred years to the height of Italian emigration to the Americas. In 1920 two Italian anarchists, Nicola

Sacco and Bartolomeo Vanzetti – by their adoptive trades in America a shoemaker and a fish peddler – were arrested and charged with having killed a guard and paymaster in a payroll robbery in South Braintree, Massachusetts. At first sight, and irrespective of the innocence or guilt of the suspects, this all too ordinary American crime might have been expected to elicit little if any interest beyond a regional or at most a state level. Instead, the initial trial and its aftermath caused an international furore and – were it not for the O. J. Simpson case of more recent memory – would definitely have been in contention (along with the Hiss and Rosenberg cases) for the honour of being the American legal trial of the century.

As in the O. J. Simpson case, with which it has superficial similarities (even if in the main radically different), the crux of the matter was indeed whether the suspects were guilty or not. Again as with Simpson's case, the ill-established facts of Sacco and Vanzetti's trial spawned a welter of further issues; most importantly, whether as poor Italian immigrants, and anarchists to boot, they had received fair treatment at the hands of the law from their arrest onwards. But unlike in the case of Simpson, their own and many other influential people's accusations that there *had* been prejudice shown in their first and only trial seem to have backfired, only further antagonizing the Massachusetts authorities. Though liberals abounded in America in the 1920s – indeed, increased considerably in number as a direct consequence of publicity surrounding this case – institutional America was probably as illiberal as in any other period of its history since or before the Revolution. Where prejudice is concerned, we might care to recall that a criminal stereotype of the 'dago' had been circulating for several decades already. In an article of 1890 in the perfectly reputable *Popular Science Monthly*, a penologist had calmly asked, 'What shall we do with the "Dago"? The knife with which he cuts his bread he also uses to lop off another "dago's" finger or ear. . . . He is quite as familiar with the sight of human blood as with the sight of the food he eats.'[28] In case we imagine that such extravagant prejudice against Italians quickly diminished as the century wore on, consider the sheer irony of a remark by Richard Nixon, documented on the so-called Watergate tapes, his recording of conversations in the White House. In deliberating with others on how they might appoint an Italian American to a top post, Nixon of all people asks dryly: 'but where would we find an honest Italian American?'[29]

To return to Sacco and Vanzetti. In spite of multiple appeals and massive American and international lobbying on their behalf, the guilty verdict was sustained, with no retrial ordered. When all possible legal process had been exhausted, the two were eventually executed by electric chair in August 1927; while outside the Massachusetts prison American and international lobby groups held a last vigil, after years of unsuccessful protest.

Many books and countless articles have reviewed the evidence in the Sacco and Vanzetti case. That is not the present aim. Creative writers also in the American tradition have been concerned with the case. John Dos Passos wrote for the original Sacco–Vanzetti Defence Committee, and Upton Sinclair wrote a novel directly based upon the crime and their trial. Another left-wing writer, Katherine Anne Porter, who had been party to the large protest movement during the 1920s, in her monograph of many years later on the affair entitled *The Never-ending Wrong*, saw the treatment of the two Italians as 'not the cause, but the symptom of a change so deep and so sinister in the whole point of view and direction of this people as a nation'.[30] This pessimism on her part was not a point of view shared by Vanzetti himself, as will shortly be seen.

Since so much of the case hinges on the initial fragilities of immigrant existence, it seems more than ever worthwhile at this distance in time to study Sacco and Vanzetti's own writings and statements for the unique record they constitute of a tremendous struggle to make good in a new country. Until the very moment of his execution Bartolomeo Vanzetti, in particular, strove to grasp the larger issues at stake, of justice in relation to the individual, of the possibilities for which – especially as an anarchist – he had all along been so sceptical.

On first reckoning, it may seem strange to offer the many letters and statements made by two immigrants convicted on a murder charge as directly representative of Italian emigrant experience, since murder charges are fortunately not the form in which the tribulations of immigrants normally come packaged. But in the quite exceptional case of Sacco and Vanzetti, once attention shifts from a review of the courtroom evidence (which is what most subsequent writing about them has attempted) and onto the hearts and minds of the two men in question, the drama is seen to be very much a crisis of immigrant experience, laid out by its protagonists in letters and statements in just such ways as cry out for analysis in those terms.

Perhaps most important of all is the issue of language – the difficulties of having to brave and master the world's worst *in a new tongue*! Most immigrants must do this just in order to struggle through each day successfully. Sacco and Vanzetti, as convicted murderers, had to do it in a heightened sense for seven years, and eventually lost their battle with the state of Massachussetts. But as a drama of achieving their identities, and acclaiming their meaning in a new tongue, there is scarcely another so triumphant as this one. And though Sacco clearly felt washed out and defeated by the end, Vanzetti's further triumph was in being able to grasp the significance of what they had achieved for the wider causes of justice, in a world beyond the terms of their own two violently truncated lives.

In support of this last contention, consider first his most famous words, often used in epigraph form on the case. Remarkably, they are not from a prepared statement, but were spoken in casual conversation with a local reporter, who immediately recorded them for posterity:

> If it had not been for this thing, I might have live out my life talking at street corners to scorning men. I might have die unmarked, unknown, a failure. Now we are not a failure. This is our career and our triumph. Never in our full life can we hope to do such work for tolerance, for joostice, for man's onderstanding of man, as now we do by an accident. Our words – our lives – our pains – nothing! The taking of our lives – lives of a good shoemaker and a poor fish peddler – all! That last moment belong to us – that agony is our triumph.[31]

The reporter's name was Phil Strong, author some twenty years later of a somewhat fêted book entitled *The Aspirin Age* (1949), in which Vanzetti's words are again reviewed. Interestingly, Strong had to defend himself against the doubts of an English writer, Edward Shanks, that Vanzetti had ever uttered these words, doubts cast largely on the grounds that the words had strong echoes in them of Lincoln's Gettysburg address. Strong defended with an adroit piece of practical criticism, demonstrating how typical of Vanzetti the words in fact were:

> It seems to me that the internal evidence of the interview is sufficient to convince any honourably disposed person of its authenticity. The change of number in the pronoun was beautifully characteristic of Vanzetti. 'I' unmarked, unknown, a failure – but 'Our' career, a triumph, work for tolerance and justice.[32]

Indeed the reporter's perceptive remarks prompt us in the direction of larger points needing to be made about Sacco and Vanzetti's use of language. Katherine Anne Porter made a start on this same ground, but only in general terms, when she claimed that 'both of them knew English very well – not so much in grammar and syntax but for the music, the true meaning of the words they used'. She went on to claim that as 'Italian peasants, emigrants, laborers, self-educated men', they had 'an exalted sense of language as an incantation. *Read those letters.*'[33]

Emphatically – as she puts it – reading Sacco's and Vanzetti's letters is a revealing experience. In other respects Porter is only half-correct. Certainly, under the acute pressures of their case – not least considering their long incarceration before final execution – both Sacco and Vanzetti repeatedly write and speak in exalted ways. But to talk of theirs as a language of 'incantation' as Porter does detracts from what the letters consistently achieve by way of processing of thoughts and emotions (and, in Vanzetti's case at least, of subtly nuanced reviews of movements in world history itself in the 1920s, as this argument will go on to demonstrate). The reporter Strong had been nearer the mark in concentrating on the eloquent internal shifts of emphasis in Vanzetti's nonetheless still far from perfectly syntactical English, as he spoke those momentous truths – on the one hand defeat, on the other triumph – of Sacco's and his real-life drama.

Sacco's and Vanzetti's letters, appeals and final courtroom pleas, published in the year after their execution and sadly now long out of print, should be known far more widely by historians, jurists and (perhaps especially) literary critics, for the remarkable collection they are: a harrowing epistolary narrative of immigrant suffering, but at the same time of persistent human striving to conquer enormous difficulties in a new land. The lesser writer of the two, Nicola Sacco, could express with solemn and uncanny accuracy in his last letter to his son Dante how their human tie would be snapped by his imminent execution. 'I never thought that our inseparable life could be separated, but the thought of seven dolorous years makes it seem it did come, but then it has not changed really the unrest and the heart-beat of affection.'[34] Interpreting such words requires more work than reading a writer of reliably correct English usage. But what is important is that the meaning at stake amply repays the greater time needed in pondering over it.

In that last claim, for instance, 'it has not changed really the unrest and the heart-beat of affection', there is a conundrum to wrestle with. Is the problem-word 'unrest' simply produced by poverty of English, or is it so exact an achievement of intended meaning that it is we native speakers who are thrown off balance? For affection may be (apart from all else) a kind of perpetual unrest, and if that is what Sacco is implicitly claiming, then what he is *explicitly* saying to his son Dante, in bidding him adieu before dying, is that not even all the pains of incarceration could really change that other unrest, of his feelings for his son. If such is the meaning, then by any reckoning it is a noble claim, for it implies there would be suffering involved in his feelings for his son – unrest, that is – even if he were living a normal life.

What this small example opens up is a consideration of crucial importance to the change of cultures and of languages that individuals undergo in the act of emigrating from one nation to another. Namely, that there may be certain creative uses of a language that are paradoxically more available – or at any rate more likely to be realized – by the wilder lunges at meaning of a non-native speaker acting under considerable duress or an urgent need to be understood. By definition, a non-native speaker who knows a new language only moderately well has not yet become habituated to the grooves of everyday usage that can tend to channel native-speaker utterances along conventional syntactic pathways and choices of word.

Under conditions that are replete with meaning – as in this case of leave-taking by a condemned man to his son – a word such as 'unrest' may be not only surprising in context but, for all its strangeness, utterly apt, and more in reach of a foreign than a native speaker. Just because all the words of the language known to a new speaker have been 'used' far less than by a native speaker – have neither been worn smooth by custom, nor lost from reach by their rarity in everyday parlance – such a person (whom we more normally suppose to be at a loss for what the French call *le mot juste*) may clutch at strange words and combinations of them that make sense, rather as some poetry does, by virtue of the very novelty of the perception couched in the unexpected phrasing. Such, it seems, is emphatically the case in this small example from the letters of Nicola Sacco.

But if that paradox of enhanced foreign-speaker articulacy is true of Sacco, how shall we account for the far more haunting utterances of his companion Bartolomeo Vanzetti – always a 'better babbler' than Sacco, to quote his own ironic judgement of the two of them in the matter of language? 'Better babbler' is itself a comparison so nonchalant in the expressing, as to be supremely moving under the circumstances, uttered as it was towards the (by then) inevitable close of his life, in his speech to the court before final sentence of death was confirmed. This particular comparison was in fact offered in explanation of why he had spoken so much longer than his co-defendant. It shows the offhand verbal wit of one who – we remember with a shock – is likewise a non-native speaker and about to have his definitive death sentence handed down by a judge he has spent so much of this speech and indeed the previous seven years comprehensively criticizing.

Already by early spring of 1922 Vanzetti's opinions on world events, written from Charlestown Prison in Massachusetts, are well worth attending to. He is shocked at the fascists coming to power in Italy, and how it reveals what he calls 'the moral lowness in which we have fallen after the war and the revolutionary over-excitation of the last few years'.[35] In April of 1923 he prophesies that fascism will lead to 'a period of insensate violences, of sterile vendettes, which would exhaust in little episodes of blood that energy which should be employed for a radical transformation of the social arrangements such to render impossible the repetition of the present horrors'.[36] Certainly, a part of this rhetoric is acquired directly from the classic anarchist texts he had read avidly for years. But the specific applications of the analysis to the early years of fascism strike me as very much his own. The prophecy is accurate and reveals a political thinker in a different league than his accusers. The prosecution in the case had made much play of his being an untrustworthy Italian and anarchist. If they had been political thinkers on anything like a par with Vanzetti himself – as evidenced in this ability to read critically the situation in Europe – they would have found the scare tactics they resorted to utterly beneath their dignities. He is, for instance, swift in his assessment of the murder in Italy of the socialist deputy, Giacomo Matteotti: 'The fascista's crimes, especially their crime against Matteotti alive and Matteotti dead, have precipitated the events – the historical Nemesis . . .'[37] Significantly, what he is showing thus early is an ability to think through criminality at the state-political level in his native land. While no attempt at all is made to draw conclusions touching his own personal case – he is simply not thinking of himself personally when writing of fascist crimes – this clarity of political temperament *will* be seen more and more in 1925, 1926 and right up to the moments before his execution in August 1927; whenever, in fact, he turns the beacon of this formidable and eloquent intelligence onto the political farce which has characterized the Massachusetts handling of Sacco's and his case.

For instance, in one letter of early 1927 he turns directly from a diatribe against 'Massachusetts' black gowned, puritanic, cold-blooded murderers' to a sweeping gaze over world events:

> Things are going from bad to worse. War in China, Nicaragua, revolution in Java, Mexico, Brazil; the Balkans on foot of war; France and Italy mobilizing one against the other; England, United States, France and Japan in a crazy rivalry of armament; South America and United States in danger of war; Italy under the fascist dictatorship; Russia under the Bolsheviki one; . . . insanity sweeping the earth. I wonder how it all will end.[38]

For him, precisely because of 'Massachusetts' black gowned, puritanic, cold-blooded murderers' it all ended seven months later, and with it the analytical perceptiveness of one of the wiser political emigrants to have graced America's shores.

Vanzetti defines his and Sacco's political epitaph, in his speech to Judge Webster Thayer in the Dedham Court House on 9 April 1927, recorded by court stenographers. In it he shows an uncanny ability to look back through the years of their original trial and long imprisonment, and to see that already the mood has changed: 'We were tried during a time whose character has now passed into history. I mean by that, a time when there was a hysteria of resentment and hate against the people of our principles, against the foreigner, against slackers . . .'[39] The first sentence reads like one that should be in the third person and spoken by someone else. It is totally dispassionate. 'We were tried during a time whose character has now passed into history.' Spoken by someone living, it defines an age that he lived through and that is no more.

And yet in one strict sense that cannot be. The final result of that trial – their execution – has not been called off just because Vanzetti declares that the age of resentment and hatred which passed sentence of death on them has itself died and passed into history. They *will* soon be executed. Vanzetti knows all this, and still insists on presenting the issue as though it is distant history. He can only do so because his very way of talking about the earlier hysteria has been highly instrumental in exposing it, politically speaking, and helping to shift it into that further historical perspective. His very discourse in other words is the kind of political speech capable of shifting the ideological ground it is also defining, and in one and the same act of language.

Probably he was right, and the original mood of the time in which they were tried had changed greatly. The support for their cause had become massive, and international in scale. They had managed to raise the stakes in all issues of what constitutes fair trial under democracy. As he was to say within weeks to the reporter Strong, the taking of their lives was now the lesser matter: 'Now we are not a failure. This is our career and our triumph.' Any analysis must line up with Vanzetti himself on this key point: that their case, and the way they had fought it, though the trial and eventually their lives were lost, had shown that two prejudicially treated Italian immigrants could be the cause of a great advance in tolerance and justice in American public life.

\* \* \* \*

The first example in this chapter was an Italo-Australian novel, almost exclusively female in its biases. The last to be taken up now is a well-known Italo-American novel which, by contrast, is characterized by what John Donne hundreds of years ago called 'masculine persuasive force'. In Donne such force was part of an offensive charm. (Take that statement how you will.) In Mario Puzo's *Godfather*, masculine persuasive force – for example, the whole ethos of offers that cannot be refused, and the ties of male friendship from which women are entirely excluded and which are themselves only ever broken by 'business' dictates (i.e. a higher law than friendship, that of making money) – is also entirely offensive, with the *obligation* this time to take both main meanings of the term. What, then, are some of the forms that exclusive maleness takes in *The Godfather* – forms which, incidentally, are mostly transposed into cinema in the series of films of the same name directed by Francis Ford Coppola, in the screenplays of which Puzo had a major hand?[40]

The characters of the novel are mostly products, even if at a one-generational remove, of 'a land that had been more cruelly raped than any in history', namely Sicily (p. 327). Curiously, the spirit of self-protection which is instituted as a consequence by these mafiosi once in America, while it is applied by dictat to the women as well, is essentially worked out in terms of friendship and solidarity between the men of the 'families'. In one place a woman even acknowledges what the book as a

**Figure 11** A 'fine funeral' – but not of Sacco's and Vanzetti's identities. Press photo from the *Boston Globe*, August 1927. Vanzetti had concluded shortly before Sacco's and his execution by the State of Massachusetts that their persecution was their 'career' and their 'triumph'. Hundreds of thousands of people took part in marches protesting against the execution in Paris, Rome, London and other cities around the globe. Republished with permission of Globe Newspaper Company, Inc.

whole implies, 'Ah, men understand friendship more than we women' (p. 44). Mothers, sisters, wives and daughters are not included in plans and consultations: indeed, they are heavily lied to throughout the novel, ostensibly to protect them from the sheer bitterness of a series of awful truths, but in effect on so systematic a basis that at all key moments they are excluded from those affective bonds and affinities which define the world of the men.

Take later events first. Don Corleone is struck by a massive heart attack in his garden, initially only in the presence of his beloved youngest son's oldest boy: 'The boy raced away to call his father. Michael Corleone and some men at the mall gate ran to the garden and found the Don lying prone . . .' The mighty Don, whom mafia hits of a concerted order have not succeeded in killing, is 'in extremis', dying in the context of a garden he has latterly retired to ('It brought back his childhood in Sicily sixty years ago . . . without the terror, the sorrow of his own father's death,' p. 407): 'He smelled the garden, the yellow shield of light smote his eyes, and he whispered, "Life is so beautiful" ' (p. 408). We realize with something of a shock that this representation of the dying Don is Puzo's idyll of a fulfilled life. Most importantly, 'He was spared the sight of his women's tears, dying before they came back from church. . . . He died surrounded by men, holding the hand of the son he had most loved' (p. 408). To be 'spared' the presence of women when dying is seen as a blessing – not, it would seem, because they mean too much to him for their presence in extremis to be bearable, but because by their weeping they deflect concentration from life's mean-ingfulness at this supreme moment, which for Corleone has to do with solidarity between men. Women are here as elsewhere defined in terms of a propensity to tearfulness, and by a churchgoingness which, because never inspected closely in the text, or dwelt upon with the sociological fascination devoted to men's gatherings, has all the hallmarks of atavism about it. The males by contrast have at least moved on a smidgen in their thinking about divinity, having had the Godfather as a peg for their understanding. As one of them remarks, 'You can't get sore at him. It's like getting sore at God' (p. 170).

Puzo is certainly not unaware of the exclusiveness of the masculinity throughout the novel. Yet every time he registers it, he allows it to be experienced more as a plenitude than as a hollowness. For instance, the singer Johnny Fantone (someone, incidentally, 'with maybe a thousand pubic scalps dangling from his belt', as the text defines him in his own masculinist interior monologue, p. 158) had, with his first wife, 'always been generous and fair'. There follows a description of almost ludicrous generosity, but which ends with the sentence, 'He had never refused her anything except the complete surrender of his own personality' (p. 177). At first one is not entirely sure if the ironies of contrast – between the long list of all Johnny *has* given her and this final and complete self-withholding – are fully in the control of the author, Puzo, because there seems to be a kind of textual justification here: of possessing the plenitude of one's own male 'personality', rather than ever 'surrendering' it to a woman. While Puzo can remark on the very next page the damage done to women – 'He had grown a thick skin about the hurts he gave women' (p. 178) – he has no full vision of the larger hurts that such self-withholding inflicts on the selves which withhold.

Key determinants of any such masculinism are the phallus and the pistol, about which we might prefer to stay silent but cannot. The main murder scene, where Michael Corleone kills the two men who are most dangerous to his father Don Corleone, requires that the subject be aired.

Michael meets the boss of another mafia family, Sollozzo, and a Police Captain, McCluskey, by means of an elaborate assignation on supposedly neutral territory in a restaurant in the Bronx. Michael must go unarmed, knowing he will be frisked by the Police Captain, who is purportedly neutral but actually in the pay of the rival Sollozzo family. His own team have managed to establish the place of rendezvous in time to hide a pistol behind a cistern, which Michael can then retrieve on a visit to the gents room some time *after* he has been frisked and declared to be unarmed.

Earlier there had been some 'tough-talk' on the part of Michael's older brother Sonny in the Corleone meeting where the killing is planned. ' "I want somebody very good, very safe, to plant that gun," he told Clemenza. "I don't want my brother coming out of that toilet with just his dick in his hand" ' (p. 146). It is a brilliant piece of smut – above all because the phallus and the pistol figure prominently elsewhere in the pages of this novel as twin instruments of mafia virility and power. Twin instruments, but patently not identical, for they have quite different potentialities, which make each useless for accomplishing the work of the other. The black humour of Sonny's remark lies in a vision of Michael disappearing into the lavatory to effect the necessary power changeover from phallus to gun, only to re-emerge still wielding the phallus, because of a hitch in his access to gun – and thus appearing ridiculous and utterly vulnerable to his enemies.

The text or subtext of pages and pages of different incidents in the novel signals that men of this stamp have compulsions of the phallus and of the gun, equally incontrovertible. And furthermore, that the work of the one and the other is a risky business, needing endless vigilance. Sometimes the phallic compulsions are interrelated with those of the gun, sometimes not. Nowhere is the subtext of connection between phallus and gun more deeply at work than in the moment before Michael's disappearance to the bathroom in the scene at the Bronx restaurant. Michael's excuse of a full bladder doesn't entirely convince Sollozzo. 'He reached over and roughly thrust his hand in Michael's crotch, under it and around, searching for a weapon' (p. 151). In a sense Sollozzo is searching in exactly the right place for 'a weapon', at least symbolically speaking – namely at the crux of masculinity for these people. But he doesn't have the privileged access we do to earlier Corleone planning, nor to the kinds of explicit interchangeability between phallus and pistol of Sonny's black humour. Hence, although by roughly thrusting his hand in Michael's crotch Sollozzo is searching in the right symbolic area, the whole trick by which the useless weapon that he *can* feel there will be supplemented by its twin and murdersome 'other' when Michael returns from the bathroom is, by definition, hidden from him. Within minutes, as a consequence, he and McCluskey are dead men.

Now it may be objected that we are supposed to see the entire novel of *The Godfather* as an indictment of the masculinist ethos in question. This, certainly, is a hypothesis that merits consideration. But there are strong grounds overall for rejecting it. On the penultimate page of the novel Kay, the Anglo-American wife of the new don, Michael Corleone, asks the family's long-term *consigliori* (i.e. *consigliere* [counsellor]) Tom Hagan to speak to her straight for once in his life about her husband's implication in mafia killing, in particular of his own brother-in-law Carlo. She hinges her appeal on something she and Tom have in common: 'I know Michael can't, but you're not Sicilian, you can tell a woman the truth, you can treat her like an equal, a fellow human being' (p. 445). Here we would seem to have – and so late in the novel that it appears like an underlining of the point – the case being made that the Sicilian ethos by which the male Corleone family members operate constitutes a grotesque exclusion of women from the category of fellow human beings. And we may care to recall at this point, for comparative purposes, another incident. When Don Corleone had conceded that an all-American meeting of mafia families take place to discuss once more entry into the drugs business, the 'Don of Detroit', essentially on Corleone's side in the stand against dealing in drugs, had taken an interesting – if to us chilling – compromise position: 'In my city I would try to keep the traffic in the dark people, the coloured. They are the best customers, the least troublesome and they are animals anyway' (p. 290). There is not a great deal of difference between the perception of another race as animals and Kay's point that in the big issues of life and death womenfolk are not treated as fellow humans by the likes of her Sicilian husband.

The novel ends with Hagan being straight with Kay, as she had implored him to be. However – and this is the crucial point – although he talks to her in ways that he claims would ensure his own death if Michael were to find out, the so-called 'truths' he actually tells Kay are a thoroughgoing justification of why Michael has engaged in a spate of killings of people near to himself and to her. The final page of the novel sees Kay returning to Michael, seeing a priest for instruction in becoming a Catholic, and then, in the final paragraphs, practising the religion not of her own forebears, but of the women of Michael's family. From being a focus of protest on Puzo's part against the principles of mafia violence, she has turned in closing towards the church, not to change the way things are in their lives, but to seek absolution for their being thus, through repentance on her own part and 'prayers for the soul of Michael Corleone' (the final words of the novel).

It might be claimed that Kay's turning from protest towards religion is part of Puzo's grim vision of how overdetermined the Sicilian American context is by that 'land that had been more cruelly raped than any in history'. But the point all along was that Kay was an outsider, able to question the old and overdetermined ways of the family she had married into. Her complete and utter capitulation at the novel's close seems to imply that the author himself has wearied of his one main principle of protest.

\* \* \* \* \*

When we tease out the implications of Puzo's meaning for larger questions of migration, and draw comparisons between *The Godfather* and the other historical examples broached in this chapter, the issues are complex but compelling. Rather than watering down their Italian conventions of male solidarity around family values, Puzo's mafia characters are portrayed as strengthening them in a new country and culture. It is something of a paradox that these very family values are ones which tend to marginalize or neuter the category of women. Puzo would seem to be implying a model not of adaptation, but of such rigid clinging to prior customs of loyalty and affinity in the mindsets of the Sicilian-Americans treated that they can only survive in America by means of a defence and perpetuation of these customs through extreme violence. Although the lines of Puzo's own analysis seem clear-cut, and can be followed even at symbological levels by the reader (as in my reading of crossover values between gun and phallus), when it comes to outright condemnation of the ethos in question Puzo goes soft. His novel is in the final analysis a vast romanticization of the rigidities of a particular fraction of Italian migrant culture, that of the mafia, rather than a more sophisticated critique of what might be involved in hybridizing old and new.

At the opposite extreme from masculine persuasive force we saw at the outset of this chapter the defeatist feminism of Cappiello's version of migrant communities in Sydney. Her novel treats of such incompatibilities between the old culture of Europe that her protagonist has grown up with, and the new country she faces, that once again, as in Puzo but for totally different reasons, adaptation proves impossible. Instead of displaying this failure to adapt by promulgating her own values through violence, as Puzo's characters do, Cappiello's migrant female protagonist experiences loss of selfhood, in common with what the author presents as a Jungian-type nightmare of total anomie for vast numbers of immigrants from many nations. As a vision of the actualities of migrant experience, this has as little appeal as Puzo's text, though as in the latter case there may be many real examples of the type.

My two historical examples of migrants that together form the centrepiece of this chapter both have the capacity to stir us with a positive sense of the possibilities of cultural adaptation. Admittedly, Lorenzo Da Ponte in the early nineteenth century never tired of complaining of his exilic lot. And Sacco and Vanzetti in the early twentieth, whether guilty of not of the crime for which they were eventually executed, were undoubtedly victims of a still highly prejudiced operation of justice in specific American states. But the more two such examples from different centuries are studied, as I have tried to do here, the more we find ourselves instancing strange triumphs on the part of individuals to adapt to the trials of a foreign culture. In Sacco and Vanzetti's case a critical analysis of the passions and convictions they expressed, whether in the form of their many letters or in speeches and interviews during the course of their years of imprisonment before final electrocution, leads us to some very unexpected conclusions as to the possible poetries of an imperfect migrant English. Reading Da Ponte's memoirs, as well as his occasional minor verses and dedications from his long American phase of resettlement, all at three major removes from his Veneto upbringing – the Viennese as well as the London years intervening – one is amazed at how much by way of sheer cultural difference a single individual can experience in just one lifetime, while still remaining true to deep-rooted Italian origins.

## Notes

1. Rosa R. Cappiello, *Paese fortunato* (Milan: Feltrinelli, 1981). In English, *Oh Lucky Country*, translated by Gaetano Rando (St Lucia, London and New York: University of Queensland Press, 1984).

2. Cappiello, *Oh Lucky Country*, p. 5.

3. See Ellie Vasta, '*If You Had Your Time Again, Would You Migrate to Australia?*': *A Study of Long-Settled Italo-Australians in Brisbane* (Canberra: Australian Government Publishing Service, 1985), p. 21, for a table showing figures of occupation by sex in Italy and upon arrival in Australia.

4. Cappiello, *Oh Lucky Country*, p. 14.

5. *Ibid.*, pp. 28–9.

6. *Ibid.*, p. 120.

7. *Ibid.*, p. 236.

8. Richard D. Alba, *Italian Americans: Into the Twilight of Ethnicity* (Englewood Cliffs, NJ: Prentice-Hall, 1985), pp. 159 and 160.

9. Mario Puzo, *The Godfather* (London: Heinemann, 1969), p. 364. (For subsequent quotations from this text, page numbers are given in brackets.)

10. Countess of Blessington, *The Idler in Italy*, 3 vols (London: Henry Colbrun, 1839–40), Vol. 2, p. 219. Quoted in Harold Acton, *The Bourbons of Naples, 1734–1825* (London: Methuen and Co., 1956), p. 660.

11. General Pietro Colletta, *Storia del Regno di Napoli dal 1754 al 1825* (Florence, 1848; numerous subsequent editions).

12. General Pietro Colletta, *History of the Kingdom of Naples, 1734–1825*, 2 vols, translated by S. Horner (Edinburgh: T. Constable and Co., 1858), Vol. 2, p. 308.

13. Letter of 20 August 1818, Public Records Office, FO 70, No. 84, Document 20.

14. Information and quotes from letters of May to July 1819, from William Parker to Joseph Planta Esq., Mr Barrow to J. Planta Esq., and from W. Hamilton to Mr Croker: Public Records Office, FO 70, No. 87, Documents 63, 76, 92 and 93.

15. Robert Pascoe, *Buongiorno Australia: Our Italian Heritage* (Richmond, Victoria: Greenhouse Publications, 1987), p. 227.

16. The best work in recent years on Lorenzo da Ponte's Jewish origins, and on his expulsion from Venice, essentially as part of a policy inspired by the powerful figure of Tron – a policy of anti-Semitism, and of surveillance and control of radicals of Rousseauean tendency such as Da Ponte – has been conducted by Felicity Baker. See her searching article, 'Lorenzo da Ponte's Witticisms: The Implication of Jewish Identity in the *Memorie*', in John Lindon (ed.), *Italian Autobiography from Vico to Alfieri (and Beyond)*, as a supplement to *The Italianist*, No. 17 (1997), pp. 42–79. All future investigation of Da Ponte's origins, of his banishment from Venice, his degree of 'assimilation' into other cultures in relation to prejudices experienced, and the complexity of the varying degrees of distance from his Jewish upbringing created by his adolescent conversion to Catholicism, would do wisely to start from Baker's analyses. From her concentration on the witticisms at the heart of Da Ponte's social and political narration of earlier experiences in his *Memorie (Memoirs)*, it is a short step, as she demonstrates, to beginning to understand his greatness as a librettist.

17. Lorenzo Da Ponte, *Memoirs*, translated by Elisabeth Abbott, edited by Arthur Livingston (1929; reprint, New York: Dover Publications, 1959), p. 390.

18. From his booklet of 1807, *Storia compendiosa della vita di Lorenzo da Ponte*, quoted in Sheila Hodges, *Lorenzo Da Ponte: The Life and Times of Mozart's Librettist* (London: Granada, 1985), p. 160.

19. See Arthur Livingston's fn. 1 to Da Ponte, *Memoirs*, p. 425.

20. *Lettere di Lorenzo Da Ponte a Giacomo Casanova, 1791–95*, edited by Giampaolo Zagonel (Vittorio Veneto: Dario de Bastiani, 1988), pp. 101–2.

21. April Fitzlyon, *Lorenzo Da Ponte: A Bibliography of Mozart's Librettist* (1955; reprint, London: John Calder, 1982), p. 194.

22. Documented in *Lettere di Lorenzo Da Ponte a Giacomo Casanova*, p. 104.

23. Quoted in Hodges, *Lorenzo Da Ponte*, pp. 157–8

24. Da Ponte, *Memoirs*, fn. to p. 264.

25. This and all earlier quotations from Da Ponte's translation, '*La Profezia di Dante' di Lord Byron*, are from the second edition (New York: R. and W. A. Bartow, 1822). The versions here of Da Ponte's Italian prose in this text are my own.

26. Quoted in Hodges, *Lorenzo Da Ponte*, p. 196.

27. The judgement comes from the dedication to Madamigella Giulia Livingston of '*La Profezia di Dante' di Lord Byron*.

28. Quoted in Alba, *Italian Americans*, p. 67.

29. Quoted in *ibid.*, p. 86.

30. Katherine Anne Porter, *The Never-ending Wrong* (London: Secker and Warburg, 1977), pp. 4–5.

31. Quoted in Francis Russell, *Tragedy in Dedham: The Story of the Sacco–*

*Vanzetti Case* (New York: McGraw-Hill, 1971), pp. 377–8.

32. Quoted in *ibid.*, p. 388.

33. Porter, *The Never-ending Wrong*, p. 9.

34. *The Letters of Sacco and Vanzetti*, edited Marion Denman Frankfurter and Gardner Jackson (New York: Viking Press, 1928), pp. 70–1.

35. *Ibid.*, p. 91.

36. *Ibid.*, pp. 92–3.

37. *Ibid.*, p. 128.

38. *Ibid.*, p. 231.

39. *Ibid.*, p. 369.

40. See Puzo's long essay 'The Making of *The Godfather*' in his collection, *The Godfather Papers and Other Confessions* (London: Heinemann, 1972), pp. 32–69.

# BIBLIOGRAPHY

## Introduction: Italy in the Cultural Cosmorama

Baranski, Zygmunt G. and Robert Lumley (eds), *Culture and Conflict in Postwar Italy: Essays on Mass and Popular Culture* (London: Macmillan, 1990).

Dickens, Charles, *Pictures from Italy*, in the volume *American Notes, Pictures from Italy, and A Child's History of England* (London: Chapman and Hall, 1891).

Eco, Umberto, *Travels in Hyperreality: Essays*, trans. William Weaver (1986 under title *Faith in Fakes*; this edition London: Pan Books, 1987).

Falcone, Giovanni, in collaboration with Marcelle Padovani, *Cose di Cosa Nostra* (Milan: Rizzoli, 1991). In English, *Men of Honour: The Truth about the Mafia*, trans. Edward Farrelly (London: Fourth Estate, 1992).

Forgacs, David and Robert Lumley (eds), *Italian Cultural Studies: An Introduction* (Oxford: Oxford University Press, 1996).

Foucault, Michel, *The Archaeology of Knowledge*, trans. A. M. Sheridan Smith (London: Tavistock Publications, 1972).

Ginsborg, Paul, *History of Contemporary Italy: Society and Politics 1943–1988* (Harmondsworth: Penguin, 1990).

*The Guardian*, 7 January 1992.

*L'Indipendente*, 19 December 1991.

Jones, Philip, 'La storia economica dalla caduta dell'Impero romano al secolo XIV', in Ruggiero Romano and Corrado Vivanti (eds), *Storia d'Italia* (Turin: Einaudi, 1974), Vol. 2, Tome 2, pp. 1469–1810.

Leopardi, Giacomo, *Discorso sopra lo stato presente dei costumi degl'italiani*, introduced and edited by Augusto Placanica (Venice: Marsilio, 1989).

Martines, Lauro, *Power and Imagination: City-States in Renaissance Italy* (1979; Harmondsworth: Peregrine Books, 1983).

*The Observer*, 29 December 1991.

Sciascia, Leonardo, *Il giorno della civetta* (Turin: Einaudi, 1961).

Sciascia, Leonardo, *L'affaire Moro* (Palermo: Sellerio, 1978). In English, *The Moro Affair*, trans. Sacha Rabinovitch (Manchester: Carcanet, 1987).

Scott, Walter, 'Memoir of the Early Life of Sir Walter Scott, Written by Himself', in J. G. Lockhart, *Memoirs of the Life of Sir Walter Scott, Bart.* Volume the First (Edinburgh: Robert Cadell, 1837).

Stendhal, *Rome, Naples et Florence (1826)* (Paris: Éditions Gallimard, 1987).

Stillwell, John, Press Association news photograph of bobbies on mountain bikes, dated 17 December 1991.

*The Sunday Times*, 3 April 1994.

## Chapter 1: Cities, Dantesque and Other

Andall, Jacqueline, 'New Migrants, Old Conflicts: The Recent Immigration into Italy', *The Italianist*, Vol. 10 (1990), pp. 151–74.

Anderson, William, *Dante the Maker* (London: Routledge and Kegan Paul, 1980).

Antico, Alessandro, 'Nidi di rondine, sakè e mafia gialla' ('Nests of Swallows, Sakè and Yellow Mafia'), *La Nazione* (Florence edition), 5 November 1995.

Augustine, *City of God*, in *Political Writings*, trans. Michael W. Tkacz and Douglas Kries (Indianapolis and Cambridge: Hackett Publishing Co., 1994).

Azevedo, Raimondo Cagiano de and Leonardo Musumeci, 'The New Immigration in Italy', *Italian Politics: A Review*, Vol. 3 (London and New York: Pinter, 1989), pp. 66–78.

Bowsky, William M., 'The Medieval Commune and Internal Violence: Police Power and Public Safety in Siena, 1287–1355', *American Historical Review*, Vol. 73 (1967), pp. 1–17.

Caesar, Michael (ed.), *Dante, the Critical Heritage* (London: Routledge, 1989).

Carocci, Guido, *Firenze scomparsa: ricordi storico-artistici* (1897; facsimile edn, Rome: Multigrafica Editrice, 1979).

Corsi, Riccardo, 'Cinesi, occorre frenare', *La Nazione*, 5 September 1990.

Cressati, Susanna, 'Non chiamatela Chinatown', *L'Unità* (local section entitled *Firenze Mattina*), 13 October 1995.

Dante, *De monarchia*, trans. Philip H. Wicksteed, in *Latin Works of Dante Alighieri* (London: J. M. Dent and Sons, 1904).

Dante, *Paradiso*, edited by Natalino Sapegno (Florence: La Nuova Italia, 1957).

Dante, epistle to Can Grande della Scala, quoted in George Holmes, *Dante* (Oxford: Oxford University Press, 1980), pp. 44–5; also in Dante's *Latin Works* (see above).

Dante, *Il convivio*, translated by Christopher Ryan as *The Banquet* (Saratoga, CA: Anma Libri, 1989).

Davis, Charles T., '*Il buon tempo antico* (The Good Old Time)', in *Dante's Italy and Other Essays* (Philadelphia: University of Pennsylvania Press, 1984), pp. 71–93.

*L'Europeo*, 13–17 March 1990.

Fallai, Paolo, report on anti-racism protest in Florence, *Corriere della sera*, 23 March 1990.

Feldges-Henning, Una, 'The Pictorial Programme of the Sala Della Pace: A New Interpretation', *Journal of the Warburg and Courtauld Institutes*, Vol. 35 (1972), pp. 145–62.

Ferrante, Joan M., 'City and Empire in the *Comedy*', in *Political Vision of the Divine Comedy* (Princeton: Princeton University Press, 1984), pp. 44–75.

Hyde, J. K., 'Medieval Descriptions of Cities', *Bulletin of the John Rylands Library* (Manchester: Aberdeen University Press), Vol. 48 (1965–6), pp. 308–40.

Hyde, Kenneth [J. K.], 'The Social and Political Ideal of the *Comedy*', in Eric Haywood (ed.), *Dante Readings* (Dublin: Irish Academic Press, 1987), pp. 47–71.

'La notte della nuova paura', *La Repubblica*, 1 March 1990.

Levey, Michael, *Florence: A Portrait* (London: Jonathan Cape, 1996).

Machiavelli, Niccolò, *The Literary Works of Machiavelli*, edited and translated by J. R. Hale (London: Oxford University Press, 1961).

Maher, Vanessa, 'Immigration and Social Identities', in David Forgacs and Robert Lumley (eds), *Italian Cultural Studies: An Introduction* (Oxford and New York: Oxford University Press, 1996), pp. 166–77.

Nannucci, V. (ed.), *Petri Allegherii super Dantis ipsius genitoris Comoedian Commentarium* (Florence, 1845), excerpt reprinted in Caesar (ed.), *Dante, the Critical Heritage* (see above).

'Note al Progetto Poggi', in the public poster entitled *Pianta geometrica della città di Firenze e tipografia de' suoi contorni con i Progetti di Ampliamento delle strade*, Litografia Toscana, April 1865.

Rose, Claire, 'Dante's Hell and the Medieval Idea of Jerusalem', *The Italianist*, Vol. 11 (1991), pp. 7–28.

Rubinstein, Nicolai, 'The Beginnings of Political Thought in Florence: A Study in Medieval Historiography', *Journal of the Warburg and Courtauld Institutes*, Vol. 5 (1942), pp. 198–227.

Rubinstein, Nicolai, 'Political Ideas in Sienese Art: The Frescoes by Ambrogio Lorenzetti and Taddeo di Bartolo in the Palazzo Pubblico', *Journal of the Warburg and Courtauld Institutes*, Vol. 21 (1958), pp. 179–207.

Simonelli, Maria Picchio, *Lectura Dantis Americana: Inferno III* (Philadelphia: University of Pennsylvania Press, 1993).

Singleton, Charles S., edition of Dante's *Paradiso* (Princeton: Princeton University Press, 1975), Vol. 2, *Commentary*.

Skinner, Quentin, 'Ambrogio Lorenzetti: The Artist as Political Philosopher', *Proceedings of the British Academy*, Vol. 72 (1986), pp. 1–56.

Squarotti, Giorgio Bárberi, 'La Firenze celeste', in *L'ombra di Argo: studi sulla 'Commedia'*, new enlarged edition (Turin: Genesi, 1992), pp. 361–95.

Touring Club Italiano, *Firenze e Dintorni* (Milan: Arti Grafiche Alfieri and Lacroix, 1964).

*L'Unità*, 13 March 1990; 1 December 1995.

Vagheggi, Paolo, 'Raid anti-neri, tutti assolti', *La Repubblica*, 4 October 1990.

Veugelers, John, 'Recent Immigration Politics in Italy: A Short Story', *Western European Politics*, Vol. 17, No. 2 (April 1994), pp. 33–49.

Villani, Giovanni, *Selections from the First Nine Books of the Chroniche Fiorentine of Giovanni Villani*, translated by Rose E. Selfe, edited by Philip H. Wicksteed (Westminster: Archibald Constable and Co., 1896).

Virgil, *Aeneid*, trans. C. Day Lewis (Oxford: Oxford University Press, 1986).

Waley, Daniel, *The Italian City-Republics*, 3rd edn (London and New York: Longman, 1988).

Woods, Dwayne, 'The Immigration Question in Italy', *Italian Politics: A Review*, Vol. 7 (1992), pp. 186–98.

## Chapter 2: Sexuality, Class and Economics: The *Decameron* as Originary Text

Abel, Elizabeth (ed.), *Writing and Sexual Difference* (Brighton: The Harvester Press, 1982).

Aikema, Bernard and Beverly Louise Brown (eds), *Renaissance Venice and the North: Crosscurrents in the Time of Bellini, Dürer, and Titian* (Milan: Bompiani, 1999).

Anderson, Perry, *Passages from Antiquity to Feudalism* (London: New Left Books, 1974).

Ascham, Roger, *The Scholemaster*, edited by Edward Arber (London: English Reprints, 1870).

Auerbach, Erich, *Mimesis: The Representation of Reality in Western Literature*, translated by Willard R. Trask (original Swiss edn, 1946; 1st edn of this translation, 1953; Princeton: Princeton University Press, 1968).

Austen, Jane, *Persuasion* (1818), edited by R. W. Chapman (Oxford and New York: Oxford University Press, 1965).

Barolini, Teodolinda, 'Dante and Francesca da Rimini: Realpolitik, Romance, Gender', *Speculum*, Vol. 75, No. 1 (January 2000), pp. 1–28.

Bergin, Thomas G., *Boccaccio* (New York: The Viking Press, 1981).

Boccaccio, *Decameron*, 2 vols, edited by Vittore Branca (Florence: Felice le Monnier, 1960). In English, *The Decameron*, translated by G. H. McWilliam (Harmondsworth: Penguin, 1972).

Branca, Vittore, *Boccaccio: The Man and His Works*, translated by Richard Monges (New York: New York University Press, 1976).

Clements, Robert J., 'Anatomy of the Novella', in Mark Musa and Peter E. Bondanella (eds), *The Decameron* (Norton Critical Edition, 1977), p. 269. This article was first published in *Comparative Literature Studies* 9 (1972), pp. 3–16.

Dante, *Inferno*, edited by Natalino Sapegno (Florence: La Nuova Italia Editrice, 1955).

Dante, *Inferno*, Vol. 1, *Translation*, and Vol. 2, *Commentary*, in *The Divine Comedy*, 6 vols, translated with a commentary by Charles S. Singleton, (London: Routledge and Kegan Paul, 1991).

De Sanctis, Francesco, *Storia della letteratura italiana* (Milan: Casa Editrice Bietti, 1960). In English, *History of Italian Literature*, 2 vols, translated by Joan Redfern (New York: Barnes and Noble, 1968).

Douglas, Gavin, Bishop of Dunkeld, *Virgil's* Aeneid *Translated into Scottish Verse*, 4 vols, edited by David F. C. Coldwell (Edinburgh and London: William Blackwood and Sons, 1957–64).

Foucault, Michel, *The History of Sexuality*, Vol. 1, *An Introduction*, translated by Robert Hurley (London: Allen Lane, 1979).

Hollander, Robert, *Boccaccio's Two Venuses* (New York: Columbia University Press, 1977).

Johnson, Barbara, *The Critical Difference: Essays in the Contemporary Rhetoric of Reading* (Baltimore and London: The Johns Hopkins University Press, 1980).

Lucas, Henry S., *The Renaissance and the Reformation* (New York and London: Harper and Brothers, 1934).

Martines, Lauro, *Power and Imagination: City-States in Renaissance Italy* (1979; Harmondsworth: Peregrine Books, 1983).

Mazzotta, Giuseppe, *The World at Play in Boccaccio's* Decameron (Princeton: Princeton University Press, 1986).

Molle, J. Vincenzo, 'La "Langue" et la "parole": contribution à une analyse des modèles idéologiques dans les nouvelles de Boccace', in François Marotin (ed.), *Frontières du conte* (Paris: CNRS, 1982).

Muscatine, Charles, *Poetry and Crisis in the Age of Chaucer* (Notre Dame: University of Notre Dame Press, 1972).

Painter, William, *The Palace of Pleasure*, 3 vols, edited by William Jacobs (1870. Reprinted Hildesheim: George Olms Verlagsbuchhandlung, 1968).

Petrarch, *Seniles*, as quoted in Bergin, *Boccaccio* (see above).

Russell, Jeffrey Burton, *Medieval Civilization* (New York: Wiley, 1968).

Sapori, Armando, 'Le compagnie dei Bardi e dei Peruzzi in Inghilterra nei secoli XIII e XIV', *Archivio Storico Italiano*, Vol. 80 (1922) pp. 5–63 (Florenze: R. Deputazione di Storia Patria, 1923).

Sapori, Armando, *La crisi delle compagnie mercantili dei Bardi e dei Peruzzi* (Florence: Leo S. Olschki, 1926).

Schevill, Ferdinand, *History of Florence from the Founding of the City through the Renaissance* (1936; New York and London: F. Ungar Publishing Co., 1968).

Toynbee, Paget, *Dante Studies and Researches* (London: Methuen, 1902).

Toynbee, Paget, *Dictionary of Proper Names and Notable Matters in the Works of Dante* (1st edn 1898), revised by Charles S. Singleton (Oxford:

Oxford University Press, 1968).

Wright, Herbert G., *Boccaccio in England from Chaucer to Tennyson* (London: Athlone Press, 1957).

## Chapter 3: 'The Architect Achieves His Victory': Renaissance and Later Ideal Cities

Adams, Nicholas and Laurie Nussdorfer, 'The Italian City, 1400–1600', in Henry A. Millon and Vittorio Magnago Lampugnani (eds), *The Renaissance from Brunelleschi to Michelangelo: The Representation of Architecture* (Milan: Bompiani, 1994).

Alberti, Leon Battista, *On Painting and on Sculpture*, translated (with Italian or Latin originals on facing pages) and edited by Cecil Grayson (London: Phaidon Press, 1972).

Alberti, Leon Battista, *On the Art of Building in Ten Books*, translated by Joseph Rykwert, Neil Leach and Robert Tavernor (Cambridge, MA, and London: The MIT Press, 1988).

Bek, Lise, *Towards Paradise on Earth: Modern Space Conception in Architecture, a Creation of Renaissance Humanism* (Odense, Denmark: Odense University Press, 1980).

Birks, Tony, *Building the New Universities* (Newton Abbot, Devon: David and Charles, 1972).

Blunt, Anthony, *Artistic Theory in Italy: 1450–1600* (Oxford: Oxford University Press, 1940).

Borsi, Franco, *Leon Battista Alberti*, translated by Rudolf G. Carpanini (Oxford: Phaidon Press, 1977).

Briggs, Asa, 'The Thinking Behind Britain's New Universities', *Architectural Review*, Vol. 134 (October 1963), pp. 233–5.

Bruni, Leonardo, 'Panegyric to the City of Florence', translated by Benjamin G. Kohl, in Benjamin G. Kohl and Ronald G. Witt with Elizabeth B. Welles (eds), *The Earthly Republic: Italian Humanists on Government and Society* (Manchester: Manchester University Press, 1978), pp. 119–75.

Burckhardt, Jacob, *The Civilization of the Renaissance in Italy*, trans. S. G. C. Middlemore from 15th German edn (no place of publication given: Albert and Charles Boni, 1935).

Choay, Françoise, *La Règle et le modèle: sur la théorie de l'architecture et de l'urbanisme* (Paris: Éditions du Seuil, 1980).

*Colchester Express*, 17 December 1964, quoted in McKean, 'University of Essex' (see below).

Da Vinci, Leonardo, *Leonardo architetto e urbanista*, edited by Luigi Firpo (Turin: UTET, 1963).

Filarete, Antonio Averlino detto il, *Filarete's Treatise on Architecture*, 2 vols, translated with introduction and notes by John R. Spencer (New Haven and London: Yale University Press, 1965).

Filarete, Antonio Averlino detto il, *Trattato di architettura*, 2 vols, edited by Anna Maria Finoli and Liliana Grassi (Milan: Edizioni il Polifilo, 1972).

Filarete, Antonio Averlino detto il, *Trattato di Architettura* (Florence: Biblioteca Nazionale, Magliabecchianus).

*Francesco di Giorgio architetto* and *Francesco di Giorgio e il Rinascimento a Siena, 1450–1500* (two exhibition catalogue volumes), edited by Luciano Bellosi (Milan: Electa, 1993).

Galluzzi, Paolo, *Mechanical Marvels: Invention in the Age of Leonardo* (Florence: Giunti, 1996).

Lawrence, D. H., 'Nottingham and the Mining Countryside', in *Phoenix: The Posthumous Papers of D. H. Lawrence* (London: Heinemann, 1936), pp. 133–40.

Mack, Charles R., *Pienza: The Creation of a Renaissance City* (Ithaca, NY, and London: Cornell University Press, 1987).

McKean, John Maule, 'University of Essex: Case Study', *Architects' Journal*, 20 September 1972, pp. 637–78.

Morris, William, *News from Nowhere: Or an Epoch of Rest, Being Some Chapters from a Utopian Romance*, 5th edn (London, New York and Bombay: Longmans, Green and Co., 1897).

Morris, William, 'The Lesser Arts', in *Selected Writings: Centenary Edition*, edited by G. D. H. Cole (London: Nonesuch Press, 1948), pp. 494–516.

Piccolomini, Aenius Silvius (Pope Pius II), *Memoirs of a Renaissance Pope: The Commentaries of Pius II*, translated by Florence A. Gragg (New York: Carpricorn Books, 1962).

Ruskin, John, *The Stones of Venice*, 3 vols, 2nd edn (London: Smith, Elder and Co., 1867).

Rykwert, Joseph, 'Universities as Institutional Archetypes of Our Age', *Zodiac*, Vol. 18 (1968), pp. 61–3.

Sloman, Albert, *A University in the Making* (London: BBC, 1964).

Smith, Christine, *Architecture in the Culture of Early Humanism: Ethics, Aesthetics, and Eloquence 1400–1470* (New York and Oxford: Oxford University Press, 1992).

Tafuri, Manfred, *Ricerca del rinascimento: principi, città, architetti* (Turin: Einaudi, 1992).

Wittkower, Rudolf, *Architectural Principles in the Age of Humanism*, 3rd revised edn (London: Alec Tiranti, 1962).

Chapter 4: 'When the Kissing Had to Stop': Eighteenth-century Venice – Apotheosis or Decline?

Addison, Joseph, *Remarks on Several Parts of Italy, &c. In the Years 1701, 1702, 1703*, in *Works*, Vol. 5 (London: Vernor and Hood et al., 1804).

Baker, Felicity, 'Lorenzo da Ponte's Witticisms: The Implication of Jewish Identity in the *Memorie*', in John Lindon (ed.), *Italian Autobiography from Vico to Alfieri (and Beyond)*, as a supplement to *The Italianist*, no. 17 (1997), pp. 66–73.

Bereford, Bruce, 'Venice Mythologized: A Seductive Maritime Playground', *Apollo*, September 1994, pp. 13–16.

Brodsky, Joseph, *Watermark* (London: Hamish Hamilton, 1992).

Byron, Lord, *Childe Harold's Pilgrimage, Canto the Fourth*, first published 1818, from *Complete Poetical Works*, 2nd vol. edited by Jerome J. McGann (Oxford: Oxford University Press, 1980).

Casanova, Giacomo, Chevalier de Seingalt, *Mémoires*, ed. Robert Abirached and Elio Zorzi, 3 vols (Paris: Librairie Gallimard, 1958–60).

Casanova, Giacomo, Chevalier de Seingalt, *History of My Life*, 6 vols, translated by Willard R. Trask (London: Longmans, Green and Co., 1967).

*Cronaca Veneziana: feste e vita quotidiana nella Venezia del Settecento*. View painting by Gabriel Bella and engravings by Gaetano Zompini in the collection of the Querini Stampalia Foundation in Venice (Venice: Fondazione Scientifica Querini Stampalia, 1991).

Da Ponte, Lorenzo, *Memorie*, 2 vols, edited by G. Gambarin and F. Nicolini (Bari: Gius Laterza and Sons, 1918).

Goethe, J. W. von, *Italian Journey (1786–88)*, translated by W. H. Auden and Elizabeth Mayer (London: W. M. Collins, 1962).

Goldoni, Carlo, *Tutte le opere*, edited by Giuseppe Ortolani (Milan: Mondadori, 1943–59).

Goldoni, Carlo, *Opere*, edited by Filippo Zampieri (Milan and Naples: Ricciardi, 1954).

Goldoni, Carlo, *The Campiello*, translated by Frederick Davies (London: Ginn and Co., 1971).

Guasti, Timina Caproni and Achille Bertarelli, *Francesco Zambeccari Aeronauta (Bologna 1752–1812)* (Milan: Museo Caproni, 1931) and *L'Aeronautica italiana nell'immagine: 1487–1875* (Milan: Museo Caproni, 1938).

Hyman, Timothy, 'A Carnival Sense of the World', *Royal Academy Magazine*, No. 44, autumn 1994, pp. 42–5.

Levey, Michael, *Painting in Eighteenth-Century Venice*, 3rd edn (original edition 1955; New Haven and London: Yale University Press, 1994).

Mariuz, Adriano, *Giandomenico Tiepolo* (Milan: Alfieri, 1971).

Monnier, Philippe, *Venice in the Eighteenth Century*, no translator given (London: Chatto and Windus, 1910).

Norwich, John Julius, *Venice: The Greatness and the Fall* (London: Allen Lane, 1981).

Norwich, John Julius, 'Venice in the Eighteenth Century', *Apollo*, September 1994, pp. 3–6.

Romanin, S., *Storia documentata di Venezia*, 2nd edn, 10 vols, reprinted on the basis of the 1st edn of 1853–61 (Venice: Giusto Fuga Editore, 1915).

## Chapter 5: Opera, Politics and Television: Bel Canto by Satellite

Ashbrook, William, *The Operas of Puccini* (Oxford: Oxford University Press, 1985).

Bianconi, Lorenzo, article on Italy in *The New Grove Dictionary of Opera* (see below), vol. 2, pp. 853–55.

Bondanella, Peter, *The Eternal City: Roman Images in the Modern World* (Chapel Hill: University of North Carolina Press, 1987).

Bosworth, Richard, *Italy and the Approach of the First World War* (London: Macmillan, 1983).

Brunetta, Gian Piero, *Storia del cinema italiano: 1895–1945* (Rome: Editori Riuniti, 1979).

Brunetta, Gian Piero, *Storia del cinema italiano: dal 1945 agli anni ottanta* (Rome: Editori Riuniti, 1982).

Callas, Maria, *Maria Callas: débuts à Paris, 19 décembre 1958*, EMI Classics Video, 1991.

Carner, Mosco, *Giacomo Puccini: Tosca* (Cambridge: Cambridge University Press, 1985).

Chappell, Herbert, quoted in *The Times*, 27 June 1990.

Clément, Catherine, *Opera, or the Undoing of Women*, translated by Betsy Wing, foreword by Susan McClary (London: Virago, 1989).

Drake, Richard, *Byzantium for Rome: The Politics of Nostalgia in Umbertian Italy 1878–1900* (Chapel Hill: University of North Carolina Press, 1980).

Eliot, T. S., 'Ben Jonson', in *Selected Essays*, 2nd revised edn (London: Faber and Faber, 1934), pp. 147–60.

Fawkes, Richard, 'Domingo's Authentic *Tosca*', *Opera Now*, July 1992, p. 56.

Gallone, Carmine, *Avanti a lui tremava tutta Roma (Before Him All Rome Trembled)*, Minerva Film (1946).

Ginsborg, Paul, *A History of Contemporary Italy: Society and Politics 1943–1988* (Penguin: Harmondsworth, 1990).

*Harry Enfield's Guide to Opera* (Ecosse Films for Channel 4, 1993).

Liehm, Mira, *Passion and Defiance: Film in Italy from 1942 to the Present*

(Berkeley: University of California Press, 1984).

Lowe, David A. (ed.), *Callas as They Saw Her* (London: Robson Books, 1987).

Martin, George, 'Verdi and the Risorgimento', in William Weaver and Martin Chusid (eds), *The Verdi Companion* (London: Victor Gollancz, 1980).

Martin, George, *Aspects of Verdi* (London: Robson Books, 1988).

*The New Grove Dictionary of Opera*, edited Stanley Sadie (London: Macmillan, 1992).

Puccini, Giacomo, *Tosca*: using the actual settings and times of *Tosca*, directed by Giuseppe Patroni Griffi, conductor Zubin Mehta (Rada Film, 1992; Teldec Video, 1993).

Rossellini, Roberto, *La nave bianca* (1941), *Un pilota ritorna* (1942), *L'uomo della croce* (1942), *Roma città aperta* (1945).

Soames, Nicholas, article in *The Times*, 9 July 1990.

Tambling, Jeremy, *Opera, Ideology and Film* (Manchester: Manchester University Press, 1987).

*The Times*, 11 July 1992.

Walker, Frank, *The Man Verdi* (New York: Alfred A. Knopf, 1972).

Weaver, William, *The Golden Century of Italian Opera from Rossini to Puccini* (London: Thames and Hudson, 1980).

## Chapter 6: Mimesis or Montage? Reflections on the Languages of Literature and Cinema

Auerbach, Erich, *Mimesis: The Representation of Reality in Western Literature*, trans. Willard R. Trask (original Swiss edn, 1946; 1st edn of this translation, 1953; Princeton: Princeton University Press, 1968).

Bassani, Giorgio, *A Prospect of Ferrara*, translated by Isabel Quigly (London: Faber and Faber, 1962).

Bassani, Giorgio, 'La passeggiata prima di cena', in *Il romanzo di Ferrara* (Milan: Mondadori, 1974).

Bondanella, Peter, *Italian Cinema from Neorealism to the Present*, new expanded edition (New York: Continuum, 1997).

Brunetta, Gian Piero, *Storia del cinema italiano: dal 1945 agli anni ottanta* (Rome: Editori Riuniti, 1982).

Calvino, Italo, 'Autobiografia di uno spettatore', prefatory section to Federico Fellini, *Quattro Film* (Turin: Einaudi, 1974), pp. ix–xxiv.

Eisenstein, Sergei M., *The Film Sense*, translated and edited by Jay Leyda (London: Faber and Faber, 1948; 1st edn 1943).

Fanon, Frantz, 'Algeria Unveiled', Chapter 1 of *Studies in a Dying Colonialism*, translated Haakon Chevalier (1965; London: Earthscan Publications, 1989), pp. 35–67. Original French title, *L'An cinq de la révolution algérienne* (Paris: François Maspero, 1959).

Fanon, Frantz, *The Wretched of the Earth*, translated by Constance Farrington (Harmondsworth: Penguin, 1967). Original French title, *Les Damnés de la terre* (1962).

Fuss, Diana, *Identification Papers* (New York and London: Routledge, 1995).

Horne, Alistair, *A Savage War of Peace: Algeria 1954–1962* (Harmondsworth: Penguin, 1977).

Irigaray, Luce, 'The Powers of Discourse and the Subordination of the Feminine': *This Sex Which Is Not One* (1977), extract in Mary Eagleton (ed.), *Feminist Literary Theory: A Reader*, 2nd edn (Oxford, Blackwell, 1996).

Liehm, Mira, *Passion and Defiance: Film in Italy from 1942 to the Present* (Berkeley, Los Angeles and London: University of California Press, 1984).

McClintock, Anne, *Imperial Leather: Race, Gender and Sexuality in the Colonial Context* (New York and London: Routledge, 1995).

Mellen, Joan, *Filmguide to* The Battle of Algiers (Bloomington and London: Indiana University Press Filmguide Series, 1973).

Overbey, David (ed. and trans.), *Springtime in Italy: A Reader on Neo-Realism* (London: Talisman Books, 1978).

Pontecorvo, Gillo, *La Bataille d'Alger*, Casbah Films Alger/Igor Film Rome (1966).

Rivière, Joan, 'Womanliness as Masquerade', *International Journal of Psychoanalysis*, Vol. 10 (1929); reprinted in Victor Burgin, James Donald and Cora Kaplan (eds), *Formations of Fantasy* (London: Routledge, 1986), pp. 35–44.

Solinas, Piernico (ed.), *Gillo Pontecorvo's* The Battle of Algiers: *The Complete Scenario* (New York: Charles Scribner's Sons, 1973).

Stern, Katherine, 'What Is Femme? The Phenomenology of the Powder Room', *Women: A Cultural Review*, Vol. 8, No. 2, autumn 1997, pp. 183–96.

Visconti, Luchino, 'Anthropomorphic Cinema', in Overbey (ed. and trans.), *Springtime in Italy* (see above), pp. 83–5.

## Chapter 7: The Triumph of Death: History in the Sicilian Context

Falcone, Giovanni in collaboration with Marcelle Padovani, *Cose di Cosa Nostra* (Milan: Rizzoli, 1991). In English, *Men of Honour: The Truth about the Mafia*, translated by Edward Farrelly (London: Fourth Estate, 1992).

Farrell, Joseph, *Leonardo Sciascia* (Edinburgh: Edinburgh University Press, 1995).

Ginsborg, Paul, 'Crisis, Compromise and the "Anni di Piombo", 1973–80', Chapter 10 of *A History of Contemporary Italy: Society and Politics 1943–1988* (Harmondsworth: Penguin, 1990), pp. 348–405.

*Keesing's Record of World Events*, News Digest for August 1997, p. 41783.

Lampedusa, Giuseppe Tomasi di, *Il gattopardo* (Milan: Feltrinelli, 1958). In English, *The Leopard*, translated by Archibald Colquhoun (London: Collins Harvill, 1960).

Leopardi, Giacomo, *Discorso sopra lo stato presente dei costumi degl' italiani*, introduced and edited by Augusto Placanica (Venice: Marsilio, 1989).

Nietzsche, Friedrich, *Untimely Meditations*, translated by R. J. Hollingdale, introduction by J. P. Stern (Cambridge: Cambridge University Press, 1983) (The second Meditation, 'Of the Uses and Disadvantages of History for Life', first appeared separately in the original German in Leipzig, February 1874.)

Paolini, Maria Grazia, 'Il "Trionfo" oggi', in *Il 'Trionfo della Morte' di Palermo: l'opera, le vicende conservative, il restauro* (Palermo: Sellerio, 1989).

Robb, Peter, *Midnight in Sicily* (Potts Point, NSW: Duffy and Snellgrove, 1996).

Sciascia, Leonardo, *Pirandello e la Sicilia*, 2nd edn (Caltanisetta and Rome: Salvatore Sciasci, 1968).

Sciascia, Leonardo, 'Il quarantotto', in *Gli zii di Sicilia* (1958: Turin: Einaudi, 1975). In English, 'Forty-eight', in *Sicilian Uncles*, translated by N. S. Thompson (Manchester: Carcanet, 1986).

Sciascia, Leonardo, *La Sicilia come metafora: intervista di Marcelle Padovani* (Milan: Mondadori, 1979).

Smith, Dennis Mack, *A History of Sicily*, 2 vols (New York: Dorset Press, 1968).

Sterling, Claire, *The Mafia: The Long Reach of the International Sicilian Mafia* (London: Hamish Hamilton, 1990).

Stille, Alexander, *Excellent Cadavers* (London: Jonathan Cape, 1995).

Thomson, Ian, 'Conversation in Palermo with Leonardo Sciascia', in Leonardo Sciascia, *1912 + 1: A Novel*, translated by Sacha Rabinovitch (Manchester: Carcanet, 1989), pp. 87–133.

## Chapter 8: 'A Fine Funeral of Our Identities'? The Italian Diaspora of the Modern Epoch

Acton, Harold, *The Bourbons of Naples, 1734–1825* (London: Methuen and Co., 1956).

Alba, Richard D., *Italian Americans: Into the Twilight of Ethnicity* (Englewood Cliffs, NJ: Prentice-Hall, 1985).

Baker, Felicity, 'Lorenzo da Ponte's Witticisms: The Implication of Jewish Identity in the *Memorie*', in John London (ed.), *Italian Autobiography from Vico to Alfieri (and Beyond)*, as a supplement to *The Italianist*, Vol. 17 (1997), pp. 42–79.

Blessington, Countess of, *The Idler in Italy*, 3 vols (London: Henry Colbrun, 1839–40).

Cappiello, Rosa R., *Paese fortunato* (Milan: Feltrinelli, 1981). In English, *Oh Lucky Country*, translated by Gaetano Rando (St Lucia, London and New York: University of Queensland Press, 1984).

Colletta, General Pietro, *Storia del Regno di Napoli dal 1754 al 1825* (Florence, 1848; numerous subsequent editions). In English, *History of the Kingdom of Naples, 1734–1825*, 2 vols, translated by S. Horner (Edinburgh: T. Constable and Co. 1858).

Da Ponte, Lorenzo (trans.), *'La Profezia di Dante' di Lord Byron* (New York: R. and W. A. Bartow, 1822).

Da Ponte, Lorenzo, *Memorie*, 2 vols, edited by G. Gambarin and F. Nicolini (Bari: Gius Laterza and Sons, 1918). In English, *Memoirs*, translated by Elisabeth Abbott, edited by Arthur Livingston (1929; reprint, New York: Dover Publications, 1959).

Da Ponte, Lorenzo, *Storia compendiosa della vita di Lorenzo da Ponte*, quoted in Hodges, *Lorenzo Da Ponte* (see below).

Da Ponte, Lorenzo, *Lettere di Lorenzo Da Ponte a Giacomo Casanova, 1791–95*, edited by Giampaolo Zagonel (Vittorio Veneto: Dario de Bastiani, 1988).

Fitzlyon, April, *Lorenzo Da Ponte: A Bibliography of Mozart's Librettist* (1955; reprint, London: John Calder, 1982).

Hodges, Sheila, *Lorenzo Da Ponte: The Life and Times of Mozart's Librettist* (London: Granada, 1985).

Pascoe, Robert, *Buongiorno Australia: Our Italian Heritage* (Richmond, Victoria: Greenhouse Publications, 1987).

Porter, Katherine Anne, *The Never-ending Wrong* (London: Secker and Warburg, 1977).

Public Records Office, Kew: FO 70, Nos. 84, 87.

Puzo, Mario, *The Godfather* (London: Heinemann, 1969).

Puzo, Mario, 'The Making of *The Godfather*', in *The Godfather Papers and Other Confessions* (London: Heinemann, 1972), pp. 32–69.

Russell, Francis, *Tragedy in Dedham: The Story of the Sacco–Vanzetti Case* (New York: McGraw-Hill, 1971).

Sacco, Nicola and Bartolomeo Vanzetti, *The Letters of Sacco and Vanzetti*, edited by Marion Denman Frankfurter and Gardner Jackson (New York: Viking Press, 1928).

Vasta, Ellie, 'If You Had Your Time Again, Would You Migrate to Australia?': A Study of Long-Settled Italo-Australians in Brisbane (Canberra: Australian Government Publishing Service, 1985).

# INDEX

Numbers in italics indicate figures.